The Professional Psychologist Today

*New Developments in Law,
Health Insurance, and Health Practice*

Herbert Dörken
and
Associates

The Professional Psychologist Today

Jossey-Bass Publishers
San Francisco · Washington · London · 1976

THE PROFESSIONAL PSYCHOLOGIST TODAY
New Developments in Law, Health Insurance, and Health Practice
by Herbert Dörken and Associates

The Jossey-Bass
Behavioral Science Series

Preface

Psychologists generally are unaware of the extent to which laws, government administration, health insurance practices, and various health service delivery models affect and will continue to affect both the discipline and profession of psychology. Perhaps this lack of consciousness is not really surprising. Only in the past few years have psychologists begun to be systematically concerned with the development of professional psychology and the welter of laws, regulations, vested interests, economic policies, and bureaucratic decisions connected with professional practice. The explosive growth of psychology, and of professional psychology in particular, has been more extensive and far more recent than is generally realized. The American Psychological Association has nearly tripled its membership in less than twenty years—from 15,000 in 1956 to about 40,000 today. More than half of the psychologists who hold Ph.D.s today received their degrees within the last ten years. The proportion of psychologists involved in clinical and counseling psychology, offering professional services to the public, has progressively increased. Psychology is no longer the small, predominantly academic discipline it was less than a generation ago. And it is no longer insulated from the legal, economic, and political realities that influence the practice of any profession.

Now more than 40 percent of psychologists see themselves as health professionals, but in a context considerably broader than that of dealing with the sick and injured. Professional psychologists concerned with disordered behavior, mental, emotional and developmental problems may seem very different

ix

from traditional health practitioners such as physicians and nurses. Yet the old and arbitrary distinctions between mental and physical health are breaking down. Mental health is increasingly seen within the larger context of human health. Therefore, psychologists are increasingly subject to the same regulations and standards that govern other health practitioners. They are (or are not) included under the same health insurance policies issued to the same clients. And they demand the same rights, privileges, responsibilities, and high standards for professional practice that are justified by their thorough professional and academic training.

It is appropriate that the distinctions between mental health and health are evaporating. Mental disorders represent the largest single category of human disability in the United States. Both medicine and psychology can now document the fact that mental and emotional factors can cause or intensify some of our most prevalent physical diseases. Almost all serious diseases, however physical in origin, have profound psychological consequences for patients and their families. Problems of emotional and cognitive development, family discord, social unrest, job stress, and economic uncertainty may develop into health problems for any of us. Psychology has both the opportunity and the responsibility to help alleviate many of these problems. Psychologists, other health professionals, and the public have become more aware of the services that psychology can offer. Academic psychology has developed a respected scientific base in the study of behavior, learning, cognition, motivation, perception, and techniques for assessment. It is time for psychology as a profession to apply this understanding to improve the health and well-being of troubled people.

The provision of mental and physical health services to the public is becoming one of the major social and political issues in our nation. Thus it involves legislators, policy makers, and the public, as well as health professionals. Psychology is increasingly recognized in legislation covering health services delivery; many of the principles and standards for professional practice adopted by the American Psychological Association (APA) and the Council for the Advancement of Psychological Professions and

Sciences (CAPPS) are being incorporated in health insurance statutes at state and federal levels. This recognition of psychology in the law has not happened by accident. Concerned psychologists have actively advocated the recognition of their profession, not only in the planning, evaluation, and organization of health services, but also under comprehensive health insurance. This involvement on the part of psychologists is crucial, for it will help to determine the shape of future health service delivery—including what services may be provided to whom, under what conditions, and at whose expense.

In *The Professional Psychologist Today*, we document the success of professional psychology in gaining recognition, setting standards, and providing services. Because the advancement of professional psychology depends on our ability to gain formal recognition in the law, in health insurance, and in health practice, we encourage psychologists to engage in constructive advocacy in public affairs. We specify, both in the text and in the annotated bibliography, sources of information that psychologists can readily use to increase the stature of the profession. And we recommend specific ways in which psychology can serve the public interest more effectively than in the past.

Although we have written this book with practicing psychologists most in mind, we hope it will also be useful to all psychologists concerned with the future of our profession. In addition, we hope the information will help other health professionals, legislators, policy makers, and planners—all of those people who have the responsibility of regulating and improving the delivery of vital health services to the public in the most effective and inexpensive ways—to recognize the contributions professional psychology can make. And, finally, we hope that psychology students in graduate schools and training programs will benefit from discussions of the forces that will influence their careers and their profession.

The book is divided into five major sections. The first five chapters examine the foundations of psychology as a health profession. Chapter One presents manpower data illustrating how deeply psychologists are already involved in health practice, and shows that graduate psychology programs are now producing a sharply increased supply of highly trained professionals to meet society's health needs. It also presents a pilot study that demonstrates the extent of psychologists' involvement in health service through full-time and part-time practice and shows that their geographic distribution is relatively well matched to the general population. Chapter Two considers the development of professional standards for practice and calls for eliminating the dual standards currently applied to public and private practice in many health professions. Chapter Three reviews federal and state laws that regulate psychology as a health profession, and explores the statutory (legal) basis of professional practice. We devote particular attention to state licensure, freedom-of-choice-of-practitioner laws, and the increasing number of states that have passed legislation in these areas. Chapter Four reviews recent federal legislation and proposals governing such restorative services as vocational rehabilitation, workers' compensation, and no-fault automobile insurance, and examines the potential involvement of psychologists in these areas. In similar fashion, Chapter Five analyzes the provisions of the major Social Security programs such as Medicare, Medicaid, and Child and Maternal Health services. We give special attention to the Ohio and New Jersey programs, which provide models for the proper inclusion of psychology, and we suggest that similar programs might be developed in all states.

The second section deals directly with the problems created by the various forms of health insurance plans, the services they cover, and the benefits they allow. Chapter Six differentiates disability, health service, hospital service, and self-insurance plans, and delineates how psychological services are and are not covered. It also examines the new health maintenance organizations and medical foundations and the extent to which they may provide for psychological services to their clients. Chapter Seven addresses the common, day-to-day problems that most practitioners encounter in dealing with health insurance companies; it offers professional psychologists specific and clear-cut guidelines for making claims, handling denied claims, safeguarding client interests, maintaining ethical standards in practice, and finding their way through the labyrinth of third-party reimbursement. Chapter Eight examines the proposed legislation establishing national health insurance and proposes a plan with specific principles and recommended levels of coverage that would guarantee inclusion of psychological services and protect the interests of both psychologists and consumers.

The third section reviews how consumers actually use psychological services in plans where such services are covered; it refutes the common argument that providing coverage and benefits for professional services by psychologists would be unnecessary, unwanted by consumers, too costly to individuals, or ruinously expensive for the insurors. Chapter Nine examines the claim experiences of the largest group health plan in the nation—the Civilian Health and Medical Program for the Uniformed Services (CHAMPUS). The data documents that consumers do use the services that psychologists provide and that the overall cost of almost unlimited mental health service is clearly feasible. Chapter Ten reports the results of an eight-year study of the utilization of mental health services in the Kaiser Northern California program, a pioneering health maintenance organization. This study adds further to the evidence that mental health services actually reduce the use of more expensive hospital-medical services and lower the overall costs of comprehensive health care. Chapter Eleven then presents a comprehensive review of other utilization and cost data for mental health and psychological services, and underscores both the feasibility and desirability of providing coverage for professional psychological services. It also points to the fact that the private sector can effectively compete with public organizations in providing care to the public.

The fourth section examines the most significant issues that professional psychologists must resolve if they are to establish their profession on an independent and self-regulating basis. Chapter Twelve introduces psychologists to the intricacies of the legislative process; it analyzes the success psychologists achieved in New Jersey, California, and Ohio in gaining statutory recognition and legal inclusion in laws governing health practices and health insurance programs. It offers psychologists specific guidelines for organizing their efforts and effectively influencing the laws that are passed, for negotiating with legislators and with competing interest groups, and for mobilizing public support for their cause. Chapter Thirteen discusses the potential impact of peer review boards on practice, develops a model plan for protecting the interests of clients by providing qualified services, and identifies the necessity for sound organization and explicit standards of practice within the profession. Chapter Fourteen provides the legal basis for refuting the argument that psychologists in health practice must be supervised by physicians. Chapter Fifteen summarizes the progress that professional psychology has made and examines the unresolved issues that will become increasingly important in the future, including the comparative advantages of private and public services to consumers; the advantages, manpower needs, and uses of health maintenance organizations compared to traditional fee-for-service methods of delivering health care; the special problems of training psychologists for professional practice; the questions of equality and staff privilege in hospitals and other health care organizations; and the transition of professional psychology from a mental health to a broader, comprehensive health orientation.

The final section is a guide to bibliographic resources. It includes an annotated description of each of the 270 references used in the book, and it will allow readers to select the information they need to support their own advocacy and professional interests.

San Francisco   Herbert Dörken
January 1976

Contents

Contributors

All authors, with one exception—a psychiatrist—are clinically trained psychologists who have been actively involved in advancing the utilization of professional psychology and its role in health care delivery systems as a primary provider. The chapters to follow reflect this personal experience and commitment. Each contributor's background is briefly summarized here.

Russell J. Bent, *Ph.D. 1960, Fordham University. Deputy Superintendent, Georgia Mental Health Institute, Atlanta. Lecturer, Emory University School of Law. Diplomate in Clinical Psychology. APA Committee on Health Insurance, 1973-1977, and Chair 1976.*

Nicholas A. Cummings, *Ph.D. 1958, Adelphi University. President, California School of Professional Psychology. Chief Clinical Psychologist, Kaiser-Permanente Medical Center (Northern California), San Francisco. APA Committee on Health Insurance, and Chair, 1966-1969. President, California State Psychological Association, 1968. APA Board of Directors, 1975-1977. Executive Committee, Council for the Advancement of Psychological Professions and Sciences (CAPPS), 1971-1974.*

Herbert Dörken, *Ph.D. 1951, University of Montreal. Adjunct Professor and Research Psychologist, University of California, San Francisco. Advisor in Program*

Development, California School of Professional Psychology. Diplomate in Clinical Psychology. Special Health Services Consultant, California State Psychological Association (CSPA). APA Committee on Health Insurance, 1971-1975 (Chair 1974-1975). APA Council of Representatives (CSPA) 1975-1977. Committee on Governmental Relations, CAPPS (Chair, 1973-1975).

Jack Dworin, *Ph.D. 1953, University of Rochester. Private practice, University Park Psychological Center since 1962. Staff Psychologist, Veterans Administration Mental Hygiene Clinic, Denver. Psychology Consultant, Blue Cross and Blue Shield of Colorado. Diplomate in Clinical Psychology. APA Committee on Health Insurance 1972-1975. Chairman, Health Insurance Committee, Colorado Psychological Association since 1968.*

William T. Follette, *A.B. 1948, University of California, Berkeley; M.D., 1952, University of California School of Medicine, San Francisco. Residency in psychiatry and neurology, Western Psychiatric, University of Pittsburgh, 1953-1956. Permanente Medical Group, Kaiser-Permanente Medical Center (Northern California), 1956 to present; Chief of Psychiatry 1964 to present. Board-certified, neurology and psychiatry, 1960.*

Durand F. Jacobs, *Ph.D. 1953, Michigan State University. Chief, Psychology Service, Veterans Administration Hospital, Cleveland. Adjunct Professor of Psychology, Kent State University. Citation, President's Committee on Employment of the Handicapped. Chair, APA, Division 22 (Rehabilitation) Legislative Committee. Chairman, Task Force on Standards for Providers of Psychological Services, report adopted as association policy, September 1974.*

David A. Rodgers, *Ph.D. 1953, University of Chicago. Head, Section of Psychology and Research, Cleveland Clinic Foundation. President, Ohio Psychological Association*

(OPA) 1972. Chair, OPA Legislation Committee 1969-1972. APA Committee on Health Insurance, 1974-1978.

A. Eugene Shapiro, *Ph.D. 1953, New York University. Private practice, Irvington, New Jersey, since 1953; vice-president, Career Consultants Inc. Diplomate in clinical psychology. APA Council of Representatives (New Jersey), 1968-1972. Committee on Health Insurance, 1969-1974 (Chair, 1973). Council, National Register of Health Service Providers in Psychology.*

J. Frank Whiting, *Ph.D. 1953, University of Pennsylvania. Ordinary Professor and Director of Research, National Catholic School of Social Services, Catholic University of America. Behavioral Science Research Consultant, United States Department of Justice, Federal Bureau of Prisons, 1975. Project Director, APA Standards for Psychological Services, 1972-1973. Deceased, April 23, 1975.*

Jack G. Wiggins, *Ph.D. 1952, Purdue University. Private practice, Psychological Development Center, Cleveland, since 1957. Chairman, Ohio Psychological Association Insurance Committee, 1966 to present. APA Division 29 (Psychotherapy) Insurance Committee, 1965 to present. APA Committee on Health Insurance, 1968-1972 (Chair 1970-1972). Executive Committee, Council for the Advancement of Psychological Professions and Sciences, 1971-1975.*

The Professional Psychologist Today

New Developments in Law,
Health Insurance, and Health Practice

1

Psychologists as Health Service Providers

Herbert Dörken and J. Frank Whiting

The role of psychology and its contributions to mental health, rehabilitation, developmental disability, and general health services are the subjects of much professional and scientific health literature today. Because psychologists are increasingly providing health services, they are expanding the scope of what was primarily an academic and research discipline a few decades ago.

Clinical psychology has been influential in the change from an academic to an applied orientation, but an unfortunate semantic difficulty has resulted. Laypersons and psychologists alike generally have identified clinical psychology with mental health. However, the adjective *mental* limits the definition of psychological services. Schofield (1969) was the first to describe psychology as a health profession without the qualifying *mental*. Like other health professions, psychology strives to assure *overall* health, which includes the emotional and mental as well as physical condition of the individual.

From an article by the same title, published in *Professional Psychology*, 1974, 5, 309-319. Republished, with update and added manpower data, with the permission of the American Psychological Association.

1

Schofield (1975) argues that as the traditional health professions increasingly recognize the emotional needs of patients, new models of health care delivery will be encouraged. Demands on traditional medical resources, as well as the high costs of health care in general, will decrease. Opportunities for alternative treatment programs already exist. What now remains is for these programs to be put into effect. Since psychology will play a crucial role in providing alternative health programs and services in the next few years, it is important to understand the composition of professional psychology personnel—what the nature, distribution, and size of this highly trained resource is. This data documents the current extent to which professional psychologists—both salaried staff and private practitioners—are involved in providing health services and indicates the possible scope of their future involvement.

Psychology's Empirical Manpower Base

In order to describe the manpower resources of psychology, we must first develop an operational definition of psychologists as providers of health services (as distinguished from those operating in research or educational settings). For our purposes, we will therefore define providers of health services as those psychologists who accept a fee for their services. Fee-for-service health care has traditionally been considered the domain of medicine and psychiatry. Now, however, psychologists are claiming professional status on the basis of widespread involvement in fee-for-service health care provision. The statistics reported in the following discussion will serve to substantiate these claims.

There are three essential contexts within which psychologists' provision of health services via private fee-for-service practice must be viewed. These contexts are the profession as a whole, the provision of health care services, and the provision of health care on a fee-for-service basis.

First, there is the professionwide context, best viewed in the data now available on American Psychological Association (APA) members from the APA 1972 survey of psychologists in the United States and Canada (American Psychological Association, 1973). Some 27,371 (77 percent) of its membership of 35,360 responded to this questionnaire. The data indicate three basic facts: (1) 6 percent, or 1,688, of the 27,371 APA members responding to the questionnaires were primarily employed in independent of group practice; (2) some 28 percent, or 7,541, performed either psychotherapy or counseling, or both, on a fee-for-service basis; and (3) nearly half, or 46 percent, of those in Category 2 were primarily employed in educational settings.

These data imply that statutory and regulatory changes affecting the practice of psychology will also affect the academically based psychologist. Further, while only a relatively small proportion of APA member psychologists are engaged full time in private fee-for-service practice, it is clear that more than one out of every four psychologists is engaged in fee-for-service activity to some degree. Fee-for-service practice by psychologists, then, exhibits an "iceberg" phenomenon; that is, full-time practitioners are only a small segment of the total group. Given the well-publicized nationwide cutbacks in training and research funds and in faculty salary support in universities (Walsh, 1970) and other educational settings, together with expanding health and rehabilitation services, psychologists will probably become more and more involved in fee-for-service practice in the near future.

Second, there is the context of human service provision. It is true that the "professional" aspect of psychology (the provision of direct services for the resolution of human problems of daily living) is only part of psychology's total activities. Many psychologists are engaged full time in teaching, research, program administration, or a combination of these activities. However, when the 1972 APA survey data were analyzed to identify member professional time in one or more of four activities (clinical service, counseling service, consultant/advisory service, and test administration and evaluation) they showed that 17,210 (63 percent) of the 27,371 APA member respondents were engaged in direct provision of human services.

The 1,688 full-time private or group practitioners constituted 10 percent of this 17,210-member group, while all of the 7,541 respondents providing psychotherapy or counseling on a fee-for-service base comprised 44 percent of this group. Moreover, more than half (52 percent), or 8,929, of the 17,210 human service providers were employed primarily in educational settings. These data allow the fee-for-service segment to emerge more clearly.

Third, there is the health service context of fee-for-service practice, as distinct from the broader human services context. Human services provision is an all-embracing concept. It involves not only health services but also educational services, employment services (including rehabilitation, social control and protection services), and many other psychological aspects of individual, familial, and community functioning in relation to the problems of daily living. However, *health* is frequently defined so broadly that it includes all aspects of life from the cradle to the grave (see Schofield, 1969).

Perhaps the clearest demarcation between "health services" and "human services" is derived through major health service settings; that is, the hospital, the clinic, and private, individual, or group practice. These settings provide an irreducible data base regarding health service provision by psychologists, which is, at the same time, inherently conservative, since it is well known that health services are provided in many other settings. Within the health setting triad, those engaged primarily in individual or group practice (N = 1,688) constituted 30 percent of the psychologists who provide services in major health settings (N = 5,554), while hospital-based (N = 2,128) and clinic-based (N = 1,738) psychologists constituted 38 percent and 32 percent, respectively, of these providing services in major health settings.

In summary, then, full-time private fee-for-service practitioners constituted 6 percent of all APA member psychologists, 10 percent of all APA member human service providers, and 30 percent of all APA member health service providers employed full time in health settings.

An Inferential Manpower Base

Some of the conclusions that could be drawn from the previous biennial surveys of psychologists reported to the National Register of Scientific and Technical Personnel (Cates, 1970) are that the majority of psychologists are employed in the field of education; that the vast majority are in salaried positions; and that only 6 percent or 7 percent are in independent practice as their primary employment.

From the 1972 APA survey, it is known that 50.6 percent of member respondents, or 13,855, are licensed or certified (Vetter, 1973). By projecting that half of the total membership of 35,360 are similarly credentialed (namely, 17,680), and by estimating that 20 percent of the non-APA members hold such qualifications, it would appear that there were about 21,700 licensed or certified psychologists in the country at that time. For example, the survey respondents included only 2,105 of the 3,261 California licensed psychologists. From the increase in APA membership by 4,000 as of 1975, one can infer that the number of licensed or certified psychologists is approaching 24,000. While each state with statutory procedures must keep public records, no consolidated, unduplicated national roster has ever been assembled (see Chapter Three). Certainly, not all such credentialed psychologists engage in private practice, let alone in health services. Certainly, not all of them are APA members nor even members of their respective state psychological associations. The panel on fee practice chaired by Peck sought to survey this provider pool in January 1968 (Peck, 1969). Based on the latest state rosters then in the APA's files and largely reflective of 1966, a pool of 8,000 was derived and each third entry was sent a questionnaire. Of the respondents, close to 37.5 percent reported no fee-for-service activity; they, in effect, were not engaged in services for which a license was necessary. Of those engaged in fee for services, 20 percent reported less than eight hours a week practice and only 10 percent (5.6 percent of total) reported full-time fee practice. In late 1973 Garfield and Kurtz (1974) surveyed every third member of the

Division of Clinical Psychology of the APA. The survey found
that the practice orientation of the clinical psychologist has increased. For 23 percent of the respondents, practice was their
main occupational setting while 47 percent engaged in part-time
private practice; together, they constituted 70 percent of the
sample.

While the full report of the 1972 survey of psychologists in
the United States and Canada being conducted by APA's Manpower Department is not yet available, Whiting and others
(1972) estimated the total of United States resident psychologists at 55,496. Whiting's tabulations suggest that of all
psychologists, 66 percent are service providers (some time), of
whom 60 percent are health service providers. Therefore, 40
percent of all psychologists render some health services. Time
accounting enabled Whiting to show that psychology had
19,800 full-time equivalent (FTE—100-percent time) providers.
Noting that service provision actually accounted for 80 percent
of the time in key health settings and applying the 60 percent
factor, we estimated that the equivalent of 14,850 psychologists
engaged in what in reality is "full-time" health service is
(19,800 X .60 + 25%). But since 40 percent of United States
psychologists, or 22,000, provide some health services, as these
data suggest, then obviously there is a very substantial proportion of psychologists now engaged in part-time health service
delivery. These data also reflect a fact of professional life—that
joint appointments are common. These data underscore the
potential for a major manpower shift with changing "market"
conditions; for example, an increase in prepaid or insured health
services or a continued shrinkage in federal grant funds. We
could well be on the verge of major further involvement of
psychology in health services. And in fact, 30, or 11 percent of
the part-time fee-for-service providers (Group B in Table 1)
reported a major expansion of their practice in 1973.

It now appears that psychology's human service resources
are on the verge of major expansion. Whereas the American
Psychological Association has reported a steady net annual
membership growth of about 6 percent in recent years, with
2,600 Ph.D.s graduated in 1973, 833 of them in a clinical or

Table 1. Regional Distribution of Service Provider Psychologists

| | 1970 census (in %) | Salaried only service provider Group A | | Fee health service provider | | | | | |
| | | | | Part-time fee Group B | | Full-time fee Group C | | Combined Groups B and C | |
		N	%	N	%	N	%	N	%
Northeast	6	47	5	20	7	2	4	22	7
Mid-Atlantic	18	170	17	61	23	11	22	72	22
East-North Central	20	185	19	50	19	11	22	61	19
West-North Central	8	94	9	23	9	1	2	24	7
South Atlantic	15	135	14	25	9	8	16	33	10
East-South Central	6	44	4	7	3			7	2
West-South Central	10	79	8	14	5	3	6	17	5
Mountain	4	68	7	14	5	1	2	15	5
Pacific	13	170	17	55	20	14	27	69	22
Total	100	992	100	269	100	51	100	320	100

professional specialty, these figures were derived from a first-year graduate student base of about 6,000. By 1970, this base had increased to 7,500, and two years later the number of first-year graduate students in psychology had reached 12,000, closely approaching the national total of first-year medical students! Moreover, there is a clear recent shift to increased professional interests among psychologists and students (Warren, 1975; Chapter Fifteen of this book). G. Albee, in a personal communication, 1974, noted that by 1977 there are likely to be over 5,000 new Ph.D.s in psychology annually.

Of special interest is Whiting's finding that the distribution of psychology's service providers does not differ significantly by region from the 1970 population census: "Psychologist service providers are distributed throughout the United States in approximately the same way that the total population of consumers of psychological services are distributed" (p. 38). Geographic maldistribution, at least regionally, apparently does not apply to psychologists. For example, omitting Los Angeles, the 1973 distribution of psychologists and psychiatrists by California county correlates with the 1970 census .96 and .73, respectively. In comparison, the distribution of psychiatrists in relation to the population does not correlate as highly. For example, although the ratio of psychiatrists to population was 1:10,384 nationally, it was 1:2,2636; 4,389; and 7,306 in the District of Columbia, New York, and California, respectively.

Another striking finding contained in Whiting's sample study is that the percentage of professional time spent in service provision varies inversely with the general size of the employment unit, whether in primary health (practice, clinic, hospital) or educational (elementary, secondary, two- or four-year college or university) settings. Moreover, while only 7 percent of these APA members were in primary independent practice, they delivered 19 percent of all services by members and no less than 30 percent of all health services by psychologists in the hospital-clinic-practice triad! Probably the economies of scale are offset in organizational size by decreased service time. Based on personal administrative experience in health services (Dörken, 1962), we project that productivity and efficiency will be maximal in relatively small service delivery units organized on a non-profit corporate basis, and minimal in units organized by local government. Productivity will be especially great when services are rendered on a prepaid "at risk" contract basis, subject to claim and peer review, whether or not the practitioner is paid on a fee-for-service or salaried basis. In their study of the cost per hour of direct services in a community mental health center, Alexander and Sheely (1971, p. 774) concluded, "This mental health center . . . could not deliver face-to-face contact any more economically on a cost-per-hour basis than the private sector. . . . As a matter of fact, physicians' services tended to be higher."

Pilot Fee Practice Survey

Such indices invite a more detailed appraisal of current fee practice. Accordingly, based on the setting and geographic distributions used by Whiting, a Twenty Questions Survey, developed by Dörken, was mailed in 1973 to a stratified sample of service providers from the 1972 national study with the objective of obtaining 1,500 respondents. The initial mailing to 2,500 psychologists was completed in mid-May and a second mailing to nonrespondents was sent out a month later. This mailing was followed by a process of replacement mailing. The response rate soon stabilized at 70 percent willing to serve as resource persons. The distribution of resource persons in service delivery at the mid-September cutoff totaled 1,312. As shown in Table 1, 992 or 75 percent constitutes Group A, full-time salaried, no fee-for-service practice; 269 or 21 percent constitutes Group B, part-time fee for health service; and 51 or 4 percent constitutes Group C, full-time fee for health service.

Group C appears underrepresented, probably because of the extent of response requested from this group. The distribution of the 269 Group B and 51 Group C providers is also somewhat skewed, with underrepresentation of the South and overrepresentation of the Pacific group. Group A, the salaried-only providers, are more closely proportionate to the census in their distribution.

It must be borne in mind that 75 percent of the provider respondents, distributed across all settings, were full-time salaried personnel having no fee-for-service practice (Group A). Of the part-time fee-for-service practitioners (Group B), somewhat more than half (57 percent) were primarily employed in educational settings; in fact, 25 percent were employed in universities. Among university psychologists (all three groups), about the same proportion as hospital and clinic psychologists (30 percent versus 28 percent) were engaged in some "extra" fee practice health services. Similarly, 36 of the full-time practitioners (Group C) claimed teaching or supervisory work of three or more hours a week.

In terms of client age, while 58 percent of the full-time practitioners saw children (ages 0-12), nearly half of the hours reported were by 16 percent of the group. All saw the young adult, 80 percent saw the mature adult, but only 26 percent reported work with those over 64, and, for the latter, only 6 percent reported averaging more than an hour a week. Thus, the survey reflects that while there are child specialists among practicing psychologists, the field of aging appears to be neglected by the practitioners; aging accounts for only 1 percent of all clients seen. Psychologists, however, are not recognized directly under Medicare (see Table 2). In a 1973 sample survey of 606 psychiatrists in private office practice, Scheidemandel (1974) reported that 92 percent of their patients were between 14 and 59 years of age, with 4 percent on either side of this age range. Respondents reported an average of 33 patients a week.

The group surveyed by Scheidemandel saw an average of 35 clients weekly, 80 percent seeing between 20 and 50 clients. In terms of broad disability categories, of the clients seen by Group C, 65 percent were reported as having a behavior disorder or neurosis; 14 percent as having a character disorder; and the remaining 21 percent were about evenly distributed among the categories of addiction (4 percent), psychoses, mental retardation (5 percent), neurological impairment, and "other." In psychiatric practice, depressive neurosis, other neurosis and personality disorder accounted for 67 percent of the patients seen, and schizophrenia added 11 percent. While about half of the

Table 2. Setting Distribution of Service Provider Psychologists

	Salaried only service provider Group A		Fee health service providers					
			Part-time fee Group B		Full-time fee Group C		Combined Groups B and C	
	N	%	N	%	N	%	N	%
Education								
Elementary	72	7	8	3	0	0	8	2
Secondary	54	5	11	4	1	2	12	4
Two-year college	55	6	10	4	0	0	10	3
Four-year college	72	7	18	7	1	2	19	6
University	185	19	72	27	5	10	77	24
Other	166	17	33	12	1	2	34	11
Subtotal	604	61	152	57	8	16	160	50
Health								
Hospital	119	12	38	14	1	2	39	12
Clinic	106	11	42	16	5	10	47	15
Practice	0	0	13	5	35	69	48	15
Subtotal	225	23	93	35	41	80	134	42
Other								
Consulting firm	9	1	3	1	0	0	3	1
Industry	18	2	2	<1	0	0	2	<1
Corrections	18	2	1	<1	0	0	1	<1
Private agency	40	4	4	1	2	4	6	2
Religious	6	<1	2	<1	0	0	2	<1
Other human service	11	1	2	<1	0	0	2	<1
Government	52	5	7	3	0	0	7	2
Military	9	1	3	1	0	0	3	1
Subtotal	163	16	24	9	2	4	26	8
TOTAL	992	100	269	100	51	100	320	100

practitioners reported regular work with cases of mental retardation or addiction, only 15 percent and 10 percent averaged five or more hours a week with these disabilities.

For the psychologist practitioner, the workweek averaged 39.5 paid hours and 3.4 donated hours. Clearly, direct clinical service was the major activity, accounting for 81 percent of the time. About 33-1/3 percent were not engaged in consultation (clinical or program), while only 6 percent and 14 percent, respectively, devoted more than an hour a week to research or administration. The median reported gross professional income was $37,500, with 25 percent of the respondents having incomes under $30,000, and 25 percent incomes of $50,000 or higher.

An effort was made to obtain information on current fees for professional services. Peck's 1968 survey (1969, p. 16) had reported that "fees are primarily based on time" rather than procedure. Over half (60 percent) now hold to a uniform hourly fee regardless of procedure. Time is somewhat elastic, however. The "fifty-minute hour" is actually 45 minutes for 25 percent of Group C, and their assessment and consultative work includes time for report preparation. For all reporting providers combined (N = 277), the modal hourly fee was $25 (see also Alexander and Sheely, 1971), the same as the median fee reported by Cuca from the 1972 APA survey (1973). Two-thirds of the fees were within the $20-$30 range (see also Vetter, 1973). By contrast, the outpatient psychotherapy visit fees charged by psychologists under the Civilian Health and Medical Program of the Uniformed Services (CHAMPUS) program in 1973 in the ten states for which such data are available, ranged from an average of $23.22 in Illinois to an average $30.95 in South Carolina; the ten-state average being $29.14, only $1.84 less than the average for psychiatry (includes California, $29.81; District of Columbia, $30.11; and Texas, $27.74; see Chapter Eleven). Fees in the $35-$50 range were charged by 51 percent of those in full-time practice (only 12 percent of Group B), with no usual hourly fee of under $20 reported by this group. Clampitt (1975, p. 4) reported a clear "tendency for those devoting less than twenty hours a week to charge lower fees." Therefore, he adopted a calculation of average fees weighted according to the hours per week in private practice. The weighted means for psychotherapy and group therapy by doctoral practitioners were $38.05 and $17.91, respectively. While there was substantial overlap in fees according to degree status, somewhat higher fees were charged by those with a doctorate. About half (54 percent) of those without a doctorate considered their fees to be below the community rate. The only evident regional variations in this limited sample were the higher fees in the Southwest and broader distribution in the Pacific. By comparison, psychiatric office visit fees, as recently reported in *Money* (Cant, 1973), ranged from $25 to $50 in four major cities and about $5 less in rural areas. In the spring of 1973, 85 percent of psychiatric fees were in the $30-$45 range for individual psychotherapy, 40 percent of all fees being $35, the median fee (Owens, 1974).

For group therapy, 80 percent of the fees clustered in the $10 to $15 per session range; 67 percent used a 90-minute session. Most couple or family therapy was at the individual rate; only two practitioners, charging more for this service, exceeded a $5 differential.

It would seem that psychology is overdue for the formulation of a rational schedule of procedures that would not only delineate the broad range of services of which the profession is capable, but also establish an internal dollar value relationship. The *Relative Value Studies* of the California Medical Association (1969) established a unit value for each procedure within broad categories such as "psychiatric services" and "consultation." A community conversion factor, when applied to these unit values, yields the "Usual Customary and Reasonable" fee for a certain service in the area.

While part-time practice income ranged widely, from $80 to $50,000 annually, the interquartile range (mid-50 percent) was $1,250-$7,500, with the median side income from this source being $3,000. Though there was substantial overlap among settings, a fee income of $8,000 or more was more often attained by university practitioners (31 percent) and by those with a doctorate (30 percent).

In terms of fee overhead, the median reported was 24 percent. One quarter of full-time practitioners reported employing psychological assistants. Two thirds of the full-time practitioners billed 100 percent of their clients directly; 80 percent undertook direct billing for at least 90 percent of their cases. For 10 percent, all or the majority of the billing was done through a medical center or group practice office. Regardless of billing method, practitioners did not often have detailed insurance claim experience at hand.

Insurance Coverage

The growing inclusion of coverage for nervous and mental disorders in group health and major medical policies and the mounting evidence, at least for the working population, that such benefits are actuarially feasible (Reed, 1974) are exerting major leverage on health care delivery. The Committee on Health Insurance of the American Psychological Association and its counterparts among state psychological associations have sustained a decade of effort with substantial success. This progress is summarized in Chapter Three.

The services of psychologists are becoming available to a progressively better insured public. But due to mental disorder deductibles, coinsurance clauses, certain exclusions (for example, alcoholism), lower ceiling, and visit limits or referral conditions, the available coverage is still decidedly limited, particularly outside of the hospital, with fewer benefits available for outpatient or ambulatory treatment and care. Moreover, psychologists all too often are not accorded parity with other health professions. Nonetheless, there is an increase in state freedom-of-choice laws (Chapter Three). Given current mental health benefit limits and restrictions, there appears to be some point in Bodenheimer's (1972) claim that the pressure for national health insurance is not so much to benefit the consumer as to assure solvency of hospitals and health empires. The presence of deductibles, coinsurance, and other devices that oblige the patient to spend money for health care turn health decisions into economic ones and mask the noneconomic deficiencies of the health care system (Hodgson, 1973).

From 1950 to 1972, the proportion of total health care costs covered by insurance increased from 8.5 percent to 26.4 percent (Committee for Economic Development, 1973). In any move toward broader insurance coverage, however, special care needs to be exercised that such plans do not become simply public subsidies for elements of the health power structure in fiscal difficulty but actually result in improved comprehensive citizen health benefits more adequately distributed. To achieve less would be a hoax (Bodenheimer, 1972).

In Scheidemandel's survey, the psychiatrists reported that 53 percent of their patients had no insurance coverage whatever for their services. In the present study, nearly half (46 percent) of the part- and full-time psychologist practitioners surveyed reported that either none of their clients have insurance coverage for their services (37 percent) or they do not know what coverage their patients have (9 percent). Only 12 percent of these practitioners reported that 60 percent or more of their clients have insurance for some of their psychological services. Only 39 percent of the part-time providers reported on their claim experience, and for that matter, only 61 percent of the full-time practitioners reported it. Nonetheless, this limited sample did cumulatively note experience with 33 commercial carriers, 5 prepaid health service organizations, and 17 employee service benefit plans. In addition, experience was reported with several government programs. Table 3 summarizes for Group C the number of practitioners having claims with specific carriers, the total of claims submitted and paid, and the proportion not paid. For Group B, the information is limited to the number of practitioners who have submitted claims to a specific carrier and a grouping of reimbursement experience. As one respondent put it, "CHAMPUS is OK, all others are a pain." Special difficulty appears to have been encountered with Blue Cross and Blue Shield, Metropolitan, and Travelers. Twenty percent of the Group C claims were denied, while of the 38 part-time practitioners reporting claims to the "Blues," 55 percent experienced some or complete claim denial. Sixteen of the respondents expressed resentment at having to accept medical supervision in order to have their claims recognized. Claim approval for services under workmen's compensation, vocational rehabilitation, and government service appears heavily dependent on having an authorized provider number or contract. A substantial increase in the involvement of psychologists in "restorative services" can be anticipated from passage of PL 93-112, the Rehabilitation Act of 1973, which recognizes psychologists as primary providers. Similarly, passage of PL 93-363 providing for beneficiary access to psychologists for covered services in all Federal Employee Health Benefit Plans, and other statutes and regulations adopted in the 93rd Congress (see Chapter Three) should heighten the involvement of psychologist practitioners in health care delivery, and related services and programs.

Table 3. Third-Party Reimbursement

Group	CHAMPUS	Blue Cross/ Blue Shield MIA, HSI[a]	Aetna, Travelers, and Metropolitan	Various carriers[b]	Government controlled, workers' compensation, and vocational rehabilitation	Medicare and Medicaid
Group C[c]						
No. citing claims	15[e]	22	16	14	7	2
Claims paid	504	284	66	485	36	15
Claims not paid	1	59	22	20	16	9
% not paid[d]	<1	21	33[g]	4	44	60
Group B[d]						
All claims paid	29	17[f]	18	33	34	8
Only some paid	2	8[f]	0	2	5	1
All denied	1	13	7	7	3	1
% having claim denied	9	55	28	21	19	20

[a]MIA stands for Medical Indemnity Association; HSI stands for Health Services, Inc.

[b]Includes 30 other commercial carriers, 17 employee service benefit funds (6 unions), and 5 health service organizations.

[c]Thirty-one in Group C provided some claim detail, 5 accept direct payment only, and 15 provided no information.

[d]104 reported some claim experience; 165 reported no information.

[e]Plus one who reported, "CHAMPUS OK, all others a pain."

[f]16 psychologists, or 15 percent of those reporting, noted medical supervision required for reimbursement by certain carriers.

[g]Aetna claim denial 10 percent; Travelers and Metropolitan, 67 percent. The latter two companies now recognize services of psychologists in all states with "freedom of choice" insurance code amendments per circular notice, effective November 1973 and August 1973, respectively.

Manpower Resources of Related Professions

The manpower base of various professions with which psychology is frequently associated will also affect the recognition of psychologists as health care providers. The anticipated expansion of demand occasioned by the proposed national health insurance programs will draw on the resources of psychiatry as a medical specialty, on psychiatric and clinical social work, and on psychiatric nursing.

In 1970, Manson (1972) reported that there were nearly 290,000 physicians in this country, of whom 19,643 designated themselves as practicing psychiatrists. Of these, 48.1 percent, or 9,458, were board certified. Similarly, though with slightly different figures, the Health Resources Administration reported (HEW, HRA, 1974) that of 323,210 physicians at the end of 1970, 90 percent were engaged in direct care of patients as their primary activity. Of this 90 percent, about two-thirds were in office practice. Child psychiatrists and psychiatrists together accounted for 7.2 percent (over 23,000) of the total physician supply. Whiting's study (1969) reported that, overall, 67 percent of all psychiatric manhours were devoted to direct patient service and that 42 percent of all psychiatrists were in private practice. Multiple appointments were common in psychiatry, with 61 percent of all psychiatrists working in two or more locations and with over 30 percent working in three or more locations.

In 1967, the changes in immigration laws led to a large increase in foreign medical graduates (FMGs). It should be noted that psychiatry, like medicine, has a high percentage of FMGs; 20 percent of the physicians in the country are FMGs; 33 percent of residents in specialty training are FMGs. The percentage of FMGs in psychiatric residencies at large state hospitals often exceeds 75 percent (Torrey and Taylor, 1972). In contrast, Garfield and Kurtz (1974) found that only 2 percent of clinical psychologists are foreign graduates. Effective interpersonal communication and an understanding of the cultural and social values of the patient, however, may be more difficult for the practitioner of foreign origin.

Social work has its own confusion in specialty delineation and requisite levels of training that can mar its acceptance as a health care resource. The U.S. Census definition of social worker includes over 240,000 personnel (Spingarn, 1974). However, only 60,000 belong to the National Association of Social Workers (NASW), which on July 1974 shifted from the M.S.W. to the B.S.W. as its standard of professional preparation. The National Federation of Societies for Clinical Social Work, however, would continue to limit membership to BSWs with several years of clinical experience.

A recent (1973) National Institute of Mental Health (NIMH) staff study of mental health manpower estimates that 14,500 NASW members are in psychiatric or mental health areas, and that there exist yet another 5,500 psychiatric social workers. Of this 20,000, about 600 are in private practice. Licensing procedures have only been adopted in four states, and certification in only nine more. Thus, this profession is internally divided on a definitional problem.

All states have "nurse practice acts," which in general allow nurses a therapeutic relation with patients. Licensing is generic but biannual registration (unique to nursing) requires specialty designation. Nursing, the traditional ally of medicine, appears to be steadily upgrading itself with the evolution of nurse specialists and will thus prove even more useful as a health care resource in the future. It is estimated that there are about 1,100,000 licensed nurses nationally, 66 percent of whom are now working. Of those who are working, 4.5 percent are in psychiatric settings, a total of 33,000 (Committee for Economic Development, 1973). In 1966 the American Nurses Association reported that 25 percent of those nurses working in mental health services had had academic specialty training in psychiatric nursing. Projected data suggest there are now about 9,000 employed, trained psychiatric nurses. Some psychiatric nurses have entered fee-for-service practice and their number appears to be growing.

In summary, psychology has the resources of a professional health care provider. Recognition of this fact is necessary for the public well-being, given the shortages apparent in related professions and the anticipated explosion of demand that will accompany national health insurance legislation.

2

Standards for Psychologists

Durand F. Jacobs

In order for a profession to assume mature stature, standards of practice are a prerequisite. Standards characterize professions sufficiently well established to define, direct, and review their own areas of practice. Historically, three basic rights assure the integrity of any independent profession: self-determination (of the qualifications for entry into the profession); functional autonomy (within the bounds established by social, moral, and legal responsibilities); and self-regulation (exercised through peer review and based on a self-promulgated code of ethics and standards of practice). With these traditional perogatives in hand, any profession is in an excellent position to influence significantly the circumstances under which its services are used. This power is assured even though the activities of the profession are further regulated by national legislation, state statute, court order, or local operating policies of an employer. Typically, the goals of a profession are to clarify and enhance its public and self-perception, and to improve the quality of its services. Psychology has made considerable recent progress in developing its standards and perogatives.

An inventory of functions in the late 1960s was so discouraging that a small group of practitioners insistently urged that the American Psychological Association (APA) develop a set of comprehensive, national standards of practice. Only definitive action by the APA in its own behalf could remedy a situation in which nonpsychologist groups wrote standards for psychologists employed in health and rehabilitation settings. Further, such action was essential if psychology was ever to gain acceptance as a full-fledged profession. The events of the last few years confirm the wisdom of encouraging and developing a set of standards.

The major policy statement, *Standards for Providers of Psychological Services* (APA, 1974*b*), is now being applied with enthusiasm in many quarters. Since the standards were adopted on September 2, 1974, facility directors have been using the statement as an authoritative reference in organizing and staffing their local psychology departments. The standards are serving as both guides and prods to more objective clinical record keeping. They have been used to support new legislation and to prevent backsliding in existing state psychology laws. They have helped to bolster the confidence of the Civilian Health and Medical Program of the Uniformed Services (CHAMPUS) officials in the competence and responsibility of psychologist providers. The standards are being incorporated into the guidelines of the national Professional Standards Review Organization (PSRO) as performance criteria for psychologists in health and rehabilitation settings (HEW, OPSR, 1974). They are being used to effect changes in national governmental and private accreditation manuals that directly affect the definition, degree of functional autonomy, and peer review of psychologists in human service settings of all kinds. In short, developing its own standards has bolstered psychology's credentials for full participant membership in this country's health care delivery system.

Any effective set of standards for professional services contains ten basic components. First, standards define the qualified service provider. Second, they describe the types of services offered and the essential organizational elements of that profession's service delivery system. Third, they define the supervisory controls that the qualified provider should maintain over professional and technical staff functioning under his or her direction. Fourth, they enumerate specific functions that are to be maintained at or above given minimally acceptable levels. Standards always represent an impetus toward improved services and tend to float at least one notch above present practices. Fifth, they define the profession's relationships to bodies that govern the setting where services are provided. In large or multidisciplinary organizations, such matters as extent of authority, staff privileges, and voting status on key committees would be included in standards. Sixth, they define relationships with other professional or administrative staffs with whom the profession interacts. Seventh, they spell out the safeguards for protecting the human and civil rights of recipients of services. Eighth, they define the methods by which the professional's services are evaluated by local peers or by those once removed from the local situation, such as PSROs and third-party payors. Ninth, they must have a built-in process for periodic review and revision. Standards are living documents, and they change as the knowledge and skill base of the profession changes—and as circumstances that influence service delivery, either within or outside the profession, change. Tenth, standards must be closely associated with some mechanism for their implementation, for they will be academic unless their widespread application and enforcement can be ensured. The APA Standards for Providers of Psychological Services have been constructed to meet each of these requirements.

Developing Professional Standards

Psychology first emerged as a health profession in the middle 1940s. At that time, mental health workers were urgently needed to help the small corps of psychiatrists meet the needs of tens of thousands of World War II veterans with mental and emotional problems. University departments of psychology rapidly expanded their clinical and later their counseling sections to supply highly trained personnel for Veterans Administration hospitals and clinics throughout the country. It is historically significant that in 1946 the VA decided to require a doctoral degree as a condition of employment for psychologists in the department of medicine and surgery. The VA also established highly competitive pay scales to attract persons qualified at this level.

In setting the qualification standard at the doctoral instead of at the more available M.A. level, the VA deliberately placed long-term quality of care above immediate pressures to provide manpower. To meet the latter requirements, the VA established the Psychology Training Program. Numerous clinical psychologists practicing today were trained in VA settings, supported by VA training funds. Many psychologists spent portions of their professional careers in these settings, developing, researching, and applying the assessment and service delivery models so familiar today. In many ways, the VA was (and continues to be) the protector of clinical psychology.

Early decisions did much to shape the present identity of psychology as a health profession. The first standard of national significance—requiring the doctoral degree (plus appropriate supervised experience) for psychologists qualified to practice in tax-supported health settings—was established by an employer agency. It would be almost thirty more years before the APA would encourage this level of competence for all persons providing psychological services in municipal, state, and federal health and rehabilitation facilities.

Another manpower crisis in psychology is building for the late 1970s. As in the mid-1940s, it will be caused by an unprecedented increase in services promised to a large segment of the public. The crisis will be triggered by passage of the first stage of national (physical and mental) health insurance. It will deepen as benefits are progressively broadened to provide a greater range of services to more citizens than ever before.

To meet suddenly increased demands for services, all health professions will have to consider major revisions in the traditional organization and staffing of their respective service delivery systems. These changes will require psychologists and other professionals to learn how best to use paraprofessionals to extend the impact of their practice (Jacobs, 1974). But the most significant effect of national health insurance in the United States on traditional service models and professional roles will be the realization that the only way to provide the public with broadly and readily available services of high quality and acceptable economy is for all qualified health professions to assume direct primary care responsibilities.

In the mid-1970s, psychology finds itself much better prepared than it was in the 1940s to enter deliberations that will shape its destiny. It is recognized as an independent profession by statute in virtually every state. As do other mature professions, it regulates the performance of its service providers through uniform written ethical standards and standards of practice. Finally, psychology in the 1970s is strengthened by recently won legislative victories supporting its rights to practice autonomously and to be freely and directly accessible to those in need of its services. To the extent that it heeds the lessons of its relatively brief history as a developing health profession, psychology can authoritatively influence how its knowledge and resources will be used most effectively in the public interest. A review of the high and low points of its thirty-year history may forearm today's leaders of American psychology for realizing the promises and avoiding the pitfalls of the future.

Between 1945 and 1955, clinical psychology built its foundations as a profession. Its role was (and is) structured by the tenor of the times, the setting for practices, the needs of the major target populations, the extent of its skills and knowledge, and its relationships to other health professions. Each of these dimensions has changed radically over the past twenty-five years. The numbers of clinical, counseling, and rehabilitation psychologists have multiplied many times. A steadily increasing proportion of psychologists have been leaving their traditional institutional settings to enter private practice. However, psychology's status as an independent health profession has not increased proportionately with these professional developments (Jacobs, 1974).

This lag does not detract from important advances that were made in self-determination and functional autonomy during the decade 1945 to 1955. Paradoxically, these advances emerged from the private-practice sector, where only a small number of psychologists were engaged, in contrast to the preponderance of those working in nonacademic institutional settings. To understand this distribution among settings, one must recall that, until very recently, the APA was committed almost entirely to advancing psychology as a scholarly and scientific discipline. Only in the past few years has the organization extended itself to professional affairs with anything approaching the investment shown for its historic commitments. Thus, professional psychology grew largely unprotected by its national parent. Its maturation and fortunes were principally influenced by the boundless energies and talents of small groups of dedicated practitioners who worked mainly through their state psychological associations.

Some parallel supportive action was stimulated by the APA Board of Professional Affairs at the national level. Between 1947 and 1953, a small group labored successfully to produce the profession's first code of ethics (APA, 1963). In 1952, the first in a series of ill-fated attempts to establish standards of practice was made. This effort extended until 1960, first under the aegis of the APA Committee on a Directory of Psychological Service Centers and, from 1954 until its demise, under the American Board for Psychological Services, Inc. (American Psychological Association, 1953). The board proposed to enhance the public image of professional psychology by publishing a directory of individuals and agencies that had voluntarily requested evaluation and that were found to meet the board's standards for providing high-quality psychological services. However, the "standards" were essentially that the independent private practitioner hold a diploma from the American Board of Professional Psychology and that the ranking psychologist in an agency hold a Ph.D. and present at least three years of appropriate supervised experience. Beyond this, virtually nothing was said about what the psychologist was expected to do or what would be minimally acceptable levels of performance.

Subsequent attempts at standard setting likewise were limited to defining the academic and experiential requirements in order for a psychologist to offer independent service. These were written into state licensing or certification laws. From 1945 (when the first psychology law was passed in Connecticut) until 1954, a total of seven states defined the psychologist in private practice. In the three five-year periods from 1955 to 1969, eight, ten, and seventeen states, respectively, passed psychology laws.

In less than successful efforts to stabilize the qualifications and functions of practitioners, the American Psychological Association offered first in 1955 and later in 1967 some well-meant basic principles and guidelines for psychologists practicing mainly as independent service providers. Unfortunately, these policies also established and reinforced a double standard that endorsed higher levels of training and experience for psychologists engaged in private practice than for those practicing in institutional settings. (The APA was later to reject this position in its 1974 policy statement on Standards for Providers.) Inadvertently, these APA positions served the selfish interests of tax-supported facilities that have deliberately recruited less trained and less expensive psychological personnel for their patients. Tax-supported facilities were protected in this stance by state psychology laws that exempted their employees from the higher requirements established for psychologists serving private citizens. These statutes will be difficult to amend.

Thus, by 1970, compared to other more established health professions, psychology had developed into something like a stork standing on one leg. It was visible and erect but lacked the firm stance expected of a mature professional group fully capable of self-determination, autonomy of functioning, and self-regulation. What psychology lacked most was comprehensive standards of practice—standards that finally would include the overwhelming majority of the country's practicing psychologists, who had been systematically exempted from the state psychology laws passed between 1945 and 1972. These psychologists were employed in tax-supported institutional settings, mainly hospitals, clinics, and correctional and rehabilitation centers. For those settings, the American Psychological Association had offered no consistent model for defining the qualified practitioner, no standards of accessibility to clients, nor the types of services to be offered within stipulated limits of autonomy and accountability.

The latest impetus for creating standards emerged from an APA executive board meeting of Division 22 (Rehabilitation Psychology) in 1966. It was noted that recent landmark federal legislation (the Rehabilitation Act of 1965) had stimulated unprecedented expansion of rehabilitation services. In addition to the influx of money for new buildings and programs, unprecedented standards-setting and accreditations manuals appeared to guide the proper staffing and operations of the new and expanded facilities. Although some manuals referred to the "qualified psychologist" in a facility as one defined as such by the American Psychological Association, the APA had not defined training level and mode of functioning for psychologists in institutional practice. As a result, some governmental and private manuals defined the psychologist in institutional settings as one "with a master's degree from an accredited university" (HEW, SRS, 1967, pp. 12; Commission on Accreditation of Rehabilitation Facilities, 1973, pp. 15).

The Division 22 executive board concluded that if this situation prevailed, psychology's dream of becoming an independent profession would be seriously curtailed. The board established a committee on standards to effect liaison with standard-setting and accreditation groups, to learn more of these developments and to influence their outcomes in a manner that would improve psychology's place in rehabilitation settings. In its first report in February 1967, the committee concluded: "If psychologists do not take the initiative [in defining their own qualifications and] in recommending how their services might best be utilized ... others will certainly make those decisions for us in a manner which might not be in the best interests of the client, the public who pays, or the profession that trains and reviews the contributions of its members." When informed of these findings, John McMillan, then APA professional affairs officer, privately responded:

> The Board of Professional Affairs [BPA] certainly shares your concern about the establishment of standards for psychologists by other groups. As you know, APA has done a great deal during the past to clarify and make more uniform the minimal professional standards for fee-for-services activities of psychologists. This, in my judgment, is real advance. However, standards for institutional employment in service roles are still very much up in the air, as the association has never really gone into this aspect of

standards in any thorough or definitive way. In fact, there has been a tendency to sidestep this by exempting institutions from standards required for independent service roles. This area certainly constitutes a very important piece of unfinished business to which APA—probably through BPA—must come to grips.

For the next two years, the Division 22 standards committee actively pursued surveys of type and numbers of psychology manpower in rehabilitation facilities with an eye to creating standards of practice. By this time, additional federal legislation had fostered similar explosive growth situations in the fields of mental health and retardation. Finally, in August 1969, the committee consolidated its findings, suggested some formal content for standards, and firmly recommended that the APA board of directors take definitive action to promulgate "Standards for Psychologists in Institutional Practice" as a matter of major APA policy. The committee emphasized that three elements were essential to any set of standards covering all kinds of psychologists in all types of institutional setting: (1) that the person designated to direct the psychology service hold a doctoral degree in psychology; (2) that there be careful specification of the nature of supervision or consultation provided to persons with master's degrees in psychology who served as staff psychologists or as acting directors; and (3) that the American Psychological Association establish standards of training and experience required for "psychology technicians" and specify the nature of professional supervision to be maintained over their activities in both institutional and noninstitutional settings.

In February 1970, the Division 22 executive board petitioned APA governance to act on the committee's report, ending with the following statement:

> While recognizing the broad and profound implications that recommendations such as these have for the profession of psychology, it is our firm conviction that APA must act to discharge its long delayed responsibility for establishing standards for the large

segment of its membership who practice in institutional settings. Although it is understood that the final form and content of such APA standards may be properly modified from those submitted as a result of further study, there can be no justification for further delay. The APA in our opinion must quickly take a definitive and public position on the matter of standards for psychologists in institutional settings since governmental and private groups have already begun to suggest their own standards in the absence of such guidelines from APA.

There are, however, even more compelling positive reasons for APA to take prompt action in this matter. Supplementing existing standards for psychologists in independent practice by a comparable set for those in institutional practice will significantly influence the content and direction of university training for the profession of psychology, and will also provide meaningful objectives for those training subprofessional technical personnel to assist professional psychologists in their work. The recommended extension of standards will better meet the profession's ethical obligation to insure competent assistance to consumers of psychological services.

Finally, the proposed extension in standards will provide a set of authoritative, national guidelines for those involved in statutory and accreditation efforts.

The first APA Task Force on Standards for Psychologists in Service Facilities was established by the Board of Professional Affairs in March 1970. Its charge was "to plan and implement activities contributing to the formulation and publication of standards that would serve to improve the quality and accessibility of psychological services to all in need of them." At its first meeting, in Washington, D.C., the task force was joined by a delegation from the Joint Commission on Accreditation of Hospitals (JCAH), which was then planning a revision of its manual of standards for psychiatric facilities. The JCAH had never before met with a professional group (outside of medicine) to seek its input prior to a revision of the manual.

Almost immediately, the task force began to speak officially on behalf of the APA on matters affecting the qualifications and functions of practicing psychologists in institutional settings. Over the years, the task force has reiterated certain basic principles and contributed some of the actual content seen in standards published by the Commission on Accreditation for Facilities for the Mentally Retarded (1973), the JCAH Accreditation Council for Psychiatric Facilities (1973), and the *Wyatt v. Stickney* judgment issued by the U.S. District Court in Alabama (1972). In 1973 and 1974, the task force joined with others representing the APA in national-level deliberations with public and private insurance carriers and in legislative activities involving definitional and quality-control guidelines for psychologists qualified to provide health services. A number of task force members were also appointed to a select APA group charged with producing model criteria for evaluating psychological services under PSRO. These interim outcomes were gratifying because they represented greater APA participation in decisions being made by others about psychology's professional identity and functioning. However, they did not replace the prime objective of formulating a set of standards through which American psychology could speak out independently and decisively on the proper qualifications, functions, and accountabilities of practicing psychologists. This objective finally was realized with the approval of the Standards for Providers of Psychological Services by the APA Council of Representatives on September 2, 1974.

A few basic principles guided the formulation of the standards. It was very strongly held that a single set of standards should cover all types of psychologists in all manner of human service settings for the guidance of all concerned parties, whether they were providers, consumers, payers, or sanctioners of services. It was further held that there should be a single generic definition of the psychologist qualified to offer independent services in whatever setting—as one holding a doctorate. Academic qualification supplemented by appropriate experience was considered the best available and most generally acceptable index of competence. It was also believed that the same stan-

dards should uniformly govern provision of psychological services in both the private and public sectors. It was felt that the
double standard sustained by licensure laws since 1945, which
had permitted a lesser level of psychological services in tax-
supported institutional settings, should be rejected. Other principles shaping the standards may be stated briefly: although the
standards should hold the psychologist strictly accountable for
the nature and quality of services provided, they must not con-
strain the psychologist from employing innovative methods and
making flexible use of support personnel. The standards should
anticipate and provide for emerging changes in patterns of service delivery. The standards should be a living document requiring continuous review and revision.

It is important to specify what the standards are *not*. A
number of queries have been received from psychologists who
are concerned that they may be in some ethical bind if they do
not immediately observe the letter of the APA standards. For
example, otherwise qualified but unlicensed psychologists employed in state and federal hospitals inquired whether they
must secure state licensing or certification. A number of industrial psychologists and clinicians were concerned that they cannot readily comply with the requirement for "a written service
delivery plan for every consumer," including evidence that
informed consent has been obtained. It is necessary to point out
that standards carry no statutory authority. They cannot super-
sede state statutes. Unlike the code of ethics, they do not even
require immediate conformance by APA members. However,
the standards do set forth official APA policy on the directions
psychologists shall take in improving their services. Operation-
ally, the standards represent a set of minimal goals toward
which each provider and facility is enjoined by APA to move
with firm resolve, honest effort, and deliberate speed. It is
understood that some will move more slowly and with greater
difficulty than will others. The principal contribution of the
standards is to illuminate weaknesses in the delivery of psychological services and to point out ways to correct them. Evaluating the adequacy of objectives, noting how quickly they are
attained, and imposing sanctions all fall within the purview of
accreditation groups and peer review mechanisms.

The mere presence of the standards does not in itself advance the professional contributions of psychology. Proper implementation of the standards must be ensured. To do so, the APA is seeking membership with national accreditation groups such as the Joint Commission on Accreditation of Hospitals and its numerous subsidiary councils. Although not yet adopted by APA governance, the following four-part affirmative action program has been recommended by the Task Force on Standards as being consistent with the "principles" set forth in the 1974 standards. First, request that chiefs of psychological services in all exempted governmental settings and chairpersons of APA-approved university departments of psychology encourage professional members of their staff who provide direct psychological services voluntarily to seek state licensing or certification; and eventually move toward state licensure or certification as a condition of employment. Second, follow up with a systematic action plan to strike from state and federal statutes and regulations all references that exempt the psychologist in government from meeting the same standards for licensure or certification as psychologists offering similar services on a fee-for-services basis. Third, require that APA take affirmative action to support freedom of choice in selecting qualified service providers by all who seek health services. And fourth, require that any constraints on the independent professional status of psychologists as providers of health services in both public and private settings be met with legal action by APA whenever appropriate, or by the APA exercising sanctions against the employment of psychologists in settings that unduly limit the psychologist's opportunities to function as an independent professional person.

Implications of APA Standards

Those APA officers and committees charged with promulgating the standards were sensitive to certain short- and long-range implications of the document for explicating the rights and duties of professional psychologists. The primary objectives guiding the construction of the standards were to improve the quality and accessibility of psychological services and to determine uniformly, for all settings, the acceptable levels for those services. The standards would, thereby, immediately constitute the basis for and facilitate more objective evaluation of services provided and outcomes achieved. This application of the standards added a new dimension of accountability for psychologist practitioners. The standards would also represent a firm step toward more uniform legislative and statutory action defining qualified psychologists and the manner in which their services are provided to the public. The standards could contribute to a national licensing law for psychologists.

Perhaps the most profound influence of the standards would be on training models for both professional and support personnel in psychology. Standards could exert a stabilizing influence on "the reigning chaos in practice and training" that has attended the explosive growth of psychology over the past thirty years. The concept of a psychological service delivery system under the direction of one or more qualified psychologists, and supported by multiple levels of differently trained service providers, would offer a viable alternative to existing models for meeting large-scale needs for psychological services.

The standards would add an indispensable measure of credibility and authority to psychology's identity and status as an independent health provider. They would help prepare psychologists for contests in state and national legislative arenas, in private and public human service settings where they seek privileges and responsibilities as independent professionals on parity with physicians, and for other interprofessional bouts that already have been joined. The standards would serve to place the prestige and resources of the entire APA behind this small, embattled group and behind others as need arose.

At its meeting in January 1975, the APA Council created and funded a standing Committee on Standards for Providers of Psychological Services. Its charge was to review and revise the standards so that they might remain timely, workable, and directed toward an unending pursuit of excellence in quality of service to the public. After thirty years, psychology at last was speaking for itself as an independent profession. Through self-definition in state and federal legislation, and by virtue of creating its own ethical code and standards of practice, it had finally assumed the firm stance of a mature profession.

3

Laws, Regulations, and Psychological Practice

Herbert Dörken

In years to come, psychology may well look back upon the 93rd Congress as the turning point in its formal recognition as a health profession. Since the late 1960s, some major insurance carriers (see Chapter Six) have recognized psychological services in their coverage; CHAMPUS (see Chapter Nine) was directed to consider the profession as a primary provider of health services in June 1970. The first federal law recognizing psychology as an independent profession entitled to engage in health practice, however, was the District of Columbia Licensing Law. Passed in 1971 by the Congress and signed into law, it helped to set the stage for later events. It remained for the 93rd Congress to pass a series of laws broadening the statutory base of psychology as a health profession.

The Veterans Health Care Expansion Act of 1973, PL 93-82, in recognizing the services of psychologists for the dependents of totally disabled veterans, opened a new area for psychologists in health services. Then, after two prior vetoes, the Rehabilitation Act of 1973 was passed. This legislation, PL 93-112, in delineating the scope of services, recognizes the services of physicians *or* licensed psychologists for both assessment and restorative services, and for physical or mental disability, within the scope of practice of these two professions. This law has a broad impact in setting standards and guidelines for all state rehabilitation programs. Extended restorative services (up to eighteen months) can be authorized when these services carry the prospect of employability or improving employment. Mental disorder is the single largest disability category and, together with mental retardation, comprised over half (50.7 percent) the clients receiving rehabilitation services nationally according to 1972 reports from the Social and Rehabilitation Services (see Chapter Four).

Following extended consideration of models to improve health care delivery, Congress passed PL 93-222, the Health Maintenance Organization (HMO) Act of 1973. Basic health care services are to include "short-term (not to exceed twenty visits) out-patient evaluative and crisis intervention mental health services." Services are also to include treatment and referral services for the abuse of or addiction to alcohol or drugs. Supplemental health services could extend these mental health services. The HMO model includes both "medical groups" and "individual practice associations." The regulations implementing this act explicitly enumerate "clinical psychologists" among the recognized health professionals (Title 42— Public Health, Subchapter J, Part 110, Section 110.101 [h][1]). The Disaster Relief Act of 1974, PL 93-288, also provided for professional counseling for mental health problems caused or aggravated by a disaster. So that health services will be more equitably available, attention is being given to critical manpower shortage areas and to the potential role of the National Health Service Corps established pursuant to PL 92-585. Proposed rules were issued in the Federal Register on January 6, 1975. Included within the definition of "assigned personnel" are such professions as "physicians, dentists, *psychologists, nurses* [italics added]." Guidelines for implementing the Head Start Performance Standards were published in July 1975. The resources that may be contracted include "Private Practitioners of . . . Psychology . . ." (HEW, OCD, 1975, p. 27). Further, this manual defines a "mental health professional" as including "a licensed psychologist."

Psychology, together with optometry (much of whose technology derives from the experimental findings and methods of sensory psychology), sought recognition as primary providers in Federal Employee Health Benefit Plans through HR 9440 (Jerome Waldie, California) and S 2618 (Gayle McGee, Wyoming) such that the employee would have free choice of and direct access to such licensed providers. The bills drew opposition from the Civil Service Commission, from the National Association of Blue Shield Plans, and from the American Psychiatric Association. As amended to licensed clinical psychologists and optometrists, S 2619 was approved unanimously by the full committee and signed into law as PL 93-363 on July 30, 1974. This law amended Title 5, U.S. Code, Chapter 89—Health Insurance, Section 8902 (j), by providing that "an employee, annuitant, or family member . . . shall be free to select, and shall have direct access to, such a clinical psychologist . . . without supervision or referral by another health practitioner." Parity for clinical psychology with other health practitioners was thus established in a nationwide program covering about 8.5 million federal employees and dependents or retirees. Eighteen states had already enacted similar freedom-of-choice statutes, since increased to twenty-three as of July 1975.

Psychological services are also recognized in tax laws. Beginning with the 1973 Federal Income Tax Form instructions for Standard Form 1040, Schedule A, itemized deductions for medical and dental expenses have included, "payments to . . . psychiatrists, *psychologists,* and psychoanalysts" ([italics added] page 10, Column 1, 1974 IRS Form 1040 instructions). This change on clarification was agreed to by the Internal Revenue Service upon request of the author.

Congress also paid attention to the problems of handicapped children. PL 93-380 amended the Elementary and Secondary Education Act, Title VI, Education of the Handicapped. This legislation includes the mentally retarded and emotionally disturbed among those handicapped who are "health impaired." The conference report clearly intends that the services for these children whose health is handicapped will include psychological processes.

Employability is a matter of concern to Congress and federal agencies. The U.S. Department of Labor regulations implementing PL 93-203, the Comprehensive Manpower Program, define psychological services within health care, ". . . to the extent any such treatment or services are necessary to enable a participant to obtain or retain employment . . . ." (Title 29, Part 94, Section 94.4[x]). In a similar vein, the Department of Labor has adopted and published regulations in the *Federal Register* (September 18, 1974, p. 43174) to implement the work incentive program (WIN) for recipients of Aid to the Families of Dependent Children (AFDC) under Title IV of the Social Security Act. Section 56.20 (b)(4) requires that the AFDC recipient shall register unless "Incapacitated, when verified by the IMU [Income Maintenance Unit] that a physical or mental impairment, determined by a physician *or licensed or certified psychologist* . . . prevents the individual from engaging in employment or training under WIN [emphasis supplied]." Supportive services include selected vocational rehabilitation services as defined by the Rehabilitation Act of 1973. Looking to the field of workers' compensation and to federal employees, PL 93-416 was signed September 7, 1974, amending Chapter 81 of Subpart G of Title V of the U.S. Code relating to work injuries compensation under the Federal Employee Compensation Act (FECA). Among other things, this law broadened the definition of both "physician" and "medical, surgical, and hospital services and supplies," to include "clinical psychologists." What may be of special significance is that, in contrast to the Rehabilitation Act, the law amending the Federal Employee Health Benefit Act (FEBHA), and the regulations implementing the HMO Act, in which cases psychology had exerted a concerted effort to secure its inclusion in these signed pieces of health legislation, the inclusion of "clinical psychologist" in PL 93-416 was accomplished essentially by "referencing in." Perhaps psychology *has* turned the corner as a health profession.

Just as in the CHAMPUS directive, federal agency decisions can have a very substantial impact. Thus, in the early 1960s National Institute of Mental Health (NIMH) regulations provided that psychologists could serve as directors of community mental health centers—after they were faced with such a fact in a number of states. More recently, the Veterans Administration has issued regulations providing that psychologists and other health professionals licensed or certified by the state may provide services on a fee basis to outpatients through VA clinics and that psychologists, among others, may be appointed to direct such facilities. The United States Department of Defense now includes psychologists in its policy, which provides that "any qualified health professional may command or exercise administrative direction of a military health care facility . . . without regard to the officer's basic health profession" (Memorandum from Secretary of Defense to the Secretaries of the Military on subject of Staff and Command Assignments of Health Professionals, May 1, 1973).

During the 93rd Congress, the national health insurance bill with the most sponsors was the Vance Hartke-Clifford Hansen (Indiana and Wyoming) S 444 bill, generally referred to as the AMA (American Medical Association) Medicredit Bill. Without any evident subsequent objection from the AMA, Senator Hartke introduced a series of amendments to this bill early in 1974, amendments that, essentially, throughout changed *medical* to *health, illness* to *disability, medical and dental services* to *professional health care services, doctor* to *licensed practitioner,* and *psychiatric* to *mental health.* And in the enumeration of professions these amendments added psychology, optometry, and podiatry. The Hugh Scott-Charles Percy bill (Pennsylvania and Illinois) S 2756, would have recognized licensed psychologists as independent providers from the outset. In 1974 the insurance industry amended its Omar Burleson-Thomas McIntyre bill (Texas and New Hampshire), S 1100, to include licensed doctors of clinical psychology. Senator Daniel Inouye (Hawaii) then introduced S 3645 to recognize psychologists as primary providers under Part B of Medicare. This move was followed on November 26 with HR 17520 by Representative James Corman (California), intended to so recognize clinical psychologists.

By the end of January 1975 both the Inouye and Corman bills had been reintroduced in the 94th Congress, with strong supporting statements. This time, however, the language of both was identical (*clinical psychologist*), and as of March, S 123 and HR 2270 had already accumulated substantial cosponsorship.

Representative Patsy Mink (Hawaii) had also introduced HR 3980, a separate bill with identical language. Soon after, Representative Spark Matsunaga (Hawaii) introduced HR 3674, amending the Edward Kennedy-James Corman Health Security Act (Massachusetts and California) to recognize the services of clinical psychologists and to increase the extent of ambulatory mental health services. In March, Senator Phillip Hart (Michigan) concerned that the national health insurance proposals being submitted did not provide for adequate mental health care, introduced S 1332, the Mental Health Act of 1975. This bill seeks "to end the discrimination between mental health care and other forms of health care." In the process it delineates a more realistic range of benefits and includes psychologists as fully recognized providers in all phases. Then, by May, the insurance industry's National Health Care Act of 1975 had been introduced, including qualified clinical psychologists as physicians (HR 5990 Burleson [Texas]; S 1438 McIntyre [New Hampshire]).

Obviously, future events are not predictable with certainty. The country's economic crisis appears likely at this time to delay implementation of National Health Insurance, perhaps for a few years. Consequently, potential changes in Medicare take on added importance, as do the establishment of national guidelines or standards for the National Workers' Compensation Act of 1975 (S 2018 Harrison Williams [New Jersey]). This bill recognizes clinical psychologists as primary providers within the definition of *physician*. Malpractice has emerged as a major problem in health care delivery by physicians and S 215 (Inouye), the National Medical Injury Compensation Insurance Act of 1975, would introduce a "no-fault" method of claim settlement. It would also include "clinical psychologists" among the designated "health professionals."

Lay organizations such as the National Association for Mental Health (NAMH) have become increasingly active, fighting impoundment of federal funds for community mental health centers, training, and research. NAMH has been equally vocal in its demands that national health insurance include realistic coverage for nervous and mental disorders and that all the major mental health professions meeting national standards of training be recognized as providers, whether in private practice or in organized settings.

The past few years have shown that if psychology is to be recognized as a health profession more will be needed than a distinguished record in the field of health research. More will be needed than the significant supply of competent professionals in positions of administrative responsibility in health, rehabilitation, mental health, and mental retardation services. Recognition will require effective advocacy. The Council for the Advancement of Psychological Professions and Sciences (CAPPS), formed in 1972, has been joined by the Association for the Advancement of Psychology (AAP), established in 1974. Both advocacy organizations are now working in cooperative "common cause"—indeed, are in the process of merging into a single organization (AAP). And psychologists—or at least more of them—have become alerted to public policy issues and the legislative process.

Licensure and Certification

In 1945, Connecticut became the first state to *certify* psychologists. In 1946, Virginia passed the first law that *licensed* those who might practice psychology. By 1972, a quarter century later, forty-six states, the District of Columbia, and six Canadian provinces had laws governing the title of psychologist or the practice of psychology. Since then, Iowa has passed such legislation, leaving only Missouri, South Dakota, and Vermont without such statutes.

The distinction between licensing and certifying is important. A licensing law is intended to define the practice of psychology and to restrict such function to qualified persons, who may be psychologists or members of other professions using psychological techniques. By contrast, a certification law limits the use of the title *psychologist* to qualified persons and may or may not include a definition of practice (APA, 1967). Twenty-six states have licensure, the remainder certification. All provincial laws (Canadian) are of the certification type. Currently, in many states psychologists are taking steps, where necessary, to secure a "practice" law, one in which the practice of psychology is properly defined.

The APA Committee on State Legislation (COSL) has monitored and provided guidance in these developments. Model conditions were outlined in the COSL report (1967). For example, using illustrative language, the report recommended that these statutes provide for privileged communication between therapist and client. As of January 1973, thirty-seven of the U.S. laws (including that passed by the District of Columbia) had such a provision for confidentiality. Then, to not unduly restrict professional mobility, reciprocity was encouraged between states with equivalent standards. Only the Arizona law fails in this respect. For licensing or certification as a "psychologist," the doctorate has consistently been recommended as the minimum standard, a standard that has vigorously been reaffirmed by key committees of APA, such as COHI (Committee on Health Insurance) and COSL, by the Board of Professional Affairs, and by the Council itself, as recently as January 1975. Iowa, Pennsylvania, and West Virginia, in enabling the licensure (quite apart from a grandfathering clause) of master's-level training, with additional experience to compensate for the lack of training, are thus in conflict with the national standards. Subsequent progress and changing conditions, however, now are leading to serious reconsideration of many "standard" provisions. Whereas exemptions from the law had typically included salaried employees of state and federal agencies—of public service—the Standards for Providers of Psychological Services adopted as APA policy by the Council of Representatives, September 2, 1974, when implemented, would require elimination of this dual standard. In effect, it is now the national policy of organized psychology that all psychologist service providers must be licensed or certified.

The statutory base of practice should be consistent with psychology's claim that it is a health profession. Critical in this regard is the definition of practice. As of January 1973, whereas forty-three statutes contained a definition of practice, psychotherapy was explicitly included in twenty-four states and in the

District of Columbia. The guideline definition, however, seems overly focused on mental disorder and to be without a key word, *treatment* (included in the California law). Thus, serious consideration should be given to securing practice legislation that ". . . includes, but is not restricted to: diagnosis, prevention, *treatment* and amelioration of adjustment problems and emotional and mental disorders of individuals and groups *and of the psychological concomitants of disease, illness, injury or disability*" [italics added]. Moreover, since psychology has provided the major impetus and leadership in the development of the behavior therapies and of biofeedback technology, it would also seem advisable to broaden the definition of *practice* so that these modes of treatment are explicitly included.

The primary purpose of this legislation has always been protection of the public and assurance of improved quality by demanding sound standards for qualification. Originally that public was more narrowly seen in the perspective of private practice. Hence, licensing was a requirement when psychological services were to be offered for a fee, monetary or otherwise. The rapid growth of health insurance and of service contracting, points to the need for a broader definition of *fee*, to include third-party reimbursement and services prepaid by premium or contract.

Psychologists, just as physicians and some other professions, have been licensed generically, with the expectation, built into the profession's code of ethics, that the licensee will limit practice to his or her area of competence. But now there is a growing public recognition that no one can be truly competent in all the specialties of a broad profession and that the recipient of services should be protected by the addition of specialty certification to the licensing process. Specialty certification should not simply be a voluntary limitation of one's practice to a specialty area—whether or not one has completed the required training or passed professional exams. Specialty certification should be issued by the regulatory state agency, with this certification and the basic license subject to conditions of continuing education for reissue. The state of Oregon, in fact, recently passed new legislation giving the Board of Psychologist Examiners the authority to require continuing education of psychologists. The first of its kind in psychology, this legislation is seen as a forerunner of general provisions to come. The current climate would suggest that clear delineation of clinical training and experience in organized health settings may become essential for continued recognition of psychologists as health service providers.

The insurance industry has shown a willingness to recognize psychologists as health practitioners, but it increasingly wants assurance that the practitioner has the requisite training and experience in health care delivery and that the services being provided are health services. A collegial relationship among health professions requires that the professions involved be health providers, not education specialists, specialized counselors, or management or vocational specialists. With such concerns in mind, the National Register of Health Service Providers in Psychology has been established. Its first directory became available in the summer of 1975, with listing made on the basis of a credentials review. Not only will this directory help to delineate the current available health manpower resources of psychology but it is also expected to facilitate claim processing and reimbursement for those listed. Indeed, the directory could well be "referenced in" as a criterion guideline by insurance carriers and agencies contracting for health services.

No unduplicated roster of state licensed or certified psychologists yet exists, not even an exact count, though estimates have been attempted (see Chapter One). Three states do not have statutory regulation of psychology—Missouri, South Dakota, and Vermont. The Iowa law is too recent (1974) to have yet provided sufficient time for the processing of those to be "grandfathered in." And, by local policy, Hawaii will advise whether a specific person is licensed there or not, but will not release a directory of its state licensed psychologists. Despite passage of the Pennsylvania law in 1972, funding uncertainties and other problems have delayed availability of a directory. Rhode Island simply does not respond to requests for such information.

Summary detail is provided in Table 1, with licensing and

Table 1. U.S. State Resident Psychologists Qualified for Practice

States	Population 1973 Census Estimates; in Thousands	Licensed or Certified Psychologists (State Residents)	Registry Date Month/Year	Registry Date Licensed/Certified	Ratio Licensed Psychologists per 10,000 Population	1973 APA Member Directory	1972 Consolidated Roster Psychologists
Alabama	3,539	112	9/74	L	.316	235	298
Alaska	330	21	74	L	.636	29	37
Arizona	2,058	318	2/75	C	1.545	323	441
Arkansas	2,037	62	1/74	L	.304	113	151
California	20,601	2,953	5/73	L	1.433	4,426	5,655
Colorado	2,437	253	1/75	L	1.021	507	763
Connecticut	3,076	293	11/73	L	.953	740	955
Delaware	576	57	4/74	L	.990	110	141
District of Columbia	746	73	73	L	.979	720	830
Florida	7,678	396	10/74	L	.516	916	1,124
Georgia	4,786	196	73	L	.410	455	581
Hawaii	832	Individual confirmation only		L	—	143	184
Idaho	770	50	74	L	.649	51	93
Illinois	11,236	1,414	8/74	L	1.258	1,879	2,448
Indiana	5,316	350	1/74	C	.658	604	782
Iowa	2,904	Directory under development		—	—	333	493
Kansas	2,279	199	11/73	C	.873	364	520
Kentucky	3,342	107	8/73	L	.320	273	374
Louisiana	3,764	161	11/73	L	.428	223	297
Maine	1,028	74	74	L	.720	120	160
Maryland	4,070	420	6/73	C	1.032	970	1,160
Massachusetts	5,818	1,212	1/75	L	2.083	1,372	1,705
Michigan	9,044	405	7/73	C	.448	1,324	1,795
Minnesota	3,897	215	3/73	L	.552	594	884
Mississippi	2,281	91	7/74	L	.399	119	156
Missouri	4,757	Nonstatutory	—	—	—	532	667
Montana	721	43	8/73	L	.600	61	92

Table 1 (*continued*)

States	Population 1973 Census Estimates; in Thousands	Licensed or Certified Psychologists (State Residents)	Registry Date Month/Year	Licensed/Certified	Ratio Licensed Psychologists per 10,000 Population	1973 APA Member Directory	1972 Consolidated Roster Psychologists
Nebraska	1,542	124	4/74	L	.804	173	237
Nevada	548	26	2/74	C	.474	68	80
New Hampshire	791	62	7/74	C	.784	110	153
New Jersey	7,361	732	2/75	L	.994	1,393	1,703
New Mexico	1,106	62	12/73	C	.561	144	179
New York	18,265	3,192	6/74	L	1.748	5,415	6,509
North Carolina	5,273	283	7/73	L	.537	537	710
North Dakota	640	40	74	C	.625	54	67
Ohio	10,731	1,342	1/74	L	1.251	1,361	1,709
Oklahoma	2,663	119	73	L	.447	247	348
Oregon	2,225	169	7/74	L	.760	318	458
Pennsylvania	11,905	(2,056) licenses issued by 5/75		L	—	2,081	2,556
Rhode Island	973	110	9/74	C	1.131	131	182
South Carolina	2,726	129	1/74	L	.473	191	267
South Dakota	685	Nonstatutory	—	—	—	41	65
Tennessee	4,126	224	11/73	L	.543	421	579
Texas	11,794	845	4/74	L	.716	1,330	1,738
Utah	1,157	157	4/74	L	1.357	181	267
Vermont	464	Nonstatutory	—	—	—	92	112
Virginia	4,811	172	73	L	.358	746	883
Washington	3,429	241	1/73	L	.703	497	733
West Virginia	1,794	84	3/74	L	.468	147	172
Wisconsin	4,569	424	4/74	L	.928	668	893
Wyoming	353	46	1/74	L	1.303	48	73
44 States and the District of Columbia	188,304	18,058	—	—	.959	30,254	38,761
U.S. Total	209,851	—	—	—	—	33,930	43,461

certification figures for forty-four states and the District of Columbia. The most current directories ranged from January 1973 to February 1975. In each instance, out-of-state residents were dropped from the count, so that the tabulation presented is unduplicated. For example, 218 residents of Maryland and Virginia, since licensed in their resident state, are not included in the District of Columbia count, which as a result totals only 73. In the seven states (Arkansas, Indiana, Maine, Michigan, Minnesota, North Carolina, and Tennessee) where licensing or certification is multilevel, only the top level, the level recognized for independent practice, was counted. Thus, by this conservative count, there were 18,058 psychologists licensed or certified for independent practice in 45 jurisdictions, a ratio of .959 such psychologists per 10,000 of population. Following the same ratio for the other three states with statutory regulation from which no information was available, the overall count would be increased to 19,508. When contrasted to the 1972 APA membership or the *Consolidated Roster for Psychology* (American Psychological Association, 1972) in the country, it is apparent that the number of psychologists qualified for independent practice by statute are but 57.5 percent of APA members and 45 percent of all known psychologists in the country. These figures are of course already outdated. By 1974, total APA membership had grown to just over 37,000; had exceeded 39,000 by mid-1975; and is projected to reach 41,500 in 1976. It may well be, then, that the number of practitioners qualified by statute is at this writing some 20 percent larger than the above derived total—say, 23,000.

Freedom of Choice

Although the APA Council of Representatives in September 1962 adopted official policy recognizing properly qualified professional psychologists as independent practitioners, it should be noted in historical perspective that the adoption was in reaction to a storm of protest from practitioners over policy adopted in 1960. In May 1960 the APA Board of Professional Affairs had recommended gaining federal acceptance of provisions for covering psychological services when deemed necessary by those having medical responsibility for the treatment of the claimant. In other words, the APA had recommended supervision by *another* profession. When that policy was adopted, the association's governance heard clearly from its clinical membership. The insurance problem became a cause célèbre.

In the mid-1960s the APA Committee on Health Insurance (COHI) encouraged state psychological associations to introduce legislation that would, by state, entitle health insurance subscribers to freedom of choice (FOC) and direct access to qualified psychologist practitioners for covered benefits without the need for referral or supervision by another profession. Twenty-three states now have such legislation, six of these statutes having passed in 1974, five in the first half of 1975. The addition of Connecticut by Public Act 75-286 on June 5th seems particularly significant, in view of the state's prominence in the insurance industry. Moreover, both the Connecticut and the new Minnesota laws mandate minimum levels of coverage for mental and nervous conditions or disorders. As already noted, comparable FOC law was passed by Congress for federal employee health plans—over considerable opposition. The current status of these statutes is summarized in Table 2.

New Jersey, in 1968, was the first state to adopt FOC legislation. The present twenty-three states cover over half the U.S. population and 12,853, or 66 percent of the 19,508 estimated total of psychologists with statutory authorization for independent practice. The 12 percent differential suggests that FOC legislation may have an effect on (or be due to) the manpower supply of psychologist practitioners. Both Illinois and Hawaii do not have FOC legislation, though they report reasonable recognition by insurance carriers and by Blue Cross and Blue Shield. Illinois, however, now has a bill active in the current legislative sessions. Similar informal local "understandings" may exist in other parts of the country. For example, the Washington law covers disability policies. A bill to extend it to all types of plans several years ago was vetoed by the governor on the assurance of local medical cooperation. Nearly two years passed, however, before all county health plans put this assur-

Table 2. Freedom-of-Choice Legislation Recognizing Psychology

State	Passed	1973 Census (1,000)	1972 APA Members	Licensed or Certified Psychologists[a]	Directory Date	Licensed or Certified Psychologists per 10,000 Population	Explanatory Note[b]		
1. Massachusetts	12/73	5,818	1,372	1,212	1/75	2.083	M	B	OS
2. New York	6/69	18,265	5,415	3,192	6/74	1.748		B	OS
3. New Jersey	68, 12/73	7,361	1,393	732	2/75	.994		B	OS
4. Utah	3/69, 75	1,157	181	157	4/74	1.357		B	OS
5. Maryland	7/72	4,070	970	420	6/73	1.032		B	OS
6. California	69, 8/74	20,601	4,426	2,953	5/73	1.433	(M)	B	
7. Virginia	9/73	4,811	746	172	73	.358		B	
8. Oklahoma	6/71	2,663	247	119	73	.447		B	OS
9. Kansas	3/74	2,279	364	199	11/73	.873		B	
10. Nebraska	4/74	1,542	173	124	4/74	.804		B	
11. Tennessee	2/74	4,126	421	224	11/73	.543		B	
12. Louisiana	74, 7/75	3,764	223	161	11/73	.428	(M)	B	
13. Mississippi	7/74	2,281	119	91	7/74	.399		B	
14. Montana	3/71	721	61	43	8/73	.600	WC		
15. Colorado	7/71	2,437	507	253	1/75	1.021		(B)	
16. Washington	71	3,429	487	241	1/73	.703		(B) on 12/74	
17. Michigan	6/68	9,044	1,324	405	7/73	.448			
18. Ohio	1/74	10,731	1,361	1,342	1/74	1.251	WC	(B*) on 5/74	
19. Arkansas	3/75	2,037	113	62	1/74	.304		B	
20. Minnesota	5/75	3,897	594	215	3/73	.552	M	B	

Table 2 (*continued*)

State	Passed	1973 Census (1,000)	1972 APA Members	Licensed or Certified Psychologists[a]	Directory Date	Licensed or Certified Psychologists per 10,000 Population	Explanatory Note[b]
21. Oregon	5/75	2,225	318	169	7/74	.760	B
22. Connecticut	6/75	3,076	740	293	11/73	.953	M B
23. Maine	6/75	1,028	120	74	74	.720	B
FEHBA (Federal Employee Health Benefit Act)	1/74	(8,500)	–	–	–	–	F B OS
Total		113,713 54.2% of	21,675 63.9% of	12,853		1.130	
National		209,851	33,930	23,000 estimated			

[a]Unduplicated, state resident, licensed or certified for independent practice.
[b]Unless otherwise specified, statute applies only to disability (health) insurance policies under the Insurance Code.
M—Mental health coverage mandatory; (M)—must be provided if requested by the insured group.
B—Specific language providing for coverage of Blue Shield contracts; (B)—included by negotiation; (B*)—governed by insurance law.
OS—Specific language requiring recognition of psychological services whether the policy issued within or outside of the state but applies to state residents.
WC—Specific language providing for coverage under Workers' Compensation Plans; (WC)—negotiated inclusion in state fund.
F—PL 93-363; applies to all federal employee plans.

ance into effect. In some states, the office of the commissioner of insurance will actively pursue delivery of coverage for insured citizens. Thus, while the Michigan FOC law does not include health service plans, the Michigan Insurance Bureau, in advising Blue Cross and Blue Shield of its 1975 program initiatives, noted that certified consulting psychologists in practice were not being reimbursed:

> Based on the nature and extent of the education received by the various specialists, the Insurance Bureau staff is of the opinion that trained certified consulting psychologists may, in almost all cases, be more qualified to provide mental health services than are most D.O.s and M.D.s not specializing in psychiatry. Blue Cross and Blue Shield's denial of coverage for mental health benefits rendered by certified consulting psychologists in solo practice appears to be based on a strict interpretation of their legal mandate to provide medical services . . . this issue seems to be centered around the acceptability to Blue Cross and Blue Shield of the professional discipline providing the service.

Such initiatives and local understandings notwithstanding, the law is a more certain vehicle. Thus, Michigan HB 5078, introduced this year, would extend recognition from simple disability policies to nonprofit medical care corporations as well.

While state insurance codes typically regulate the disability (health) policies of the insurance carriers, disability is but one major segment of the market. To assure that a freedom-of-choice statute will be broadly applicable, it is necessary to also cover self-insured employee welfare benefit funds, hospital corporation plans, and health service plans (see Chapter Six; also, Table 2), which, depending on the state, may fall under the labor, health and welfare, government, or other code. Moreover, it is not sufficient simply to cover policies or plans issued, amended, or renewed in the state, but also policies, wherever issued, that are delivered within the state or apply to residents or employees of a state. The "out-of-state" problem applies principally to the disability policies and to health service plans that are designed for national coverage of a particular group.

The "corrective" potential of this type of legislation is well illustrated by the New York Court of Appeals decision (*Moore v. Metropolitan*, 1973). As one outcome of that judicial decision, the state insurance commissioner instructed the home office of Travelers to pay all claims of New York psychologists treating New York patients, retroactive to 1969 (the date the law was enacted). In November 1973, Travelers issued a circular memorandum (S. A. Maher, Vice President, Group Policies) to all group health insurance policyholders, which stated, in part: "For purposes of compliance with these statutes, effective immediately, medical care and treatment under medical, comprehensive medical and major medical expense insurance coverages will be considered to include the services of a licensed or certified clinical psychologist when acting within the legal scope of his practice . . . for psychological testing and for psychotherapy in connection with a mental or nervous illness or disorder to the extent benefits would have been paid if the psychotherapy had been performed by a psychiatrist." Then, faced with a class action suit by the California State Psychological Association, Metropolitan Life decided to reimburse psychologists, effective August 1973, for services covered by one of the largest single health insurance plans in California, namely the North American Rockwell Health Plan (Rockwell International). These were important breakthroughs, but more was to come.

The nature of contract insurance law is such that the conditions in the state of issue are to apply wherever delivered unless there are explicit provisos to the contrary. Thus, for example, a master policy issued in New Jersey, which has an all-encompassing, strong freedom-of-choice law, should recognize the services of licensed psychologists in another state, whether or not that state has FOC legislation. Counsel for the New Jersey Psychological Association recently put this question to the Equitable Life Assurance Society and received a January 22, 1975 reply, which stated, in part: "Under this law recognition of psychologists will be provided in all States unless in a particular State a psychologist is not recognized under State law, that is, there is no certification or licensing act for a psychologist."

Even prior to PL 93-363, this matter was discussed with the U.S. Civil Service Commission whose director of the Bureau of Retirement, Insurance and Occupational Health Thomas A. Tinsley, on March 12, 1974, noted that Commission policy is that its insurance carriers must comply with applicable state law. "We have advised our carriers that they should not rely on their contracts with us to avoid a State law and that if they pay benefits to comply with a state law, such payment would be an allowable charge to our contract." The Group Health Association in the District of Columbia had confirmed that Blue Cross and Blue Shield was paying psychologists on a par with psychiatrists as of January 1, 1974, under FEHBA (Federal Employee Health Benefit Act) contracts.

Some consideration has been given to mandating the inclusion of coverage for mental disorder in all health insurance policies issued or renewed within or outside a state. The Massachusetts law (SB 1985, Daniel Foley) appears to cover all types of policies from January 1974 and includes, "consultations or diagnostic or treatment sessions, provided that such services under this clause are rendered by a psychotherapist (physician, practicing psychiatry) or by a psychologist licensed (in Massachusetts)." At the close of 1973, AB 49 (Frank Lanterman, California) became law and now requires that every group health insurance plan (all types) "shall offer to every member of the plan coverage for mental and nervous disorders in such coverages and limits as the member/insured/employee may select." Thus, if requested by the insured group, such coverage must be offered in California. The provider component was then made explicit in 1975 by passage of AB 991 (Walter Ingalls, California): "Each prepaid health plan shall provide the services of a psychologist and psychiatrist when the . . . contract requires the provision of mental health services." Moreover, it is later specified that the "enrollee may be seen initially by either a physician or a psychologist." The Connecticut law that had mandated certain minimum mental health benefits in group plans

was revised in 1975 to recognize the services of licensed psychologists. The new mandatory Minnesota law of 1975 requires
that where in-hospital mental disorder coverage is provided, a
group contract must henceforth provide for ambulatory mental
health benefits. There is no distinction in level of benefits
whether the services are rendered by a qualified practitioner or
by an organized health facility.

Specialized or limited freedom-of-choice provisions may
also apply to various states. It is reported that in Illinois, state
employee plans must recognize the services of psychologists.
California, effective September 1974, adopted a pilot program
for its state employees extending a broad range of services for
the care and treatment of alcoholism. This program provides for
outpatient care "up to 45 visits" as well as inpatient and day or
night controlled residential care. The licensed psychologist is
one of the designated providers with fees at parity.

Program Direction

It is one thing to be qualified for or licensed to practice. It
is quite another to have the authority for policy and program
determination or program direction. In the public sector
psychologists and some other nonmedical health professions
have moved into positions of program responsibility. A 1970
national survey (Dörken) reported that psychologists held or
could hold high-level positions within a state agency or department—such as director, commissioner, deputy director, or assistant commissioner—in ten states. According to informal data,
such positions were held by psychologists in an additional five
states by 1975: Illinois, Massachusetts, Colorado, Minnesota,
and Nevada. Posts of a statewide divisional level such as community mental health or mental retardation programs were actually
held by psychologists in half the states in 1970. Further positive
change has since occurred here too. The past five years have also
seen an increase in the number of states where psychologists are
or can be directors or superintendents of state mental hospitals
or retardation facilities; from four to at least seven and from
twenty-three to at least twenty-five, respectively. For example,

in 1975 Virginia dropped the physician requirement for head of its state hospitals. However, the class specifications for positions of program leadership—whether exempt, under civil service, or set by regulation—still warrant close review and potential revision.

Psychologists were actually directors of community mental health centers in a majority of the states in 1970, while a current estimate exceeds the 80 percent mark. Such developments have been strongly resisted in some states such as California, where it has taken no less than four successive laws since 1971 to make the conditions explicit. Thus, while the 1971 law (Petris SB 725) called for regulations enabling the director of local (county) mental health services, when not the local health officer or medical administrator of the county hospitals, to be a psychiatrist, psychologist, or clinical social worker and also called for the adoption of standards for these three professions employed as program chiefs, further legislation became necessary. SB 542 (Nicholas Petris, California) of 1972 was explicit in stating that, "No regulations shall be adopted which prohibit a psychiatrist, psychologist or clinical social worker from employment in a local mental health program in any professional, administrative or technical positions in mental health services." Further statutory clarification was passed in 1973 and 1974, but as of this writing the complete set of implementing regulations had still not been presented for hearing by the department of health and counties continued to advertise vacancies for director and program chief as restricted to psychiatrist, in direct and open violation of the law—even when the violation was brought to their attention.

In recent years, there has been a shift from disciplinary to programatic organization of services in public mental institutions. This shift has brought with it a reorganization of hospital services where specific competence and experience rather than discipline in itself become the requisites for appointment as program or service director (Dörken, 1973). This shift has occurred not only throughout many major state services but in facilities of the Veterans Administration as well. When given the opportunity, members of clinical disciplines appear to be equally competent in administration—a skill for which few are rarely trained.

Because of the shortage of competent, clinically trained administrators—especially in circumstances that foreclose the possibility for all but physicians and given the notion that the clinician should be saved for direct patient service—an anomaly appears to be developing in public service. On the one hand, there is little incentive in terms of higher status or pay to reward demonstrated clinical expertise. On the other, there seems to be an increased receptivity to program managers having business administration or comparable training, even though they do not have the experiential background really to understand, from the delivery standpoint, the services they administer. Such prospects appear self-defeating. It is not enough that the trained health professional may be allowed to make the clinical decisions and be responsible for the treatment program. Ultimately, whoever controls the dollar controls the program.

Competency Determination

There are further marks of recognition which the psychologist claims. Pacht and others (1973) have reviewed the status of the psychologist as an expert witness. *United States* v. *Jenkins* (307 F 2d637, U.S. App. D.C., 1962), in which the appellate court for the District of Columbia established the acceptance of the psychologist as an expert witness, is generally considered to be a landmark case. By 1971, eighteen states (including New York, Florida, Texas, Illinois, Michigan, and California) and the District of Columbia clearly accepted the testimony of a psychologist as an expert witness. It would appear that this acceptance will extend to other states, particularly where the profession is recognized through licensing or certification. Examples of recent case law recognizing psychologists as independent experts for diagnosis or treatment include *United States* v. *Brawner* (471 F 2d 1190, 4th Cir., 1969); *Hogan* v. *Texas* (496 SW 2d 594., Crim. App. Texas, 1973); and *United States* v. *Green* (373 F Supp., 149 ED Pa, 1974).

Congress is currently considering a reform of the federal

criminal law code to clarify the distinction between those responsible for their behavior and those who lack the capacity to appreciate their conduct, the so-called distinction between the "mad" or "bad." The M'Naghten rule held that a defendant is criminally responsible unless it can be proven that because of mental illness he did not know the nature and quality of his acts. The Durham decision of 1954 held that the defendant is not criminally responsible if his unlawful act was the product of mental disease or defect. This ruling facilitated the introduction of expert testimony by psychiatrists and, later, clinical psychologists. The history of this development is succinctly reviewed by Miller (1975).

During the time that the 700-page Criminal Justice Codification, Revision and Reform Act is under consideration by the 94th Congress (S 1) it is likely to be mirrored by similar considerations in state legislatures. As an illustration, after extended staff and committee consideration, the California legislature passed a bill (AB 1529, Frank Murphy) amending the Penal Code and the Welfare and Institutions Code. The intent of this law was to change various procedures relating to a person's "sanity" in a criminal proceeding to a person's "mental competence." It changed the definition of "gravely disabled" for purposes of hospitalization to include one who is deemed mentally incompetent, who is named in an indictment charging certain felonies, and who, as a result of mental disorder, is unable to understand the nature and purpose of the proceedings. Such a person cannot be tried or adjudged to punishment while mentally incompetent. During the deliberation on provision for expert testimony, it was possible, due to the definition of practice in the Psychology Licensing Act and to prevailing recognition of the profession, to gain the inclusion of psychologists. Thus, in a trial by court or jury on the question of mental competence, Section 1369 of the Penal Code as of September 1974 now states, in part: ". . . the court shall appoint two psychiatrists, licensed psychologists, or a combination thereof . . . ." This inclusion provides for a major entry into criminal law for the profession of psychology in California. The 1974 Hawaiian penal code amendments enabled even broader use of certified psychologists or physicians as consultants to the state court system for examinations with respect to "physical or mental disease, disorder or defect"; acquittal or such grounds; application for discharge or conditional release; or "pre-sentence psychiatric or medical examination."

Civil commitment has also been the subject of recent consideration, even though many states have passed a "Bill of Rights" for the mentally disordered (Baynes, 1971). Baynes points out that the majority of states do not have a statutory definition of mental disorder nor is there mention of "medical or psychological terminology" (p. 491). In effect, the statutes for the most part refer to "behavioral aspects, that is, personal acts or characteristics" (p. 492) as the paramount mode of definition. Thus, the determining factors are nonmedical, for such terms as mental illness and mental disease are defined by "behavioral characteristics in a perpetual statutory circus" (p. 492). Baynes concludes from his review of fifty-one statutes that they are really not criteria or guidelines but, rather, "conflicting labels that are the social excuse for incarcerating the gauche" (p. 495). Given such a situation, the determination of either insanity or mental competence hardly falls within the exclusive province of psychiatry or medicine—or of psychology, for that matter.

It is not surprising, then, that the laws relating to the commitment of mentally disordered or mentally retarded persons are gradually broadening to enable the participation of a recognized psychologist in this legal process. In 1970 (Dörken) the involvement of a qualified psychologist was required in the commitment process of the mentally retarded in twelve states and accepted in another fifteen. Minnesota, in 1967, was the first state to adopt such a statute. With regard to mental disorder, such participation was possible in only four states at the time. Generally two signatories are required. Over the past five years five additional states have adopted laws enabling a psychologist to be one of the signatories in involuntary commitment (Colorado, Nevada, Oregon, South Carolina, and Washington). This subject clearly warrants consideration by psychology in those states where the profession is a nonparticipant. With passage of SB 349 in Colorado in 1975 licensed physicians or psychologists can commit mental patients to hospital. Also in 1975 Nevada legislation enables emergency and temporary commitment by a licensed psychologist.

The classic *Wyatt* v. *Stickney* case in Alabama (1972) is likely to have widespread repercussions on the right to treatment, institutional conditions, minimal staffing requirements, and related matters. Of special interest to psychology is the fact that the doctoral psychologist, among several other disciplines, was recognized as a "Qualified Mental Health Professional."

Other State Laws

Other areas of state law have an effect on the practice of psychology. These areas have not been approached in a systematic fashion comparable to that attention given licensure and freedom of choice. With limited resources, priorities do have an effect. The next several years are likely to see significant change in state Medicaid programs, workers' compensation laws, and prepaid health plans—among the areas of vital concern to clinical psychologists. It is also probable that there will be an increase in consumer-oriented legislation. In California, AB 3250 (Henry Waxman, now Congressman for California), the Health Insurance Disclosure Act of 1974, which becomes effective January, 1976, is one such example. This law requires the development of a standard disclosure form to include the exceptions, reductions, and limitations of the policy.

There is also a need for law facilitating collegial relations among the various health professions rather than fostering isolation. Practitioners must, of course, be licensed. They may also incorporate individually. And a group of practitioners may form a professional corporation. At that point, given current state law, the enterprise must ordinarily be unidisciplinary. Professional corporation law, then, prevents professionals of several disciplines from having membership and owning stock in such a corporation. In 1974, Hawaii Revised Statutes amended Section 416-146 to read in part: "Shares of capital in a professional corporation may be issued only to a licensed person . . . provided, that notwithstanding . . . any psychologist certified under the provisions of chapter 465 may own stock in a medical corporation as long as . . . the sum of all shares not held by a physician in a medical corporation does not exceed forty-nine per cent of the total number of shares . . . ." A broader model has been extant in the state of Washington since 1969. There, professional service corporations may be composed of shareholders or professional employees all licensed "to render the same professional services as the corporation" (Chapter 18.100). To the extent that the same services are rendered, more than one discipline may be involved. These are models for private-sector corporate health practice, but they require enabling state legislation. Entitlement of qualified psychologists to hospital staff privileges is another area overdue for closer attention by organized psychology and, possibly, remedial legislation. In California, for example, AB 1570 (Paul Carpenter—a California psychologist), if enacted, would require recognition (under certain criteria) of psychologists as members of the hospital's professional staff, in accord with criteria of the Joint Commission on Accreditation of Hospitals.

To be effective in the legislative process will require a substantial investment of time and talent by state psychological associations. Since the law is a basic determinant of the scope and nature of practice, however, such an involvement in state legislative activities should be accepted as a fact of life. Moreover, sound recognition in state law is generally given consideration in the formulation of federal law. A "grass-roots" network is vitally important to effectiveness at the national level.

4

Disability and Rehabilitation Services

Jack G. Wiggins

Restorative services refers to treating people with mental or physical conditions so that they may return to work or work at more productive levels than previously. It is an important area in which psychologists may provide health care, and the government is now taking an active interest in how psychological expertise can help people gain, or raise their level of, employment.

Governmental concern about the hiring of individuals who have had treatment for nervous and mental disorders is not just altruism. If an individual is not working, he or she is not paying taxes, may have to be subsidized by welfare payments, and in other ways may become a burden to taxpayers. Therefore, this discussion will define restorative services as the process of restoring the individual to the working force, rather than of rehabilitating the individual to a state of mental well-being.

Enlightened self-interest has prompted the federal government to allocate funds for the restoration of individuals with mental conditions. In 1943, the Barden-LaFollette Act included mental rehabilitation in the vocational rehabilitation program. Vocational counseling, training, and employment services were made available to those who had been mentally ill. Prior to this act, the federal government's involvement in mental conditions was primarily through the military, where servicemen and disabled veterans required professional care. In the civilian area,

59

the federal government operated St. Elizabeth's Hospital as a mental hospital for the residents of the District of Columbia. Before 1943 the bulk of the care and treatment for the mentally disturbed was left to state institutions and private facilities. Even after the passage of the act, until the mid-1950s, the state mental health programs were primarily a series of custodial institutions in which the individual received little vocational training beyond housekeeping duties, food service, or farming on a state farm. Thus, providing federal funds for vocational rehabilitation of those with mental conditions was a major step. However, it took another thirty years after the initial enactment for those with mental conditions to receive the same benefits as those with physical conditions in rehabilitation programs.

Vocational Rehabilitation

Until the Rehabilitation Act of 1973 (PL 93-112), passed in 1974 to become effective January 1975, mental restoration was subsumed under physical restoration. States had widely varying interpretations of how mental restoration should take place. Not until the mid-1960s was systematic study of the effects of vocational rehabilitation for individuals with mental conditions reported. If vocational rehabilitation services were made equally available to those with mental conditions as well as physical conditions, a more accurate reporting and accounting undoubtedly could be developed.

By 1972, 41.7 percent of the 326,138 rehabilitated persons who had some kind of nervous or mental disorder had received restorative services in state vocational rehabilitation agencies. (*Rehabilitation* is defined as able to obtain or retain employment in the competitive labor market [HEW, SRS, n.d.]). From fiscal year 1968 to 1972, the rehabilitation of the mentally handicapped individual was the most rapidly expanding area in vocational rehabilitation. Whereas the proportion of persons classified under epilepsy and mental retardation only increased from 12.5 to 13.1 percent over this five-year period, the increase in the "mental illness" category was from 19.6 (40,156 persons) to 28.6 percent, accompanied by a marked change in the character of this group. Psychotic disorder, once 33 percent of this group, had declined to 19 percent, "while the proportion of those in the all other mentally ill groups rose to 43 percent" (HEW, SRS, RSA, n.d.). Thus, by 1972 character, personality, and behavior disorders accounted for one of every eight rehabilitated clients. They were the largest subcategory; mental disorder was the largest category. By 1974 "mental illness" accounted for 30.4 percent of all persons rehabilitated, almost 110,000 persons. On a person basis this was about a 275 percent increase in such rehabilitations over the seven-year period, reflecting the establishment of vocational rehabilitation services at state mental hospitals as part of the state rehabilitation plan in many states and the generally broader acceptance of cases of mental disorder for rehabilitation services.

The vocational rehabilitation program is administered by the Rehabilitation Services Administration (RSA) of the Social and Rehabilitation Service (SRS) of the U.S. Department of Health, Education, and Welfare (HEW). This broad-based program provides matching funds to state rehabilitation agencies that provide restorative services to help individuals with physical or mental handicaps obtain or retain employment. Federal grants are made to vocational rehabilitation agencies of the states on a basis of matching funds, 80 percent being provided by the federal tax monies and 20 percent by state tax monies. A formula establishes the maximum amounts of federal tax monies that can be allotted to each state. In order to obtain the federal grant money, each state must submit a plan providing rehabilitation services for the mentally and physically handicapped. Vocational rehabilitation services include the following, as quoted from "Vocational Rehabilitation Programs and Activities, Interim Regulations Implementing the Rehabilitation Act of 1973," (*Federal Register*, January 3, 1974) Volume 39, No. 2, Part II, (z) (1):

> "Vocational rehabilitation services" means: (i) evaluation of rehabilitation potential, including diagnostic and related services, incidental to the deter-

mination of eligibility for, and the nature and scope of, services to be provided and including, where appropriate, examination by a physician skilled in the diagnosis and treatment of emotional disorders, or by a licensed psychologist in accordance with State laws and regulations, or both; (ii) physical and mental restoration services; (iii) counseling, guidance, and referral services; (iv) vocational and other training services, including personal and vocational adjustment, books, and other materials; (v) maintenance during rehabilitation, not exceeding the estimated cost of subsistence; (vi) transportation in connection with the rendering of any vocational rehabilitation service; (vii) interpreter services for the deaf; (viii) reader services, rehabilitation teaching services, and orientation and mobility services for the blind; (ix) telecommunications, sensory and other technological aids and devices; (x) recruitment and training services for handicapped individuals to provide them with new employment opportunities in the fields of rehabilitation, health, welfare, public safety and law enforcement, and other appropriate public service employment; (xi) services to members of a handicapped individual's family when such services are necessary to the adjustment or rehabilitation of the handicapped individual; (xii) placement and followup prior to case closure; (xiii) postemployment services, including follow-along; (xiv) occupational licenses, tools, equipment, and initial stocks and supplies; and (xv) such other goods and services which can reasonably be expected to benefit a handicapped individual in terms of his employability.

Subpart (i), consistent with the law, provides parity recognition to psychologists nationally, thereby overturning the guidelines of those states that previously did not recognize the involvement of psychologists in restorative (treatment) service or else made such service conditional to medical referral.

State agencies determine the eligibility for services for each individual on the following basis: (1) the individual must have a physical or mental disability, (2) the disability must represent a substantial handicap to employment, and (3) there must be reasonable expectation that the rehabilitation services will lead to gainful employment. There is no federal requirement that the handicapped must show financial need in order to be eligible. On the other hand, the state may elect to establish conditions whereby an individual contributes to payment for services, except for the evaluation, counseling, guidance, and placement services. The federal regulations do provide that if pension compensation or insurance payments are available, they shall be used to meet all or parts of the cost of services other than the counseling, guidance and placement.

The federal government also purchases services from state rehabilitation agencies for selected recipients of Social Security benefits with Social Security trust funds. Individuals who are classified as totally and permanently disabled are eligible for Social Security benefits. They may be authorized to receive restorative services under the state vocational rehabilitation program. Disabled Social Security recipients constitute about 10 percent of the caseloads of vocational rehabilitation agencies.

It is curious to note that psychological reports, based on testing and interviews, are considered medical evidence for the establishment of the mental impairment in a disability determination under the Social Security Act. Since disabled individuals are covered under Medicare, the psychologist is unable to treat the mentally disabled person under the benefits provided under Title XVIII. However, if the individual is declared eligible for vocational rehabilitation, then the psychologist can provide the necessary services for mental restoration. In fact, the Social Security Administration (SSA) has used psychologists as expert witnesses in compensation cases for more than a decade, since they provide a more equitable determination of disability than do witness testimony or medical records alone (Hannings and others, 1972).

The federal government also provides project grants to state rehabilitation agencies for innovative service programs. Federal funds for project grants for the expansion of services in state and local agencies as well as nonprofit private organizations are available. There are special funds for programs to recruit and prepare handicapped persons for careers in public service. The federal government also contracts with businesses, trade associations, and similar organizations capable of providing training and employment opportunities for the handicapped in realistic work settings. Start-up funds for public and non-profit private rehabilitation facilities are available through federal grants to assist organizations in meeting the initial costs of compensating professional and technical staff as well as in improving the professional services or management of their rehabilitation services.

With the wide array of federally sponsored or funded rehabilitation services, there are many opportunities for treatment for those with mental conditions. Cost estimates of mental health services in vocational rehabilitation programs run as high as $151,000,000 annually (Burnell, 1971). These cost estimates may be imprecise. Accurate cost estimates are difficult to obtain because the reporting systems used by the various states are based on the unique standards for eligibility for services in each state. An inspection of the frequency of services to the mentally ill, the mentally retarded, and the epileptic revealed a wide variation from state to state (HEW, SRS, n.d.). The range is from about one-third of the caseload in Indiana to approximately two-thirds of the caseload in Arizona. Illustrative of one state provision for psychological services is that of the Montana State Division of Social and Rehabilitative (DSR) Services. Its revised DSR Code of October 1973 established a schedule of procedures for psychological services. For example, $30 are paid for psychotherapy sessions of 50 minutes. These procedures authorize a maximum of twenty-two hourly visits to a licensed clinical psychologist, or the equivalent, in a fiscal year. Physician referral or supervision are not required and the limit can be extended on prior authorization when justified.

A profile of rehabilitation services may be gleaned from a variety of sources. The Rehabilitation Services Administration of the SRS publishes *Statistical Notes* periodically, describing the types of services available, clients served, and the results obtained. The *State Data Book, Federal-State Program of Voca-*

tional Rehabilitation for fiscal year 1972 (HEW, SRS, n.d.) provides information regarding the types of mental conditions treated and relative costs of the treatment of these conditions in state rehabilitation agencies. Overall, mental conditions (including psychotic disorders, psychoneurotic disorders, alcoholism, drug addiction, and other character, personality, and behavior disorders) comprised 28.6 percent of the caseload. Mental retardation contributed another 11.6 percent of the caseload of rehabilitation agencies. Epilepsy constituted 1.5 percent; drug addiction, 9 percent. A separate information memorandum (HEW, SRS, 1971c) reports a rehabilitation rate for drug addicts of "52 percent, considerably lower than the 76 percent rate for all other clients."

Of particular interest is a high degree of variability of the percentage of cases attributed to "mental illness" among the various states. In Arizona, the percentage was 53.2; while in Indiana, it was 7.5 percent. Alcoholism represented 14 percent of the caseload in California and only .3 percent in Idaho. Drug addiction cases ranged from 6.7 in Connecticut and 7.4 percent in the District of Columbia to .1 percent in Oklahoma. Arizona was again high in the category of "other character, personality, and behavior disorders," with 35 percent; Indiana was again low, with only 1 percent of the vocational rehabilitation caseload represented in this category. Mental retardation represented 20.7 percent of the caseload in Missouri and only 3.6 percent in West Virginia. It is unlikely that these differences in rates for various mental conditions are representative of the unique populations residing in those states. Rather, these differentials in rates of conditions treated in the various states represent differences in the regulations of the various state agencies. The high degree of variability leads to the speculation that if mental conditions were given their proper priority, there would be an increase in the caseload ascribed to mental conditions rather than to mental retardation or other categories. For example, while Indiana had the lowest frequency of mental conditions (7.5 percent), it had the second highest percentage in mental retardation and the highest rate diagnosed as epilepsy (4 percent). Thus, there seem to be variations not only in the diagnostic classification of mental conditions among the various states but also in the identification of mental conditions.

The average cost of case services by major disabling conditions for persons served by state vocational rehabilitation agencies was reported for fiscal years 1968 to 1972 (HEW, SRS, n.d.). These data provide relative costs for various kinds of mental conditions. The average costs for all rehabilitated cases in the year 1969 was $666. By 1972 this figure had increased to $771. The average cost for the rehabilitation of individuals with mental conditions was $581 ($666 in 1972). For individuals with mental retardation the average cost was $678 ($788 in 1972). These figures indicate that the cost of rehabilitating individuals who have mental conditions or are mentally retarded is reasonable compared with the cost of rehabilitation for other conditions. A further breakdown of costs by type of mental condition for individuals receiving rehabilitation services in 1969 is revealing: psychotic disorder, $693; psychoneurotic disorders, $641; alcoholism, $386; drug addiction, $900; and other character, personality, and behavior disorders, $537. While these data do not reflect the current increases in cost of services, they do illustrate some relative costs of treatment of mental conditions. The variations in costs also suggest that more detailed analyses might reveal the most effective treatment modality for each of the types of mental conditions.

In 1971 the SRS published "A Profile of Mentally Ill Persons Rehabilitated in the Fiscal Year 1969" (HEW, SRS, 1971a). The rehabilitated mentally ill cases averaged only about one year younger than all the other clients rehabilitated. However, the mentally ill tend to be concentrated in the 20- to 44-year-old range. While men comprise 55 percent of the caseload, higher rehabilitation rates were noted for women. About one-third of the mentally ill were in tax-supported public institutions at the time of acceptance for vocational rehabilitation. In most cases, the institution was a mental hospital, although there is a trend toward an increased number of referrals from correctional institutions. Seventy-nine percent of the mentally ill clients were not employed as wage earners or homemakers at the time of their acceptance, compared to 69 percent of all other clients. Persons employed at the time of acceptance for rehabilitation tended to have higher rehabilitation rates than the unemployed.

The most dramatic statistic in the report is the amount of increase in earnings from time of acceptance to time of closure. Mean weekly earnings for the mentally ill were $11.47 at acceptance and were $69.41 at closure, a gain of $57.94 (HEW, SRS, 1971*a*) per week per client (a gain of $68.01 per week in 1972–HEW, SRS, 1975). In constrast, clients other than those with mental conditions had mean weekly earnings of $13.67 at acceptance and $58.66 at closure, a gain of $44.99. This gain is dramatic proof that vocational rehabilitation does pay, not only for the physically disabled but to an even greater extent for the mentally handicapped individual. These increased earnings, if projected on an annual rate, would produce new tax monies that would offset the costs of treatment in approximately one and a half years. The projected return underscores the value of rehabilitating the mentally ill rather than allowing them to remain in tax-supported custodial institutions or on welfare rolls of local government. In fact, on introducing S 3108 on March 5, 1974, to amend the Rehabilitation Act of 1973, Senator Stratford stated, in part (*Congressional Record,* S 2778): "One of the strongest arguments used in support of the Rehabilitation Act of 1973 was that it [rehabilitation] returned an estimated $3 to $5 on every $1 the government invested by enabling the handicapped individual to earn a living."

In a second report, the Rehabilitation Services Administration published "A Profile of Mentally Retarded Clients Rehabilitated During the Fiscal Year 1969" (HEW, SRS, 1971*c*). Those classified as mentally retarded comprised a younger age group, approximately two-thirds of them being under twenty years of age. They were referred primarily through educational institutions. Only 13 percent of the mentally retarded clients had jobs at the outset, and 91 percent had earnings at the point of closure of the case. Prior to entering the rehabilitation program, the mentally retarded were being supported primarily by their families rather than by welfare. The mean weekly earnings for the mentally retarded were $3.70 at the outset of rehabilitation and $51.27 at closure, a gain of $47.57. In comparison, mean weekly earnings for all other clients were $14.36 at acceptance and were $62.40 at closure, a gain of $48.04. Thus, the mentally retarded showed about the same amount of gain in weekly earnings as the nonretarded case clientele of rehabilitation agencies. Since the mentally retarded tended to remain in rehabilitation programs longer, the costs of rehabilitation were somewhat higher ($678 versus $668). Nevertheless, the increased tax monies on these new earnings would offset the costs of rehabilitation in a little over one and a half years. Therefore, appropriate services must be made available to the mentally retarded on the same basis as to any other citizen.

The wide variations in standards from state to state and the need for additional services in certain states tend to result in new amendments to the Rehabilitation Act in each session of Congress. Part of the pressure for amendment comes from the states that are not in compliance with federal guidelines. Although noncompliance with federal guidelines is usually a temporary matter, it tends to persist since the federal guidelines are changed with each Congress. This situation creates an atmosphere of change in vocational rehabilitation in which there are increased opportunities for innovative programs for mental restoration.

In spite of the large dollar outlays for the restoration of individuals with mental conditions, one major obstacle for the employment of those rehabilitated has been employers' reluctance to hire the mentally handicapped. If applicants reveal they have received treatment for a mental condition, they may be refused employment without an opportunity to demonstrate that they are able to perform. The other alternative is to falsify job applications by denying they have ever received treatment for a mental condition. It was not until 1974 that the United States Civil Service Commission deleted from its standard application form the infamous Question 29, relating to a person's history of nervous or mental disorders. A person's current mental status and capability should be the sole criteria for being hired. If states, local governments, and industry will follow similar progressive employment practices, vocational rehabilitation of individuals who have received treatment and rehabilitation services will be much easier and will benefit not only the individual job applicant, but also the employer and the taxpayer.

Workers' Compensation

Workers' compensation programs are becoming a type of no-fault insurance plan providing necessary health care services to workers following an industrial injury or work-related disability. The traditional concepts of tort liability for negligence or of accident are outmoded when there may be indeterminate physical and toxic hazards, combinations of job stress, and other interacting forces that may precipitate, aggravate, or perpetuate employment-related disability. The costs of workers' compensation plans are borne by a special tax to employers. Each state has established a workers' compensation commission to administer the state programs. In addition to basic health care, these state plans authorize income maintenance and pay for restoration of the injured worker to productive employment. In the event that individuals are no longer able to perform the work that they were performing at the time of injury, they can be trained to perform jobs for which they are suited. In the event that the injured individuals are no longer able to work, they can be provided with disability benefits. Compensation is provided to families in the event the industrial accident or illness results in death.

According to the *National Commission Report on State Workmen's Compensation Laws* (1972), in 1970 over one billion dollars of medical and rehabilitative service benefits were provided under the workers' compensation acts of the various states. Of the five million claims filed each year, four million require immediate medical attention, but claimants are not disabled long enough to be eligible to receive cash benefits. Among the one million claimants who are more seriously injured, the record of workers' compensation laws is very uneven for the rehabilitation and restoration of workers to gainful employment.

There are also federal laws providing for workers' compensation to special job classifications. For example, longshoremen and harbormen are covered under the Longshoremen's and Harbor Workers' Compensation Act. Federal employees are covered by a Federal Employees Compensation Act (FECA). A recently enacted amendment to the federal plan (PL 93-416) recognized clinical psychologists as qualified providers of services for work-injured employees.

As might be expected, there are wide variations in laws governing workers' compensation among the federal and state programs. State workers' compensation laws are a curious mixture of health care, legal maneuverings, and bureaucratic administration. A sixty-day delay from point of filing before any benefits are received by an injured or ill worker is not uncommon. Resentment of the compensation system instills in the injured worker an attitude of trying to get everything he or she is entitled to from the state. The worker may nurture any illness or injury, since the amount of the compensation award will be directly related to the degree of injury. This nurturing tends to increase legal maneuvering, which in turn slows down the bureaucratic process. The resulting delay causes the individual to focus on symptoms and condition, creating a state of "compensationitis." One of the most frequent use of psychological services is to help determine the extent to which mental attitude may be affecting return to the work force.

Trade unions have attempted to establish federal guidelines for workers' compensation laws. The Occupational Safety and Health Act of 1970 (PL 91-596) authorized the National Commission on State Workmen's Compensation Laws. The report of this commission was submitted on July 31, 1972. One of the commission's findings was that there were arbitrary restrictions on services available to the worker under workers' compensation. Some of these restrictions involve variant interpretations of state statutes that authorize payments for "all reasonable and necessary medical, surgical, and hospital care." In current legalese, the services of a psychologist fall under the category of "Medical Care and Physical Rehabilitation." Workers' compensation agencies in seventeen states and Puerto Rico currently use a narrow interpretation of this language and therefore deny payment for certain types of practitioners or health care institutions. For example, some states will not pay for services by rehabilitation centers, home health care programs, occupational therapists, osteopaths, registered nurses, or psychologists. Generally, six states were reported as not paying for the services of psychologists (Alabama, Louisiana, New York, Ohio, South Dakota, and Utah) as of January 1972 (Rosenblum, 1973).

In order to correct these deficiencies, the commission made eighty-four recommendations, nineteen of which are considered essential. Two are of particular interest in the present context. First, "R 4.1 We recommend that the worker be permitted the initial selection of his physician, either from among all licensed physicians in the State or from a panel of physicians selected or approved by the Workmen's Compensation Agency." (The executive council of the AFL-CIO at a conference in Chicago, August 1972, endorsed this principle of "free choice of physician by injured worker." Twenty-four jurisdictions allow the injured worker to choose his own physician. The legislative trend is toward employee choice, as opposed to employer choice. Moreover, "there are no significant differences between medical costs in different states on the basis of their methods of physician choice.") Second, "R 4.3 We recommend that the Workmen's Compensation Agency have discretion to determine the appropriate medical and rehabilitation services in each case. There should not be arbitrary limits by regulation or statute on the types of medical services or licensed health care facilities which can be authorized by the agency." (For "whatever reason," the commission found that there were a greater number and variety of specialists available to injured workers in employee-choice states.)

The commission did recognize the mental and emotional aspects of industrial injury and disease in its statement of objectives of medical care and rehabilitation: (1) definitive medical care must be provided to restore the patient's abilities or functions; (2) vocational counseling and job retraining if the worker suffers a loss of endurance or skills needed to perform his previous duties; and (3) the worker's actual return to productive employment. In concluding, the commission also stated, "It is perhaps even more important to begin promptly to prepare patients *psychologically* [emphasis added] for recovery of their capabilities and morale, before apathy or despair becomes deeprooted." Clearly, we would support such objectives, and note the introduction of S 2018 (Harrison Williams, New Jersey) in the 94th Congress. This National Workers' Compensation Standards Act (of 1975, if enacted) would substantially broaden the concept of injury, mandate minimum standards, and recognize the services of clinical psychologists.

The Occupational Safety and Health Act (OSHA) of 1970 also required a systematic recording and reporting of work-related injuries and illnesses. OSHA regulations have resulted in many new rules and safety requirements for industry. Industry has made marked strides in conforming to the new regulations; however, at this writing, it is difficult to get accurate figures pertaining to mental health. Yet data on other diseases does suggest some areas in which psychology may be able to provide health services. Bulletin 1798 of the U.S. Department of Labor (1973) listed a distribution of illnesses by type, including diseases of the lung; poisonings; respiratory conditions caused by toxic agents; disorders caused by repeated trauma; disorders caused by physical agents; skin diseases or disorders; and all other illnesses. Skin disease was the most frequently reported class of condition, comprising about one-third of the illnesses, another one-third being accounted for by the other diseases listed above. Manufacturing generated the most work-related injuries and illnesses on a per capita basis, and construction appeared to be the most fatal occupation. On May 13, 1974, the administration's *White Paper on Workers' Compensation (A Report on the Need for Reform of State Workers' Compensation)* was released. The white paper noted that since the commission recommendations there has been a flurry of state legislative activity (400 bills in 1973 alone) to strengthen various aspects of workers' compensation. "There is a strong social and economic case for improving rehabilitation services since the available evidence indicates that vocational rehabilitation is more cost-effective for workers' compensation claimants than for the general client population of the Federal/State Vocational Rehabilitation programs" (p. 7).

It is hard to determine the cause of many disabilities. Some diseases are almost solely related to occupation, but there are also conditions "which occur frequently in the general population but which can be aggravated by work conditions" (*White Paper,* 1974, p. 2). The concept of microtrauma, however (that is, an accumulating job stress resulting in job-related emotional or mental disability), has gained but limited recognition. Nevertheless, there is growing recognition of the psychosocial aspects of physical injury. There is increasing evidence that the worker's attitude toward his or her job-related injury or illness is a major factor in rehabilitation. William R. Halliday (1971), Chief Medical Consultant for the Department of Labor and Industries for the State of Washington, reported that industrial accidents and illnesses cost the taxpayers of the state of Washington one hundred million dollars a year. Detailed analysis of the medical budget revealed that 40 percent of the money was going to about 3.5 percent of the beneficiaries of the program. About one-third of these victims had a serious injury. The primary problem constituted about .5 percent of the workforce, who had trivial injuries and minimal if any objective impairment, but nevertheless had an overwhelmingly apparent disability. Eighty-five percent of these cases complained of low back pains. It was found that medical examination was of little benefit in determining the person's capabilities, and the most effective way to rehabilitate these workers was through psychosocial intervention by dealing with the psychological aspects of the illness or injury. Psychologists have also been used as expert witnesses in compensation cases.

Montana, in 1970, was the first state to recognize the need for psychological rehabilitation in its Workmen's Compensation Act by guaranteeing parity of psychological services. In other states, workers' compensation agencies are establishing the worker's right to diagnosis and treatment by a psychologist (*Martin* v. *Lever Brothers,* California, 1970). However, even in states that allow workers the right to choice of practitioner, industrial claims may be obscured and the worker's health care paid for by other health insurance programs, thus inflating basic health costs and underutilizing the compensation fund. Thus, even though there may seem to be a legal basis for the reimbursement of the services of the independently practicing psychologist under workers' compensation acts, much remains to be done in the actual use and recognition of the psychologist's expertise and professional skills in this program, since the program is reluctant to move beyond evident or gross on-the-job trauma, macrotrauma such as head injury, dismemberment, or disfigurement. However, where these injuries result in a reduction of mental competence, loss of self-esteem, or fear of the job situation or of further injury, there is an obvious job-related, mental injury or disability.

No-Fault Automobile Insurance

The personal liability and medical expense coverage of automobile accident insurance provides for the treatment of the injured. The rapidly escalating cost of automobile insurance due to personal injury awards has prompted a review of automobile liability claims. It has been reported that only one-third of the premium dollar for personal liability is returned to the accident victim, and that two-thirds are spent on court litigation, including court costs and attorneys' fees (*Cleveland Press,* May 2, 1974). This finding has prompted a demand for no-fault automobile insurance to eliminate litigation and to provide equitable compensation and treatment for injured parties. Such insurance provides for the treatment of traumatic neuroses and aggravated mental conditions so that the person may be restored to gainful employment and health. In at least one state (New Jersey), psychologists are listed as eligible providers of these services under no-fault automobile insurance.

At the present time, at least twenty-three other states are considering no-fault automobile insurance, and there are two proposals for a federal no-fault automobile insurance. The federal bills propose both physical and mental restorative services to the victims of automobile accidents. The fate of these particular pieces of legislation is as yet undetermined. There is strong sentiment that some form of no-fault automobile insurance be enacted that will provide restorative services for mental conditions.

In summary, it would seem that the development and expansion of rehabilitation programs in a variety of areas will require increasing attention to mental health services. Governmental agencies are recognizing that the cost of rehabilitation for mentally disturbed patients is extremely low compared to the cost of maintaining such patients with tax monies. Similarly, the cost of health insurance, particularly of workers' compensation for disabilities, can be substantially reduced by using psychologists systematically in both the assessment and treatment processes of rehabilitation. The stage is set for psychologists to serve a major and collegial role as a health profession in these services. The opportunity must be taken. The objectives of rehabilitation and of the professional psychologist are the same—to maximize human effectiveness.

5

Major Social Security Programs

Jack G. Wiggins, Herbert Dörken,
Jack Dworin, and A. Eugene Shapiro

Although Medicare, Medicaid and Child and Maternal Health programs involve psychologists only to a limited degree, these programs represent major social legislation with far-reaching public impact. Thus, psychologists who are concerned about the delivery of health care in general must be aware of some of the problems that various health services pose, for future policy decisions in relation to such services obviously will affect the role of psychologists. A major problem is the cost of social security programs. The costs of Medicare and Medicaid more than tripled in the first four years of these programs' existence. Since it is difficult to gather data proving that the investment is worthwhile, and since it is difficult to eliminate or reduce programs once underway, legislators are understandably cautious about expanding such programs (to include the services of psychologists, for example). Moreover, a variety of problems associated with these programs demand immediate attention: achieving equal access to services; providing quality controls; involving consumers in planning and decision making; developing accurate projections of use and cost; and balancing the distribtion of health manpower. Some recent federal legislation, aimed at producing basic changes in health programs, addresses these problems.

The Health Maintenance Organization and Development Act of 1973 (PL 93-222) is one step toward organized and comprehensive health care service delivery, with community-wide integrated facilities and group practice, on proscriptive prepaid rates. The Bennett amendment to the Social Security Act (PL 92-603), through the Professional Standards Review Organizations (PSRO), lays the basis for quality control through peer review. This placing of controls on the provider rather than on the consumer is long overdue. The Health Manpower Training Act, the Hill-Burton Hospital Construction Act, the Community Mental Health Centers Act—these and others are all likely to undergo substantial change in 1976. But no previous health legislation is likely to equal the potentially profound impact and implications of PL 93-641.

The National Health Planning and Resources Development Act of 1974 (PL 93-641) was signed on January 4, 1975. This legislation can be viewed as the product of much accumulated experience focused to ensure comprehensive change and development of health services. The law called for the establishment of health systems agencies (HSAs) across the country. Moreover, within 120 days (May 3, 1975) of enactment each governor was to submit (to the secretary of HEW) the proposed boundaries of health service areas in his or her state. These program boundaries were published in the Federal Register within 210 days of enactment. The HSAs replaced the current comprehensive health planning and regional medical programs; and they are responsible, among other things, for reviewing and approving or disapproving all federal health and mental health grants and contracts, loans, and loan guarantees made under the Public Health Service (PHS) Act, Community Mental Health Center Act, and the Alcohol Act. The Hill-Burton Act is replaced by a new Title XVI of the PHS Act, Health Resources Development. Part B of Title XVI provides that not more than 20 percent of a state's allotment from the federal government in any year may go for inpatient facilities to serve areas of rapid growth, and that not less than 25 percent shall go to outpatient facilities for the medically underserved populations, half of this (12.5 percent) to rural populations. Moreover, there will be funding for comprehensive planning on the basis of capitation (a uniform per capita fee), and for the development of non-provider control. Unfortunately, psychologists are not among the designated providers in this law. It is another major issue that the profession must solve.

One can speculate about the conditions that prompted such an act. Perhaps we have learned that money alone does not produce quality care and may even divert personnel from providing good service. More broadly, in terms of community health, the effects of direct health care are seldom visible. Developing community health services requires social involvement (Dörken, 1971). We do know some of the history of this act. The Office of Economic Opportunity (OEO) programs of 1964 brought consumer participation into local service delivery programs. The Model Cities effort tried to change health—and everything else. The New Careers program focused on performance rather than on professionalism. The Economic Development Act of 1965 focused on regional concerns, laying a basis for comprehensive planning. At the same time, the federal government, through Medicare and Medicaid, became involved in funding health facilities run by others. The later categorical fundings of programs for alcoholism, drug abuse, and the aged were all piecemeal, separate, and without comprehensive planning. State departments that ran health services became involved in planning but this involvement largely proved to be self-serving. PL 93-641, Title XV, calls for national planning. The intent of this bill is to mouth fewer promises and to develop a sound base for future health care delivery. The history of health services under Social Security programs illustrates some of the problems involved in developing such a base.

Medicaid, Title XIX

Although Medicaid funds were available to states under the basic authorization of the Social Security Act of 1965, not until 1973 had all fifty states implemented programs for those eligible. While many states attempted to establish programs immediately, others required two, three, or more years for the necessary enabling legislation to secure money to match federal funds. As with all new programs, Medicaid has been troubled by duplication, confusion, and intradepartmental as well as interdepartmental rivalries within states for control over the programs. Because of the options available to each state in establishing benefit programs (for example, options in selecting eligible providers and standards of service), many programs were slow in becoming established. In Ohio, for example, the Medicaid program was not functioning effectively until 1970. Other states experienced similar difficulties in establishing their programs for Medicaid. Some states have not provided for services for mental conditions in their Medicaid programs. The Social Security Amendments of 1972 (PL 92-603) authorized federal matching funds for care of Medicaid beneficiaries in mental hospitals. By the end of 1972, thirty-four states had included the mental health option in their Medicaid plans.

While Medicaid was designed as a federal-state program to pay for health services to all recipients of categorical assistance (welfare), states at their option could also include the "medically indigent." As of 1972, persons aged 65 and over accounted for 19 percent of all Medicare beneficiaries and 30 percent of benefits paid. Hospital and nursing home costs accounted for 70 percent of all Medicaid costs; physician services accounted for 13 percent. By 1974, state governments were expending four and a half billion dollars on their Medicaid programs; the federal government contributed about five and a half billion dollars that year (Clarke, 1975), these funds coming from general revenue. Whereas benefits in some states were minimal, the Medicaid programs of twenty states generally provided equal or better coverage for nonwelfare, medically indigent families than the Administration's national health insurance (NHI) proposal of 1974. Moreover, by 1972 the number of Medicaid recipients had become sizable, approaching eighteen million persons (about 9 percent of the national population). There was wide variation among the states, from less than 3 percent of the Wyoming population to over 18 percent in California (New York, 15 percent). The extent of coverage, then, despite state program variation, warrants close professional attention.

Programs of this magnitude and cost quite naturally raise concerns for cost as well as quality control. Roemer's (1975) study of overall health services to Medicaid patients in California shows that a prior authorization requirement reduces the frequency of doctor office visits. Copay requirements further and measurably reduce ambulatory care but consequently increase hospitalization, with a net increase in cost. There seems no reason to believe that mental health services will not follow the same pattern.

Medicaid has become a major resource for paying for the care of elderly patients in mental hospitals; as of 1969, the federal share in thirty states was 53 percent of $306,700,000, covering nearly three fifths of all such patients in the country (DHEW, SSA, ORS, 1971). Clinic service, currently an optional service, has been adopted by thirty states and Washington, D.C. to include mental hygiene clinics and community mental health centers. Medicaid then, has become the largest plan of third-party payment for mental health benefits in the United States. Clearly, such a program should be of major concern to professional psychology. Nevertheless, it has not drawn the attention it should from psychologists at the state level. This federal program is permissive and open to wide variation, depending on state plans. Part 249, Services and Payment in Medical Assistance Programs, mandates·that for services delivered to the categorically needy the plan must include the first five items of 249-10 (b) or any seven of the items in (b)(1) through (14). Certain of these items clearly provide for the recognition of psychological services, as in the following quotes (with emphasis supplied). Section 249-10 (b)(4)(i) defines "skilled nursing home services . . . which are provided under the direction of a physician *or other licensed practitioner* . . . as defined by state law." Section 249-10 (b)(6) seems especially pertinent in recognizing "medical care and *any other type of remedial care* recognized under State law, furnished *by licensed practitioners* within the scope of their practice as defined by State law. The italicized words mean . . . services *other than physicians'* services." Further clarification is given in 249-10 (b)(13): "other diagnostic, screening, preventive, and rehabilitative services . . . by a physician or *other licensed practitioner.*" Finally, Section 249.11 was added to the Code of Federal Regulations, effective April 2, 1970: "Free choice of providers of medical services: State plan requirement. A State plan . . . under title XIX . . . must provide that any individual eligible for medical assistance under the plan *may obtain the services* available under the plan *from any* institution, agency . . . *practitioner* . . . qualified to perform such services."

Title XIX of the Federal Social Security Act of 1968 (Medicaid) provides for the health care of indigent persons who are on welfare and who cannot afford their own treatment. In the initial provisions of this act, each participating state would be reimbursed by the federal government for 50 percent of the monies expended. As the law was written, each state could use the services of any licensed health profession in that state. Certain basic services and professional providers of service had to be included by a state to achieve eligibility under the act. However, psychologists were not among the required professions and the federal publication SSA 74-10050, "Your Medicare Handbook," does not refer to the profession.

Psychologists' interest in Medicaid has involved attention to the Social Security amendments establishing Medicare. Many psychologists assumed that since Medicaid was a federal program, the necessary modification to include psychologists must take place at the federal level. Many psychologists were unaware that the states determined the categories of health providers who would be eligible to render services under the Medicaid program. Furthermore, those psychologists who were aware were discouraged from participating in the program by the backlog of unpaid billings by state Medicaid programs. For example, in Ohio, at one point, payment for services required nine months from submission of billings to receipt of payment. Additional confusion was created by unclear state departmental regulations. Sometimes the services of a psychologist would be paid for and sometimes not. Inquiries addressed to local offices for public assistance produced confusing answers, varying with the person who was answering the phone or writing the letter.

The role of psychologists in Medicaid throughout the

nation is difficult to establish and clarify. Repeated surveys have brought forth different opinions and different information at different times. Indeed, it has been difficult even to find out what the procedures are, and what is covered. For example, the results of an informal survey conducted late in 1972 by the American Psychological Association's Committee on Health Insurance indicated that five states (Connecticut, Kentucky, Maine, Montana, and New Mexico) had accepted qualified psychologists as independent providers of services. In a few states, psychologists were accepted with limitations, such as for psychological testing only (Massachusetts and Minnesota); or for either testing or therapy, but only if referral was by a medical doctor (California; Georgia, which has a $250 therapy limit; Kansas; and Nevada). Since that survey, psychologists have been recognized by agreement in Tennessee; by regulation enacted in New Jersey (1973), Ohio (1974), Minnesota (January 1975), Washington (April 1975), and Oklahoma (effective July 1975) to include the coverage of psychologists under Medicaid as independent providers; and in Hawaii (April 1975), but only on physician referral. The state plan in Colorado has recognized psychologists at three levels of qualification and lower fees for mental health services since June 1972, but only under medical direction. This latter restriction may be reconsidered with fiscal year 1975 to 1976. In 1974, the APA, upon reviewing Item 6 of Section 3 of state Medicaid plans, found psychologists recognized for therapy in eleven states. This review cast some doubt on the situation in Kentucky and Kansas, but added New Hampshire, New York (except New York City), Oregon, and Utah. Nevada psychologists reported that they were not paid as primary providers under that state's plan. Certain aspects of the New Jersey program are described in Chapter Twelve. In Ohio, a licensed psychologist with a "vendor" number is reimbursed on a UCR (usual, customary, and reasonable) fee basis—up to a limit, the maximum being whatever fee 75 percent of the providers charge for similar services. The services recognized are specified in a currently relevant broad schedule of procedures. The Ohio plan deserves close consideration by other states. The Minnesota policy recognizing licensed consulting psychologists for both assessment and treatment services also recognizes a broad range of procedures that include up to ten individual psychotherapy visits per year; up to two hours per week, not over twenty weeks for psychotherapy of two family members; and for three or more family members, up to twenty-six sessions per six-month period. In New York and Oregon prior authorization from the state agency is required. In Montana, coverage is extended only to the services of a clinical psychologist, and is limited to twenty-four hourly visits per year. In New Hampshire, the maximum paid for psychological services is limited to $500 per year.

However, states are beginning to report that excessive cost controls are more costly than the savings achieved. For example, when the new administration in California found that $900,000 had been expended to reject $300,000 in claims via prior authorization for services beyond two visits a month, the prior authorization process was largely removed from the Medi-Cal program (but retained for dermatology and psychiatry). Similarly, Utah expended $100,000 to reject $20,000 in claims. More effective means of cost control and quality assurance clearly must be evolved.

In comparing the results of the two surveys, we find that several states that had stated that psychologists were accepted as independent providers of services now apparently no longer reimburse qualified psychologists. What happened in these states? Why is this situation so clouded? Direct communication with the Social Security Administration (SSA) by two investigators (Wiggins and Dörken), pursued over several months, drew a blank. They were advised that this information was not available in the state plans filed with the SSA and were referred to the individual states. Moreover, when the use of psychologists as independent vendors under Medicaid was studied by contract (BLK Group, 1975), initial information provided by a federal agency proved grossly inaccurate, while at the state level use and cost data were scarce and often inconsistent for purposes of interstate comparison. In four states (Maine, New Jersey, Nevada, and Montana) the payments to psychologists as a percent of total vendor payments in 1974 averaged only .17 percent of the Medicaid budget in those states.

One state, Minnesota, has attempted to estimate its total

Medicaid mental health program costs. Thus, inpatient psychiatric services in psychiatric hospitals, in acute care hospitals, and in long-term care facilities is at an approximate current annual expenditure rate of $12,000,000 or 5.1 percent of total Medicaid costs. By contrast, the outpatient mental health services of the 96 vendor clinical psychologists (13.6 percent of these expenditures), 180 psychiatrists, community mental health centers, and outpatient hospital services collectively amount to $660,000 or .28 percent of total Medicaid costs. Expenditures for mental health services then account for 5.38 percent of program costs.

The records and response are not the only thing amiss in the federal administration of this program. The *Washington Report on Medicine and Health* (1975), for example, found from a survey of eight states that apparently only about 3 percent of eligible welfare children were getting the health screening care mandated by Medicaid's Early and Periodic Screening, Diagnosis and Treatment program.

Since several of the major national health insurance proposals, if enacted, would embrace Medicaid, it becomes strategically important for each state to gain recognition through administrative agreement, regulation, or legislation so that psychologists would be accepted as qualified, independent providers of services. It is obvious that unemployment (Brenner, 1973), financial difficulty, and perhaps poverty (all of which might be expected from persons eligible for treatment under Medicaid) can break down one's tolerance of stress. Treatment of such persons should not be limited to physicians or psychiatrists. In twenty-three states (see Chapter Three) there are laws that provide freedom-of-choice of practitioners for persons covered by health insurance contracts. Programs for the indigent that place special restrictions on access to care thus are guilty of setting a discriminatory double standard. Furthermore, in 1974 Congress passed legislation that cited clinical psychologists as qualified, independent providers of services under all Federal Employees Health Benefit Act plans (PL 93-363). The government pays the majority of the premium under such plans. Why should the indigent not have the same benefit, especially when the same government is paying most of the cost of their health insurance bill?

Medicaid Negotiation in Ohio

Since many state psychological associations have not yet attempted to have psychologists included in their Medicaid program, the details regarding the negotiations of the Ohio Department of Public Assistance, Division of Income Maintenance, may be instructive. Once it was agreed that the Ohio Psychological Association (OPA) would attempt to secure the recognition of psychologists as eligible providers, additional time was required to select a negotiating team, attempt to obtain some documentation of the regulations on the services by other professions under the Ohio Medicaid program, and to distribute material and obtain feedback from the individual negotiating team members. This work required approximately four months. Another two months were required to write a letter of request for the inclusion of psychologists as eligible vendors, to obtain a reply, and to establish a meeting time.

In the initial meeting, representatives of the (Ohio) Division of Income Maintenance made clear that dealing with the request to include psychologists was merely another demand on their time; they were busy enough trying to get their computerized billing program to work. They had over $1,000,000 in unpaid bills, bad newspaper publicity, and interdepartmental struggles. From the discussion it was learned that psychological testing was already an includable benefit in the Title V program of the Social Security Amendment, which provides evaluative services for crippled children. This information reduced one source of confusion, since under the Crippled Children's Program, Title V, a child could be evaluated, though the treatment services rendered to that crippled child would have to flow through Medicaid, Title XIX, channels funds. Thus, some of the payments for services of psychologists had apparently come out of Title V funds. Nonetheless, there were separate vendor lists for Title V and for Title XIX, even though both sets of funds were administered through the Division of Income Maintenance.

The Division of Income Maintenance had promised a reply to the OPA's request for vendor registration for psychologists under Title V and under Title XIX. Received after a lengthy delay, the reply proved unsatisfactory. Meanwhile, the efforts of individual psychologists to register as vendors under the Title V program were unsuccessful. The Division of Income Maintenance then questioned the cost of increased benefits caused by including licensed psychologists as eligible vendors. The vague and evasive letter incorporating this question indicated that the division had chosen to delay decisions, and that further negotiations might be attempted.

Deep internal problems within this state division caused wholesale resignations and reassignments. This reshuffling allowed the OPA to make presentations to a new cast of players from the Division of Income Maintenance, who proved to be much more sympathetic. For one thing, they did not have to defend past decisions and mistakes; and secondly, they were in the position of trying to please everyone, or at least trying not to make enemies. Furthermore, the OPA negotiating team was now experienced and had done their homework. In addition, there was data showing the distribution of psychologists and psychiatrists providing services in Ohio, which demonstrated that under the present regulations, about half the counties in Ohio had no practicing psychiatrists registered with the Division of Income Maintenance to supply mental health services under the Medicaid program. The inclusion of psychologists would provide the opportunity for approximately 25 percent of those eligible for Medicaid to receive services, now denied because there were no eligible vendors in their locale. Once this information was documented, personal assurances were given that the Ohio Medicaid program regulations would be amended to include psychologists.

The OPA then began a series of negotiations on writing the necessary regulations handbook, and drawing up the necessary computer code, service classifications, and fee schedules. Even in this favorable climate, a period of ten months from writing to publishing the regulations elapsed before the first psychologist could be registered as a vendor. Even though no major problems were encountered during this period, delays were caused by interpretations of language, clarifications, time off, the pressure of other issues, and attention to detail.

The process was typical of what happens with low priority items that receive the official attention of all interested departments. Even after the implementing regulations were officially approved by the division, they still required clearance from ten other individuals to be sure that there was no other regulation with which these would conflict; that the funds necessary for starting the program would be available; and that the claim supervisors would be properly trained for the administration of claims for psychological services. Fortunately, Edgar Crough of the Division of Income Maintenance, chief negotiator for the division, was experienced in claims administration procedures and was instrumental in establishing this program for psychology.

Contrasted to the general situation in state Medicaid plans, the Ohio effort represents a sophisticated approach to claims review and reimbursement for services rendered. Of course, as in all new programs, there will be unforeseen difficulties. The Division of Income Maintenance has agreed to hire a psychological consultant to handle these contingencies. So far the Ohio Medicaid program has been implemented with minimum difficulty. Other states have used the Ohio experience in establishing psychologists as vendors in their state's Medicaid program. There is sufficient documentation in the *Ohio Medicaid Handbook for Psychologists* (1974) to allow adaptation of the program to other states.

In retrospect, analysis of the distribution of Ohio psychologists in urban and rural areas proved to be the most potent argument for inclusion. Pilot studies (Dörken and Whiting, 1974) indicated that the distribution of psychologists was generally more parallel to the population than that of psychiatrists and that psychologists are more apt to serve rural areas than are psychiatrists, who are heavily urbanized in their practices. The question of the availability of needed health services in rural areas has been effective in other states for other professions as well. For example, in Pennsylvania the optometrists were able to show that they provided services in rural areas, whereas opthalmologists tended to be urbanized. As a result, optometrists were then authorized to use medication for the examination of eyes, where previously this procedure had been restricted to opthalmologists. Webb's study (1974) of the distribution of psychologists within Ohio, showing that 49 counties had no practicing psychiatrist qualified to deliver mental health services, stimulated psychologists to find opportunities to serve these counties. Webb reported that 79 percent of the psychiatrists in Ohio are found in five metropolitan areas as compared with 59 percent of licensed psychologists. By contrast only 43 percent of the population is found in these areas. Also, on comparing the patients of the two professions (February 27, 1974 letter to Congressman Donald D. Clancey), he found, "... virtually no differences in the type or severity of pathology." The use of Medicaid funds for psychological services in these underserved areas has accelerated the progress made to date.

New Jersey Medicaid Experience

Licensed psychologists, recognized as vendors by the (New Jersey) Division of Medical Assistance and Health Services, have been able to provide .a broad range of procedures to Medicaid recipients since January 1974. Maximum hourly rates for reimbursement have been established at $26 for psychological generalists and $37 for specialists (ABPP [American Board of Professional Psychology] Diplomate or eligible). (The BLK final report [1975] noted that a survey by the Prudential Insurance Company, the fiscal intermediary, had shown the average rate for psychologists in the state to be slightly more than $35 an hour in 1974.) Prior authorization is required for services exceeding $300 in a year to any beneficiary.

Nine months into the program, less than 300 psychologists —under 40 percent of the state resident licensed psychologists— had requested and received vendor status. Collectively, they had submitted somewhat over 1,400 claims and had been reimbursed about $107,000 or almost $75 per claim. These claims constituted .07 percent of all claims made in that period. By comparison, the 582 vendor psychiatrists submitted close to 30,000 claims and had been reimbursed about $1,750,000 or almost $61 a claim. The psychiatric claims constituted 1.47 percent of all claims submitted. Together, the services of psychologists and psychiatrists to this program constituted only 3.89 percent of all reimbursements and 1.54 percent of all claims. Psychologists submitted less than 5 percent of these mental health service claims. Clearly, the cost of including psychologists in this Medicaid program was minimal.

Medicare, Title XVIII

Title XVIII of the Federal Social Security Act of 1968 (Medicare) provides services to the aged and certain other groups of impaired or disabled persons. Medicare, however, gives preferential benefits for inpatient treatment. If treatment under Medicare takes place in a general hospital, there is no difference between the benefits for mental disorder or for other disability. For care in a psychiatric hospital (under Part A) though, there is a 190-day lifetime limit. Perhaps this limit may account for the 9 percent decrease in certified beds in psychiatric hospitals between July 1973 and July 1974, a net loss of 21,000 beds (HEW, SSA, 1975b). Effective January 1975, the Medicare hospital deductible has been increased to $104, the Social Security Administration's calculation of the average cost of one day of hospital care. Then, for outpatient treatment under Part B, psychiatric care may be furnished by physicians in outpatient departments, in a physician's office, the patient's home or a skilled nursing facility. Payments for these services are limited to a maximum of $250.00 or 50 percent of reasonable charges, whichever is less, after the $60 deductible is met, in a calendar year. Obviously, for the senior citizen, the outpatient benefit, with its $60 deductible and 50 percent cost-sharing may preclude early therapeutic involvement, at the time when therapy can often be most helpful. Psychologists, moreover, are not included as therapists under the Medicare provisions of this act. The services of psychologists are limited to psychological testing on medical referral, either on an inpatient or outpatient basis. Inpatient testing is the more common and is typically billed through the hospital. Outpatient testing is frequently done for disability determination for Medicare benefits.

A report on the financing of mental health care under Medicare and Medicaid (HEW, SSA, 1971) delineates certain constraints, statutory inconsistencies, and utilization data. Thus the $250 maximum is derived from 80 percent of the statutory limit of $312.50. If the $60 deductible has not otherwise been met, then the limit for outpatient psychiatric service is $202. Psychological services are reimbursable to the extent they are "incidental" to a physician's service. In order to be "incidental to," the practitioner must be located in the same service facility and under immediate physician supervision. Under such circumstances, ironically, psychological services would not be restricted to the reimbursement limit of $250 on psychiatric services.

From 1967 to 1969 the relative proportion of reimbursements for psychiatric services under both Medicare and Medicaid declined (though there was a substantial rise in absolute expenditures). By 1969, 1.4 percent and 7.6 percent of reimbursement, respectively, went to these programs for psychiatric services—collectively, only 3.7 percent. For those with supplementary medical insurance in 1967 only 0.2 percent utilized outpatient psychiatric services. Much of the picture of psychiatric utilization in these programs is unknown and current data are apparently not available.

While the distinctions in coverage are explicit, the reporting apparently is not. Thus, attempts to secure cost data from regional offices of the Public Health Service and from the Social Security Administration, while yielding data on total cost of services in psychiatric hospitals and on average cost per admission and per diem, do not show the cost for psychiatric services in residential facilities covered under Part A. Moreover, data on outpatient physician costs attributable to "psychiatric care" under part B are apparently not available. It is hard to reconcile the logic of higher cost presumed for psychiatric services with the lack of cost data.

In 1972, the Medicare act was amended in great detail. While psychologists were not directly recognized as independent providers of services, PL 92-603 did authorize the secretary of HEW, within two years, "... to determine whether the services of clinical psychologists may be more generally available to persons ... under ... this Act in a manner consistent with quality of care and equitable and efficient administration." Regulation 755.25, Services of State Licensed Practitioners, appears to enable psychological participation by stating "medical care or *any other type of remedial care* recognized under state law, furnished by licensed practitioners ... provided within the scope of practice as defined by state law ..." (emphasis supplied). The Social Security Administration's interpretation is that psychological services under Medicare are restricted to those deemed to be "incidental to" a physician's services. Senate Report 92-1230 regarding the amendments of 1972 refers to the "Conditions of Coverage of Services of Clinical Psychologists" (Section 284 of HR 1) and notes that their services are available as part of hospital or extended care services under direct physician supervision. The committee would, however, liberalize Part B for outpatient coverage provided, again, that the services were under direct physician supervision. Such services would be included in and limited by the same overall $250 annual limitation on outpatient treatment of mental disorder. After objection from psychology this proposed amendment was dropped and provision made for a special study under Section 222(a)(b)(I) of PL 92-603, the Social Security Amendment of 1972. This authorized the secretary of HEW either directly or through grants or contracts to engage in experiments or demonstration projects "to determine whether the services of clinical psychologists may be made more generally available for services under titles XVIII and XIX of this Act in a manner consistent with quality of care and equitable and efficient administration."

In the 1974 Congress, bills were introduced in the House (HR 17520, by Representative Corman) and in the Senate (S 3645 by Senator Inouye) to include psychologists' services in the supplementary medical insurance benefits established under Part B of this Title as independent providers of services under

Medicare. While these bills were introduced late in the session, and therefore not acted on, they have been reintroduced into the 1975 Congress on behalf of clinical psychologists in both houses by these same authors, as S 123 and HR 2270, and they are gathering impressive cosponsorship. Mink has also introduced an identical bill (HR 3980), as have Representatives Edward Patten, New Jersey (HR 4796) and William Broomfield, Michigan (HR 6901). Corman's statement of introduction is succinct justification (*Congressional Record,* January 28, 1975, E 193-194) and cites supportive legislation passed by the 93rd Congress. Senator Inouye's statement of support (*Congressional Record,* January 15, 1975, S 194-195) notes its sound implications for national health insurance. Then, Senator Hartke, with an extensive statement supporting recognition of the services of psychologists, introduced S 1748 to amend licensed or certified psychologists into both Medicare and Medicaid (*Congressional Record,* May 15, 1975 S 8270-8275). He stated that the inclusion of psychological services "would not be costly," since it would not "add any new costly service, . . . would put an end to unnecessary and costly referral . . . [and would] merely . . . utilize qualified and available mental health manpower to provide services already covered . . . . Psychologists are geographically distributed in such a manner as to assure access by those in need . . . ." The resistance to the recognition of psychological services is usually on the basis of predicted substantially increased costs and utilization. Available empirical data does not support such a view (see Chapter Eleven). Moreover, the third-party intermediaries contacted who process Medicare claims do not even tabulate data on present outpatient psychiatric services. The actual use and costs of such services nationally must then be an unknown—and fear of the unknown may account for part of the resistance to extending coverage.

Comparison of the cost effectiveness of the Social Security Administration's Division of Direct Reimbursement with private fiscal intermediaries indicates an advantage for the private sector. Whereas a bill processed through the division averaged $12.39 in cost, the cost reported by four contract intermediaries was: Travelers, $7.31; Mutual of Omaha, $7.38; Chicago

Blue Cross, $3.38; and Maryland Blue Cross, $3.55 (*Medicine and Health,* October 1975, No. 1477).

Based on the Administration's proposed 1976 fiscal year budget, Medicaid and Medicare would account for more than 59 percent of all federal health outlays under the Department of Health, Education, and Welfare. This fact gives added perspective to the magnitude of these two programs, projected at $7,200,000,000 and $15,000,000,000 respectively. In fiscal year 1974, for persons aged 65 and over, Medicare alone accounted for 62 percent of hospital expenditures and 52 percent of their doctor bills (HEW, SSA, 1975).

Child and Maternal Health

Title V of the Social Security Act is administered by the Social and Rehabilitation Service of the Department of Health, Education, and Welfare under the provisions of PL 92-345. This statute covers: (1) services for reducing infant mortality and otherwise promoting the health of mothers and children, and (2) medical, surgical, corrective, and other services; and services, and facilities for the diagnosis, hospitalization, and care of children who are crippled or suffering from conditions leading to crippling. The program gives special recognition to the need to reduce the incidence of mental retardation and other handicapping conditions. For the purposes of this act, a crippled child is defined as an individual under 21 years of age who has an organic disease, defect, or condition that may hinder the achievement of normal growth and development.

Under its present scope, Title V rules out mental conditions that have no demonstrable organic basis. While this definition may be unnecessarily narrow for the diagnosis and treatment of some mental conditions, there are provisions for psychological testing. Evaluation is an accepted practice and is billed to the Title V plan by institutions. Direct billing by an independent provider of psychological services is becoming more commonplace.

The act authorized expenditures up to $350,000,000 a year for Title V programs for the fiscal year 1974. Evaluation of the psychological aspects of crippling conditions is subsumed under the total evaluation of the child, and no precise estimates on the extent of psychological services used under the Title V program are available. While there are provisions for recognition of psychological problems and mental conditions in the act, actual treatment services for these conditions must be supplied through Medicaid funds. Since a major focus of this act is aimed towards prevention, there are provisions for research and training funds that presumably can be used for dealing with psychological aspects of crippling conditions.

Other Social Security Programs

Under Title II, psychologists have been actively and increasingly involved as vocational experts in disability determination (Hannings, 1972). The determination and availability of employment for which the claimant has a capacity or transferable skills require an appreciation of the psychosocial factors both in disability and in the job market. The emphasis is on the actual situation rather than on the possible. Therefore, rehabilitation potential is not a component of disability determination. Where rehabilitation is indicated (see Chapter Four) assessment and therapy also is provided frequently by psychologists under state vocational rehabilitation services. When these measures are insufficient to fill claimant needs, there is a supplemental income program under Title VI.

This overview of Medicare, Medicaid, and Maternal and Child Health programs indicate that, with the exception of several state Medicaid programs, psychologists are currently involved only in a minor way. Yet, these programs are the forerunners of national health insurance programs. Hence, concerted effort to have psychologists recognized as providers of health services now will pave the way for recognition when health programs are developed for much wider segments of the population.

6

Forms of
Health Insurance

Herbert Dörken

Five major types of health ben-
efit plans are available to people who might become clients of
psychologists. These types are (1) stock and mutual health
insurance companies, such as Aetna, Occidental, Prudential, and
other members of the Health Insurance Association of America;
(2) such "nonprofit" open-panel hospital service or medical
service corporations as Blue Cross or Blue Shield; (3) such
closed-panel group practice plans as the Kaiser Foundation
Health Plan (currently cited as the health maintenance organization [HMO] prototype); (4) the newly emerging foundations
for medical care, consisting of fee-for-service practitioners feder-
ated into a foundation; and (5) employee beneficial indemnity
plans wherein the company or union in effect, is self-insured.
Although there is wide variation between states, only the first
and fifth categories typically come within the purview of a
state's insurance code. Hospital or medical service corporations,
or foundations for medical care may be governed by the government code, business and professions code, or health and welfare
code, depending on the particular state.

Most insurance companies have four major departments:
actuarial, underwriting, marketing, and claims. The actuarial
department statistically determines the premium cost of policies
for benefits provided. The underwriting department is essen-

tially responsible for the design of the insurance policy, for implementing and authorizing new lines of coverage, and for monitoring the benefit experience of the policyholders. The marketing department is responsible for the sale of the various policy lines. The claims department evaluates individual claims to determine whether or not they comply with the requirements of the provisions, definitions, limitations, and exclusions of the health insurance contract and pays or denies benefits accordingly.

Policies are issued under a variety of labels, such as "basic," "supplemental," or "major medical," "health catastrophe," "disability," and so on. Even in "basic" health plans, benefits are often only available to the insured after an initial deductible or coinsurance clause is satisfied. For example, a policy may require that the first $150 of expenses per calendar year are to be borne by the insured or subscriber and that subsequent expenses above a certain limit are to be shared, 80 percent by the insurer and 20 percent by the insured. Benefits may differ for employee and dependents. In most plans there are fewer limitations and more extensive benefits for inhospital than for outpatient services. Each policy states limits of liability in specifying the coverage or benefits. Some policies have relatively low maximums, such as $5,000, while others may exceed $50,000. In many, benefits may renew after time. In the past year catastrophic limits of $350,000 have been introduced in some plans. Many policies (fortunately, a decreasing number) have special exclusions or limits regarding the diagnosis and treatment of nervous, mental or emotional disorders, alcoholism, drug dependence, or self-inflicted injury. Coverage for mental disorder and recognition of the professional services of psychologists vary among the types of insurors, between individual or group plans, and from contract to contract. It is necessary to check the actual policy to clearly determine what health and professional services are covered; what amount of coinsurance, if any, is required; what number of visits are permitted; whether there is a referral or supervision clause; and what the contract benefit limit is.

The marketplace for buying health insurance is immense,

comprising over 1,000 commercial companies, 74 Blue Cross associations and 71 Blue Shield associations writing a variety of policies (Boroson, 1974). Further, as of mid-1974 there were 177 operational HMOs in the country (*Washington Report on Medicine and Health,* 1974). Health insurance is big business. In 1972, health insurance premiums paid totaled almost $25,750,000,000—55.6 percent of this amount was paid to the insurance companies, the balance to Blue Shield and Blue Cross and other hospital-medical plans. The dollar volume had doubled since 1966. Americans spent 3.2 percent of total disposable personal income in 1972 for health insurance premiums. Total personal-consumption expenditures for health care were $61,000,000,000 in 1973 or 76 percent of the amount spent by Americans on all personal needs. The United States population averaged five physician visits per person per year. This average does not include visits to dentists (an average of 1.6 visits) and other practitioners. Not only were general health insurance coverage and health care costs rising, but the use of public mental health services had increased progressively, from .63, 1.03, 1.20, to 1.99 percent of the population, in 1946, 1955, 1963, and 1971, respectively.

Health insurance coverage, though still far from adequate, has been increasing rapidly both in terms of persons covered and the extent of coverage available. This progress is summarized in the *Source Book of Health Insurance Data 1974-75* (Health Insurance Institute, n.d.*b*). Thus, a 1973 survey found that seventy-eight insurance companies were insuring almost 67,000,000 people under group major medical policies. Eighty-five percent were covered for treatment of mental and nervous disorders, though the maximum benefits for outpatient visits were usually limited to $500 per year and $10,000 per lifetime. Of these policies, 91 percent had coverage for alcoholism and many group policies continued the insurance on disabled dependent children into adulthood, thereby providing coverage to the mentally retarded.

One limitation on the diversity of health care delivery models is the restrictive legislation that exists in about half the states in the country against salaried, closed-panel group practice and, in some of these states, against group practice per se. As of 1973, there was specific statutory exemption from restrictions on the corporate practice of medicine in only twenty-four states. But by the time PL 93-222, the HMO Development Act of 1973, became law, fewer than ten of the remaining state laws effectively prohibited formation of an HMO (Clarke, 1975). National health insurance may preempt or override such restrictive state laws, as did PL 93-222. One approach to competition in the health field and to choice for the consumer is the mandating of a dual-choice option, as in this law. Another common limiting condition, particularly in individual health insurance policies, is that policies often exclude or severely restrict coverage for mental disorder. Group health plans often require a differentially lower ceiling in coverage for mental disorder or require the insured to pay a higher proportion of the costs of professional services received (coinsurance). In Connecticut, Maryland, Massachusetts, and Minnesota (as of June 1975), however, mental health coverage is mandated in all group health contracts. Comparable legislation has been introduced in Colorado and Tennessee and is under consideration in other states. The Minnesota law and the Colorado and Tennessee proposals seek to assure equal coverage for mental disorder. In Georgia, if mental health benefits are not included, a disclaimer must be written across the face of the policy and recent California law required that if the insured group requests coverage for mental disorder it must be provided. Mandatory legislation of this type, however, if it only establishes a minimum benefit "floor" for mental disorder, could have a paradoxical outcome, the floor becoming the ceiling. In any event, in contrast to basic plans, mental health benefits are generally included in "major medical," "comprehensive coverage," or "extended benefits" contracts underwritten by the commercial carriers or in "supplemental benefits" programs in Blue Cross and Blue Shield subscriptions.

A major review of current coverage for nervous and mental disorder is contained in Reed, Myers, and Scheidemandel (1972). This survey clearly documents the feasibility of insurance coverage for mental disorder for the working population, and is perhaps the best compendium of actuarial data available. Back in 1963, after an experimental trial (Avnet, 1962), Group Health Insurance of New York offered psychiatric benefits for families at $.60 per month (Dörken, 1963). Now, twelve years later, the Health Insurance Plan of Greater New York has found it can provide unlimited mental coverage to families for an additional premium of $2.70 per month.

Reservations about insurance coverage for comprehensive mental health care typically have focused on the relatively large proportion of benefit (costs paid) to a small proportion of the insured. But is such coverage any different from those with such chronic or long-lasting disabilities as heart disease, diabetes, or cancer? (See also HEW, SRS, 1975.) Moreover, the point may be made that patients who begin receiving service under a medical diagnosis (physical or physiological) often are treated more favorably than those labeled with a specific psychiatric diagnosis. And this differential coverage is facilitated by the benefit structure of many policies. Perhaps it is time to think in terms of levels of functional disability rather than diagnosis.

When there is an organized consumer concern, the insurance industry can be responsive, even to chronic or long-term disability. In October 1968, for example, the Health Insurance Association of America, in cooperation with the National Association for Retarded Children (NARC), formulated a "model bill" to provide uniform guidance to all states. Most family plans and employer group insurance contracts now contain a provision that terminates a child's coverage on attainment of age nineteen (unless a full-time student, in which case coverage is terminated at twenty-three). The proposed model NARC bill would set aside this limiting age if the child continues to be "both (a) incapable of self-sustaining employment by reason of mental retardation or physical handicap and (b) chiefly dependent upon the employee or member for support or maintenance."

Such changes in the approach to health insurance are seriously needed, for nearly all the forms of insurance currently available do not adequately deal with problems of mental health. To prepare for a discussion of what is needed, therefore, we will first describe the major provisions for mental health in various common types of policies.

Indemnity Benefit Plans

Commercial insurance companies commonly indemnify (reimburse for loss) up to but not exceeding such limits as a per diem rate for semiprivate hospital care; a dollar value by visit for office, home, or hospital professional services; and a total dollar limit on reimbursement. Characteristically, much broader benefits are available through group than individual policies because the risk can be distributed and more predictably estimated for group policies. Premium costs may vary according to the nature of the insured group (which is "experience-rated") or of the particular community ("community-rated"). Adverse risk selection is moderated in group plans. Data from "experience-rated" plans suggest that the utilization rate for nervous and mental disorder is largely a function of the kind of group served rather than of who the providers of services are. However, insurance is a complex and varied field—as mentioned, there are more than 1,000 health insurance companies in the United States, with various benefits, exclusions, and deductibles, all of which produce variations in policies (NHI Reports, December 30, 1974, p. 3).

These industry group health plans pioneered the adoption and extension of mental health benefits. Thus, data from eleven major companies for the period 1930 to 1950 show that mental disorder comprised about 6 percent of disability claims, a volume that was generally exceeded by cardiovascular conditions and malignant neoplasms (Society of Actuaries, 1953). Later, the Health Insurance Institute of New York reported in 1962 that of the new group health insurance underwritten by forty-four companies (which wrote almost 75 percent of such plans for 1961), 96.6 percent provided coverage for nervous or mental disorder. In a 1962 bulletin the Life Insurance Agency Management Association reported that, for 133 companies from which survey information was obtained, group policies seldom excluded coverage for mental disorders. Among individual policies this category was excluded in 13, 24, and 40 percent of the disability income, basic hospitalization, and major medical plans, respectively. But exclusion among these classes applied to only 2, 6, and 7 percent of the group plans, respectively. Basic hospitalization, when offered by group plans, was ordinarily provided for "this condition the same as any other covered illness." A relative reduction in outpatient mental health benefits was fairly typical, with higher coinsurance, a limit on professional visits, and allowed expense per visit. Nonetheless, the majority of member companies pioneered in underwriting coverage for mental disorder and today some 1,000 companies reportedly underwrite disability health insurance. An American Psychiatric Association memo (1975), entitled "Recent Data Documenting the Feasibility of Nondiscriminatory Coverage of Mental Illness," included reference to data from the Bureau of Labor Statistics, that "148 large employers and/or unions in major industries (the group included such industrial giants as General Motors, U.S. Steel, IBM, Goodyear, and ITT) showed that in 1974, 68 percent of these firms provided the same hospital benefits for mental conditions as for other conditions . . . outpatient (office) care, 41 percent of the plans provided the same care of mental as of other conditions, 45 percent had reduced benefits for mental conditions, and 8 percent had no outpatient coverage . . . . The remaining 5 percent . . ." provided outpatient benefits only for mental disorder.

In 1962, 60 percent of eighty companies made direct payments to professionals for therapeutic services, recognizing only physicians. In addition, however, 41 percent, or 33 companies, made payments to psychologists when involved on a referral basis and 15 percent made such payments when psychologists were consulted directly by the insured. These data show that there *has* been progress in the past decade. Court decisions have supported the extended coverage, by following the principle of "reasonable expectations." For example, decisions in Ohio and New Jersey have required that disability benefits must be accorded a liberal construction in favor of the insured.

Major Medical Policies

Following the development of group health insurance plans, emerged "major medical" policies of the commercial carriers and "supplemental benefits" plans of medical service corporations. These policies initially provided for treatment of physical ailments when the services were performed by a physician licensed to practice medicine and surgery. When the insurance carriers, under pressure from various concerned groups, began to provide benefits for the treatment of emotional problems, they proceeded cautiously. Such basic concepts as "illness" and "cure" were difficult, if not impossible, to define. Therefore, the carriers commonly limited coverage for mental disorder to services in general hospitals, restricted professional services to those of medical doctors, and placed more restrictive limits on the benefits to a claimant. For example, many policies paid 80 percent of medical expenses after satisfying an initial deductible of, say, $500, while benefits for mental health services required a 50 percent coinsurance. Health benefits having a maximum reimbursability of from $15,000 to $50,000 might limit mental health benefits to a lifetime aggregate of $500 to $1,500. Nonetheless, some policies today make no distinction in benefit limit by type of disability, and coverage under more recent "comprehensive" major medical policies shows a clear trend to broadening mental health benefits.

Since psychologists were increasingly involved in the treatment of mental and emotional problems, the early major medical policies, by not reimbursing patients of psychologists, placed undue hardship on both the patient and the psychological practitioner. Through their insurance committees, the American Psychological Association and affiliated state associations began to address this problem by directly negotiating with carriers, major corporations, and labor unions. While some gains were achieved, overall results were modest until recently. Nonetheless, some insurance carriers did accept psychologists as providers of services and their actuarial figures clearly indicated that the inclusion of properly qualified psychologists in no way led to overutilization nor created an expansion of special risk for the insurance industry. Companies reporting lack of adverse experience included Occidental Life, Massachusetts Mutual, Continental, Prudential, and Aetna. Excerpts from letters of industry executives are illustrative. In January 1968 an actuary of Continental Assurance Richard Sieben wrote to Oliver Kerner, chair of Insurance Committee of the Illinois Psychological Association, that "there have been no problems in claim administration . . . not . . . any significant increase in claim levels. We are satisfied with our experience at Continental . . . . Helped us to extend coverage to our own employee group." Later, in November 1971, Donald Hawkins, vice-president of the policy benefits division of Occidental Life noted in a letter to John Armer, insurance consultant to the California State Psychological Association, that in "claims involving services of psychologists . . . this benefit has not created problems in claim administration or in overall case experience . . . . We have seen no need for changing our computer program in order to segregate experience with psychologists." On December 1, 1971, a Massachusetts Mutual vice-president C. G. Hill wrote to Rogers Wright (CAPPS) that "our overall observations do not indicate that inclusion of coverage for treatment by clinical psychologists has had an adverse effect on our overall claim ratio." Then, on January 11, 1972, Richard Hellman, vice-president of Prudential, wrote to Jack Wiggins (chair, Committee on Health Insurance, APA) reviewing the experience of several years. He noted: "In 1967, we began to accept charges for out-patient psychotherapeutic services rendered by a licensed or certified clinical psychologist on the same basis as those by a psychiatrist . . . . None of the various methods of recognition . . . have resulted in any significant expansion of the risk assumed . . . . This applies both to over utilization . . . as well as to increase in claims for psychotherapy which could be attributed to the inclusion of clinical psychologists." Guardian Life and Liberty Mutual have also voluntarily included psychologists as autonomous providers of services in many of their contracts.

In April 1974, Frances Atorick of Aetna wrote to Myron Singer (Warren, Michigan) about claim costs for mental and nervous disorder in 1971 and 1972 in their federal employee government-wide indemnity program. From 1972 Aetna recognized the services of psychologists without medical referral. While total claims increased 16 percent in 1972 over 1971, and mental and nervous costs increased 15 percent, the proportion of mental disorder claims to total claims actually declined from 8.6 percent to 8.5 percent.

Following repeated inquiries by the American Psychological Association and by states such as New Jersey, and following an increase in the states with freedom-of-choice legislation, Ronald McPhee, vice-president of TIAA/CREF (Teachers Insurance and Annuity Association, and College Retirement Equities Fund) notified Kenneth Little of the APA that effective August 20, 1974, TIAA/CREF would recognize psychologists as independent providers: "We have adopted the policy of no longer requiring a physician's prescription or order for a psychologist's charges to be covered under TIAA Major Medical plan . . . . The new practice . . . will be implemented on an administrative basis until we can conveniently amend group contracts." In October 1974 the company sent a circular notice advising the officers of all institutions with TIAA/CREF major medical coverage of this change. TIAA/CREF ranks among the top ten insurance companies offering insurance and major medical programs in 80 to 90 percent of private colleges and universities and as an option in about 40 percent of public institutions—in all, some 2,700 nonprofit organizations. About 400,000 individuals have subscribed (Walsh, 1974).

Individual major industries are responding to the same trends. For example, General Electric recently announced (*Employee Handbook*, 1973) that its insurance plan will cover the fees of psychologists in the same manner as the fees physicians or psychiatrists charge for treatment of illness or injury. This change, which was originally scheduled to go into effect in January 1976, was later made to apply retroactively from January 1970, as a result of a study of various legislation relating to coverage of psychologists' fees under group health insurance plans. Similarly, in November 1973, The Travelers (Hartford, Connecticut) issued a circular memorandum to their group policy holders advising that "compliance with these [freedom-of-choice] statutes, effective immediately, . . . Treatment under medical, comprehensive medical and major medical expense insurance coverages will be considered to include the services of a licensed or certified clinical psychologist when acting within the legal scope of his practice." The states that have passed freedom-of-choice legislation (see Chapter Three) are cited in this memo. Major companies such as the White Motor Corporation, in turn circularized their affiliates and offices that their contracts would "be amended accordingly in the states that have changed their laws."

Health Maintenance Organizations

According to current federal definition (HEW, HSMHA, 1971a), any prepaid health plan (PHP) that markets to only one buyer or segment of service is not a health maintenance organization (HMO). In principle, HMOs are distinguished by prepayment for health care; group practice by the professional staff; integration of health facilities; voluntary client enrollment; and emphasis on preventive health services. Within the service area, the insured usually can only exercise benefits if he or she uses a "member" provider of services. Ordinarily, limited out-of-area emergency benefits are covered. While the HMO concept has received recent wide publicity, its prototype is the Kaiser Foundation plan dating back to World War II. The concept is also preceded by the health cooperatives of the midwest. The Health Cooperative of Puget Sound (Washington) is rather unique, being a subscriber-owned HMO corporation, and offers both prepaid and fee for service health care. The development of HMOs is proceeding rapidly, albeit not under the HMO Development Act of 1973 (PL 93-222). Rothfield (1973) reported 80 HMOs in operation, with a comparable number under development. As of March 1975, there were 179 operational HMOs in the country with another 314 in planning or formational stages (Wetherille, 1975). It is estimated that more than 7,000,000 Americans are members of HMO-type organizations and that about 20 percent of the population lives within their service areas (Clarke, 1975). Apart from government development grants, this type of delivery system is attracting private capital, insurance industry, and other forms of involvement. While the HMO "movement" may be growing, it should be noted that as of February 1975 there were no "qualified" HMOs in the sense of PL 93-222 and only one facility that had received a loan (as distinct from grants to study feasibility). Ten feasibility grants, however, have been awarded in California alone. According to the *Washington Report on Medicine and Health* (June 1975), only 5 percent of the country's HMOs are qualified under the HMO Act of 1975. Some 29 new facilities serving 400,000 people have opened with federal aid in the past four years (Iglehart, 1974). The combination requirements (community rating; comprehensive coverage with eight basic services; no limits on time or cost of services; subscribers not over half to be Medicare or Medicaid beneficiaries, annual open enrollments; a dual-choice provision, a governing board to include one-third consumers) are such that premium costs cannot be competitive with other current group health plans. And providers may not yet be ready for all the complexities of such plans. However, this law, analyzed by Dorsey (1975), and other laws such as Pl 93-641, the National Health Planning and Resources Development Act of 1974, do lay the groundwork for eventual National Health Insurance.

A health maintenance organization contracts for a prepaid premium to provide a specified array of health benefits to plan members. The prepayment links providers and consumers. The model would be equally applicable to coverage on a capitation basis. Since the providers of service, the closed-panel or member staff, can share in the risk, the motivation for an efficient, economical operation is enhanced. In effect, early preventive care, emphasis on ambulatory care, prescreening and control of hospitalization, and quick rehabilitation are held to yield a more competitive operation. Thus, in theory, the concept of such a prepaid health plan, where the provider has an incentive to keep the patient population healthy, is in contrast to ordinary solo or fee-for-service group practice, or to indemnified services, in which the provider of services only earns a fee or reimbursement after services are provided. Compared to the group health plans of Blue Cross and Blue Shield or those of the commercial insurance carriers, the mental disorder benefit package of the HMOs is generally more limited. In only a few plans do all enrollees receive mental health treatment as part of their basic health benefits. Thus, "about one-fourth of the HIP membership have mental health coverage, and the various Kaiser plans make mental health services available through a rider to only about one-third of their enrollees . . . . At the present time only three of the largest prototype plans—Group Health Cooperative of Puget Sound, Group Health Association of D.C. and the Kaiser Foundation Health Plan of Portland, Oregon—provide mental health treatment for all enrollees" (HEW, HSA, 1974). These programs appear, however, to be moving toward a benefit package formula of 20-45-90; that is, twenty outpatient mental health visits, forty-five days of hospitalization and ninety days of partial (day or night) hospitalization. Moreover, the staffing guideline of one full-time mental health professional to each 10,000 covered enrollees, used by Kaiser for many years, is changing, with a ratio now of almost 1:7,000 in Kaiser's Southern California mental health service. In the federal employee, high-option Kaiser group, the mental health utilization rate was 2.21 percent, though for the high-utilizing age group (females ages twenty to forty-four) it was about double (4.12 percent) the average for all eligible enrollees.

As far as psychologists are concerned, HMO plans quickly bring to light the fact that many people seeing physicians, if not a majority, are essentially there because of emotional or mental problems per se or because of such problems related to a physical disability. As a result, a number of HMOs have recognized that both sound economics and good health care call for direct treatment of the emotional problem (Follette and Cummings, 1967; Goldberg et al., 1970) rather than for treatment of only the physical or physiological components, often by tranquilizers or palliative medication. Since early short-term psychotherapy may avoid later hospitalizations, the importance of a pool of trained mental health professionals become obvious. Psychologists, with their clinical training, are a natural resource for building such a pool.

Owing to recent tax law favoring a professional corporate structure and the public demand for broad coverage, corporate practice appears to be increasing and small local partnerships declining (Harsham, 1973). Corporate law and tax law is a highly specialized field. Generally, however, in a professional corporation licensed to practice, all shareholders must be of the same discipline (the corporation holds a practice license). In California, at least, an HMO must be nonprofit at the top. This nonprofit corporation, however, if not licensed to practice, need not be a professional corporation and may contract for management services, with a profit or nonprofit corporation or partnership. The management group, multidisciplinary or unidisciplinary, advises the holding corporation on its subcontracts with provider groups or with separate professional corporations (each unidisciplinary). The contracts can, however, require an integration of services—that is, cooperative coordination among members of the different professional corporations in service delivery. Clearly, there can be many variations in corporate structure.

Blue Cross and Blue Shield

Blue Cross and Blue Shield are "nonprofit, franchised" companies that technically are not considered insurance companies but rather hospital-medical service corporations and, therefore, are usually regulated under other statutes than those covering insurance companies. However, Blue Cross and Blue Shield together own a series of insurance stock companies known as Health Services Inc. and Medical Indemnity Association (HSI/MIA). Health Services Inc., an Illinois corporation, is wholly owned by the Blue Cross Association, while the Medical Indemnity Association is a stock insurance company wholly owned by the Blue Shield Group. Whether a specific contract would be underwritten by the Blue Cross Association or by HSI would depend on local law and other circumstances. Thus, it appears that state insurance codes, affecting commercial carriers, apply typically to HSI/MIA contracts as well. In any event, HSI/MIA underwrite the majority of the "Blues" major medical policies. When functioning as health service plans rather than insurance corporations, the "Blues" have about a 3 percent tax advantage over the industry. This advantage is due to their nonprofit status, which exempts them from taxes, negotiated contracts with member hospitals, and payment of physician services according to UCR rates rather than fees charged. In either event, as Iglehart (1974, p. 1830) has noted, "the sole product of Blue Cross/Blue Shield is health insurance." Thus if Congress enacted a national health insurance program in which the federal government had the primary role of providing insurance, all this business would be lost. Resistance to such a form of national health insurance could logically be anticipated.

The national associations of Blue Cross and Blue Shield are headquartered in Chicago. There are seventy-eight affiliates that provide health coverage for 68,000,000 Americans (Schorr, 1970). Each state has at least one Blue Cross or Blue Shield organization, with substantial variance locally in coverage and benefits. Generally, Blue Cross pays for expenses associated with hospital care; Blue Shield covers the cost of physicians' and other specified providers' services and of out-of-hospital benefits. In a few states, either may offer a combination plan. One such plan is the Blue Cross plan for the University of California. It provides limited "mental benefits" and recognizes both licensed psychologists and psychiatrists as independent practitioners. This, however, is not national Blue Cross policy.

Both "Blues" have their own independent service corporations. Their boards are usually dominated by physicians and their practices reflect medical thought and attitudes towards other professions. While this situation is changing and some boards (Oklahoma, Colorado, Pennsylvania, and some others) now have a majority of lay representation, the predominance of physicians can result in such requirements as "medical referral and supervision." This condition obtained in the government-wide Federal Employees Health Benefits plan until set aside by PL 93-363, signed July 30, 1974. Where plans include benefits that may be provided by licensed or certified clinical psychologists or optometrists, this law entitles the insured to freedom of choice and direct access to such practitioners. Indeed, the

Mental Health Report, a form issued by Blue Cross and Blue Shield in December 1974, relative to their government-wide federal employee Service Benefit Plan, states "Therapy provided by a qualified clinical psychologist is a covered service under Supplemental Benefits without supervision, direction or referral from a physician." This development reflects the recent constructive legislation.

Hospitalization is the most expensive form of health care and the area in which costs have shown the greatest recent increase. Thus, control of hospitalization can reduce health care costs. The practice of psychology is primarily oriented to ambulatory care and outpatient treatment and diagnosis. It is of interest, then, that some Blue Shield plans (for example, Colorado and Maryland) have recognized the contribution of psychologists and have voluntarily accepted qualified psychologists as independent providers of service. Maryland Blue Shield has recently issued an outpatient mental health endorsement providing "for the care of any mental or emotional illness, when such care is rendered on an outpatient basis by a licensed psychiatrist or psychologist." There are both low and high options ($400 and $1,000, respectively). Payments are on the basis of usual, customary, and reasonable (UCR) fees. The intent is to cover therapy where significant amelioration or improvement can be expected. A psychologist is defined in this endorsement as a person having a "doctoral degree in clinical psychology or behavioral science who is certified or licensed to practice as a psychologist in the State in which the Covered Services are rendered." In 1973, the Maryland Legislature amended its freedom-of-choice laws to include medical service corporations. Mental health hospital benefits are often paid under a Blue Cross contract section known as Rider "J" (Joint). This rider is a joint service of Blue Cross and Blue Shield. The intent of Rider "J" is to encourage diagnostic procedures and emergency treatment of disabilities outside of the hospital setting—in effect, a more economical approach. In Colorado, panel psychologists are recognized as independent providers under the panel physician plan, without referral or supervision by a physician.

Local option is a major factor in coverage for mental disorders and emotional problems. Blue Cross generally pays only for routinely available inpatient procedures when billed by the hospital. Often the services of a psychologist practitioner will be paid by Blue Cross if billed by the hospital. Psychologists have been paid by Blue Shield in those states where laws (insurance codes) mandating parity and freedom of choice of practitioners apply to the Blue Cross and Blue Shield plans. Only in a few states at this time, however, has Blue Shield implemented voluntary parity for psychologists. Optional services are usually covered only in major medical policies under the supplemental benefits section of the Blue Shield plans.

Blue Cross and Blue Shield also underwrite "major" health policies, usually as major medical plans or supplemental benefits under major medical plans. Industry-wide or national account policies are negotiated by the national associations of Blue Shield and Blue Cross in Chicago. When a plan is agreed upon with a major consumer, the various affiliated Blue Cross and Blue Shield organizations administer the plan in their state. The state affiliates are usually bound by the terms of the master contract. For example, the United Auto Workers Blue Cross and Blue Shield contract has a referral clause and limits psychological services to testing. On the other hand, Blue Shield serves as the fiscal intermediary in many areas for the Civilian Health and Medical Program of the Uniformed Services (CHAMPUS), which covers about 7,800,000 people and since 1970 has offered full parity for the services of psychologists. When the purchaser of a contract insists that qualified psychologists be reimbursed for servicing a covered condition, Blue Shield or Blue Cross can comply. In 1969 it became Blue Cross policy to include benefits for mental or nervous disorders for all ages in all high-option plans. Of the 60,000,000 members enrolled in Blue Shield plans in 1966, three-quarters were covered for such inhospital physician visits but less than 14 percent for outpatient psychotherapy (HEW, SSA, 1971).

In general, psychologists seem to have found the National Association of Blue Shield Plans to be more resistant than other carriers in accepting psychologists as fully independent health practitioners. But conditions appear to be changing. Utah reported that early in 1973 Blue Shield agreed to pay for psychological services following medical referral only (no longer requiring medical supervision). Many physicians recognize that the health services that psychologists perform are necessary and effective. Progressive physicians do not want the supervision-and-referral function imposed on them or on their patients. In addition, these imposed features can add additional or "feather-bedded" costs to the premium without adding additional benefits to the consumer. Indeed, they can result in a paradoxical situation in which the physician, having referred the patient to a specific psychologist whom he considers to have expertise in the treatment of mental disorder, has to state that he is supervising the psychologist (to whom he made the referral) in order for the patient to be reimbursed under the contract. This issue was highlighted in the June 14, 1972, United States Senate Report from the Committee on Post Office and Civil Service. Testimony regarding the services of clinical psychologists indicated "that Blue Cross/Blue Shield is the only insurance carrier of significance which does not cover such mental health services without the certification by a doctor of medicine who supervises the treatment . . . . There is little if any benefit . . . other than the earning of money by doctors of medicine and the avoidance of payment by Blue Cross/Blue Shield." PL 93-363 has changed this situation, at least for federal employees, effective January 1975.

Reed (1974) analyzed utilization experience for mental disorder under the Blue Cross and Blue Shield Plan for Federal Employees, reporting data for 1966, 1969, and 1972. Benefits paid for mental disorder as a proportion of total benefits for all conditions had increased from 4.8 to 7.3 percent. Still, even under the high-option plan, which provided mental disorder benefits virtually equal to those for other conditions, the total benefits paid in 1972 amounted to only $11.92 per person covered. Another review of this group health plan noted that the benefit cost for mental disorder "leveled off in 1971 at 7 percent. For the last three years, the percentage has remained at 7 percent, auguring well for coverage of mental illness without upper limits" (Morris Associates, 1974).

Foundations for Medical Care

Following the lead of the San Joaquin Foundation for Medical Care (headquartered in Stockton, California), the foundation movement has attracted growing interest and emulation among county and state medical societies. Eisenberg's review (1971) reported that thirty-five foundations for medical care (FMCs) had been established. The rapid further development then predicted has occurred and an American Association of Foundations for Medical Care has been established (Box 230, Stockton, California, CA 95201). In the fall of 1974 the association issued a directory listing eighty-two member foundations, of which forty-six are "comprehensives" and thirty-six "review" foundations. The review FMCs perform only a peer review or PSRO-like function under agreement with various group health insurance plans. Foundation officers have been active supporters of the PSRO concept. The "comprehensives," in addition to ongoing peer review functions, render professional services to various insured groups (and, in some plans, do so on a proscriptive, prepaid basis, where they are at risk). It is of interest that the comprehensives have achieved successes comparable to closed-panel, salaried practice HMOs in reducing hospital usage to 325 to 375 days annually per 1,000 insured, a figure said to be half or even less, than the utilization rate being experienced by Blue Cross and indemnity plans.

Although described by some as the local medical society's response to Kaiser and to the specter of national health insurance, the federation of fee-for-service providers into an organizational entity that can contract to provide designated services on a prepaid basis within a geographical area gives the foundation the attributes of the HMO. In fact, in the Health Maintenance Organization Act of 1972, S 3327, the foundations were defined in the following Senate debate as "supplemental health maintenance organizations." In PL 93-222 they are clearly recognized as HMOs, being designated "individual practice associations." Since foundations can engage in capitation forms of payment and modified risk sharing, while at the same time retaining an incentive reimbursement to the provider, they can be quite flexible in handling group and individual health problems. With their emphasis on peer review and quality control, they are able to exert strong leverage on their members in requiring quality health services. The March 22, 1973, *Congressional Record* contains an excellent review of the foundation movement (Dominick, 1973).

The basic standards of the FMCs, however, have until recently limited recognized providers to duly licensed doctors of medicine, dentistry, osteopathy, and podiatry. By unanimous vote, May 1972, the San Joaquin Foundation's board of directors voted to expand this definition to include duly licensed doctors of psychology. A category of cooperating membership for psychologists was established and a special application form developed. The form requires that psychologist applicants have a doctorate, be state-licensed, be a member of the state psychological association, hold professional liability insurance, agree to practice in keeping with the APA code of ethics, and be familiar with and agree to the bylaws and policies of the foundation. As of February 1973, there were seven psychologist members and three applications in process. While this number may seem small, since there are only ten psychiatrist members, the addition nearly doubled this foundation's mental health manpower in serving its four-county area. The psychology group is responsible for determining its own UCR fees in the area and must agree to accept foundation reimbursement as reimbursement in full for services rendered. Psychologists (the same as other practitioners) may charge less than their schedule of fees but not exceed that level. They must also agree to participate in peer review and must agree to the fact that all their claims will be reviewed. As for other providers, there is no membership fee and membership is for the year of application only. The foundation is not obligated to accept an applicant in a subsequent year.

All contractees were notified April 1973, and the new minimum standards for psychologists applied to all plans in which this foundation participated from July 1973. It is hoped that this formal recognition of professional psychologists as autonomous but collegial practitioners may be extended to other foundations in the coming year. Indeed, in September

1973, the Orange County Foundation for Health Care recognized psychologists as primary providers in its MediCal contract with the state. Some half dozen other foundations in California and several in other states currently have the matter of psychologist membership under consideration. The foundation movement has been described in greater detail by Dörken (1974b).

Principles for Health Insurance

Based on a report of an APA Task Force on National Health Care, prepared in conjunction both with the APA Committee on Health Insurance and with the APA Board of Professional Affairs, the American Psychological Association adopted a position statement (1971) on *Psychology and National Health Care.* Then, the Council for the Advancement of Psychological Professions and Sciences (CAPPS) enumerated twelve *Principles for National Health Insurance* (1973). The key eleven principles succinctly stated in these two releases are consolidated and amplified from the perspective of this review.

The first three deal with the concept of health per se. First, psychology views health as far broader personally and professionally than medicine or medical services. The philosophy of the World Health Organization is wise in declaring that health should be regarded not just as the absence of disease, but as a positive state of well-being. Second, a national health plan must be universal—that is, it must apply to all residents. Third, since emotional or mental disorders are a precipitating or concurrent presenting complaint in the majority of visits to the "gatekeeper" of well-being (Gurin and others, 1960), mental health ought to be an integral component of all health services and not subject to an exclusion or explicit restriction of benefits that is not applied to other common disabilities.

The next set of principles deal with restrictions on the patient and professional. The fourth principle holds that clients in need of mental health services should have freedom of choice among qualified practitioners. In the face of an avowed shortage or maldistribution of health manpower, and the major published contributions of psychology to the advancement of knowledge in the field (see *Action for Mental Health,* 1961; of the ten Joint Commission on Mental Illness and Health reports, six were written by psychologists, a seventh coauthored, 1958 to 61), it is logical to recognize the state-licensed or -certified psychologist with training and experience relevant to the health field as a potential provider of service on an independent basis. Requirements for prescription, referral, or supervision by another profession function as a restraint of trade on the one hand, and as featherbedding of the cost of services on the other. Fifth, it is the position of professional psychology that all major scientifically based and licensed health professions that are graduates of nationally accredited schools, including schools of psychology, should be recognized as appropriate providers of services in both basic and supplemental health benefit and insurance plans. This principle applies to individual and family health (disability) policies whether on a group or individual basis, and to major medical, supplemental, or catastrophic health plans. Sixth, whether in a hospital, mental health center, clinic, or private practice setting, the principles of competence and ethical practice, rather than any discipline per se, must determine the recognition of psychologists and members of other health professions for treatment or leadership responsibilities in health service.

The seventh principle holds that all persons should have equal access to all needed health and mental health services. The consumers as well as the providers of health care should have a fair opportunity not only to participate in the development of health services, but also to determine local specific needs and review the quality of care provided. The consumer must have a dual-choice option between not less than two alternative and competing health care plans.

The remainder of the principles deal with quality of care. Eighth, quality control of services is best achieved through professional peer review. It is in the public interest that the primary controls be placed on the provider rather than on the consumer. Continuing education for relicensure and prior authorization for extended services are further mechanisms to achieve quality care. Ninth, the services should be sufficiently broad and comprehensive enough to meet the public need for mental health care, including early intervention and health maintenance. Deductibles, coinsurance, arbitrary limits, and other restraints upon the consumer that convert health needs to economic decisions should be eliminated. Further, the health care services should not merely be sufficient, but also should protect individual rights, dignity, and confidentiality. Tenth, there must be provision for program evaluation, assurance of quality care, the integration of new knowledge into health care delivery, and the training of needed health manpower. Eleventh, there must be incentives and controls to achieve a redistribution of health resources—personnel, facilities, and funds—toward community based ambulatory care and alternatives to hospitalization in a manner proportionate to population and needs, taking account of community differences. To accomplish this goal there must be an organized structure for health planning, proscriptive rate setting, and service prepayment.

In summary, there are two major common obstacles to proper utilization of professional services under mental health benefits in health insurance plans, whether publicly or privately funded and to which continuing exception must be taken. There should not be a segregation between physical and mental health services either through a specific exclusion of mental health services or through benefits that discriminate between physical and mental health service reimbursement formulas nor should there be contract provisions that favor certain types of treatment or practitioners (for example, inhospital benefits as opposed to ambulatory care). Moreover, attempts to control access to health services, by imposing physician referral "gatekeepers" or economic restraints on health care, are not in the public interest.

The growth of health insurance, substantial as it has been, has essentially been limited to the employed. Coverage has varied considerably. Furthermore, the coverage in general has been substantially less than the cost. For the poor, health insurance is almost nonexistent, while for the indigent, as in Medicaid, coverage varies widely among the states. The incentive structure of this admixture of both public and private financing with private and public administration has led not only to multiple standards of care but also to emphasis on expensive hospital care with out-of-pocket discouragement of ambulatory care. Some, such as Bodenheimer (1972), view present coverage as a hoax—the coverage being primarily for the benefit of facilities and providers. Others are concerned lest the cost controls typical of most health insurance convert health decisions into economic decisions (Hodgson, 1973).

Perhaps we are turning the corner. The health maintenance organization does set a prototype model for coordinated health care delivery in an organized setting. Professional standards review organizations can establish a means of effective peer review. The National Health Planning and Resources Development Act of 1974 does call for consumer involvement in the planning and organization of health systems areas within each state. And the proponents of National Health Insurance (NHI) are many. There were twenty-three NHI bills before the 93rd Congress, perhaps five were model front runners: 1) the AMA plan, voluntary private purchase with government subsidy for the poor; 2) the administration plan, building on existing mechanisms to offer a standard plan through Medicaid for the poor by states, through insurance companies by employers and through the federal Social Security Administration for the Medicare population; 3) the Long-Ribicoff plan, an expansion of the Social Security program to cover catastrophic illness and replacing Medicaid; 4) the Kennedy-Mills plan, an expanded Social Security system to include health care for those under sixty-five with retention of Medicare for the elderly and with insurance companies serving as third-party intermediaries; and 5) the Kennedy-Griffith plan, a single, mandatory, comprehensive plan, financed by tax revenue and federally operated. The extensive congressional debate and hearings on NHI moved toward a consensus on the benefits (coverage of health service entitlement) but agreement could not be reached on program financing or administration. As the *Consumer Reports* excellent review (1975) so aptly pointed out, "The significant difference among plans is not the total cost, but who pays it and how." And further, "a system operated by the Federal Government could be . . . inaccessible and unresponsive to the consumer and public interests." From the consumer perspective *Consumer Reports* maintains that an NHI plan must meet five minimum goals: coverage must (1) be universal and mandatory; (2) have no relation between personal income and the quality or extent of care; (3) be progressively financed, by a method open to public scrutiny; (4) include incentives for efficiency, cost control, quality, and innovation in health care delivery; and (5) have an administration that is accountable to the public and that includes consumers.

The benefits, costs, and consequences of national health insurance have been thoughtfully analyzed by Davis (1975) from the perspective of social economics. She notes a substantial commonality of goals in the major bills before Congress and with relatively little difference in real cost. There are marked differences, however, in methods of financing, administration, and the reimbursement of providers. Health services are now an industry of more than $100,000,000,000. National health insurance would be social legislation of very major proportions. Consensus has obviously not yet been reached on how to achieve the desired outcomes.

7

Health Insurance and Psychological Practice

Jack Dworin

The insurance industry has grown phenomenally in the past several decades. Life and property insurance has increased, and there has been a major acceleration of automobile and other liability insurance. With the spiraling costs of health care, prepaid health insurance has developed. The first such coverage was for physical health and accidents. Public demand, coupled with indices of feasibility and effectiveness, however, has led to progressively broader coverage for emotional and mental disorders. The recognition of psychological services under insurance coverage, quite a recent phenomenon, has been accelerated by licensing and freedom-of-choice statutes (see Chapter Three).

Since 1955, professional liability (malpractice) insurance has been available to practicing psychologists. Developed with the approval of the APA Insurance Trust, a nationally available policy of the Interstate Fire and Casualty Company (Chicago) provided up to $1,000,000 protection (per claim or in a year) against "any and all claims in a case of alleged liability in rendering or failure to render professional service," for a premium of $60 annually. During the ensuing twenty years, only one case has come to court (California, 1974; license revoked). A number of claims were filed in 1975, however. With understandable concern about increasing risk in the malpractice area, the insuror has decided to withdraw from this liability area and will

120

not renew at the close of the policy year in February 1976. At this time, negotiations are underway with a new carrier.

Perhaps these events also reflect the impact of increased practice by professional psychologists. As more states (now twenty-three) enacted freedom-of-choice laws, and as more insurance companies reimbursed their patients for the services of psychologists, a more specific definition of a psychologist became necessary. Insurance companies were willing to reimburse qualified psychologists for their services, but they asked, "How do we recognize a qualified psychologist?"

Insurance companies generally were as willing to reimburse the patients of psychologists as any other professional, if the service was provided for in their contract. However, two limitations were very important to them: namely, first that the psychologist be a recognized *health* professional; and, second, that he or she be performing a health service, rather than an educational or "social" service. After several years of development, in September 1974, the APA council of representatives adopted, as policy, the *Standards for Providers of Psychological Services* (American Psychological Association, 1974b). These standards define a qualified psychologist as having "a doctoral degree from an accredited university in a program that is primarily psychological, appropriate experience in the area of service offered, and either a license or certificate by state statute or endorsement by the state psychological association through voluntary certification" (pp. 4-5). The doctoral degree is also required for full membership in the APA. However, in states with statutory certification or licensing of "grandfathered" psychologists at the master's level with appropriate experience, they too are considered qualified for practice. In the 1974 session of Congress, bills submitted by Representative Jerome Waldie of California and Senator Gayle McGee of Wyoming were passed that included psychologists as eligible practitioners under the Federal Employees Health Benefits Plan, and cited clinical psychologists as appropriate providers "without referral or supervision by a physician." This landmark legislation, PL 93-363, defined a clinical psychologist as licensed or certified in the state in which he resides or practices and in which the standard was a doctoral degree as well as one or more years of supervised experience. The new *National Register of Health Service Providers in Psychology* (1975) while providing for those who were grandfathered, essentially requires the doctorate and two years of supervised experience in an organized health setting as a minimum standard for listing. Listing will be on the basis of a credentials review and should make it easier for qualified listed practitioners to gain reimbursement for their services.

Psychologists are also bound by a code of ethics since 1953. The "Ethical Standards of Psychologists" ([1953] 1963) include such matters as competence and misrepresentation in principles 2c and 4c respectively. These principles state that:

> The psychologist recognizes the boundaries of his competence and the limitations of his techniques and does not offer services or use techniques that fail to meet professional standards established in particular fields. The psychologist who engages in practice assists his client in obtaining professional help for all important aspects of his problem that fall outside the boundaries of his own competence. This principle requires, for example, that provision be made for the diagnosis and treatment of relevant medical problems and for referral to or consultation with other specialists .... The psychologist avoids misrepresentation of his own professional qualifications, affiliations and purposes, and those of the institutions and organizations with which he is associated. A psychologist does not claim either directly or by implication professional qualifications that differ from his actual qualifications, nor does he misrepresent his affiliation with any institution, organization, or individual, nor lead others to assume he has affiliations that he does not have. The psychologist is responsible for correcting others who misrepresent his professional qualifications or affiliations.

Thus, any psychologist who practices outside of the areas of his or her competence, or who misrepresents his or her qualifications or ability is subject to being dropped from membership in the APA, his or her state association, and, more importantly, to having his or her state license to practice professionally, revoked. It should be noted that in the twenty years that malpractice liability insurance has been nationally available to psychologists, only one case has gone to court.

The ethical psychologist is obliged to abide by the APA Code of Ethics, or be subject to disciplinary action for violation. This obligation includes restricting one's practice to areas of competence and utilizing referral or consultation with other professionals when it is indicated. For insurance purposes, this obligation includes properly reporting claims to the insurance carrier, maintaining the confidentiality of the client-therapist relationship, not rendering unnecessary service, and charging appropriate fees. To practice ethically, and in the client's best interests, the psychologist must be acquainted with the prevailing insurance regulations in his locale. As of the beginning of 1975, eighteen states had passed freedom-of-choice laws requiring that if an insurance policy provides for reimbursement of services within the scope of a psychologist's practice, it must reimburse the client of a psychologist. (For a discussion of freedom-of-choice laws, see Chapter Three). It is the responsibility of the psychologist to be acquainted with state law and to advise clients when their insurance does not cover psychological services. The ethical principle, that the rights of the patient are paramount in the entire relationship, must be followed.

In states where there is no freedom-of-choice law, some insurance companies do reimburse patients for the services of a psychologist, but may require either referral by a physician or supervision by a physician. This requirement is rapidly disappearing, and independent practice is now becoming the rule rather than the exception. If consultation is recommended, by a physician as in the patient's best interest, the interprofessional relations are collegial. Supervision required by a third party becomes an intrusion into the treatment process. It may add unnecessary cost for the patient, as well as disrupting the therapy. The ethical duty of the psychologist is to point out such factors to the patient, from the outset, and to refer the patient elsewhere if indicated.

Client Information

The ethical responsibility of the professional psychologist is to ensure the well-being and rights of his patients. At times, special problems may arise where the fee is being paid, either entirely or partly, by a third party. It is important, therefore, that the psychologist discuss the clients insurance coverage as early in the treatment as possible. The patient is of course responsible for paying his own bill, whether he receives reimbursement by an insurance company or not. Some policies provide for direct assignment to the practitioner. In any event, the patient has the right to expect the psychologist with whom he consults to be aware of insurance reimbursement procedures and to advise clients in these matters when necessary. Clearly, the psychologist should be acquainted with the various insurance forms, fill them out promptly, and instruct his patients on how the forms are to be submitted, and to whom payment is to be made. Practitioners often fail to determine whether the client has several levels of coverage. Benefits for mental health services, for example, may not be included in the client's basic health insurance policy but may be available through a complementary "major medical insurance."

Psychological practice is predominately oriented to ambulatory care. There are sound fiscal and human benefit reasons for this orientation to be encouraged. However, the majority of group health plans today still provide more extensive coverage for inhospital service. Where appropriate, proper follow-through may involve some hospitalization and the acquisition of hospital staff privileges for the psychologist practitioner (see Chapter Fifteen). The issue of hospital staff privilege is important not only to treatment continuity but to the broadening involvement of psychologists in general health care delivery. Psychological consultation in the hospital is frequently needed in pediatric, surgical, and other services.

Completing insurance forms should be a fairly simple,

routine matter. The Health Insurance Council (HIC) developed a uniform special form for this purpose in 1967. There are now 327 member insurance companies in the Health Insurance Association of America and the Health Insurance Institute (Health Insurance Institute, n.d.*b*). These companies issue approximately 85 percent of the health insurance policies written by the insurance companies in the United States and recognize this simplified claim form, which is also approved by the Council on Medical Service, American Medical Association (AMA). In June 1974 the AMA developed its own uniform health insurance claim form. It was the intention of the AMA to simplify and standardize reporting of professional services for reimbursement and to have a form that would be adaptable to computers. The Health Insurance Association of America has recommended that its member companies adopt the form. The Social Security Administration has also approved its use for Medicare and the National Association of Blue Shield Plans have adopted a motion supporting the concept of a uniform claim form. Acceptance and use will, however, vary among localities.

Now, in most states, psychologist's patients have the right of privileged communication, which means that whatever is said or done in the patient-therapist relationship can only be released following the consent of the patient. The privilege of confidentiality belongs to the patient, with few exceptions. The case of *Tarasoff* v. *The Regents of the University of California* (Supreme Court 405694, SF 23042) would appear to have established a precedent that the therapist is required to warn other persons in danger even if such knowledge was acquired in the course of treatment. (The psychologist-therapist, knowing that his patient had homicidal intent, tried to arrange for commitment and notified campus police, but the chief of psychiatry had the records withdrawn. The victim was later murdered.) Said the court, "Privilege ends where the public peril begins" (Simmons and others, 1975, p. 12). Comparable decisions have been rendered in cases of child abuse and communicable disease.

Sending out information to an insurance company constitutes giving out information about the patient, so the psychologist should be certain beforehand that the patient approves. Most insurance forms have a section that the patient must sign, to allow for this release of information to the insurance company. However, if the form does not have such a release section, the psychologist should obtain one in writing from the patient. The psychologist should also be aware of where the form is to be sent and to whom the information in it will be revealed. Some insurance forms require that the patient's employer fill out a section of the form before it is sent to the insurance company. In order to preserve maximum confidentiality, the therapist should try to have the patient and the patient's employer fill out their portions of the form first, so that after completing his section, the psychologist can send it directly to the insurance company. In this manner, although the method is not foolproof, confidentiality will be better protected, and the patient's personal information will not be revealed to his employer.

Some forms ask the practitioner, "Do you accept assignment?" If the psychologist indicates that he will accept assignment, he receives payment directly from the insurance company. Where the fee schedule of the insuror is less than the practitioner's fee or where there are coinsurance provisions, a differential, or balance owing, will result. Charging the patient the difference between the carrier's reimbursement and the psychologist's fee can prove awkward and should be carefully explained and mutually agreed to beforehand.

In some insurance plans, however, notably the Blue Cross and Blue Shield Panel Practice Plan, and in some of the foundations for medical care and group practice contracts, participating psychologists agree (by agreeing to participate or by "accepting assignment") that they will accept the fee provided by the company as payment in full. Assignment is a condition of participation. In these contracts, the patient is not to pay any additional fee.

Diagnosis is a critical item on the insurance form. Insurance companies certainly have the right to request this information. They need it in order to know whether the health condition for which the bill is submitted is reimburseable under the terms of the insurance policy. It is therefore important to make the diagnosis as accurate and as specific as possible. Defining a mental disorder as "problems relating to people," may result in claim rejection if the company does not reimburse for problems in living. Some practitioners tend to underdiagnose on insurance forms with a view to protecting the patient. However, if the condition is going to require intensive treatment the accurate diagnosis should be stated, as the insurance carrier may question why a "milder" diagnosis requires such care. Some therapists prefer to list "transient situational reaction" rather than any major neurotic or psychotic condition, and then are upset when the insurance company questions why a "transient reaction" is taking months rather than weeks for remediation. Accurate diagnosis is a professional responsibility, and it is a disservice to the patient to do otherwise.

It must also be recognized that some diagnostic labels or words carry a connotation that may be upsetting to the patient or could be detrimental to his employment if this information is not kept confidential. For this reason, it is recommended that the numbers of the categories found in the *International Classification of Mental Disorders* (ICMD) be used, or that the numbers from the *Diagnostic and Statistical Manual of Mental Disorders* (DSM-II, American Psychiatric Association, 1968) be used (the DSM-II includes the ICMD numbers). Insurance companies are familiar with the diagnostic categories contained in these manuals, and if the code number is written in where diagnosis is required and if the code numbers are followed by initials of the manual from which it is obtained (for example: "300.4, DSM-II"), the diagnosis will be clearly understood by the insuror. These circumstances hold for the present although major changes may be in the offing. There is a growing awareness that the diagnosis in these classification systems are often quite unreliable and offer little guidance in prognosis or therapy. Tarter and others (1975) report that apart from organic disorders, highly experienced and competent psychiatrists agreed poorly on other major diagnostic categories—less than 50 percent of the time in the case of neurotic and personality disorders. It is not surprising, then, that in its five-county program evaluation study, the California Department of Health (Hanson,

1974) found that the professional staff of these community mental health services could not reliably distinguish between a mental disorder and a life crisis. There is a serious need to develop a functional or problem-oriented classification of mental or emotional disability.

The Insurors' Perspective

Insurance companies and health service plans serve a very useful and necessary function for the public. Carriers that issue health insurance policies, both for groups and individuals, provide, through prepayment and a relatively nominal "administration" fee or "retention" factor, protection against the high cost of disability and treatment. Insurors can provide this protection because the risk is spread among those insured. Insurance companies and nonprofit health service corporations are not in business, however, to lose money. Thus benefit options that are open to some choice, will carry premiums based on actuarial predictions. Those contracting for policies select from plans and options available. As yet, not all policies cover treatment for emotional disorders, not all policies cover outpatient treatment, and some have rather severe limitations or coinsurance features. But insurance carriers are interested in public goodwill and, for this reason and to be competitive, they will generally be responsive to what the public wants. Then, although increasing the number of eligible providers—as with the recognition of psychologists—does not increase the incidence of disability, it probably will have three outcomes that are not predictable with certainty. Client access to appropriate service probably will be improved by the increase in the provider pool and the necessity of artificially imposed referral and supervision requirements will evaporate. On the other hand, the possibility of interprofessional competition will emerge.

The actual cost of outpatient treatment for mental and emotional disorders has not been as predictable as most companies would like, though favorable utilization data is increasingly available (see Chapter Eleven). With pressure from legislative, professional and lay groups such as the National Association for Mental Health and its state associations, coverage of nervous and mental disorders in health insurance contracts is becoming more extensive. Indeed, in 1973 the state of Massachusetts, and in 1975 the state of Colorado, mandated certain minimal coverage for nervous and mental conditions in all hospital and health policies issued or renewed in that state (see also chapters Three and Six). It should be added also that while the per hour cost of procedures such as outpatient psychotherapy may seem high, in contrast to a brief office visit to a general practitioner, there is not only a substantial time differential, there is also the fact that hospitalization and surgical procedures—regularly and extensively covered—are many times more costly. The intention of health insurance is not to dictate the types of disabilities clients will have.

The insurors are interested in prompt and efficient reimbursement for valid claims and in giving their subscribers all of the benefits to which they are entitled. However, they will *not* pay for benefits that are *not* in the contract. To this end, the carrier has the right to insist that charges for professional services be limited to qualified practitioners as defined by the health insurance contract (policyholder agreement) or state law. The companies also have the right to insist that the provider charge only his usual, customary, and reasonable fee for that particular service and that he provide only the appropriate treatment for the condition. If there is any unusual item or charge on the bill, the psychologist, like any other provider of services, should indicate on the bill the reason for the unusual item, or be prepared to justify it to the insurance company.

The psychologist has an ethical responsibility to the insurance company as well as to his patients. Care should be taken that the period of treatment is not extended, nor fees increased, simply because the patient is not paying the entire amount. Overdependency and overutilization should be avoided. Excessive charges are a disservice to the insurance companies, to the patient, and to the public. The results are increased costs to everyone concerned, a lowering of respect for the profession, and a disservice to the patient.

On submitting a first claim to a particular insurance company, especially Blue Cross and Blue Shield or other nonprofit franchised companies that use this procedure, the psychologist should request a user or provider number from the carrier. Once the provider number is assigned to the psychologist, it is filed in the computer and facilitates processing of all future claims.

Handling Denied Claims

As mentioned earlier, the psychologist should be prepared to help his patient deal with denied claims. He should be familiar with the health insurance statutes and procedures as they exist in his particular state. The laws, and circumstances, at present differ from one state to another. In twenty-three states, the legislature has passed laws making it mandatory for insurance companies to reimburse patients for services by psychologists, if treatment for the condition is covered in the contract. In eighteen of the twenty-three states, the statute has been extended to cover not only insurance companies, but also the nonprofit health and hospital service plans such as Blue Cross and Blue Shield. Additionally, many large, major health insurance carriers have voluntarily agreed to provide nationwide coverage for reimbursement for services of psychologists in their contracts. The psychologist should contact the health insurance committee chairperson of his state association for information regarding local conditions in the state, and should report any special difficulties in securing claim reimbursement.

In general, the insurance carriers deny claims when they believe that the contract definitions have not been adequately met. For example, claims are usually denied, either in full or in part, for one, or all, of the following five reasons. First, a claim may be denied if the condition is not a covered mental disorder. For example, health insurance policies are unlikely to provide reimbursement for marital counseling or for special education services. Second, a claim may be denied if the treatment procedure is not a usual and customary one. For example, many insurance companies do not reimburse for encounter or sensitivity groups and may not reimburse for techniques such as primal scream therapy. Third, claims may be denied if there is question as to whether the practitioner's profession is covered, or whether the practitioner is qualified. For example, some contracts do not reimburse for the services of a psychologist; the claim can be denied for this reason in states without freedom-of-choice laws. Or, some contracts may limit reimbursement to designated providers—for example, to clinical psychologists. Fourth, claims may be denied if the frequency or duration of the treatment seems beyond the usual and customary practice for similar conditions. Fifth, claims may be denied if the charges or fees seem to be beyond those customary in that area.

Technically, redress to a denied claim should be initiated by the patient. The insurance contract is between the insured (patient or employer) and the insurance carrier. The psychologist is simply the service provider. Nonetheless, where reimbursement is a "reasonable expectation" and within those included in the policy benefits, the psychologist should try to help a client secure claim settlement.

One unfortunate consequence of an attempted claim denial is that while the client is seeking reimbursement, he may be under financial pressure, and may have to make a decision to terminate therapy. This pressure can result in additional stress. Such a situation underscores the importance of ascertaining and explaining insurance coverage, from the onset of professional services, where possible. Some specific procedures are useful in seeking redress for denied claims. First, if the claim appears covered by the policy and there is apparently no reason for its being denied, the psychologist should contact the local group claims manager of the insurance company involved. Sometimes, the claim has been denied by a clerk in the company, not aware of changes in providers, in the law, or in the specific policy and the group claims manager can usually settle such a matter quickly. Second, the psychologist should contact the chairperson of his state association committee on health insurance. That person may have some particular knowledge that can be helpful. Even if he cannot help in a particular instance, the communication keeps him appraised of ongoing difficulties and provides the state association with information on which to take corrective action.

Such situations should be discussed with the patient, and the available options described. If the insurance policy is an individual one, the patient is at a better advantage in working through the insurance agent. If it is a group policy that is part of an employment benefit the patient should try to have his employer, personnel officer, or union representative take up the matter. Even if the contract does not cover that particular condition or professional, pressure from the employer or the union can sometimes result in a contract change. Another way of seeking redress for denied claims is a formal complaint to the state insurance commissioner. His job is to protect the public against misrepresentation, unwarranted claim denial, or other such questionable practices by insurance companies. If the commissioner believes that a law has been violated, or that the carrier has been unduly restrictive, he can make his position known to the carrier. Since the commissioner has the right to determine who can sell insurance in the state, such an inquiry can carry considerable weight. The insurance commissioner can also take legal action, although he rarely does so, since in most instances a ruling in favor of the patient (without going to court) usually results in reimbursement for the claim. In the event that the commission will not act or the insurance company still refuses to accept the claim and provide reimbursement, the patient always has the option of taking the matter to court. Most insurance companies do not like to have cases go to court, since they might result in a precedent-setting decision. However, the advice as to whether the patient should press the case with legal action should come from an attorney. The successful use of small claims courts by clients has been reported in Florida and New York. See Clark (1973) regarding procedures and state limits.

Professional standards review committees have now been established in forty states and in the District of Columbia. These committees cannot rule on whether a condition is, or could be, covered by a particular company or contract. However, if the claim has been denied because there is some question as to whether the fees are usual and customary, whether the treatment modality is appropriate, or whether the practitioner is qualified (meaning whether he has the appropriate credentials, not whether he is competent) the case can be submitted to the committee. Either the patient, the psychologist, or the third-party payor has the right to request a ruling by the state professional standards committee. Usually, when the parties agree to submit the question to peer review procedures, they also agree to accept the findings as final and binding. (See also Chapter Thirteen.)

A longer-range but ultimately better solution is the passage of state laws that entitles clients to direct access to, and freedom of choice of, psychologist practitioners for covered conditions. Some states have such laws, but with loopholes that need amendment. For example, some companies may insist that they are not liable for reimbursement because "the contract is old" (predates the law) or has been issued out of state. Guidance and consultation for state associations is available from the American Psychological Association, through its Committee on Health Insurance (COHI), Committee on State Legislation (COSL), and state legislative affairs specialists. The more states that develop freedom-of-choice laws, the more the insurance companies will find it economical to recognize all qualified psychologists for reimbursement, nationwide.

8

Mental Health Services in a Comprehensive National Health Plan

Russell J. Bent and A. Eugene Shapiro

O_{nly} within the past decade has professional psychology developed a systematic approach to third-party health service support systems. These systems have often excluded psychologists as independent, authorized, health service providers. The recognition of psychologists as primary health service providers under health benefit plans was a primary concern of professional psychology during these early days. Over the past several years, however, attention has shifted to broader concerns. One fundamental principle now being advocated by various professions and citizen groups is the inclusion and delineation of mental health benefits within health insurance. As with any entitlement, insurance management must assure quality services within optimal benefit-cost constraints. The sincerity of the insurance industry and their desire to provide a broad range of quality services to the public within reasonable cost limits has been impressive, particularly in the face of a relative dearth of basic and systematic knowledge on which to base mental health benefits. The rationale for such benefits and their management have either developed out of various agency and governmental mental health programs or, more often, out of existing models for physical health insurance. Little creative thinking has been done and few innovative demonstration projects exist. Billions have been spent on the same old thing and "A penny for your thoughts" on new approaches.

Psychologists are often asked how existing health service support systems or how a particular support system might be improved. It became evident that organized psychology had to shift from emphasizing inclusion to emphasizing the promotion of sound mental health benefits and the development of an effective management system.

In the spring of 1973, representatives of the American Psychological Association (APA) met with the Health Insurance Association of America (HIAA) to discuss mutual concerns. HIAA develops and coordinates broad industry policy for the member insurance firms across the nation. Daniel W. Pettengill, then chairman of HIAA and vice-president of Aetna Life and Casualty, and other HIAA members held a frank and open meeting with representatives of psychology. The receptive interest by HIAA in developing a more reasonable, workable approach to mental health benefits stimulated a continuing dialog and effort by psychology to formulate a sound mental health benefits plan. Not only HIAA and its national health insurance bill but also the many other proposed national health insurance plans had to be met constructively, with a sound mental health system proposal that represented the thinking of organized psychology. In order to accomplish this objective, the Health Benefits Task Force was established, consisting of the APA Committee on Health Insurance (COHI)* and selected consultants from the California State Psychological Association and the APA. The authors of this chapter served as cochairpersons of the task force, and were principally charged with reporting the wealth of information, ideas, and directions the workshops produced.

---

*This chapter represents the personal views of COHI members and the authors, as individuals; basically, the information herein is the report of our findings as COHI members. It is without endorsement or review by the APA and in no way should be construed as a policy or position statement.

In essence, the task force held that all persons have a right to comprehensive health services and that since emotional or mental disorder is a primary or concurrent problem for the majority of persons seeking health care, broad mental health services must be included as a basic part of health services. Furthermore, any national health plan should be based on the principle that the consumer should have direct and equal access to licensed doctoral health providers who meet national standards of accreditation. Also, a national health plan should encourage pluralism in health service delivery systems—the consumer always should have the option of selecting between at least two competitive systems of health delivery and support. In summary, the task force advocated universal coverage, integration of mental health into the mainstream of health care, consumer freedom of choice among qualified providers of all health professions, and consumer choice among competitive health plans.

A Comprehensive Health Care System

First let us consider essential elements of a comprehensive health care system. Such a system should include a comprehensive range of health service benefits available in organized systems of service delivery. To assure utilization—not simply availability of benefits but actual service delivery—the health needs of the individual will require screening and periodic evaluation, together with preventive services, including positive health education. As personal health problems are identified, a specific treatment plan for each disability based on a schedule of established procedures of demonstrable effectiveness should then be implemented. To gain quality assurance, all services must be subject to program standards and peer review, backed up by a standardized, unified, automated management information system. That system must assure coordination of services, cost control, and proper confidentiality. Inherently, such a system requires that the predominant controls be placed upon the provider. In addition to ongoing peer review, proscriptive treatment planning, and prior authorization for certain services, it is in the public interest to establish a biennial renewal of provider certification based, in part, on continuing education. National and regional registries of qualified health service providers would be available to interested parties. To provide a broad range of mental health benefits, the emphasis should be placed on health maintenance, early intervention, and alternatives to costly twenty-four-hour residential (hospital) services. Independent practitioners and various health facilities and organizations should be components of the comprehensive mental health system and should be closely integrated with general health services.

System control and quality regulation can be achieved through national standards, regional program review, mental health management support organization, and peer review procedures. In particular, peer review would emphasize constructive consultation, continuing education, and health system information rather than simply setting arbitrary numerical limits on utilization. Consumer use or demand patterns, of course, would greatly determine the development and delivery pattern of mental health services.

The mental health service program should include mental health education and prevention, mental health screening, consultation services by mental health specialists, and direct mental health services. The education and prevention component would focus on the availability of service and new developments, on information and training in positive skills that enhance mental health, and on positive environmental influences that support the maintenance of mental health. The mental health screening component would involve an early detection system, a recognition of conditions responsive to early intervention methods, and a means for information and early intervention specific to high-risk populations. Consultation services by mental health specialists would include advice to persons, groups, or systems regarding the benefits of treatment and available resources together with public education. These critical indirect service elements, added to direct service and treatment, would provide a solid framework for a mental health service program.

Practitioners have typically been preoccupied with direct mental health services. Here, too, there are general principles that guide benefits and benefit controls. To maximize effectiveness and proper utilization, access to early intervention services should be stressed with almost no barriers of any kind to early, immediate access by the consumer. Rather, controls primarily should be placed on service providers through a process of prospective and concurrent peer review and mental health program management organizations and should require almost no arbitrary limitations on benefits. The services should emphasize community-based alternatives to hospitalization and other high-cost options. Furthermore, services should emphasize evaluative study of the feasibility of implementing a unit value system providing flexible and interchangeable alternatives within available resources. A full range of mental health services should be available, not only to individuals, but also to families, and social groups, with reasonable provisions for innovative techniques. Virtually all services should readily be accessible on the community level.

In terms of specifics, utilization data suggest two cutting points for outpatient services. First, up to six units of service (which might include determination of disability, detailed service planning, consultation, crisis service, or brief psychotherapy) could be provided without prior peer review authorization and without prior filing of a service plan. Typically, half of all cases are served within this limit. For service units beyond the initial six units and up to fifteen units (covering 80 to 90 percent of all cases), the provider should file a plan, subject to peer review, detailing service objectives and the procedures to be employed in order to meet those objectives. Pretreatment authorization should be required for service units beyond fifteen. Such long-term or unusual service plans would require prior peer review and authorization before initiation. Request for such prior authorization should be possible any time after the initial contact. However, the request should present an individualized service plan, including the span of time and extent of services anticipated to attain the service plan objectives. Authorized plans would be reviewed on a periodic basis suitable to the particular plan. Significant changes in the service plan, a new plan, or an extension of the plan beyond the time authorized would require another presentation to the peer review committee.

For optimum effectiveness and cost control, use of residential services will need close monitoring, particularly to shift current utilization patterns. Except for life emergencies, hospital services should be available only after pretreatment authorization (certified hospital admission plan), subject to review within seventy-two hours. There should be a review of all hospital services every fourteen days to make sure that therapy is progressing and that alternative services are not warranted. Partial hospital services and alternatives to residential services are to be encouraged with review every twenty-eight days. As indicated, the cost of the generic prescription of psychotropic drugs should be covered for both inpatient and outpatient services and reviewed periodically.

In summary, the direct mental health service system should allow the provider much professional latitude during initial phases of service (with monitoring by audit procedures); should permit a moderate latitude for more extended service primarily through provider profile analysis and exception reporting; and should exert close control over extended services through proscriptive and concurrent peer review processes.

Management and Administration

The general structure of the management and administration of the proposed mental health benefits assumes consumer freedom, pluralism of service provider systems, program management organization, peer or program review procedures, and state and national policy- and standard-setting councils. The consumer should be able to spend benefits as he or she chooses within an environment of authorized mental health providers and provider management organizations wherein the provider is subject to review of both service quality and quantity. Although the review should be carried out by small committees of the providers themselves, the development, support, and organization of the review process itself should be coordinated through specialized management organizations. These organizations should be designed to support the review process and manage the total mental health benefit program with consumer involvement.

All consumers should be "credited" with the benefits previously described. The consumer selects a provider system from one of two or more systems through which he or she readily can receive these benefits. At stipulated time periods the consumer has the option of continuing with the provider system selected or of changing. Within a given dollar benefit amount provider systems will have a priority to render direct service benefits and certain other services as stipulated. More efficient management of the provision of direct services will allow a wider range of related services to be developed, which, in turn, should decrease the need for direct service. The provider system that more responsively, efficiently, and innovatively uses the flexibility allowed in developing cost-effective services to meet consumer needs will be more competitive and more likely to grow through the consumer's freedom to choose that system. A diversity of consumer use patterns should encourage a diversity of provider systems that more realistically can provide effective service without forcing a highly bureaucratic "model" upon the public.

A mental health service provider system is defined as the pattern of relationships established among specified providers and the consumers, allowing access to such providers in relation to the proposed mental health benefits. Such a system should accommodate a diversity of client and provider relationships ranging from the "independent" professional or facility, to groups of professionals and facilities such as the comprehensive community mental health center, to organized, total health care systems such as some health maintenance organizations and foundations for medical care. Since service providers making up the provider service system in this plan would be certified as providers and subject to biennial review and recertification, minimal standards for mental health program management organizations (the provider service systems) would be designated and listed in a national registry of mental health program management organizations (MHPMO).

Assuming that mental health providers can be more effective and efficient if combined into voluntary, cooperative systems, authority and management support must be vested in some organizational structure, preferably nongovernmental and nonprofit. The MHPMO is envisaged as an autonomous corporate body whose board and staff would plan, manage, and implement the comprehensive mental health service benefits authorized under the national health care plan. The MHPMO should then elect its board of directors and indicate its functions, organizational structure, management staff, provider arrangements, "subscriber" population, and other relevant information within broad state and federal regulations. It is to be responsible for such activities as provider support and education, the development and implementation of the review process, including technical assistance and monitoring of the review process, standardized data sets and automated management information applications, provider and patient monitoring, evaluation and program research studies, coordination activities, community education, operations information, procedures for assuring compliance with basic standards and benefits, as well as cost-utilization studies and assurances of proper fiscal management. To accomplish all these objectives, it must be a dynamic, flexible organization encouraged to develop diverse organizational patterns so as to be maximally adaptable and innovative in providing the mental health benefits. Essentially, the successful attainment of the benefit objectives, not the organizational structure of the MHPMO, would be emphasized in evaluation. Consumer satisfaction as reflected in their selection of MHPMOs also will serve as an important evaluative index of effectiveness.

A prime component in the evaluation of provider effectiveness is the peer review process that applies collective professional judgment to determine and monitor the necessity, quality, and effectiveness of mental health services. Peer review's major function is managerial, designed to develop and insure the effective and efficient distribution of mental health services within resource availability constraints and with the least interference by bureaucratic control. It differs from the usual retrospective claims review process in that its emphasis is upon prospective and concurrent review. Peer review should be directed toward the coordination and most effective use of resources and educational and consultation outputs that affect the mental health providers' performance. Particularly when mental health services are provided in noninstitutional settings, peer review should be flexible enough to adapt to patterns of practice that may differ from those typical of physical health services. This more functional definition of peer (a person engaged in the service a mental health provider renders) often might lead, for example, to a mixed-discipline composition of a mental health peer review committee, particularly in group or interdisciplinary practice settings.

It is anticipated that a national health care plan on a state or national level would be administered through some form of health review councils or similar bodies responsible for the total national health care program. The mental health benefit system integrated in the national program should nonetheless be also reviewed through a mental health program committee or similar body within the health review council, the chairperson of the committee being a member of the council. The history of mental health programs within physical health programs strongly suggests that unless authority, delegation, integration, and the coordination of mental health benefits in a total, comprehensive health program receives separate specialized attention, the highly complex (in size and function) mental health program and its special aspects are not adequately addressed. Therefore, both the health review council and that council's mental health program committee, at their appropriate levels, would carry out such functions as policy development and administration, program evaluation, make recommendations for improvements, coordination and integration of programs, make annual reports, and advise and assist the secretary of HEW in the administration of the program.

A Dual Plan

In order to provide a broad range of services that will both meet health service needs and be supported realistically, there should be two concurrent and coordinated, but independently managed and funded, mental health components of an overall health system addressed to a mental health service program on the one hand, and a mental health supportive living program on the other. The mental health service program would be involved with the "acutely disabled," disabilities that essentially respond to short-term mental health treatment and temporary resource use—that is, the mental health benefits proposed above. The mental health service program is seen as an integrated, basic part of the national health program. Those persons requiring continued care due to mental disabilities, perhaps multiple in nature, which result in a continued inability to work and live independently without special support would receive services from the mental health supportive living program. Whereas the mental health service program would rely most heavily on the independent and "noncustodial" sectors of the nation's mental health resources, the mental health supportive living program would develop active, continued care programs predominantly in the community to replace the passive custodial system and the practice of "dumping" persons with chronic disabilities into marginal living arrangements and unsupervised community living. Since rehabilitation would be a continuing central objective, this program would provide and coordinate, in accord with individual capability, for vocational training and support, supportive community-based living arrangements as alternatives to institutionalization, and planned socialization opportunities to sustain persons with long-term disabilities. Extensive involvement with educational, vocational, and welfare programs would be encouraged. Individualized, goal-oriented, continued-care service plans should involve consultation services from the mental health service program.

Stated in other terms, it seems unwise to impose a welfare model upon a health delivery model. Government involvement has predominantly been for those least likely to benefit—working from the bottom up. A preventive, active treatment orientation in the private sector has and can address the majority of resolvable clinical health problems. There is no compelling indication that their "federalization" would result in improved service or cost. Indeed, the reverse seems more likely and would add a further layer of government bureaucracy to health services.

Financing

Detailed considerations for the financing and administration of a national health plan lay beyond the primary focus of the Health Benefits Task Force. In formulating its proposal for integrating mental health services in a national health plan, however, some consideration of financing could not be avoided; administration, funding, and service delivery, after all, *are* related. In brief then, the mental health service program could be financed by various means ranging from employee-employer prepaid premiums to a "health tax" on income up to a level of proportional cost, or by general federal revenue. Any of these approaches could carry tax credit entitlement of their cost and graduated federal financing based on levels of need. The federal government might pay all or portions of the costs of benefits, depending on income levels. The fiscal intermediary could be the insurance industry, the Bureau of Health Insurance of the Social Security Administration, or a newly established special agency.

As a group, the task force membership favored maximal involvement of insurance industry and health service corporation resources. It was skeptical of the long-run effectiveness of a federalized or national administration of health service delivery, of the public service model for health care. The setting of minimal entitlement standards, providing incentives for change and innovation, and more equitable distribution of health manpower and their training—such roles were seen as only feasible for implementation at a federal level.

These, then, are the broad outlines of a mental health service plan that could mesh efficiently with the proposed models for a national health insurance plan. While this proposal may need modification in response to future developments, it is offered as a sound working model having the perspective of professional psychology. And it anticipates the national debate on health services.

9

CHAMPUS Ten-State Claim Experience for Mental Disorder

Herbert Dörken

Broad and comprehensive utilization data on insured mental health services are rare. Some reports are available on frequency of utilization and proportion of total cost (see chapters Ten and Eleven). What makes the data discussed in this chapter truly unique is not only the indices of visit frequency categorized by type of mental disorder and whether such visits were in- or outpatient service, but also the basic data categorized by procedure, by provider, and by state (for ten states), together with fee information. The Civilian Health and Medical Program of the Uniformed Services (CHAMPUS) is the only program for which such complete data are available, for the fiscal year 1974.

CHAMPUS with 7,830,000 people insured, is the single largest group health insurance plan in the Nation. While the Federal Employees Health Benefits Act (FEHBA) plans have a greater total number of lives insured (about 8,800,000), they are distributed over some forty plans, with the two largest, Blue Cross and Blue Shield (the Blues) and Aetna, covering about 5,500,000 and 1,500,000, respectively, or 80 percent of federal

Presented in part to the Annual Meeting, California State Psychological Association, Anaheim, California, March 1975.

employees and beneficiaries. In the majority of regions in the country, the Blues (also Mutual of Omaha) serve as the fiscal intermediary for CHAMPUS. CHAMPUS benefits were set by Congress in 1966 to be not less than that of the largest FEHBA plan (Blues, high option). Recent testimony before Congress (United States House Armed Services Committee, 1974) notes the rapid increase in the size of the retired community (retirees and dependents) from 2,400,000 in 1964 to 3,200,000 in 1974, though the active duty personnel are decreasing. For a summary outline of the CHAMPUS program, its objectives, and recent changes, see Penner (1975).

CHAMPUS experience with benefits for nervous and mental disorder in terms of professional services (procedures) rendered, providers involved, ages of beneficiaries served, diagnoses reported, and fee rate variance by region and provider, takes on special significance in terms of future benefit planning and the imminence of national health insurance. Inasmuch as psychologists have been recognized as independent providers in the CHAMPUS plan since June 1970, under direction of the Office of the Assistant Secretary for Defense, the data are of special interest to this profession. The Civilian Health and Medical Plan of the Veterans Administration (CHAMPVA), the Veterans Administration's equivalent program, was established by the Veterans Health Care Expansion Act of 1973 (PL 93-82) and it, too, recognized the services of psychologists practicing within the scope of their license. That program covers nearly 300,000 lives (including wives, widows, and dependents). The report to follow is based solely on CHAMPUS fiscal year 1974 (July 1973 to June 1974) claim experience in ten states (processed through September 1974) estimated at 93 percent of claims for the twelve-month year. As of September 30, 1974, there were already 56,837 users (unduplicated count) who received some mental health service charged to CHAMPUS.

The author especially appreciates the courtesy and cooperation of the CHAMPUS Office of Policy in informally providing a copy of their computer printout of claim experience for this period and in clarifying certain policy controls on cost. It should be understood, also, that any interpretations and conclusions reached are those of the author and should not be construed to reflect official procedure or policy of CHAMPUS. The Denver office also provided helpful clarification on claim processing, fees, and coinsurance. Thus by the end of September 1974 only 93 percent of claims had been processed due to delayed billing and a 25 percent return and reject rate existed, largely due to incorrect or incomplete submissions. The fees listed here are the fees charged as negotiated (usual, customary, and reasonable—UCR) but the coinsurance has not been deducted; therefore, the government cost is less than the fees and charges shown.

Large as it is, CHAMPUS is, of course, a select group derived from uniformed personnel. The dependents of active duty personnel (nationally, 44.7 percent of all insureds) pay a 20 percent outpatient coinsurance, whereas all others (nationally, 55.3 percent), the retired military personnel and their dependents and the dependents of deceased military personnel pay a 25 percent coinsurance (all services). The proportion varies somewhat with the age of the beneficiary, the state, and the diagnosis.

The utilization reported here is not necessarily the total mental health service utilization of the beneficiaries, for several reasons. Some beneficiaries, such as retired military personnel now employed by the federal government, have other additional coverage by virtue of their current employment. This coverage must be used first before claims are accepted by CHAMPUS. Then, acute (only) psychiatric care may be available to military dependents at some installations. Such utilization would not appear in the CHAMPUS claim experience. Also, it is possible, that even though coverage is available, some beneficiaries for personal reasons may choose to seek care without submitting any claims to CHAMPUS. Thus, the utilization is underreported to an unknown degree. "The House Appropriations Committee ... showed that in FY 1972, 48% of all inpatient days under CHAMPUS were for the treatment of mental ... conditions ... the cost of inpatient psychiatric care represented 24% of the total funds spent for inpatient care ... only 9% of the beneficiaries who received inpatient care under CHAMPUS" (Penner, 1975, p. 21).

Benefits

The CHAMPUS mental disorder benefits available in fiscal year 1974 were extensive, compared to most other group health programs. Inpatient benefits could run the entire year, with the dependents of active duty personnel paying $25 per hospital admission, or $1.75 per diem (increased to $3.50 in January 1974), whichever was greater. The original professional fees, where necessary, were brought into line with UCR rates. The inpatient fees shown include the deductible or the 25 percent coinsurance for retirees and their dependents, whichever was greater. The outpatient services for 30 days prior and up to 120 days following hospitalization are merged for the same period of disability. This merging obviously augments the inpatient professional services reported to an unknown degree (outpatient and inpatient recording of costs are now separated). The fact that the dependents of active duty personnel do not pay the 20 percent coinsurance when hospitalized may also add somewhat to reported inpatient utilization. Apart from a $50 per insured per year deductible (maximum $100 a family) for outpatient services (this cost not being included in the data) and the coinsurance, the health benefits were essentially unlimited. Effective July 1974, CHAMPUS annual benefits for mental disorder were reduced to 120 days for inpatient services and forty outpatient visits, for a period to enable establishment of utilization review procedures. The computer printout data suggest instances of overutilization, perhaps due to unorthodox providers or excessive charges. While the collective cost effect of overutilization seems only a small proportion of total claims, overutilization does have a very direct bearing on program quality, as noted in the Senate hearings during the summer of 1974, when there were cries of alarm that the costs of psychotherapy had reached nearly 20 percent of total mental expenditures (all 50-minute outpatient psychotherapy accounted for 21 percent of such costs). It would, therefore, seem in the interests of all concerned for the major professions to assist CHAMPUS in establishing peer review and other suitable controls on providers and utilization.

Outpatient special education services were terminated as a benefit on August 31, 1973, and from July 1, 1974, services in residential facilities were only recognized when accredited by the Joint Commission Council for Accreditation of Psychiatric Facilities. In September 1974, the 120-day forty-visit limits were replaced by a review process. After 120 days' hospitalization, a psychiatric panel is to determine whether further inpatient treatment would be beneficial. Outpatient mental health benefits will also be subject to review after sixty visits (United States House Armed Services Committee, 1974, p. 16) ". . . with provision for recommendations for care in excess of these amounts to be professionally evaluated." Marriage, child, and pastoral counseling services were terminated as a benefit on February 27, 1975. Further changes were announced on March 7, 1975, in an effort to bring program costs into line with the available appropriation. Psychologists continue to be recognized as independent providers, however. Reimbursement for their services on a fee-for-service basis is now restricted to licensed psychologists with a Ph.D. in clinical psychology and with two years of supervised experience in an organized health setting (essentially, this is the definition contained in the insurance industry's proposed National Health Care Act of 1975; HR 5990-Omar Burleson, Texas; S 1438-Thomas McIntyre, New Hampshire). Other psychologists and all other therapists will be subject to physician prescription for their services, with physician review and recertification every thirty days. The services of psychological assistants will not be recognized.

It should be noted here that where the number of visits to any provider did not equal at least 1 percent of the services rendered and where 1 percent of the beneficiaries (or N) was less than 100, the claim costs are not cited.

Procedures

The CHAMPUS schedule of procedures, with some additions, closely follows that for psychiatric services developed by the California Medical Association in its *Relative Value Studies* (1969). Individual psychotherapy, the 50-minute "hour" was by far the most common procedure, and was rendered to 58 percent of all clients receiving any mental health service (see Table 1). Note, also, that this one procedure accounted for 79.4 percent of all outpatient visits to all providers. Half-hour (25-minute) psychotherapy involved 14 percent of the clients. The briefer forms of psychotherapy (25 minutes and 15 minutes) were more commonly on an inpatient basis. Psychiatrists provided 78, 83, and 80 percent of all inpatient psychotherapy visits of 50, 25, and 15 minutes duration, respectively. The only other category of providers delivering more than 10 percent of this inpatient psychotherapy was the attending physician (commonly, the family doctor). On an outpatient basis, the psychiatrist was again the major psychotherapy provider, participating in 57 and 73 percent of visits with a duration of 50 and 25 minutes, respectively. It appears that psychologists and social workers, although providing 26 and 5 percent of this hourly outpatient therapy (attending physicians and clinics, 6 and 2 percent), are rarely engaged in brief therapy (15 minutes) and collectively provide only 11 percent of the short (25-minute) outpatient visits (see Table 2). Psychologists, social workers, and clinics, however, each provided more than 10 percent of their hourly psychotherapy to those under ten years of age and about 32 percent of their services to those aged ten to nineteen years.

Much has been written of the cost-benefit effectiveness of group therapy. However, it is apparently more often read about than practiced. Only 6 percent of all clients served were involved in ninety-minute group therapy sessions (all providers) and 5 percent in hourly group therapy. Psychiatrists provided 81 and 53 percent of the inpatient and outpatient 90-minute group therapy, while psychologists and social workers provided 26 and 9 percent of such therapy on an outpatient basis.

Psychologists may be surprised to learn that they provided only 48 and 59 percent of the psychologic testing on an inpatient and outpatient basis, at least insofar as billing was concerned. Psychiatrists and attending physicians are shown as providing 46 percent of inpatient testing and 24 percent of such outpatient testing. More likely, much of such testing is at their

Table 1. Psychiatric Procedures and Visits: Fiscal Year 1974

Main Procedure (only)	Time (in minutes)	Clients	Inpatient Visits	Outpatient Visits	Total Visits	Average Visits per Client
Psychotherapy	50	39,171	83,281	400,535	483,816	12.4
	25	9,547	59,131	24,167	83,298	8.7
	15	2,176	14,368	–	17,495	8.0
Group Therapy	90	4,346	14,857	43,319	58,176	13.4
Other Psychotherapy	?	3,818	6,298	20,127	26,425	6.9
Psychologic Testing	?	4,013	–	6,411	8,242	2.1
Convulsive	?	1,047	9,325[b]	–	10,133	9.7
Totals (9/30/74)	–	68,082[a]	234,949[b]	504,188[c]	739,137	10.9
Unduplicated User	–	56,837	–	–	739,137	13.0
Corrected to 100%		73,206	272,562	535,231	807,793	11.0

Based on fiscal year 1973: [a] = 93% of total utilization, [b] = 86.2%, [c] = 94.2%. No count entered for cases where visits totaled less than 100. In certain cases (?) no time was specified for average visit length.

Table 2. Mental Health Service Visits to Major Providers, by Site, Number of Visits, Average Fee and Clients

Procedure (minutes)	Clients	Site	Attending M.D. Visits	Attending M.D. Average Fee	Psychiatrist Visits	Psychiatrist Average Fee	Psychologist Visits	Psychologist Average Fee	Social Worker Visits	Social Worker Average Fee	Clinic Visits	Clinic Average Fee	Total Visits (All Providers)
Psychotherapy 50	39,171	in	8,888	32.45	65,518	31.57	3,115	33.28	21,881	25.98	7,425	29.27	83,281
		out	23,398	34.94	230,165	35.79	103,701	33.41	–	–	–	–	400,535
25	9,547	in	8,840	17.88	48,838	17.78	–	–	–	–	899	18.34	59,131
		out	2,707	19.34	17,588	20.24	1,896	18.11	709	14.69	928	16.00	24,167
15	2,176	in	2,433	14.99	11,447	14.42	–	–	–	–	–	–	14,368
		out	–	–	2,213	12.73	–	–	–	–	–	–	3,127
Group Therapy 90	4,346	in	1,722	14.52	12,002	16.18	357	15.15	3,751	15.08	461	14.86	14,857
		out	–	–	22,440	17.85	10,829	16.62	–	–	440	13.12	42,319
60	3,393	in	736	10.57	2,390	10.60	136	11.69	–	–	131	10.67	3,393
		out	–	–	–	–	–	–	–	–	–	–	
Other Psychotherapy ?	3,818	in	329	26.96	4,426	31.26	1,278	26.61	127	22.63	–	–	6,298
		out	–	–	2,982	34.84	14,583	29.05	2,143	25.28	–	–	20,127
Psychologic Testing ?	4,013	in	135	43.09	712	36.37	873	66.75	–	–	–	–	1,831
		out	387	37.71	1,154	40.50	3,763	55.66	177	25.50	521	35.30	6,411
Convulsive Therapy ?	1,047	in	1,407	31.29	6,163	31.75	–	–	–	–	196	25.29	9,325
		out	160	30.22	579	30.46	–	–	–	–	–	–	808
All Procedures ?	68,082	in	–	–	–	–	–	–	–	–	–	–	234,949
		out	–	–	–	–	–	–	–	–	–	–	504,188

Client, same as beneficiary or user, unduplicated number = 56,837. No count entered in cases where visits totaled less than 100. In some cases (?) no time was specified for length of visit.

request or direction either by salaried personnel or on a unit cost basis, or they billed for the services provided on referral. Clinics provided 8 percent of the psychological testing on an outpatient basis. Though an average of 2.1 visits are reported for psychological testing (all providers), it is probable that this figure frequently represents hours of service rather than separate visits.

"Not otherwise classified psychotherapy" was provided to 5 percent of the beneficiaries. Of such inpatient visits, 70 percent were made by psychiatrists, while psychologists accounted for 72 percent of such outpatient services. Of those receiving mental health services, 1.5 percent had convulsive therapy (electroshock or drug-induced). Insulin shock therapy appears to have nearly disappeared from treatment with but .0004 percent of the beneficiaries involved in 1974, whereas psychoanalysis was only *billed* for as such in .005 percent of the visits.

Apart from psychological testing, of the major therapies listed in Table 1, the average number of visits by client ranged from 6.9 to 13.4 visits. Neither the degree to which specific clients received more than one form of therapy (procedure) nor the extent of services by client, nor the index of their effectiveness per spell of disability, can be determined from the data. The fact that a total of 68,082 beneficaries, however, are reported in the printout, when there are known to be but 56,837 unduplicated users, would indicate that 16.5 percent of the procedures were additional procedures rendered to certain users (see also below and Table 5).

Fees

Interestingly, the fees of attending physicians were somewhat higher than those of psychiatrists for psychotherapy and testing on an inpatient basis (see Table 2). This fact again raises the possibility that some fees include both the services of the physician and an assistant. When the average outpatient fees of the mental health trilogy are contrasted for 50-minute psychotherapy or 90-minute group therapy, they are: for psychiatry, $35.79 and $17.85; for psychology, $33.41 and $16.62; and for social work, $25.98 and $15.08, respectively. Clearly, there is substantial overlap among these three providers in group therapy fees and psychologists appear to be approaching parity (less than $2.38) with psychiatrists in their outpatient hourly psychotherapy fees. Fees charged by clinics (organized facility and salaried personnel, but no differentiation between public and private) for these two procedures are less than the average fees of practitioner psychologists. Psychologists' fees for testing are roughly double those for their hourly psychotherapy, probably reflecting the time required.

The fees reported here are certainly higher than those found in a small (N = 277) national sample survey of psychology providers (Dörken and Whiting, 1974) at close to the same point in time. Thus, while psychologists' average fees under CHAMPUS were $33.41 and $16.62 for hourly outpatient psychotherapy and 90-minute group therapy, respectively, Dörken and Whiting's sample study reported a modal hourly fee of $25.00 (two-thirds in the range of $20 to $30) and 80 percent of group therapy fees clustering in the $10 to $15 per session range. Attention was drawn there to the somewhat higher fees of the Southwest, the greater range in the West, and the fact that those in full-time practice tend to charge more than the part-time practitioner. In the CHAMPUS data, 62 percent of all outpatient visits reported were in California and Texas (another 17 percent in the District of Columbia). This geographic weighting may be a factor and the largest proportion of psychologist services to CHAMPUS beneficiaries are probably rendered by full-time practitioners. Judging from personal reports, however, the modal fees of established psychologist practitioners in urban centers of California appear to cluster currently in the $35 to $45 range (hourly therapy or assessment). Also, in November 1974 the newsletter of the Florida Psychological Association (FP, 1974) reported, on the basis of a survey, that the median fee for individual psychotherapy was $40 per hour and that the results had been accepted by Blue Shield of Florida as a basis for paying CHAMPUS claims. (Some Florida areas did report lower median fees.)

Diagnosis, Hospitalization, and Outpatient Service

The fact that there were 14,296 diagnosed beneficiaries, accounting for 46,592 admissions, indicates that multiple admissions are common. The neuroses and transient situational disturbances account for 49 percent of beneficiary diagnoses and 58 percent of hospital admissions (see Table 3). Personality disorders, special symptoms not elsewhere classified, and childhood behavior disorders account for an additional 14 percent of the diagnoses, but for only 6 percent of the admissions. On the other hand, whereas schizophrenia accounted for 17 percent of the diagnoses and admissions, alcoholism accounted for 10 percent of the diagnoses and 12 percent of the admissions. Diagnoses more common among the aged are not evident for the reason that CHAMPUS benefits are rarely provided to persons over sixty-four. The law restricts such provision to only those not eligible for Medicare.

The average duration of hospital stay was 14.1 days. This average, however, reflects the longer average duration of stay of those with childhood behavior disorders, personality disorders, and transient situational disturbances, at 96.6, 48.2, and 36.5 days, respectively. Young clients contributed heavily to long-term hospital utilization. For example, those diagnosed schizophrenic and aged one to fourteen years, while 4 percent of all admissions for this diagnosis, accounted for 12 percent of the hospital days with an average stay of 89 days in contrast to the overall average stay of 17.5 days for this diagnosis. Similarly, 15 percent of personality disorder admissions accounted for 41 percent of all hospital days, with an average stay of 133 days, in contrast to this disorder average of 48 days. The average duration of stay with an affective psychosis was 14 days. Of even shorter duration were the average stays of those with neurosis at 6.4 days and alcoholism at 4.9 days. However, average stay per admission is one thing and number of admissions quite another. Thus while alcoholism showed the shortest stay per admission, the multiple admissions led to an average of 18.6 days hospitalized in the year, neuroses 28.8, and so on. Note also that the

Table 3. Hospital Admissions by Diagnosis, Duration and Cost

| Diagnosis | Clients | Hospital Admissions | | Average Hospital Cost per Day | Admissions per Client | Professional Visits | Visits per Client |
		Number of Admissions	Average Stay				
Schizophrenia	2,385	7,705	17.5	57.66	3.2	73,333	30.7
Affective Psychoses	376	575	14.0	75.09	1.5	4,616	12.3
Neuroses	5,329	23,735	6.4	69.19	4.5	149,213	28.0
Personality Disorder	907	1,518	48.2	50.11	1.7	14,430	15.9
Alcoholism	1,438	5,397	4.9	57.26	3.8	10,487	7.3
Not Classified	154	298	15.8	43.80	1.9	3,151	20.5
Transient Situational Disturbance	1,742	3,218	36.5	51.41	1.8	29,934	17.2
Behavior Disorder, Childhood	978	993	96.6	49.79	1.0	13,774	14.1
Nonpsychiatric with Physical Condition	420	1,267	18.2	40.85	3.0	4,028	9.6
Total	14,296	46,592	14.1	56.76	3.3	316,996[a]	22.2

[a]Report is 35 percent higher than visits in tables 1 and 2 and includes professional services other than "psychiatric." Conversely, these visits average 26 percent more than purely "psychiatric" visits.

professional visits per client averaged 7.3 and 28 for these disabilities, though overall 26 percent of the professional visits were "nonpsychiatric."

When outpatient services are compared by diagnosis, the average number of visits per client are seen to range from 7.4 (affective psychosis) to 14.7 (neurosis). The neuroses and transient situational disturbances together account for 65 percent of all professional visits. Note that 22 percent of the overall outpatient visits in Table 4 are "nonpsychiatric." Note also, that

Table 4. Outpatient Service by Diagnosis and Visits

Diagnosis	Clients	Professional Visits	Visits per Client
Schizophrenia	3,011	411,747	13.9
Affective Psychoses	463	3,412	7.4
Neuroses	20,864	307,532	14.7
Personality Disorder	3,054	37,812	12.4
Alcoholism	330	2,482	7.5
Not Classified	4,021	42,553	10.6
Transient Situational Disturbance	9,815	112,348	11.4
Behavior Disorder, Childhood	5,993	69,140	11.5
Nonpsychiatric with Physical Condition	1,293	15,844	12.3
Total	50,240	643,638[a]	12.8

[a]This figure is 28 percent higher than visits in tables 1 and 2 and includes professional services other than "psychiatric." Conversely, these visits include 22 percent more than purely "psychiatric" visits.

the total clients or beneficiaries in tables 3 and 4 at 64,536 is less than the clients in Tables 1 and 2. The data tabulation thus differs somewhat between dimensions. Recall also that as of the September 30, 1974 date, only 94.2 and 86.2 percent of the expected total billings for inpatient and outpatient services had been recorded.

Utilization

The number of persons covered by CHAMPUS in these states has been estimated by the U.S. Department of Defense at 3,262,206 (41.6 percent of their insureds in the program), with 40 percent of the sample in California, 20 percent in Texas, and

13 percent in Florida. At the time of this report, there had been 56,837 unduplicated users, with an estimated 93 percent of the data in. Thus the total number of unduplicated users is likely to reach 61,116 for fiscal year 1974. On this basis, it can be estimated that 1.87 percent of the eligible beneficiaries actually used the available mental health benefits. The total fees of all providers for all mental health services (to September 30, 1974 billings) were $7,630,000 for inpatient services, $19,740,000 for outpatient services (the $50 deductible per person not included) or $27,370,000 in professional service fees. Hospital services costs (patient and government) were $37,290,000, or 58 percent of the total cost of mental health services provided, outpatient professional services accounting for 30.5 percent, or less than one-third of the cost. The 56,838 users received mental health services at a total cost of $64,660,000, an average of $1,138 per user per year in these ten states. The CHAMPUS (government) costs were less by the amount of the estimated coinsurance, $11,970,000; an annual government cost of $927 per each user. The projected utilization rate (for mental health services) at 18.7 per 1,000 insureds, less than 2 percent, is remarkably comparable to the $19.89 per thousand total national annual rate of users of public mental health services reported by the biometrics branch of National Institute for Mental Health (NIMH) for 1971 (Kramer, 1973). On this per capita basis, the mental health services had an average per-person-insured annual cost of 19.82 (CHAMPUS cost was $16.15 per each, or $1.35 a month). With a total program cost of about $413,000,000, the CHAMPUS cost for mental health service at around $53,000,000 absorbed 12.8 percent of the total health benefit funds. While instances of extensive overutilization and questionably appropriate services are of concern both to CHAMPUS and to Congress, it would appear that in general a very broad range of mental health services for this group is both feasible and within realistic and reasonable expectations.

In 1962, Avnet reported on the landmark Group Health Insurance Study in New York. There was a 6:1,000 annual utilization rate of mental health services; 96 percent of these patients received individual office psychotherapy; and for 80 percent it was their only form of treatment. Of those hospitalized, 6 percent of the project cases had a 22.8-day average hospital stay. Fink (1971) reported a mental disorder utilization rate of under 2 percent with a 15-visit average. The United Auto Workers studies of the mid-sixties (Glasser and Duggan, 1969) found a 6.4:1,000 first-year outpatient utilization rate, with an average of 8.5 visits. By contrast, at this time, one Kaiser group (Green, 1969) reported a utilization rate of about 23:1,000, though outpatient visits averaged 7.8 in a year. The Health Cooperative of Puget Sound (Kogan and others) in a 1969 to 1972 study, found comparable utilization in outpatient services between its prepaid and fee-for-service groups. The number of users per 1,000 persons covered ranged from 35 to 42 from 1970 to 1972 with the mean number of visits being under 4 in any year and the median mental health visits per user ranging from 6.8 to 5.6. No data is provided on inpatient services.

Considered the most comprehensive review on this subject, a study by Reed, Myers, and Scheidemandel (1972) noted that, back in 1969, the high-option Blues plan had a 5.6:1,000 mental disorder hospitalization rate, with an average stay of 16.3 days under basic benefits, 19 days under supplemental benefits (NIMH at that time reported an average 17 days of stay per discharge in all nongovernmental general hospital psychiatric visits). In contrasting ten plans, Reed noted a substantial case rate range from 5.5 to 21.9 per 1,000 covered persons and an average number of visits per case, ranging from 4.2 to 18.8 among these plans.

In reporting on their 1973 FEHBA claim experience, Aetna and the Blues show a mental disorder utilization experience of 1.2 and 1.1 percent. Both plans note a higher utilization rate among the younger ages and among dependents. They also find that outpatient mental health visits are disproportionately higher in the Washington, D.C., area than in other parts of the country; conversely, hospital usage was lower (approximate ratio 3:2 versus 1:2, District of Columbia:other states, outpatient:hospital, respectively). For 1973, the Blues report an average duration of hospital stay for mental disorder of 17.8

days. Both report an absolute and relative increase in mental disorder claim costs. For the Blues, it increased from 5.4 to 7.3 percent of total claims from 1967 to 1973. Aetna's 1973 cost experience was 12.5 percent (as opposed to 8.5 percent in 1972 reported elsewhere). In line with the "spreading the risk" concept of insurance, it is worth noting that for the Blues, only 43 percent of their covered population in this plan received any benefit in 1973. Thus the CHAMPUS 1973 experience, even with virtually unlimited benefits, of an average hospital stay for mental disorder of 14.1 days, an average of 13.0 total "psychiatric" visits per unduplicated user and an 18.7:1,000 utilization rate, is within the range of already reported experience in other plans, albeit towards the upper limits. This conclusion, while based on 93 percent of the expected billing, seems likely to be representative of total utilization.

It is also of interest to contrast fiscal 1974 with 1973 costs and utilization. While the overall cost of mental health services increased from 63.1 to 64.7 million dollars, the increase in unduplicated users from 52,709 to 56,837 resulted in a decreased average cost per user from $1,213 to $1,138. The ratio of utilization per 1,000 insureds rose from 17.5 to 18.7. On a per diem basis, the average hospital costs increased from $47.77 to $56.76 or 19 percent. The average fees of major providers increased also, but at a rate more in keeping with the general economy. The average fees of psychiatrists, psychologists and social workers for 50-minute outpatient psychotherapy increased 6.6, 5.6, and 7.8 percent, respectively. Thus the rate of increase both proportionately and absolutely ($2.22, $1.76, and $1.89) was least in the case of psychologists.

The location of CHAMPUS beneficiaries does not follow state civilian population but rather the location of uniformed personnel and retirees. This is evident by contrasting the number of insured in California, New York, and Florida to state population.

Detail on the four major providers is listed in Table 5. The proportion of visits (services) provided by any one profession varied widely among the ten states. The professions involved were affected whether the services were on an inpatient or out-

Table 5. Ten-State Visit Distribution to Major Providers

State	Insureds/M		Site	Visits	Attending M.D.		Psychiatrist		Psychologist		Social Worker	
	Number	%			% Visits	Average Fee	% Visits	Average Fee	% Visits	Average Fee	% Visits	Average Fee
Alabama	121.8	3.7	in	8,656	35.0	$15.43	48.2	$18.27	—	—	—	—
			out	5,076	18.1	20.90	29.0	26.99	21.4	$30.92	—	—
California	1,300.3	39.9	in	84,203	18.7	28.30	73.0	31.08	1.9	33.69	—	$27.71
			out	310,885	7.8	27.25	39.1	33.01	24.1	32.27	12.1	24.66
District of Columbia	167.2	5.1	in	16,608	—	—	93.8	26.19	2.0	33.01	2.2	18.56
			out	110,617	—	—	67.1	34.51	18.4	32.95	9.7	24.34
Florida	418.8	12.8	in	60,684	10.7	21.78	76.6	24.48	2.4	27.75	4.9	19.79
			out	61,213	7.1	29.20	47.8	31.40	24.4	28.20	8.1	21.00
Illinois	142.9	4.4	in	8,137	28.7	18.80	64.9	27.06	2.1	29.61	—	—
			out	9,973	10.9	21.40	42.7	30.91	10.2	31.25	5.8	25.45
New York	169.4	5.2	in	3,683	—	—	84.2	29.83	—	—	—	—
			out	24,020	1.2	27.34	72.8	36.57	17.3	29.92	2.9	28.49
Ohio	105.7	3.2	in	10,034	34.0	14.61	58.3	20.12	1.4	29.41	—	—
			out	10,379	12.9	20.95	40.6	30.16	36.4	29.94	3.1	28.54
Rhode Island	30.5	.9	in	2,259	24.4	32.89	69.8	35.50	3.1	31.64	—	—
			out	8,280	7.6	27.89	23.5	31.60	5.0	31.40	2.9	20.74
South Carolina	166.0	5.1	in	10,356	26.6	14.16	68.1	17.27	2.5	30.01	1.1	23.37
			out	15,032	10.5	23.27	46.3	32.57	22.0	35.72	7.5	26.20
Texas	639.5	19.6	in	112,378	22.9	16.36	62.9	19.49	3.5	39.63	2.1	39.35
			out	88,173	10.7	24.22	38.4	31.40	28.3	34.12	6.6	33.22
10 States	3,262.2[a]	100.	in	316,998	19.1	20.11	69.8	24.59	2.5	35.17	2.0	27.60
			out	643,638	2.0	26.26	45.9	33.13	23.1	32.20	9.7	25.20

[a]Unduplicated users equal 56,837. No count is given in cases where visits totaled less than 100.

patient basis. Thus, while attending physicians and psychiatrists accounted for 89 percent of inpatient services and psychologists and social workers together provided only 4.5 percent of such services (6.5 percent by all other providers), the physicians and psychiatrists provided just less than half (47.9 percent) of the outpatient services. Psychologists and social workers delivered 32.8 percent of such services, all other providers delivering the 20 percent balance.

Whereas the proportion of inpatient services provided by psychologists in these states ranged from less than 1 to only 3.5 percent, their delivery of CHAMPUS outpatient services ranged from 5 to 36 percent (overall averages 2.5 and 23.1 percent). These data underscore the importance to psychologists of acquiring hospital staff privileges. Interestingly, when psychologists are engaged in inpatient services, their average fees are higher than those of psychiatrists in seven of the states. This fact suggests that their inpatient involvement may be more in the nature of special consultation or for particular expertise. Overall, the ratio of psychiatrist to psychologist outpatient services is 2:1, but it is 8:5 in California and only 15:4 in the District of Columbia, but approaching 1:1 in Ohio. The highest proportion of visits to psychiatrists are evident in the District of Columbia and New York, areas with the highest concentration of psychiatrists (see Chapter One). The states also varied widely in overall utilization, particularly of outpatient mental health services, ranging from a low of 41.7 such visits (all disorders, all providers) per thousand insureds in Alabama to 662 in the District of Columbia. The overall ten-state ratio was 197 outpatient visits per thousand insureds (239 in California, almost half the ten-state reported visits).

Outpatient visits are about twice as frequent as inpatient visits overall in these ten states. No certain explanation can be offered for the greater frequency of inpatient versus outpatient visits in Texas and Alabama—surely not Southern hospitality! Both types of visits are also comparable in number in Florida and Ohio. Perhaps the licensing standards for such facilities in these states may be a factor. Also, this situation hardly seems compatible with the current emphasis on need for ambulatory care. The highest proportional utilization of psychologists in outpatient services occurred in Ohio (where they are known to be well distributed relative to population), and for social workers in California, where the clinical social worker is licensed.

The average fees reported in Table 5 are for all procedures and therefore differ somewhat from the ten-state averages for "hourly" psychotherapy listed in Table 2. They do reflect actual provider fees—those prevailing July 1973 to June 1974. When the average outpatient fees of psychiatrists and psychologists are contrasted by state, one notes that overall the psychologist is less than $1.00 per visit short of parity, but the differential runs to $6.65 in New York, $0.74 in California, while in South Carolina and Texas, psychological fees are apparently somewhat higher.

Social workers provide only 9.7 percent of the outpatient services (range from less than 1 to 12.1 percent among these states), perhaps a reflection of the fact that they are only licensed or certified in thirteen states. When their average outpatient fees are compared to those of psychologists, fees for social workers are found to be lower in every state, the differential ranging from $1.40 (Ohio) to $10.66 (Rhode Island).

It should be emphasized that the fees, although showing substantial variation between states and professions, do so on an average, even though they have been adjusted by CHAMPUS to UCR rates. Local economy, custom, and provider expertise, and some variance in third-party intermediary reimbursement practices, undoubtedly are factors leading to intra- and interprofession and interstate variance. For example, in Florida (psychiatry-psychology differential $3.20), the Miami area was reimbursing psychologists at 75 percent of the rate for psychiatry. Blue Shield of Florida has since complied with basic CHAMPUS instructions and retroactive adjustment of unauthorized fee cuts was approved.

Though limited to the ten sample states and to this select group of beneficiaries, and though affected by some merging of outpatient visits with inpatient services and some underreporting, these CHAMPUS data nonetheless provide an unusual perspective on the utilization of fee-for-service practice in the treatment of mental disorder. The mental disorder benefits, apart from a minimal deductible and moderate coinsurance, were essentially unlimited. Utilization rates appear consistent with reports of national utilization and within the upper limits of experience of other significant group health insurance plans with broad benefits. To the extent that any future controls may be necessary, it is suggested that they be placed on the providers via peer review, proscriptive treatment plans, and prior authorization for extended services, rather than on the consumer.

10

Brief Psychotherapy and Medical Utilization

Nicholas A. Cummings and William T. Follette

It has been suggested that hospital overutilization is caused partly by the very nature of hospital insurance benefits—services are reimburseable if done in hospital, but not in the practitioner's office. Pacific Mutual's five years of experience with a health maintenance plan in Southern California (Gamlin, 1975), administered through the Orange County Medical Foundation (see Chapter Six on foundations for medical care) clearly supports this view by demonstrating that when the traditional benefits are reversed, there is an actual decrease in dollars paid out. Contrary to common practice, the foundation placed a $100 deductible on hospital stays while offering first-dollar coverage for outpatient physician's services. Claims increased 30 percent but dollars paid out decreased. This refutation of traditional fears has been demonstrated by the Kaiser Health Plan for years as illustrated in the eight-year follow-up study reported in this chapter.

In the first of a series of investigations into the relationship between psychological services and medical utilization in a prepaid health plan setting, the authors (Follette and Cummings, 1967) found that (1) persons in emotional distress were significantly higher users of both inpatient and outpatient medical facilities as compared to the health plan average; (2) medical utilization declined significantly in those emotionally distressed individuals who received psychotherapy as compared to a

165

control group of matched emotionally distressed health plan members who were not accorded psychotherapy; (3) these declines remained constant during the five years following the termination of psychotherapy; (4) the most significant declines occurred in the second year after the initial interview, and those patients receiving one session only or brief psychotherapy (two to eight sessions) did not require additional psychotherapy to maintain the lower level of utilization for five years; and (5) patients seen for two years or more in regular psychotherapy demonstrated no overall decline in total outpatient utilization, since psychotherapy visits tended to supplant medical visits. However, there was significant decline in inpatient utilization in this long-term therapy group from an initial hospitalization rate several times that of the health plan average, to a level comparable to that of the general adult health plan population. In a subsequent study the same authors (Cummings and Follette, 1968) found that intensive efforts to increase the number of referrals to psychotherapy by computerized psychological screening with early detection and alerting of the attending physicians did not increase significantly the number of patients seeking psychotherapy. The authors concluded that in a prepaid health plan setting already maximally employing educational techniques for both patients and physicians, and already providing a range of prepaid psychological services, the number of health plan subscribers seeking psychotherapy reached an optimal level and remained fairly constant. During the entire period of the study, as well as in the insured years before and after the eight years of this study, the utilization of mental health services was consistently .5 per 1,000 insureds for inpatient (hospitalization), and 9 per 1,000 insureds for outpatient services. The average length of hospitalization remained under eight days, and the average outpatient psychotherapy series remained at 6.6 visits.

Sixteen years of prepayment experience demonstrates that there is no basis for the fear that an increased demand for psychotherapy will financially endanger the system. It is not the number of referrals received, but the manner in which psychotherapy services are delivered, that determines optimal cost-therapeutic effectiveness. The finding that one session only, with no repeat psychological visits, could reduce medical utilization by 60 percent over the following five years, was surprising and totally unexpected. Equally surprising was the 75 percent reduction in medical utilization over a five-year period in those patients initially receiving two to eight psychotherapy sessions (brief therapy). The data offered no conclusive reason as to how and why this early, brief psychotherapeutic intervention resulted in a persistent reduction in medical utilization throughout the following half decade. The authors speculated that the results obtained demonstrated a psychotherapeutic effect, inasmuch as the clinic procedure was to offer early and incisive intervention into the patient's crisis problem, to get beneath the manifest symptoms to his or her real concerns, and to offer understanding and therapy in the very first session. Such a hypothesis would suggest that a patient's understanding or appreciation of his or her problem and its relationship to symptoms would diminish the somaticizing of emotions, and consequently reduce medical visits. This speculation is in keeping with the experiences of providing psychotherapy under national health care in Great Britain (Balint, 1957). Perhaps a less satisfactory, but an equally plausible hypothesis might be that the patient attained no mastery over his problems and that after the psychological visit he found ways other than visiting the doctor to express emotional distress. The present eight-year follow-up tried to clarify the effect of brief psychotherapy previously reported.

It is important to describe the setting in which the past and present studies were conducted. The Kaiser Foundation Health Plan of Northern California is a group-practice prepayment plan offering comprehensive hospital and professional services on a direct-service basis to 1,250,000 subscribers in the greater San Francisco Bay Area. Professional services are provided by the Permanente Medical Group, a partnership of physicians that uniquely and effectively utilizes an impressive number of nonmedical doctors (such as clinical psychologists and optometrists) as primary health service providers. The San Francisco Kaiser-Permanente Medical Center, where the studies were conducted, is one of ten centers in the San Francisco Bay Area offering direct and indirect mental health services. Its staff of six clinical psychologists, four psychiatrists, and two psychiatric social workers reflects the fact that throughout the Northern California facilities it is typically the nonmedical, and particularly the psychological personnel that provide the bulk of the psychotherapy and consultation. Working on an equal patient-responsibility level with their psychiatric colleagues, clinical psychologists and psychiatric social workers assume full responsibility for their patients; admit and discharge from the hospital; provide consultation for nonpsychiatric physicians and consultation in the general hospital; participate in twenty-four hour "on call" duty; and make determinations of mental health emergencies (such as suicidal attempts and acute psychotic episodes) appearing at night in the emergency room of the general hospital. The ability of a psychologist or social worker to function effectively as a primary health service provider with full patient responsibility is a condition of employment at Kaiser-Permanente, San Francisco.

As the original health maintenance organization (HMO), one of the heretofore unique aspects of this setting is that it tends to put a premium on health rather than on illness, by making preventative medicine economically rewarding. The same principle holds true for the delivery of mental health services where there is a constant search for the most effective and specific methods of treatment. Consequently, effective cost-therapeutic techniques have been developed for the treatment of alcoholism, suicidal activity, drug abuse, heroin addiction, and a variety of other conditions often excluded from insurance coverage. To deny psychotherapeutic intervention in these problems merely results in having to medically and surgically treat their expensive physical consequences. On the other hand, traditional intake procedures, waiting lists, and protracted therapies have been eliminated in favor of rapid, immediate intervention with individual and group psychotherapy, which is most often relatively brief, but which occurs in programs specifically designed to promote maximum patient recovery to his effective state. All therapists perform long-term psychotherapy when indicated, but other dynamic modalities are most often the treatment of choice.

The present study investigated the question of whether the reduction in outpatient and inpatient medical utilization following brief psychotherapeutic intervention reflects a positive, or therapeutically defined change in the patients' behavior. The hypothesis can be stated simply: if the reduction in medical utilization is the result of the patient's having coped more effectively with emotional distress, then the presenting symptom (called the "manifest problem") should disappear, and the patient should have an awareness of the real or underlying concern that produced his or her symptom.

The psychotherapy charts of the eighty patients seen for one session only and the forty-one patients seen for brief therapy (a total of 121 patients seen eight years previously) were drawn and reviewed for the following information obtained from the psychotherapists' notes:

1. What is presenting symptom, problem, or "manifest" reason why patient was referred or is here?
2. What is underlying psychological reason for patient's symptom, problem, or complaint?
3. Did the therapist suggest that patient return, or did he or she ask patient to return? Did patient express an interest in returning? Did patient make return appointment?
4. From the therapist's notes, did you get the feeling anything was dealt with by the patient that would be of value? Was patient unduly resistive, angry; or was patient friendly, impressed?

This information was necessary as background orientation for a telephone questionnaire conducted by a masters-level psychology assistant. Whenever possible each patient, when located, was individually interviewed. It was not possible to locate all patients after eight years, as over 50 percent of each group were no longer members of the health plan, a typical situation in the highly mobile California labor force. Meticulous tracing, often out of state and sometimes as far away as the East

Coast, resulted in telephone contact with fifty-six of the eighty one-session-only group, and thirty-one of the forty-one brief-psychotherapy group. The telephone interviewers employed the following questionnaire as a guide:

Telephone Call to Patient

(Try to record extensively patient's exact words.)

I am _____ , a psychologist at Kaiser-Permanente. We are following up on some of the people we saw sometime back, and would like to know how you are getting along.

1. Do you remember your appointment or visit with a psychotherapist? How long ago was it?
2. Do you remember whom you saw?
3. How did you know of our service? Did a doctor refer you, or did you ask for a referral?
4. What was the reason you consulted a psychotherapist? (If patient says something to the effect that "my doctor wanted me to go," try to elicit the reason (such as symptom, complaint, problem) why the doctor thought the referral a good idea. We are interested here in what the patient remembers, whether he focuses on the manifest problem or the psychological problem).
5. What do you recall was discussed with your psychotherapist? (if this has not been spelled-out in No. 4 above).
6. Do you feel the visit with a psychotherapist was of any benefit to you? If so, how? If not, why not?
7. How have you been getting along? (Here if the patient has not recalled the manifest symptom or complaint, remind him and ask about it. If he has not recalled the psychological problem which was discussed, remind him and ask about it.)

In the telephone interviews the researchers were interested in whether the patient recalled the presenting symptom (manifest problem) as the reason for having consulted a psychotherapist, or whether, instead, he or she remembered the actual focus and direction taken by the therapist in bringing to awareness the patient's real concern as the reason for the consultation. Of importance, also, was the patient's own perception of the degree of help derived from the single consultation or brief series of sessions. Of the eighty-seven patients located and interviewed, only two refused to cooperate. A third who initially refused cooperation changed her mind after verifying the legitimate nature of the research project.

All 85 patients contacted and who were diagnosed in terms of anxieties, phobias, somaticization, depression, and psychosis in their presenting problems could readily be categorized in terms of the actual problem that was creating the symptom, and on the basis of even one interview. They could be classified as marital difficulties, problems with children or pregnancy, alcohol or drugs, job problems, and so forth, and all cut across psychodiagnostic categories. The therapist was quick in eliciting the patient's immediate life problem, but it must be emphasized that often he was also able to formulate for the patient the immediate crisis in terms of his dominant psychological dynamics and life-style. This formulation was made without fostering long-term dependency or plans for a complete personality overhaul, and within the context of immediate, brief, incisive therapeutic intervention.

The telephone interviews found that although all but one of the eighty-five persons responding remembered seeing a psychotherapist, only two could recall the therapist's name. There was a tendency to underestimate the eight years elapsed since the last session, with "two or three years ago" being the response in almost 60 percent of the cases. The patients were nearly equally divided between those who recalled being referred by a physician (forty-four) and those who were self-referred, or by the spouse, a relative or a friend (forty-one).

The crucial question was whether the patient remembered

the manifest or the actual problem in recalling the interview. The results are unequivocal, for seventy-eight patients, or 92 percent, recalled the problem discussed (marital, familial, job, and so forth) rather than the presenting symptom as the reason for the referral. In fact, when these seventy-eight patients were asked directly about the presenting symptom (such as, "Did you ever have severe headaches?"), all but five denied ever having consulted a doctor for such a complaint. Thus the patient seems to have understood that the problem was more "real" than the symptom.

In view of the latter finding, it is somewhat surprising that the patients generally felt their psychotherapeutic contact had not been helpful. This trend existed in spite of the response that they were getting along well and had either resolved the psychological conflict or were coping with the problem. The response elicited were as follows:

		Yes	No
1.	Do you feel the visit with the "psychiatrist" was of any benefit to you?	9	76
		Well	Not well
2.	How have you been getting along (in regard to the psychological problem)?	83	2

The patients tended to attribute their coping with the problem to their own, rather than the therapist's solution, with "I just worked it out" being the frequent answer. On further consideration, this finding need not be surprising, as real insight becomes part of the patient's own belief system.

In several instances the patient reported being very angry with the psychotherapist, but in each case the patient added that, "He made me so mad I realized I had to solve this myself." Two illustrative cases might be helpful.

Case 1

Mrs. W., age thirty-nine, married sixteen years, with three children, was referred by her internist for severe headaches that had become less and less responsive to medication for the past ten months. She was seen by a psychologist three times, during which time her anger at her husband (whom she reluctantly said was seeing his secretary) was discussed, along with her feelings of being old at thirty-nine and unattractive. Between the second and third sessions she blew up at her husband, put her foot down regarding his staying out at night, and was surprised to find he was remorseful and eager to make amends. On telephone interview eight years later she denied ever having suffered from severe headaches, and recalled clearly that she consulted a psychotherapist for a marital problem. She did not find the sessions helpful, and stated flatly that she and husband worked it all out and they have been happier than ever.

Case 2

Mrs. S., age fifty-four, office worker, divorced after one year of marriage at age forty-seven, has no children, and lives alone. She was diagnosed as an involutional psychotic after being referred by her internist for delusions in which her neighbor was wiring her house to kill her with electricity. She saw the psychiatrist only once and left in a rage when, after discussing her lifelong loneliness, isolation and feelings of uselessness, he suggested she was envious of a neighbor woman's happy marriage, her four older children, and her new baby. On telephone interview eight years later she expressed frank hostility toward her psychiatrist and was outspoken in stating he made her worse. On the other hand, she recalls discussing her loneliness, denied ever having had her delusion, and insisted the neighbor had always been her best friend. In fact, the patient was the neighbor's frequent and only babysitter and had become "like a member of the family." At the conclusion of the interview she could not resist adding heatedly that "psychiatry is bunk; they try to make lonely people think they're crazy."

The results suggest that the reduction in medical utilization was the consequence of resolving the emotional distress being reflected in symptoms and doctors' visits. The modal patient in this eighth-year follow-up may be described as follows: "He denies ever having consulted a physician for the symptoms for which he had been originally referred. Rather, he recalls the actual problem discussed as the reason for the "psychiatric" visit, and although he reports the problem is resolved, he attributes this to his own efforts and does not give credit to his psychotherapist." This description reaffirms the contention that the reduced medical utilization reflected the diminished emotional distress expressed in symptoms presented to the doctor.

The findings suggest that the expectations of the therapist influence the outcome of psychotherapy, for if the first interview is merely "evaluation" or "intake," not much of therapeutic value is likely to occur in the first interview. If the therapist's attitude is that no real help is forthcoming from less than prolonged "intensive" psychotherapy, he may be right (for his own patients). Malan (1963), in his classic study of brief psychotherapy, was able to examine honestly the prejudices of his group of psychiatrists about brief therapy and the kinds of benefit possible, the kinds of patients who could utilize it, the permanency of the results, and so forth. He concluded that traditional attitudes about very brief therapy were mostly in the nature of unjustified prejudices. It would appear that therapeutic effects of brief therapy that can be labled "transference cure," "flight into health," "intellectualization," and other derogatory terms can often be long-lasting and result in a major change in the person's symptoms, relationships, and even lifestyle. Many of the patients in this study would undoubtedly be called "poorly motivated for treatment" or "dropouts from therapy" in many psychotherapy clinics.

Immediacy of availability and treatment is probably a very important aspect of this study. The results tend to support the crisis-clinic thesis that a great deal more can be done in less time during a time of emotional disturbance than during a period when a patient is relatively comfortable (such as often occurs after being on a waiting list for several months). The lack of "intake procedure" and the beginning of psychotherapeutic intervention in the first interview—sometimes even in the waiting room before the first interview—are probably crucial in obtaining psychotherapeutic results in a minimum amount of time and maintaining cost-effectiveness as well.

11

Utilization and Costs of Mental Health Services

Jack G. Wiggins

The need for insurance coverage for mental health services has been a growing concern over the past twenty years (Auster, 1969; Avnet, 1969; Gibson, 1972; National Institute of Mental Health, 1973, 1974). Early efforts to point out this need were directed toward identifying the frequency of mental health problems and illustrating the need for mental health services (Bennett, Hargrove, and Engle, 1953; Davidson, 1957). Avnet (1962) presented one of the first systematic studies of utilization, costs, and feasibility, concluding that the treatment of mental conditions could be financed as part of the health service benefits under a group health plan. Using Avnet's data, Dörken (1963) estimated that the demonstration project services could be provided at a mere $.36 per month. These benefits, including outpatient visits, were later added by Group Health Insurance of New York at a cost of $.35 per month for single persons in the high-risk group ($.15 per month for limited-risk cases). Although the data base is still relatively narrow, there is increasing evidence that, in spite of early fears of excessive costs to a health insurance plan, mental benefits are very reasonable. In fact, there is some evidence that mental health services can offset other health costs (Follette and Cummings, 1967; Goldberg, Krantz, and Locke, 1970).

Public acceptance of mental health services is recorded by Follman (1970) and Scheidemandel, Kanno, and Glascote (1968). Concern about financing care has led to various estimates of the total costs of treating mental conditions (Conley, 1973, and Conley, Conwell, and Arrill, 1967; Follman, 1970; National Institute of Mental Health, 1973; Rice, Knee, and Connell, 1970; HEW, SRS, 1972*a* and *b*; and HEW, SSA, 1971). In 1970, it was estimated that the cost of mental conditions in the United States was about $21,000,000,000 per year. The greatest cost of identified mental conditions was not the cost of direct treatment services, which accounted for only about $4,000,000,000 but rather were caused by the loss of economic productivity, estimated at $17,000,000,000. The majority of the productivity loss was in terms of wages lost due to sick time, which were paid by industries to workers off the job. These wages amounted to about $10,000,000,000 per year. Lost jobs and unemployment by those with mental problems also resulted in the loss of tax monies. Additional government expenditures in the form of income supplements to those out of work and to the families of the mentally disabled were about $7,000,000,000 per year. Thus, the estimated indirect costs of mental disorder are approximately four times as great as the costs of direct services. Stated otherwise, if mental health services are made readily available, effective diagnosis and treatment for mental conditions could return $4 to society for each $1 that is spent on the diagnosis and treatment of mental conditions. These results may be compared to the nationwide outcome of rehabilitation services, which have returned $3 to $5 to the economy for every dollar invested (see Chapter Four). Mental disorder is the single largest disability category in this federal-state program. Thus, the breakeven point of $1 returned for each dollar spent on direct treatment services would adequately justify equal coverage for mental conditions in all health insurance contracts. In a national health plan one can properly be concerned with such a broad impact, even though the merit may be obscure for a single group health plan today.

In addition to the direct and indirect costs of identified mental conditions, there is growing evidence that undiagnosed, untreated mental conditions may equal or exceed the cost of diagnosed conditions. The overutilization of medical-hospital services by individuals who have mental conditions masquerading as physical symptoms could amount to as much as $10,000,000,000 per year for misdiagnosis and ineffective treatment. Sick time and lost wages attributable to mental conditions (including alcoholism, but not identified as such) and underemployed individuals classified as mentally retarded (Conley, 1973) could amount to another $10,000,000,000, and an additional $2,000,000,000 in lost taxes on these reduced earnings. These data suggest that we cannot afford to be permissive regarding the inclusion of mental health services in a health insurance plan, nor can we tolerate passive acceptance of mental conditions without some attempt at active intervention for the well-being of the individual as well as for society.

The public's need and demand for mental health services is expressed by the use of services. Utilization data is typically expressed in terms of benefit use frequency per thousand of enrolled policyholders or subscribers, average number of visits per case or episode, cost per case, and proportion of total health plan costs subsumed by mental disorder. Although all such figures are meaningful and relevant, they tend to vary widely, depending on the groups served. For example, groups with higher education tend to have greater outpatient utilization rates. Other variables affecting utilization rates are age, sex, ethnic or racial background, occupation, the magnitude of initial consumer cost barriers, and range of services available in the program. As might be expected, those programs with more generous benefits and a wider range of services report a greater rate of utilization. Frequency of utilization is therefore not directly related to number of visits on an outpatient basis, the number of days spent in a hospital, or costs per case. At first glance, available statistical data on utilization of mental treatment may appear to be an actuarial nightmare. However, careful review of the data begins to reveal some patterns of utilization among the employed. About 2 percent of this insured population is likely to use mental health services in any given year, the average number of outpatient visits being fifteen or less, and inpatient days averaging about twenty-one (Myers, 1970).

Using the fact that almost 2 percent of the population (4,009,506 episodes) were reported to have used some form of mental health service in 1971 in an organized setting, Kramer (1973) estimated the manpower (among four professions) that would be necessary to deliver certain levels of service. His estimate of unmet need at the 2 percent utilization level suggests that those under eighteen and over sixty-four are not adequately served. Not included in Kramer's data are the private-sector office visits to practitioners, the outpatient psychiatric services of Veterans Administration hospitals, care in day treatment centers, and residential treatment centers for emotionally disturbed children. Drawing on estimates of psychiatrists, clinical psychologists and psychiatric social workers in full-time equivalent private practice (20,000) at an annual visit load of 1,500, each episode averaging six visits, one can infer another 5,000,000 episodes in private practitioner office therapy. Overall, then, utilization of mental health service in 1971 apparently involved somewhat over 4 percent of the total population.

Usage, when insurance benefits are available, appears consistently higher for dependents, who are "time rich." A sound level of short-term ambulatory mental health benefits is not broadly provided for the elderly, the unemployed, the indigent, or children. It is not unreasonable to anticipate, then, that with total population mandatory coverage in a national health insurance program, the overall mental health utilization would reach a 5 percent level, even with good controls.

Comparative Utilization

In order to place mental health utilization in perspective, it is meaningful to compare frequency of hospitalization for individuals diagnosed as having a mental condition with hospitalization rates for all other individuals. This comparison was made for Medicare patients for the period of July through December 1966 (Rice, Knee, and Connell, 1970). Diagnosed mental conditions constituted 1.4 percent of all diagnosed conditions entering general hospitals during the period. The average length of stay for all other diagnoses was 12.9 days, and the average length of stay for mental conditions was 15.1 days. Utilization rates of outpatient mental health services for the calendar year 1967 for individuals enrolled under part B of Medicare indicated a 2 percent utilization rate, constituting only about .3 percent of the total supplementary medical insurance outlays. Although the provisions for mental services under Medicare are quite limited, they do not show overuse of either outpatient or inhospital services, a possibility that had been feared by many (Eisdorfer and Lawton, 1973; Hess, 1966).

Another comparison of mental health to physical health utilization has been under the government-wide plan for federal employees (Reed, Myers, and Scheidemandel, 1972). These plans tend to be more generous than those available under Medicare and tend to have different utilization experiences, depending on the amount of service benefit available. Blue Cross and Blue Shield plans underwrite over half the federal employees. Equal coverage for inhospital treatment of mental disorder is provided by the Blue Cross plan, with the exception of care provided in nonmember psychiatric hospitals, which is not covered. Basic benefits include 365 days of hospital care for admission under the high-option plan and 30 days under the low-option plan, in contrast to 190 days of lifetime benefits under Medicare. The services of the attending physician are covered for inhospital treatment under the basic health plan. Outpatient or inoffice services are covered under supplementary benefits, which pay for 80 percent of the charges beyond an annual deductible of $100. The Aetna government-wide indemnity benefit plan, which covers approximately 20 percent of federal employees, covers 100 percent of the first $1,000 of hospital and room and board charges per calendar year, plus 80 percent of the balance in the high-option plan. In Aetna's low option plan, the first $500 and 75 percent of the charges thereafter are covered. Outpatient services of psychologists and physicians are covered, subject to an annual deductible of $50, with the plan paying 80 percent of the remaining covered charges in the high-option and 75 percent in the low option categories.

Frequency of utilization was greater in the federal employee high-option plans than in the low-option plans. This finding was not too surprising, since families with histories of major illnesses and disabling conditions tend to choose those plans that will serve them best, and these are likely to be the high-benefit programs. Thus, the Blue Cross and Blue Shield frequency of hospital utilization for mental conditions was 5.6 per thousand, representing 4.1 percent of all admissions in the high-option plan; and 3.1 admissions per thousand, representing 3.3 percent of admissions in the low-option plan. The average number of days of care per thousand population under Blue Cross was 89.3, representing 8 percent of the days of care under the high-option plan; and 39.1 days of care per thousand, representing 6.4 percent of the days of care under the low-option plan. Cost comparison of mental disorder benefits (7.2 and 7.3 percent) for all conditions in 1972 and 1973 suggest a plateauing of utilization in this plan (American Psychiatric Association, 1975). Per capita in terms of covered persons, $13.73 went for mental benefits in 1974 and $175.22 went for all other care. The mental benefits then were equivalent in cost to $1.15 per month per covered person.

In the Aetna plan, hospital utilization rates were somewhat lower, 4.1 admissions per thousand, or 3.1 percent of all admissions on the high-option plan and 2.7 admissions per thousand, representing 2.7 percent of the admissions in the low-option plan. However, Aetna experienced much longer hospital stays under its program, having the greatest number of days of hospitalization recorded among the federal employees' plans. Under the Aetna high-option plan, there were 153 days of hospitalization for mental conditions per thousand population covered, representing 15 percent of the total days of care. In Aetna's low-option plan, there were 64.3 days of hospital care per thousand population covered, representing 10.4 percent of the total days of hospital care.

Of the thirteen federal employee health programs reporting, the admission rates ranged from .8 per thousand in the Group Health Association to the 5.6 per thousand reported by the high-option Blue Cross and Blue Shield plan. The percentage of admission of mental conditions compared to all admissions to hospitals ranged from 1.1 percent in the Group Health Association to 4.1 percent in the high-option Blue Cross plan. The Hawaii Medical Service plan reported the lowest number of days of mental hospital care, at 6.9 per thousand, representing 1.6 percent of the total days of hospital care. The Aetna high-option plan, at 153 days per thousand, representing 15 percent of the total days of care, was the highest reported. The average number of days of hospitalization for all conditions in the other nine plans reporting ranged from 5.7 in the Hawaii Medical Service to 10.9 in the American Federation of Government Employees' high-option plan. The lowest average number of days of care for mental conditions was reported by the Kaiser-Permanente Northern California Group (7.7) and the highest was reported by the American Federation of Government Employees at 42.6 days.

Comparable costs per case between physical and mental conditions were reported in eight of the nine listed federal employee programs. The only substantial disparity was in the Health Insurance Plan of Greater New York, where psycho-analysis is in vogue. Here, mental conditions cost nearly twice as much per case as all other conditions. The range in cost for physical conditions for the nine reporting plans was from $485 in the Hawaii Medical Service to $915 in the Health Insurance Plan. The range in per-case cost for mental conditions was from $455 in the Hawaii Medical Service to $1972 in the Health Insurance Plan.

Data on the federal employees' plan for outpatient services does not provide a comparison of utilization rates for physical and mental conditions. However, outpatient use rates are reported for certain plans. The federal employees' Blue Cross and Blue Shield high-option plan reports that the average rate of utilization was 12.5 per thousand covered beneficiaries with an average annual cost of $2.84 for outpatient services. Highest rates of utilization were for the group aged nineteen to thirty-four. The group aged thirty-four to forty-four had the next highest utilization rate with utilization rates declining significantly thereafter. Outpatient charges per covered person for mental claims range from $7.16 for ages nineteen to thirty-four, to $.29 per year for those aged sixty-five and older.

It is noteworthy that although private insurance carriers underwrite the majority of coverage for mental conditions, the most frequent reports of mental health service utilization have been by health maintenance organizations. For example, the Group Health Association of Washington, D.C., reported a utilization rate of about 2 percent, with an average number of visits per case of 4.2 (Goldberg, Krantz, and Locke, 1970). The Community Health Association in Detroit reported a utilization rate of 1.5 percent, with an average number of visits per patient of 5.7 (Glasser and Duggan, 1969). Reports by insurance companies typically have been anecdotal, with limited statistics (American Psychological Association, 1968a). Insurance carriers have viewed this data as proprietary, as if publication of their experience might detract from their competitive position. In a small, unpublished study of utilization of mental health services by presidential employees, a .6 percent outpatient use rate was reported. The experience in major state employee health plans has gone unreported.

The Health Insurance Plan (HIP) of Greater New York has been one of the more prolific reporters of utilization experience (Fink and Shapiro, 1966; Fink and others, 1967, 1969; Fink, Goldensohn, and Shapiro, 1970; Goldensohn, 1972; Goldensohn and others, 1967; Goldensohn, Fink, and Shapiro, 1969, 1971; Health Insurance Plan of Greater New York, n.d.). The HIP annual adult consultation rate was 1.1 percent, with a treatment rate of .75 percent, averaging 14.2 outpatient visits per case. Utilization rates for children under age fifteen were approximately the same levels as for the adult case load, with a referral rate of 1.26 percent, a treatment rate of .86 percent, and an average of 14.5 consultations per case. Higher rates of utilization were reported for women, for those in the age range of twenty to twenty-nine, for people who had entered college, and for those who were Jewish rather than Catholic or Protestant, and white rather than black. Among the enrollees who applied for mental treatment, 65 percent were self-referred and only 26 percent of the case load of the mental health unit were referred by the HIP doctor who had been caring for the individual. These data strongly suggest that patients with emotional problems do not discuss them with their family doctor and report only physical symptoms to their doctors. Also, reliance on family physicians is apparently not an effective way to obtain needed help for emotional problems. The HEW Health Services Administration (1974) review of utilization in HMOs, found the highest rates among females between thirty to forty-nine years of age. With regard to inpatient care this report notes that 90 percent of patients needing such care can be treated within thirty days.

Green, Haar, and Hyams (1972), in studying the psychosocial aspect of medical practice, found that "a common pitfall of medical authorities is characterized by repetition of the same prescription—usually a mild sedative or psychotropic drug—over a period of years. The primary physician, trained in illness-centered medicine could not achieve much, but he kept on trying anyway—attested to by the high frequency of multiple diagnoses in this group." The primary treatment of the typical physician when confronted with emotionally disturbed patients is to provide physical examination and reassurance. The second choice is to provide an opportunity to ventilate problems, and a third choice is to give advice. Drugs are listed fourth. Typically, the physician is very cautious in the use of drugs. Although the typical physician would prefer to refer the patients with emotional problems than to treat them himself, only 31 percent of the doctors in the study referred more than two patients in a six-month period. These data support the view that relying on a primary physician to refer individuals with mental conditions is not effective in getting people needed treatment.

Goldensohn, Fink, and Shapiro (1969) reported additional utilization experience in the Health Insurance Plan. The referral rate remained 1 percent. The most common treatment was psychotherapy, with 24 percent receiving medication. Of the diagnosed cases, 70 percent were classified neurotic, with 28 percent listed as depressed, 24 percent listed as having anxiety reaction, 17 percent having adolescent behavior disorders, and 13 percent involved in family conflicts. Nearly 40 percent of the children receiving treatment had another family member who was also in treatment. Thirty percent of the diagnoses reported were classified as psychotic—either as depressed or schizophrenic.

The Health Cooperative of Puget Sound, a health maintenance organization, reported an average number of visits for mental health services at 3.98. This average was approximately the same as reported for medical consultation, 4.01 per enrollee, in 1970 (Sachs, 1972).

The early experience of the St. Louis Labor Health Institute reported that 6.5 percent of the new patients in 1958 were admitted for mental conditions, a utilization rate of .8 percent of the eligible enrolled group (Tureen, 1959). The St. Louis data on improvement rates showed that 20 percent of the sample improved with one or two consultations and that 75 percent improved after three or more consultations. The overall improvement rate was 53 percent. Improvement rates are reported by diagnosed conditions with the highest improvement rates in the nonpsychotic categories.

The vocational rehabilitation data previously presented in Chapter Four, on restorative services, compares the utilization of outpatient mental health costs to the cost per case for physical conditions (HEW, SRS, RSA, n.d.). Although vocational rehabilitation services are not entirely comparable to utilization of health services, the average case cost for mental conditions ($581) compared favorably to the average cost of all other conditions ($666).

While out-of-hospital utilization experience is not available for most federal employee plans, some previously unpublished figures for outpatient experience under the CHAMPUS program indicate a favorable utilization rate for outpatient services rendered by both psychologists and psychiatrists. In 1971, the average cost per case for outpatient services was $122 for psychologists and $128 for psychiatrists. The cost per case for inpatient services was $136 for psychologists and $256 for psychiatrists. An analysis of the CHAMPUS ten-state utilization experience for mental disorder in fiscal year 1974 is presented in Chapter Nine.

CMHC and HMO Utilization

One of the significant features of the Community Mental Health Centers (CMHCs) Act of 1963 (PL 88-164) was that the act required program evaluation of the centers. Since that time, data has slowly been accumulating on the costs of services in community mental health centers, on a fee-for-service basis, and in health maintenance organizations—HMOs (Feldman and Windle, 1973; Ozarin, Taube, and Spaner, 1972). The data accumulated on costs and utilization in community mental health centers has not been systematic and is frequently inflated or distorted by startup costs, unique overhead situations, costs of supervision, training and research (HEW, SRS, 1972a and b). Thus, comparable figures on the costs of fee-for-service, HMOs, and Community Mental Health Centers as delivery systems of mental health services are not readily available. Nevertheless, since mental health services are provided through all three financing mechanisms, it may be concluded that in the view of most health professionals, mental health services are needed as part of a total health delivery plan and are economically feasible.

Under the Health Maintenance Organization Act of 1974 (PL 93-222) mental health services for acute conditions are a prerequisite for an HMO. The HMO need not provide these services, but may subcontract to other health professionals. The pattern of subcontracting mental health services by an HMO is illustrated by the Group Health Association (GHA) of Washington, D.C. A study of 781 Medicaid patients reported by GHA (1975) did not report any unusual costs for mental conditions because of the subcontracting procedure. Although the small number of cases studied and a time frame of only nine months limits the conclusions that can be drawn from this study, the rates are probably fairly representative. The utilization rate was 2.5 percent, with an average cost per case of $103 for psychiatry and $80 for psychology. In addition, there was a 2 percent utilization rate for neurology and neurosurgery, with a per-case cost of $67. One of the primary GHA findings regarding this group was a 30 percent reduction in number of hospital admissions, a 32 percent reduction in hospitalization days, a 15 percent reduction in visits to physicians, and an 18 percent reduction in the use of prescription drugs. GHA estimated that the cost savings per patient in the GHA plan versus fee-for-service averaged 21 percent for fiscal years 1972, 1973, and 1974. Since the benefits package to the Medicaid group included dental care, transportation and prosthetic devices, GHA estimated that if the fee for these services had been omitted, as they typically are in most health plans, the cost savings would have been 37 percent. Clearly, the primary reduction in costs was in lowered hospital utilization. Since the data for mental conditions are not separated from those for physical conditions, it is assumed that the cost savings of outpatient services over inpatient services would also apply to mental health services.

In contrast to the GHA study on Medicaid patients, the United States General Accounting Office reported "that per capita payments for Medicaid patients enrolled in prepaid health plans in California exceeded the average fee-for-service costs on one of two pilot projects studied." Thus, more extensive comparative cost-benefit studies by type of service delivery model are sorely needed ("Pre-Paid Plan's Cost Exceed Fee-for-Service, GAO Reports," 1974). Spiro and others (1975) compared a cost-financed mental health group practice plan to fee-for-service insurance as dual options for a single blue-collar worker population. Over a four-year period only 2.73 percent of the population at risk used the mental health benefits (1.3 percent in the final year). Cost remained well under $.50 a month per enrollees and the "removal of restrictive deductibles and early coinsurance features produced none of the predicted dire effects" (p. 140). There was however, a marked difference in hospitalization between plans. While 34 percent of the cost financed clinic patients were initially seen as potential hospital cases, only 3 percent were hospitalized, whereas 47 percent of those seen in the fee-for-service system began their treatment career by being hospitalized.

Utilization rates of mental health services of other HMOs have been reported. The Kaiser-Permanente Group inhospital admissions for Northern California were 1.5 percent of total admissions and for Southern California were 2.7 percent (Green, 1969, 1973). These figures represented 3.2 percent and 5.5 percent of total days of hospital care, respectively. Average length of stay was 7.7 days in Northern California and 15.4 days in Southern California. Costs were reported only for Southern California and represented 3 percent of the total charges to the plan, with an annual charge of $1.36 per covered person in comparison with $44.30 for inhospital services for all other conditions. The average charge per case for mental conditions was $764, as compared to $685 for all other conditions.

Green (1969) cites the Southern California Permanente Medical Group experience with mental conditions. The group's experience over an eight-year period of serving the general population as well as federal employees led him to conclude that there is a vital need for mental health services in a health maintenance organization and that patients will not flood an HMO with unnecessary requests for mental health care. He also states that patients accept mental health professionals in an HMO the same way as they do in private practice. Green concludes that psychologists and social workers offer competent psychotherapeutic services, and that psychiatrists are no better at providing these services than are psychologists and social workers. It is interesting to note that because of the established competence of psychologists and social workers, mental health services are *not* delivered by a "team approach," but rather by an individual therapist who is assigned to each case. Green notes that "we cannot afford to have three people making a decision that one is competent of making."

The need of the team approach for the delivery of mental health services to control costs by controlling utilization is also questioned by the experience of the CHAMPUS program (unpublished, 1970-1971). Comparing the year prior to dropping the requirement of medical referral for psychological services with the year following this decision, the per case cost for psychiatry was $125 and $128, respectively. For inpatient services, the per case cost for psychology was $134 in 1970 and $136 in 1971 and for psychiatry in the same periods it was

$252 and $256, respectively. Thus, dropping the requirement for medical referral did not alter the pattern of costs per case. There was some shift in outpatient utilization toward increased services of psychologists as a result of dropping the medical referral requirement.

Fee-for-Service and Clinic Utilization

A study in Southern California remarkable for its paradoxical outcome is reported by Cohen and Hunter (1972). They compared a fee-for-service indemnity plan and a comprehensive mental health center. From 1961 to 1966 the Retail Clerks Union (Local 770) were served by the Southern California Permanente Group when a separate Mental Health Development Center was established. This center was moved into the same offices in which the union offices were housed. The Mental Health Development Center had a broad range of services and included individual psychotherapy, hospitalization benefits, both total and partial day and night hospital services, a wide range of group therapy activities related to particular problems of retail clerks and their families, family therapy, psychoeducational services (including tutoring associated with therapy to learning problems), parent-child education, vocational guidance, marriage counseling, and psychological testing and evaluation as required for treatment planning. This benefit package was intended to provide saturation level services and, not unexpectedly, it resulted in a higher frequency of utilization. But, interestingly enough, it also resulted in a lower cost per eligible person served. The program also had a low utilization rate of inhospital services. This experience of Local 770 in California was compared with the utilization of other Retail Clerks locals as part of a merged trust covered by an indemnity benefit program, and the Retail Clerks Local 889, also located in Southern California. The utilization rate for Local 770 was 6.5 percent of eligibles, compared to 1.6 percent in the merged trust, and 1.0 percent in Local 889. The cost per case was $246 for Local 770, $346 for the Merged Trust, and $453 for Local 889. The average hospital days per case was 21 for Local 770, 49 for the Merged Trust, and 31 for Local 889. Thus, the more generous benefit package for outpatient services appeared to result in a 33 percent to 50 percent reduction of inhospital utilization. The cost per year per eligible under the generous Mental Health Development Center benefit package was $13.80, compared to $3.88 for the indemnity benefit plan. The difference in the costs to the subscribers resulted in discontinuation of the center in favor of the health insurance indemnity plan. The value of ambulatory services to the subscriber appeared to be less important than the direct cost. The differential would have been approximately $16 per family per year in the indemnity benefit program, versus $70 per family per year in the mental health center. Thus, even though there was a reduction in average cost per eligible, and even though the Mental Health Development Center was more frequently used by eligible families, we are forced to conclude that the 94 percent of the eligibles who did not use the mental health services were unwilling to finance these services for the 6 percent who did use the center. Apparently, most people do not feel that they or their families are going to need mental health services during their lifetime, and that other people may be "a little bit crazy"—not them.

Another comparison of fee-for-service with community mental health centers (CHMC) costs is provided by Alexander and Sheely (1971), who compared the per-hour cost of CHMC staff with the UCR charges of psychologists, psychiatrists, and social workers in the community. At the time of the study, the going rate for psychiatrists in the community was $30 an hour, $25 for psychologists, and $20 an hour for social workers. During the diagnostic phase, the clinic cost for physician time was $41.81, for psychologist time was $32.20, and for social worker time was $29.37. The costs per hour of the treatment phase were: staff physicians—$32.06; contract physicians—$40.06; social workers—$18.26; and psychologists—$20.26. Alexander and Sheely concluded that the clinics were unable to provide services less cheaply than on a fee-for-service basis. The data also indicates that, contrary to some people's expectations, the costs of diagnostic evaluation by psychologists using tests and interview methods are not significantly different from the costs of other diagnostic services.

Costs of Supervision and Training

Another interesting feature of the presentation by Alexander and Sheely is the cost of supervision and training. It is generally assumed that the relatively low rate at which trainees are paid adds to the cost-effectiveness of the mental health unit. Contrary to expectations, after the time of training, supervisory time, and conference time were applied to the basic salaries of social work trainees functioning as full-time social workers, costs were not substantially lower. The cost per hour of service delivered by trainees was $26.34 during the diagnostic phase and $14.26 during the treatment phase, as compared to staff social workers' base of $29.52 during the diagnostic phase and $18.26 during the treatment phase.

This finding regarding training costs is also supported by a study by Karon and Vandenbos (1975). In case care by trainees, the initial hospitalization time for schizophrenics was for a shorter period than for experienced therapists. The days of initial hospitalization for the trainees were 64.5, with correspondingly less amounts of investment in psychotherapy. However, rehospitalization required an additional 81.7 days. Initial hospitalization days for experienced therapists were 86.3 and rehospitalization required 6.2 days. The psychiatric trainees were hired at $8 an hour and psychological trainees at $6 an hour, as compared to $35 an hour and $25 an hour for experienced psychiatrists and psychologists. Nevertheless, cost savings by experienced therapists were achieved by having an increased therapeutic contact with the patient during the initial phase of the treatment, with lesser investments of time in rehospitalization. The major difference in this study was only in the amount of psychotherapy that the patient received, not in the medication program or the care that the person received during the hospital stay.

For 1972, Van Buskirk (1974) reported cost per hour of

direct service rates in an established community mental health center served by sixty professionals and twenty trainees. The average cost for staff or students for long-term therapy was the same, at $35, but for consultation or short-term therapy it was $43 and $44 per hour respectively. Relative to training costs the author comments: "It is apparent that students differ wide-ly . . . . Psychology trainees . . . are efficient apprentices whose volume of clinical work repays both the community and their teachers for the investment . . . . At the other extreme are the medical students . . . [at] $108 for an hour . . . . Social work . . . students fall . . . between these extremes in cost per hour of service . . . ."

Comparison of the effectiveness of psychologists versus psychiatrist in the Karon and Vandenbos study (1975) indicated a saving of 29 percent by employing psychologists rather than psychiatrists. This saving was accounted for primarily by the difference in cost per hour for hiring a psychiatrist at $35 an hour, as contrasted to a psychologist at $25 an hour. Thus, the psychiatrists and psychologists appeared to be about equally effective in psychotherapy, achieving about an equal reduction in the utilization of hospital services. This finding and the cost differential held on completion of the study (Karon and Vandenbos, 1975). Most impressive, however, was the effectiveness of psychotherapy in contrast to medication in the treatment of hospitalized schizophrenics. Case cost for psychotherapy was less not only due to shorter duration of hospital stay but to substantially less rehospitalization in the two-year follow-up period.

Delivery Systems

Although there is great concern about treatment effectiveness, there is no consensus as to what is the most effective mental health delivery system. Historically, mental hospital programs were the first public services offered and inhospital benefits were the first insurance benefits underwritten. Inhospital coverage for mental conditions appears in over 90 percent of all new group health insurance plans underwritten. Outpatient services for mental conditions were an added benefit, underwritten with a great deal of trepidation regarding overutilization. At the present time, about 36 percent of inoffice visits to psychiatrists or psychologists are at least partially reimbursed by some third-party payment mechanism (Myers, 1970). Although outpatient services are costly on a per hour basis, the total professional time of inhospital services greatly increases the overall cost of private psychiatric hospitalization. The cost of room, food, overhead, attendants, and all of the related services creates a further cost of somewhere between $100 and $150 per day for inpatient services in urban general hospitals. By the end of 1974 and as of this time, California MediCal and the vaunted Short-Doyle local mental health programs are in serious financial crisis. The recent five-county cost-effectiveness study of these mental health services (Hanson, 1974) show why. Of all treatment episodes, about 49 percent were in inpatient services, while 74 percent of all outpatients received five or less units of service. Moreover, 38 percent of persons admitted to hospital were rated as not being impaired to the extent of requiring substantial supervision!

Until recently, the focus of concern of program planners, legislators, and actuaries has been on the costs of treatment rather than on the benefits obtained from treatment. Studies of case management pertaining to treatment effectiveness must take into account all benefits accrued from the treatment of mental conditions. Efficient case management must provide maximum treatment benefits with the cost of that treatment in mind. In the last few years, renewed attention has been given to designing effective therapeutic programs for the management of mental conditions (Burnell, 1971; Goodwin and Rosenblum, 1972; Harper and Balch, 1975; Malan, 1973; Spiro, 1969).

The orientation of mental health care has changed from custodial care to one of therapeutic intervention into dysfunction and rehabilitation of the individual to a functioning member of society. The use of psychotherapy, behavior therapy, tranquilizers, token economies in mental hospitals, and other recent therapeutic innovations (such as biofeedback) have created a new optimism for the treatment of mental conditions.

Unfortunately, program evaluations of the effectiveness of these innovations have been piecemeal, and no uniform method of reporting or recording is generally agreed on. Therefore, outcome data are often "one-of-a-kind" efforts and are difficult to compare. There have been many attempts to develop models for program evaluation. Actual collection of data is a difficult and an expensive task. McCaffree (1967) compared the costs of custodial care to intensive mental health care. The costs he considered were: (1) subsistence of patients, depreciation and maintenance of physical structures; (2) treatment costs of professional services and supplies; (3) loss of income; and (4) transfer of payments—that is, any economic costs that may result from taking an income from one unit of society and giving it to another. His data indicated that intensive care, including psychotherapy, cost 30 percent less than custodial care in the Washington State mental hospital system.

Karon and Vandenbos (1975) found that for schizophrenic patients there was also a 30 percent reduction in hospital usage when psychotherapy was used as part of the treatment program. In this study, they compared a treatment program of psychotherapy plus medication and one of medication alone. Follow-up of these patients two years later revealed that the individuals who had received psychotherapy averaged 78 days of hospitalization versus 113 for the patients who had received medication only. Thus, psychotherapy resulted in a significant cost reduction.

In a cost-benefit analysis of a token economy program, substantial cost savings were found when the system of behavior modification was applied rather than the routine custodial care patients had received. In a study by Foreyt and others (1975), seventy-four "untreatable" backward patients in a custodial institution were given rewards for demonstrating competence and for suppressing bizarre behavior. In one and a half years, 91 percent of these individuals were living in the community. During this period of time, only nine of the patients had to return to state mental hospitals, compared to a 49 percent return rate for the hospital as a whole. The entire cost of the program was a little over $29,000, with an estimated cost savings in subsistence, maintenance and staffing of $3,000,000. Thus, cost savings were $108 of costs saved for each $1 spent on a program of token economy for acceptable behavior. If these regressed individuals had spent the rest of their lives as custodial patients without therapeutic intervention, the estimated cost of custodial care for their lifetime would have been $8,800,000—representing a cost savings of $302 for each $1 spent on the token economy program.

Other attempts have been made to study the financing of various models of mental health delivery. In an important effort at program evaluation, Binner and others (1973) compared the return on investment of varying intensities of therapeutic involvement with individuals with slight, moderate, marked, and severe mental impairments. The treatment status was classified according to percentage of time the patient would actually be involved in treatment in a typical twenty-four-hour day over a seven-day week. These classifications included: inpatient, medical-surgical, day care, halfway house, evening care, home care, family care, lodge, outpatient, and special hospital leave. It was found that the best return on dollar investment occurred when there was maximum utilization of outpatient and partial hospitalization resources and a minimum use of inpatient care.

Taylor and Torrey (1972) provide support for Binner's conclusion that less intensive treatment intervention provides the greatest return per dollar invested when they state, "Psychiatric hospitalization is less effective as a means of dealing with mental problems than are a number of less expensive alternatives." Per case costs cited are outpatient crisis intervention, $162; acute hospitalization averaging 8.6 days, $943; and extended hospitalization averaging 58 days, $1,922. They go on to state, "With this emphasis on psychiatric hospitalization and use of psychiatrists as primary providers of outpatient service, traditional psychiatric care will not be able to meet the demand generated by a national coverage plan."

In another study, Halpern and Binner (1972) did an output analysis for various diagnosed conditions, including acute and chronic brain syndromes; involutional affective disorders; schizophrenia; paranoid schizophrenia; paranoid reactions and other psychotic conditions; psychoneurosis (except depression); neurotic depression; transient situational disorders, personality pattern disorders, and special symptoms; mental deficiency; and other disorders. Acute paranoid reactions and other psychotic conditions and categories of psychoneurosis showed the greatest return on investment. Mental deficiency and acute and chronic brain syndromes showed the least response. While the output value index methodology is still a rudimentary tool, it does provide a basis for comparison of costs incurred in program evaluation of various aspects of mental health services. And it is a tool that can be applied without great difficulty. It takes into account innovations and variations in local costs so that they can be compared to one another. It does not take into account increased productivity and many of the other benefits that can accrue from psychotherapeutic intervention. In its present form, it does not take into account the return to hospital rate; the costs of readmission deserve increased attention. Nevertheless, it does provide a fresh approach to cost benefit evaluation from which we can assess the state of the art.

The studies that report information on utilization and costs per condition generally tend to support one another. For example, they report that psychotic conditions cost more to treat and rehabilitate than neurotic conditions and that hospitalization is usually less effective than vocational rehabilitation for mental retardation. However, caution must be exercised in evaluating these studies regarding the costs and effectiveness of services by type of condition. Psychiatric diagnostic categories are crude classifications at best and are subject to disagreement. In a study of reliability of psychiatric diagnosis, Tarter and others (1975) found only 48 percent agreement among five experienced psychiatrists. In fact, the five-county cost effectiveness study (Hanson, 1974) found that California "clinicians are unable to clearly differentiate between Life Crisis and Mentally Disordered target groups." Clinicians did, however, show a 87.6 percent agreement on the problems manifested by the patient. Therefore, as interesting as the data on cost by condition is, it must be considered as suggestive only. Until our behavioral classification system is revised by reorienting it toward specific impairments in behavioral functions such as inability to sustain friendship (rather than generalized behavioral patterns—for example, schizophrenia) the cost benefit of treatments for various mental conditions remains unspecified. The lack of a reliable functional classification of disability, enabling proscriptive treatment planning and outcome predictions, will hamper behavioral science applications in peer review and professional standards review organizations as well.

One of the major shortcomings of cost benefit analyses has been a tendency to overemphasize costs of treatment programs rather than to emphasize benefits derived from them. The problem of obtaining outcome data has limited the execution of these studies. There are indications that psychotherapy does significantly alter the course of human events and results in increased earnings, as cited in an earlier chapter. Individuals with mental conditions receiving vocational rehabilitation have an average weekly increase of earnings of about $58 per week (HEW, SRS, 1971a). Mentally retarded individuals had increases of $47.50 per week following rehabilitation (HEW, SRS, 1971b). Conley (1973) estimates that underutilization of employable skills of individuals who are classified mentally retarded reduces the gross national product by $7,000,000 a year. Thus, rehabilitating the mentally disordered or mentally retarded into productive lives not only reduces the tax burden, but also makes these individuals contributors to the total economy of the nation. Since the purpose of vocational rehabilitation is designed to get the disabled individual back to work, the increase in earnings is not too surprising. Even the finding that the new tax monies of these increased earnings would offset the cost of treatment in one and a half years may not be unexpected. However, other studies also indicate that psychotherapy tended to increase the incomes of individuals receiving treatment even when there was no direct attempt to increase vocational or employable skills of the individual. Thus, these increased earnings are viewed as a measure of the increased effectiveness of the individual receiving treatment. Reiss (1967) studied a sample that had an average weekly income increase of $29. This increase would have offset the costs of their treatment in only one and a half years. And Ross (1968) found that the daily wages of "problem-free employees" averaged 16 percent more than wages of employees with identifiable problems. This difference amounted to about $21 per week. Employees identified as having miscellaneous problems had an absentee rate seven times greater than that of the "problem-free employees." Suspected problem drinkers had an absentee rate sixteen times greater than the "problem-free" sample. Ross concluded that aggregate corporate costs of employees with personal problems or suspected drinking problems are twice as much as those for "problem-free" employees when measured by costs of health compensation claims, number of grievances, days absent, medical and clinic visits, and efficiency on the job.

In a study (Kennecott Copper, 1972) of the Insight program for Kennicott Copper employees, the researchers found the most common problems among employees could be classified as family, alcohol, legal, marital, absenteeism, and financial problems. Once the problems were identified, about one-third of the problems were dealt with in a single interview. It was estimated that 7 percent of the workforce had difficulties with alcoholism, which is a comparable figure for experiences of other heavy industry. In a study of thirty-seven employees identified as problem drinkers over a one-year period, the company experience showed an absenteeism rate five times greater, a sickness and accident cost five times greater, and medical and surgical costs three times greater than the average employee.

Then comparisons were made between 150 Kennicott employees who undertook psychotherapy and 150 employees who were identified as needing treatment but not participating in psychotherapy. Those receiving psychotherapeutic treatment improved their attendance by 52 percent. Weekly indemnity costs decreased by 75 percent and health, medical, and surgical costs decreased by 55 percent. Consulting actuaries estimated that the employees with unresolved mental problems were 20 percent less effective on their jobs than were the average employees.

Using community resources for treatment and rehabilitation, Alander and Campbell (1975) have reported on an alcohol and drug recovery program at Oldsmobile's Lansing plant. The postprogram behavior of the three experimental groups (total of 117 employees) showed in follow-up a substantial decline in lost man-hours, sickness and accident benefits paid, and disciplinary action. Collectively, wages lost decreased 52 percent. For the control group there was an increase of 10 percent in wages lost in the one-year follow-up. Clearly such intervention pays off for both the employee and the company.

Halliday (1971, 1973), in his report on workmen's compensation for Washington State, described a situation in which individuals with relatively minor injuries accounted for a high percentage of the disability cases. These cases are frequently called "low back cases." He described a program of vocational rehabilitation, emphasizing the psychosocial aspects of the worker's conditions. The psychosocial rehabilitation of eleven cases to gainful employment obviated the necessity of pensions that would have required pension reserves of $583,000! Thus, failure to rehabilitate the injured worker is obviously more costly than any direct treatment services.

Studying payments for accidents, absenteeism, and sickness among problem drinkers, Maxwell (1959) matched forty-eight problem drinkers by age, sex, length of service, type of job, and ethnic background with two other employed groups in a given company. In order to assure accuracy of matching, he actually created two control groups. The problem drinkers had two and a half times as many episodes of illness or injury causing job absences of eight days or longer than did the control groups and two and a half times as many days of absence. The cost of sickness payments to the thirty-two problem-drinking men was $88,000 compared to $24,000 for the controls, a ratio of 3.3 to 1. For women, the sickness payments for alcoholics and controls produced a ratio of 2 to 1. Overall, problem drinkers cost three times as much in sickness payments as did the controls.

A differential occurred in the data regarding on the job accident rates of problem drinkers after the age of forty, which is almost identical to that of controls. But before age forty the problem drinkers experienced twice as many on the job accidents as the controls. Maxwell felt that the high on-the-job accident rate of early problem drinkers compared to that of older problem drinkers was because older workers were identified as accident prone and placed in an area where they would have fewer accidents. This conclusion was supported by the frequency of off-the-job accidents. Among the group of older alcoholic men, there were a total of twenty-one off-the-job accidents requiring an absence of eight days or more; there were none for the control groups. When the on- and off-the-job accidents were combined for both men and women, the total number of accidents recorded by problem drinkers was 3.6 times as large as that of the controls. These data suggest that substantial cost savings to an employer could be obtained if therapeutic intervention was provided for these individuals with drinking problems.

The United States General Accounting Office (1970) estimated that somewhere between 4 to 8 percent of federal employees suffer from alcoholism. They estimated the costs of alcoholism to the federal government because of lost sick time, inefficiency, and related conditions as ranging from $275,000,000 annually, based on a 4 percent alcoholism rate, to $550,000,000, based on an 8 percent alcoholism rate. The comptroller estimated that if an effective governmentwide alcoholism program for federal civilian employees could be installed, there would be an estimated cost to this program of $15,000,000 annually, but that the government might achieve employer cost savings ranging from $135,000,000 to $280,000,000 annually. The report also cites a statistic that 30 percent of the individuals in state mental hospitals have either a primary or secondary diagnosis of alcoholism.

Of 5,800,000 arrests in the United States each year, 1,900,000 of these are for alcoholism or for the misuses of alcohol. Thus, public drunkenness accounted for about 24 percent of the arrests in the United States, adding a significant burden to the cost and time of law enforcement. Additionally, 50 percent of the fatal motor vehicle accidents are associated with the use of alcohol. In a private communication, Richard I. Phillips, Official Community Relations Advisor at the Occupational

Programs Branch of HEW, reports that the employee with a drinking problem is temporarily absent from his work place sixteen times more often than average and is subject to the garnisheement proceedings seven times more often, and is frequently involved in job grievance procedures. He goes on to say, "However, empirical research, based on in-depth analyses of personnel and medical records, has led us to believe that the cost to employer will equal nearly 25% of the base average salary of the employee in trouble with alcohol, from the first interference with his job performance to the end of his work career. These costs are made up of such items as lost time, accidents, administrative costs, fringe benefits used, grievance procedures, and even the cost of replacing the employee."

Effective July 1974, the state of California initiated a broad-range pilot program for its employees for the care and treatment of alcoholism. Among the benefits are: up to twenty-one days of inpatient care and up to forty-five visits of outpatient care, maximum $25 per visit. Licensed psychologists are among the recognized primary providers. The project seeks to obtain utilization data and given current data, we may expect further support for therapeutic intervention.

Mental and Medical Utilization

Other investigators, notably Follette and Cummings (1967), found that medical utilization by individuals who received psychotherapy decreased significantly and that over a period of years these savings in medical utilization offset the costs of psychotherapy. In their 1967 study, the long-term benefits of therapy of one session or consultation only were not apparent after one year, but were progressively more significant over a period of five years. This change was not a function of substituting psychotherapy for medical treatments. Rather, it represented gains that were sustained after psychotherapy had been completed. Short-term psychotherapy resulted in substantial reductions in outpatient medical utilization and in savings. There was a trade-off in costs between long-term psychotherapy and outpatient medical services. Long-term psychotherapy, however, lowered costs for inpatient utilization even after one year. The obtained results were consistent regardless of whether the therapist was a psychiatrist or a psychologist. Cummings and Follette also said that their efforts in early detection of emotional problems did not generate more mental health service patients but that they were generated through routine medical practices. Among the high medical utilizers, neurotics tended to use outpatient services. Individuals diagnosed as psychotic often manifested baffling symptoms that resulted in a high incidence of hospitalization for medical diagnostic studies. Goldberg, Krantz, and Locke (1970) did a study similar to that of Cummings and Follette and found in their sample of Group Health Association subscribers that there was a 30 percent reduction in medical utilization following mental health consultation. Reduction in costs appeared to be primarily a function of less use of diagnostic, x-ray, and laboratory studies.

The study conducted by Kogan (1974) at the Puget Sound Cooperative compared base rates of utilization of medical services for treated and untreated individuals with nervous and mental disorders. He found that therapeutic intervention did not reduce medical utilization below that for the control group. He did find that there were periods of high utilization of medical services in both groups, but that they tended to subside over a period of time. Presumably, the control group had found other means of coping with their problems without using mental health services. Interestingly, however, he noted that utilization did not differ between prepaid and fee-for-service clients.

The high frequency of utilization of medical services by individuals with mental conditions has been a concern of the general practitioner for a long time. It has been estimated that perhaps 70 percent of the visits to general practitioners' offices have a major psychological component. The high frequency of utilization of medical services by individuals diagnosed as having mental conditions was clearly involved in the experience of treating patients in a rural area comprised of two villages and one kibbutz reported by Wamocher (1973). The individuals classified as disturbed averaged 8.7 visits to the doctor per year. This average was nearly two and a half times the consultation rate of those classified as undisturbed, who averaged 3.7 consultations per year. Thirty percent of the individuals studied were classified as disturbed.

In a study of the interaction between physical and mental states, Goshen (1969, 1970) found that a cost savings of 25 percent was possible if psychological conditions were routinely diagnosed along with physical conditions. This finding corresponds favorably to the findings of Follette and Cummings (1967) and of Goldberg, Krantz, and Locke (1970). Goshen (1969) reported his findings to the hospital staff and found that there was a 53 percent reduction in the costs of diagnostic procedures for psychiatric patients, representing an average cost savings of $212 per patient. He concluded that medical diagnosis without any accompanying mental evaluation merely forced the patient with functional disturbances to develop new complaints and caused the doctor to order more laboratory studies. In an earlier study of thirty-six patients with known psychiatric conditions, Goshen (1963) found that nearly $10,000 was spent on unnecessary laboratory studies only to confirm (negatively) the diagnosis already made by the psychiatrist. These costs would have offset the salary of a full-time psychiatrist for four months. These unnecessary laboratory tests were an additional expense superimposed on the costs of psychiatric services.

These data confirm the need to take into account the psychological state of the individual in any health treatment program. Failure to do so leads to unnecessary costs and wasteful procedures. Further supportive evidence is provided by Ley. In reviewing sixty-eight studies of the effectiveness of medical treatment, he found that the median of reported rates of patients not following medical advice was 44 percent! Of nine studies reviewed regarding the utilization of psychiatric drugs, again 44 percent of the patients did not follow medical advice. These findings suggest that patients' cooperation rates for mental or physical conditions are similar. In interviewing patients within a half hour after a visit to the doctor, Ley (Ley [1966, 1972a and b], Ley and Spelman [1965, 1967]) found that only 86 percent could recall the diagnosis given, only 62 percent could recall other information they were given, and only 44 percent remembered the instruction for treatment that they'd been given. A follow-up study by Ley and others (1973) found that they could increase the recall of medical diagnosis and treatment as much as 50 percent. Thus, the psychological aspects of medicine are not confined to those who are diagnosed as mentally disturbed, but rather impinge upon a high percentage of all individuals seeing the family doctor.

While these findings regarding patient cooperation demonstrate that health care is a cooperative venture between doctor and patient, we have only begun to scratch the surface of the psychological aspects of health care. In his study of 800 chronic complainers and problem patients who tended to overutilize medical services in a hospital, Lipsitt (1971) found that 86 percent of the isolated somatic symptoms represented components to a single syndrome, that of masked depression. In being given an opportunity to talk about himself to the doctor, the patient learns that his acceptance by the doctor does not depend on the intensity of his symptoms. Thereafter, the patient's complaints diminished. Thus, the patient who is a problem to the general practitioner often is merely a person for whom mental health care is indicated but unrecognized.

Carey and Kogan (1971) attempted to study whether or not the recognition of an emotional problem in a patient would affect the frequency with which the doctor referred the individual for mental health care. Emotional problems were identified in 822 of the 10,667 enrollees (8 percent) who had had health checkups. Half these cases were made known to the examining physician and half were not. Even when the doctor was informed that the individual had an emotional problem, his pattern of referral did not alter. Carey and Kogan found the general practice group was the greatest prescriber of psychotropic drugs, while the surgical specialist group was the most frequent prescriber of placebo drugs. The highest referral rates were among medical specialists, who tended to refer to other medical specialists.

It appears then that there are two significant areas warranting further development of psychological services. First, those individuals who require special handling in order to gain their cooperation and active participation in the treatment of their health conditions, whether they be mental or physical should be identified early by health programs. Second, patient management programs should be developed to gain better cooperation of patients in adhering to prescribed medication schedules and other health regimens. Providing necessary health services under a program of national health insurance without the cooperation of the individual receiving those services is naive and wasteful. Since the general practicing physician tends to ignore appropriate referral for mental conditions in a high percentage of cases and is not prepared to evaluate his patients' compliance with his prescriptions, additional means must be sought to heighten patient cooperation. The inclusion of psychological specialists as primary providers in health insurance plans would facilitate identification of mental and physical conditions and thereby improve treatment effectiveness and cost savings. Failure to include qualified psychologists as primary providers would jeopardize the adequacy and effectiveness of our nation's health care resources.

This review of the research establishes that the rates of admissions to hospitals and the numbers of outpatient services for mental conditions are not especially high and do not represent an inordinate burden upon hospital and health care programs in terms of financing or facilities. Neither do they represent an inordinate cost per case as compared to the costs of all other conditions. Mental conditions are, according to the data available, an insurable risk, deserving the same financial support of preventive, diagnostic, and treatment services as any other health condition. It can be estimated that the total combined inpatient and outpatient utilization rate, all modalities, all resources, is likely to be around 5 percent of the population at risk in any given year. Utilization rates reported appear to be fairly constant over a period of years (Brenner, 1973; Blue Cross Association, 1969; Fry, 1972; Locke and Gardner, 1969). Thus, present levels of utilization reported are approximately those that were obtained from samplings of some years ago. This fact tends to discount fears that if mental treatment gains widespread public acceptance there will be a marked increase in the use of mental health services. Failure to include mental health benefits in standard health insurance program benefits represents an unwillingness to recognize mental conditions as health problems and as part of the facts of life.

Although the data on utilization and cost effectiveness of mental health services are still far from complete, certain summary statements can be made with varying degrees of certainty. First, it is more costly to leave mental conditions untreated than to treat them. Second, psychotherapy increases personal effectiveness and results in increased earnings, which produce new tax monies sufficient to offset the cost of treatment in one and one-half to two years. Third, the cost per case for treating mental conditions is reasonable and is about the same as the per case treatment costs for physical conditions. Fourth, contrary to often-expressed reservations, the very large majority of mental health treatment episodes are of short duration. Fifth, the frequency of mental conditions in the general population requires that necessary treatment be made routinely available to the public. Sixth, utilization rates tend to be fairly stable over time, while ranging from about 1 to 8 percent for the combined inhospital and inoffice services, depending on the group. Seventh, contrary to fears, overutilization of mental health benefits has not occurred in fee-for-service, indemnification financing, cost-financed group health practice, or capitation-based financing. Eighth, medical diagnosis alone contributes little to the outcome of treatment or rehabilitation of the individual with mental problems. Ninth, dependence on general practicing physicians to diagnose and treat or refer to mental health specialists would be costly and ineffective and appears to deprive individuals of necessary mental treatment. Tenth, concomitant mental evaluation must be made in order to promote the most efficient use of health services and obtain the proper care for individuals with mental conditions. Eleventh, inpatient mental health services tend to be overutilized, while outpatient services are underutilized and underinsured. Twelfth, the mental health "team" model is a costly and inefficient means of providing mental health services. Thirteenth, the effectiveness of psychotherapy depends more on the amount of training and experience of the therapist than on the professional discipline of the therapist. Fourteenth, psychotherapy reduces high medical utilization by individuals with emotional problems masquerading as physical symptoms. Fifteenth, whether in therapy, treatment innovation, program evaluation, geographic distribution of its practitioners functional competence of its interns, or cost and duration of its clinical mental health services, psychology appears—on the record, at least—the equal of any of the other mental health disciplines. Indeed it may hold a cost-benefit advantage, range of competence, and distributional advantage, enabling it to better serve the general population. And sixteenth, treatment of mental conditions can result in significant cost savings and other benefits to industry, including increased productivity and reduced absenteeism; payments in sickness benefits; costs of medical utilization to health service benefit plans; accidents on the job; grievance, garnisheements, and other paperwork costs; employee turnover; and training costs.

12

The Legislative Process

A. Eugene Shapiro, Herbert Dörken,
David A. Rodgers, Jack G. Wiggins

Legislative processes are complex and, to be successful, require a measured balance of public interest, professional objective, the support of advocacy, congruence with the mood of the legislature, and consensus. A pragmatic view is reflected in the saying, "Politics is the art of the possible." The passage of laws and regulations (which when adopted have the force of law) follows a legislative process. Events do not "just happen." Initiative is taken, objectives are delineated, sponsorship is gained, compromises are considered, and selective maneuvering guides each bill through to its destination.

In a bicameral (two-house) legislature, any bill accepted for introduction is first assigned to a committee in the house of origin. In state legislatures, it typically passes through two or three committees on that side (the third deals with fiscal implications, if any) and then goes to the floor (entire senate or entire assembly). The bill then proceeds through several committees on the other side and then to that floor. If the bill is amended in the second house, then it must go back to the house of origin for concurrence. Finally it goes to the governor who can veto. On the federal level, in Congress, the comparable course is sketched in Figure 1, prepared by the Council for the Advancement of Psychological Professions and Sciences (CAPPS). Separate (companion) bills, however, can proceed

Figure 1. The Path of a Bill in Congress

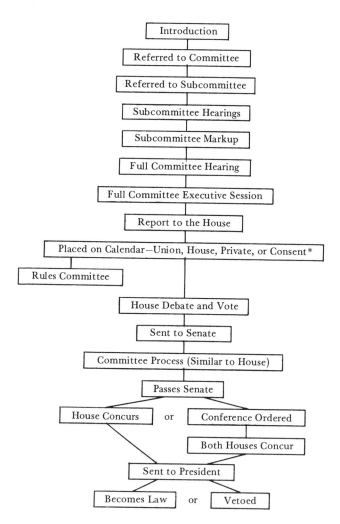

NOTE: A bill can originate in either the House or the Senate, except for certain revenue bills, which must originate in the House. This chart traces a measure originating in the House.

*Most bills of interest to psychology either appropriate or authorize money and are therefore on the Union Calendar.

through the Senate and the House of Representatives, go to conference committee for reconciliation of any differences and on to the president. Each elected representative has staff assistance and all major committees have staff. Legislative staff are responsible to the elected representatives (their employer) and they in turn to their constituents. Committee staff (distinct from legislative staff) develop substantial expertise in the areas of their concern and, because of this expertise and their appreciation of the potential interrelatedness of a bill to other law or pending legislation, may often exert substantial influence on its destiny. Legislative advocates (the "third house" or lobbyists) also monitor all bills in their area of concern.

If we consider how many hands each bill passes through and the potential for amendment or defeat, we can see that the handling of health legislation, which typically carries significant social and fiscal implications, is hardly a casual matter. Therefore, we will be describing the legislative process in some detail, in order to provide useful perspective for influencing that process.

In establishing legislative contact, one usually has initially but five or ten minutes to make an impact and get key points across. If one is referred to staff, more detailed and concrete communications, supplemented with written material, are then in order. If one initiates follow-up by letter the legislator, instead of providing a form response, will usually provide a more articulate reply that he or she will usually review before releasing. Quite naturally, the legislator will be more responsive if there is a prior, friendly, personal contact or if the issue raised is central to his or her platform. Selection of legislators and contact psychologists should therefore be based on known resources.

Given a receptive legislator and a responsible (preferably constituent) psychologist seeking law that is in the public interest, it is usually not too difficult to get a bill introduced. But to steer a bill through to enactment is a long process requiring close involvement, trade-offs, potential compromises, the gathering of support, defense against opposition, and appreciation of the climate of the times. The committees to which the bill is assigned and the stature of the authors or cosponsors are also important factors that will govern its progress. Whereas advocacy is typically public, opposition is often privately lodged. Careful monitoring and the development of a communication network are part of working with the legislative process.

Few state psychological associations have the personnel and resources successfully to sponsor and monitor more than several bills a year. Bills of concern to psychology will be introduced and passed only if psychologists are willing to devote the necessary time and energy. However, until the establishment of CAPPS in 1971 and the Association for the Advancement of Psychology (AAP) in 1973, psychology had no advocacy organization at the federal level. Few state associations have the assets to afford more than a part-time legislative advocate.

Psychology has, moreover, allocated relatively minimal fiscal resources to advocacy. The total operating expenses for CAPPS in 1974, including staff, amounted to just less than $124,000. On January 1975 the APA council, in its most concerted effort ever, only voted to donate $50,000 to AAP for 1975. And most state associations, if they have any legislative funds at all, are dealing with several hundred or thousand dollars annually, with occasional special "assessments" for a particular cause. Given the low fiscal input, psychology has done incredibly well in the legislative arena in recent years.

Unfortunately, the majority of psychologists (in contrast to physicians, chiropractors, dentists, or optometrists) seem to be disinterested and naive regarding the legislative process. Typically, psychologists are preoccupied by professional, scientific, and academic work. But the legislative process can and often does change the extent and nature of a profession's involvement in health care delivery and of its training and research support bases. Legislation can support, thwart, or broaden horizons. To become fully professional, psychology must therefore become aware of and intervene in the laws that shape our working environment.

Legislative Effectiveness: The New Jersey Model

Since 1967 the New Jersey state association has achieved consistent success in its legislative efforts. Five major pieces of legislation were introduced on behalf of psychology—and successfully passed into law. In addition, a number of bills have been amended to include properly the profession of psychology. Although many other states have also been successful with legislative efforts, the New Jersey Psychological Association has developed an organizational style that most effectively uses its own membership. This style, of course, has kept legislative costs to a minimum.

New Jersey is a small state, ranking forty-sixth in size geographically. But it is a relatively populous state, ranking eighth in the nation and first in density of population, with a total population of 7,168,164 according to the last census. The statehouse in Trenton is centrally located. The bicameral system of government (an assembly and a senate) reflects population distribution. There are eighty assemblymen and forty senators. New Jersey is made up of twenty-one counties. Population varies widely within these counties, from a high of 932,526 population in Essex County to a low of 59,554 in Cape May County. The more populous counties, following the one-man, one-vote rule, have a larger representation in the state legislature.

Now, the fact that the distribution of licensed psychologists is nearly parallel with the general population, first suggested by Whiting (see Chapter One), can prove to be a substantial asset. The gross maldistribution reported for some of the health professions is not a problem for psychologists. To the extent this parallel holds true in a particular state, psychologists are in a position to have political influence throughout the state and to have ready access to all legislators.

Organizing for Action. Perhaps the single most important element in any successful legislative effort is the choice of the person to chair the legislative committee of the state psychological association. This individual must be committed to the passage of a designated bill and willing to dedicate his or her energies towards that goal. No other committee calls for this degree of singlemindedness of purpose and dedication. This person must have the goal-oriented character of a successful insurance salesman. The chairperson also needs a *strong* committee, people who are willing to devote a considerable amount of time and work to the legislative process. Members should represent important elements within the profession and should reside in well-distributed geographical areas. With the mandate of the state association, the legislative committee can both develop the bill(s) and implement the legislative (political) strategy.

In the state of New Jersey, the legislative committee appointed county chairpersons. Thus, each county had at least one psychologist with responsibility for legislators in his own area. This approach had several advantages. Each county chairperson was not a distant lobbyist, nor a representative of a large organization, but rather the legislator's constituent, whose family and friends vote at elections.

The essence of any legislative program is a sound piece of legislation. Of course, no single bill can meet all conditions for all time. However, time and energy can be saved if the legislation is properly constructed in the first place. It is extremely important, therefore, to review related experiences before writing the bill. Previous legislation should be reviewed and reevaluated. Experiences in other states, both good and bad, should be reviewed. The central office of the APA, a repository of much excellent information on the subject, should be consulted. In addition, the APA Committee on Health Insurance (COHI) and the APA Committee on State Legislation (COSL) are also excellent resources.

When related material has been thoroughly reviewed, the intent of the legislation and the public benefit clearly defined and the potential danger signals earmarked, a competent attorney, experienced in writing legislation, must be consulted. In New Jersey, the shortcomings of not having adequate legal counsel for early legislative efforts were soon evident. For example, though New Jersey passed the first bill (1968) in the United States that mandated reimbursement for the patients of licensed practicing psychologists by insurance carriers for covered conditions under major medical plans, the state association had modeled the bill after one successfully promoted by the optometrists of New Jersey. However, it became necessary to introduce three bills in 1972 in order to close all the loopholes that had not been anticipated. In reality, in 1967 there were no other models to work from since this optometry bill was the first law of its type. The state association assumed that the optometric model would work for psychology.

After a bill is properly written, the choice of a legislator as sponsor can be an extremely decisive factor. Careful selection at this point in time can save many headaches along the legislative route and improve its reception. One might assume that psychologists, with their scientific background and their knowledge of people, *should* have a relatively easy time in the legislative arena. But one must know who the legislators are, whom they represent, what their relative power is within their own political party and within the legislature, and what their "track" record is. Will the sponsor who introduces the bill enhance it, or will he become a liability? Is he on a committee to which the bill may eventually be sent, so that his strong voice can help the committee's deliberations? Is he sufficiently interested in the bill to push it to its conclusion, or will he merely introduce it, as a public relations gesture? Many bills are introduced, but relatively few become law. Will the sponsor be willing to encourage bipartisan cosponsorship—an important factor for vote getting? Such necessary political considerations merit close evaluation.

After the introduction of legislation, someone close to the statehouse and close to the sponsor-legislator should follow the bill through the legislative morass. It is very easy to lose control of a bill. A bill may wind up in a committee, never to be heard from again. It may be amended from the floor and so weakened and distorted that it would be best not passed at all. Or it can be defeated. To avoid these pitfalls, constant monitoring of the sense of the legislature is necessary. A properly chosen sponsor is the best person to guide the bill through the legislative maze. Effective communication between the bill's sponsor (or his legislative aide) and the state psychological association legislative chairperson (or designate) is essential to timing in the use of the psychological association's support and its development of effective testimony.

The New Jersey state psychological association has operated with the philosophy that state psychologists are the most effective tool. The association has followed Stanley Milgram's

"Small World" concept (1967). Milgram found that on the average, five intermediaries, individuals who have a first-name relationship, will enable contact with anyone in the United States. The association sought to find out who knows the legislator on a first-name basis and has consistently found that the "acquaintance" resources within our profession amaze us. Invariably some psychologist, or a good friend of a psychologist, or a relative of a psychologist has an excellent personal relationship with a needed legislator. And almost invariably, when the chips are down, the association has been able to find someone who knows a key legislator well enough to make a *personal* appeal. Personal, meaningful, direct appeal, on a face-to-face basis, not only conveys the message most effectively, but also often provides immediate feedback as well. Establishing this personal contact became the task of the twenty-one county chairpersons. It was their responsibility to try and secure an "aye" vote from each of their representatives. The legislative committee kept an ongoing tally, through the county chairperson, as to the number of assured "aye" votes that would be recorded when the vote was taken. The degree of interplay between the psychological association and the sponsoring legislator was crucial. Unless sufficient "aye" votes were guaranteed, the bill would not have been brought out for vote.

The New Jersey association has used lobbyists sparingly. In one of our early legislative efforts, the association expended a total of $500 for a part-time lobbyist to help the psychologists understand the political scene and to guide them at critical points in the legislative procedure. In effect, he was more of a teacher and mentor than an active lobbyist on behalf of a particular bill. For the most recent legislative efforts, the association employed a law firm that also engaged in lobbying. However, although the lobbyist had an important effect, the most important and critical issue was the impact of the individual psychologist. Each state association, will have to consider the fiscal and personal involvement of its psychologists, their distribution, and the location of the capital (among other factors) in deciding whether a lobbyist is necessary.

Whether a lobbyist should be used or not often depends on

the makeup of the state. Some state associations, such as New York, have made major use of a well-paid, well-respected lobbying firm. For example, in New York, a majority of the psychologists are in New York City, whereas the state legislature is in Albany. Such distance adds difficulty to the monitoring process. A paid or full-time lobbyist may be necessary, in such circumstances.

A lobbyist can be an excellent asset or a costly hazard. Close consideration must be given to how well the lobbyist can represent psychological interests, who else he represents, and what respect he commands in the legislature. It is rare that a lobbyist alone can get a bill for psychologists passed. The profession simply does not have the power or the influence to arm any lobbyist to such an extent. The legislative power of psychologists lies in their ability to make personal contacts as constituents of their representatives and to represent the public interest, and in their personal integrity and the soundness of their legislative proposals.

One of the important roles of the state association's legislative committee is to review, combine, and disseminate appropriate support material for the legislative effort. This material may have to be distributed in various forms to legislators and key psychologists. Obviously, since legislators are busy people, the material sent to them must be succinct and straightforward. It must also reach them in such a manner as to compel their attention. The material for the psychologists can be more comprehensive. Each psychologist who meets with a legislator should be familiar enough with the situation to be able to respond directly to questions that are raised. The legislative committee may want to develop a catechism of questions and answers, or even engage in role playing so that the psychological representatives are thoroughly informed. The representatives should be able to speak from experience and to underscore the public advantage of the proposed legislation. Furthermore, whatever material is transmitted must be reliable and absolutely accurate, since the legislative process proceeds on shared objectives and trust. Inaccurate information will destroy support for future legislation.

In the communication process and in developing support letters from recognized public agencies, professional and lay associations or their offices can prove effective. Direct testimony from the officers of such groups can also be important. However, legislators assign mass letter writing and telegrams by psychologists minimal impact and consider such efforts stereotyped self-interest correspondence.

The referral of a bill to a committee of the legislature for consideration is the beginning of the legislative process. The committee to which a bill is assigned is often of critical importance. If the members of the committee are "hostile" to the bill, rather than "friendly," it may never be released. On the other hand, a sympathetic membership will facilitate its release from the committee with a recommendation for favorable action. Here again, the sponsor may play a key role in committee assignments. Now, the legislative committee and particularly the chairperson must be prepared to testify at the committee hearings and to distribute supportive and explanatory material to the committee membership and staff. At hearings, proponents and adversaries of the legislation are heard. Although it has been the practice of the New Jersey association to have a written statement available for the committee where possible, it is by far preferable to have the bill's author (legislator) introduce it and speak on its behalf. Testimony may or may not be necessary. When indicated, it is often best to submit a statement for the record, confining the verbal presentation to a summary of the highlights and leaving time for questions. The New Jersey experience has been that most hearings of state legislatures are informal and that much can be accomplished in the question-and-answer exchange. It is well to be prudent and follow the principle of parsimony, exchanging needed information, but mindful that the purpose is to win friends and votes—not necessarily arguments. The tenor of interaction should always be at a high level of regard for others.

Psychologists Under Medicaid. To fully understand how psychological services became available to New Jersey Medicaid recipients in 1973, some history of legislative developments that established psychology among the health providing professions is necessary. Only in 1967 were psychologists licensed in New Jersey, although prior to that time they had functioned in many professional settings, including private practice. A second major legislative event transpired one year later—New Jersey became the first state to pass a law mandating that insurance carriers reimburse their insureds for covered conditions when treated by a licensed psychologist functioning within the scope of his or her practice. (In 1974 this bill was amended to remove some loopholes and to make it stronger and two related bills were passed, one covering individual policyholders and the other covering medical corporations such as Blue Cross and Blue Shield. The original legislation had only covered group disability insurance policies.)

Against this background, in 1972 the executive committee of the New Jersey Psychological Association requested that its insurance committee (chaired by the author), explore the inclusion of psychologists as providers of services under the state Medicaid program. A special subcommittee of the insurance committee was established for this purpose.

Now, according to the enabling federal legislation, each state may include the services of any health profession recognized by state statute in its Medicaid plan, which is filed annually. Therefore, the decision on including psychologists, if not preempted by state law or regulation, can be made by the administrative authority for the state's Medicaid program. Generally, no state legislation process is necessary. The most pertinent permissive sections of the Social Security Act, Title XIX, are 249.10 (b)(4), (6), and (13). (See Chapter Five for further details on Medicaid.)

In 1973, representatives of the New Jersey Psychological Association, with their legal counsel, met with the commissioner of institutions and agencies. Also present was the director of the Medicaid program, his assistant, and the director of the department of mental retardation, a psychologist. In fact, it was through this psychologist that the meeting was arranged. Such a meeting could otherwise have been arranged; however, the cordial, task-oriented focus of that meeting was largely a product of this psychologist's presence, an internationally known figure in the area of mental deficiency who has been a respected civil servant in the state of New Jersey for many years.

The psychologists were under the impression at the initial meeting that the director of the Medicaid program had been instructed by the commissioner to determine the feasibility of including psychologists under the state plan. The director, however, believed that the decision to include psychologists as providers of services should be made by the state legislature, not by the department; that is, a law should be passed. After further discussion (occasionally heated) the commissioner maintained that the decision was his and that he would not pass the buck to the legislature. The director of the division of medical assistance and health services (department of institutions and agencies) then delegated negotiation to his medical director and staff. Several productive meetings were held. The major stumbling block was recognition of psychologists as *independent* health providers. It appeared that there would be no difficulty in including psychologists if medical referral (not necessarily supervision) would be acceptable to the profession of psychology. Another major concern of the medical administrator was identifying those licensed psychologists competent to provide health services. He was concerned that some psychologists who were licensed but not necessarily qualified to provide health services, would function outside of their scope of competence and seek reimbursement under Medicaid. Finally, there was concern that by admitting psychologists, other professions, such as chiropractors, would seek similar rights.

In response, the association presented strong opposition to a referral clause. It attempted also to reassure the administrators that as an independent profession, while having collegial relations with other health professions, psychologists could not accept mandatory referral as a condition of relationship to the Medicaid program. The association suggested that mandatory referrals can lead to featherbedding, that is, an unnecessary referral to a physicial for rereferral to the psychologist in order to meet such a reimbursement criterion. In the discussion, the association noted that functioning beyond levels of competence could hold true for any profession and that the professional association would be available to monitor any abuses of the program should they occur. All psychologists seeking to be providers under Medicaid would have to fill out applications (as did other professionals) indicating their professional background. In addition, the association offered its services to establish a liaison committee to assist the commission in provider selection. The concern that the admission of psychologists as providers of services might open the door to other professions, was one the association felt should be decided on each professions' merits.

Another concern, which did not prove to be a major problem, was the fact that a number of psychologists with master's degrees had been licensed in New Jersey. Originally, the Medicaid medical administrators felt that only doctoral graduates should be able to provide services. They pointed out that all of their providers of services, regardless of professional category, had doctoral degrees. The association informed them that psychology is a new profession and that the licensing law grandfathered a number of highly competent professionals who had a minimum of eight years of experience (in 1967 when the licensing law was passed) and who at this point in time had a minimum of fifteen years of experience. In addition, a threatened suit against the administrators by a group of master's-degree licensed psychologists seemed to have a distinct impact on the decision to include them as providers.

Finally, a psychologist's services manual was agreed on. It is consistent with services manuals for other provider professions in New Jersey. One of the more interesting developments that occurred in New Jersey was the creation of the "psychologist specialist" category (as differentiated from the psychologist generalist category), to maintain consistency with other professions in which a differential fee schedule was established for those providers of services who were board-certified or board-eligible. The two-level categorization does not seem to have created any undue hardship. However, a number of psychologists in this state have now begun to apply to the American Board of Professional Psychology (ABPP) for diplomate status.

As of this writing, the inclusion of psychologists under

New Jersey Medicaid services has been in effect close to one year. No major problems have been encountered. Psychologists, as in the past, have proven to be responsible and ethical professionals. The inclusion of psychological services in the state Medicaid program has clearly added to the scope of comprehensive health care for needy individuals in New Jersey.

On a more personal note, we would like to share our own experience in dealing with the Medicaid population. Most private patients are at least moderately affluent, or else are covered by a major medical policy that provides significant mental health benefits. Previously, physicians who referred patients to private practitioners had been unable to refer their Medicaid patients, since the services of psychologists were not covered. These patients, then, had to be referred to a clinic. Since clinic facilities, at least in our areas, are often inadequate, undue delays and often inadequate services prevailed. We have personally found the Medicaid population to be particularly rewarding. After many years in the private practice sector, one may lose contact (other than for periodic voluntary clinic services) with this portion of the socioeconomic population. In many respects, serving the Medicaid population continually confronts one with the basic reality of our complex society and hopefully keeps us from a more narrow perception of the world as often seen in private practice.

Some California Legislative Experience

Just as society is in a continual state of change and evolution, so too is professional practice. Guidelines for both are reflected in law. The legislative process is not one that can be ignored, nor can it be dealt with on a one-time, total-solution basis. It is a continuing process in which psychology must participate as a major reality of professional life. To round out the illustrations in this chapter, examples have been selected of rational compromise, veto, amending onto major bills, and regulatory hamstringing of legislative intent.

Freedom-of-choice Legislation. In the mid-sixties psychologists in California and some other states succeeded in gaining recognition for their services, at least in some major group health plans (disability policies) underwritten by several major insurance carriers. With this encouragement and a sympathetic legislator (Assemblyman Leo Ryan, now in Congress), the California State Psychological Association (CSPA) introduced a bill amending the insurance code to require recognition of and direct consumer access to licensed psychologists in policies including benefits within the scope of psychological practice. The insurance commissioner, following the bill's passage in 1969, issued a memorandum of instruction so advising all carriers doing business in California.

Psychology's enthusiasm with this accomplishment, like New Jersey's, was soon dampened, however. First, a significant number of companies carried on as if the law never existed or offered various rationalizations such as "We insure medical costs, not health services," or "The master policy was issued out of state." Second, despite entreaties, the insurance commissioner refused to enforce the law maintaining the statute, and his advice was "sue the company." The cost, the many carriers licensed in California, and the time required made such litigation impractical. Third, the CSPA soon learned that the insurance code does not cover health care service plans (for example, Blue Shield, HMOs, and FMCs) that are regulated by the government code in California. Fourth, the CSPA learned that hospital corporation contracts and self-insured employee welfare benefit plans, although within the province of the insurance code, had not been included in the bill.

So the CSPA went back to the drawing boards with a senator who had demonstrated concern about mental health services and consumer benefit. California Senator Nicholas Petris previously had coauthored the Lanterman-Petris-Short Act (community mental health services legislation). In 1974 the senator introduced SB 2002 at the request of the CSPA. In California, many Blue Shield plans are written by Physicians Services, Inc., a stock insurance company. Together with the insurance companies these plans collectively cover about two-thirds of the market, one-half of this written out of state. The HMOs, FMCs, employee benefit plans, and Blue Cross or Blue Shield policies comprise the one-third balance. SB 2002 as introduced would have covered everything. No sooner was the bill calendered, however, than representatives for the Kaiser-Permanente Group and the state department of health both pointed out that as written, the bill would place an unworkable condition upon health maintenance organizations. Such a condition had not been intended and a friendly amendment was agreed to: "Nothing in this section shall be construed to allow a member to select . . . [a psychologist] . . . who is not directly affiliated with or under contract to the health care service plan . . . ." The bill cleared its first committee but got stuck in its next committee. The CSPA soon learned that the insurance industry objected to the extraterritoriality provision and in effect had the bill "locked up." Discussions with industry representatives were to no avail for passage in that form. With elimination of the out-of-state issue section, they "would have no problem with the bill." The CSPA opted for "half a loaf" rather than fight with no chance of winning.

The bill then finally cleared its senate committees and the floor. On to the assembly. The log jam of bills slowed progress and resulted in some unexpected shifts in the hearings calendar. The bill came up in its second assembly committee on short notice and at a time when the author could not be present. It proved to be a "short" (incomplete) committee and the bill was voted down. Six signatures from committee members, necessary for reconsideration, were secured, not without a lot of foot work, but with the senator present at the rehearing the bill passed on to the ways and means committee. The session was almost at a close and the bill, calendared for the final day, was ultimately heard and passed at 10 P.M. Finally, the governor signed the bill.

At every committee where the bill passed, in both houses, the senator was present to promote and defend the bill, with CSPA representatives present as backup. Though seldom needed, they had to be there, as well as at the prior meetings with the senator's staff, senate counsel in drafting the bill, discussions with those who introduced amendments, and prior contact with the key legislators (votes) on every committee.

There was no medical opposition though this possibility had been checked out with their representatives and several other groups. In summary, SB 2002 did not "slide" through. Nor does psychology have any overpowering presence in the legislature—far from it.

Workers' Compensation. California provides a broad range of compensation, health services, and rehabilitation for workers injured in the course of employment. Psychologists are not included in two pertinent sections of the labor code. Broadening the definition of *physician* by one word—*psychologist*—and enabling an employee to require a psychologist to be included in the physician panel from which he or she might select a practitioner would achieve the desired result. Senator George Moscone introduced the bill in 1973 and carried it to passage. It even received support from staff in the State Department of Industrial Relations. But during the session, the senator became a declared candidate for governor in 1974. The CSPA bill and most others sponsored by the senator were vetoed by the governor. With a new, consumer-oriented governor, the bill has been reintroduced in 1975 (AB 2538, Paul Carpenter) and is certainly congruent with the recommendations of the National Commission on State Workmen's Compensation Laws.

Competency Determination. Both the chairperson of CSPA's Legislative Committee and the author were well known to the chief of staff in 1974 for the California assembly ways and means committee. Extended consideration had been given over several years to the matter of "sanity" in criminal procedures with wide bipartisan agreement to change various provisions in the penal codes and welfare and institutions codes pertaining to criminal proceedings to relate instead to a person's "mental competence." Committee staff were giving consideration to final markup changes for the bill's fifth amendment, sixteen months after its introduction. The CSPA learned of this staff meeting by coincidence and an informal on-the-spot discussion was arranged with the staff committee. In a discussion lasting not more than five minutes, they agreed that licensed psychologists do indeed have expertise in the matter and a further amendment was written into AB 1529 (Frank Murphy), which a few months later, in the fall of 1974, became law, providing a major entry for psychologists in criminal law proceedings in California. The key section reads: "A trial by court or jury of the question of mental competence shall proceed in the following order . . . . The court shall appoint two psychiatrists, *licensed psychologists or a combination thereof. One of the psychiatrists or licensed psychologists* may be named by the defense and one *may be named* by the prosecution" [amendment emphasized]. There are two messages in this success. First, it is critically important to monitor all ongoing pertinent legislation. Second, the development of trust and a working relationship with key staff facilitates objectives of long-run mutual interest and can open up opportunities not otherwise available.

Regulatory Amendment. A legislature generally prefers to write a law broadly, leaving the implementation of legislative intent to regulation and administrative directive. This broadness allows more ready accommodation to change over time. At times it is possible to gain specific inclusion in regulation where the statute is only permissive. This fact was illustrated in the HMO Development Act of 1973 (see Chapter Three). At other times, regulations can undo a seeming legislative victory.

In 1957, California became the third state to pass community mental health legislation. This, the Short-Doyle Act, called for psychiatric direction when the program director was not the county health officer or administrator of the county hospital. Back in 1970 a national review (Dörken) showed that psychologists were or could by law be directors of local community mental health programs in three-quarters of the states—but not California. However, in 1967 the Lanterman-Petris-Short Act and the Short-Doyle Act revised set parameters for major change in mental health service delivery in the state. The Lanterman-Petris-Short part gave primacy to the county mental health plan and protection to the civil liberties of patients. It was pioneering legislation that broke new ground. The CSPA participated in the development of this law. The revised Short-Doyle Act throughout used such phrases as "the professional person in charge" and "mental disorder." The Conference of

Local Mental Health Directors, given approval authority over regulations, lost little time in defining the professional in charge as a psychiatrist and by regulation insured that every service— outpatient, rehabilitation, consultation, and the rest of the ten services in federal law, would be defined as psychiatric services. In 1971 Senator Petris gained passage of SB 725, remedial legislation that opened the position of program director to psychologists and social workers as well as psychiatrists, when not held by the county health officer or hospital administrator. The Conference of Local Mental Health Directors redrafted their regulations to honor the letter but not the spirit of the law by insuring that all services would still be under psychiatric direction. The next year, the aggravated senator introduced SB 542 calling for elimination of the conference's approval authority—later dropped on assurance of conference cooperation—and requiring that, "No regulations shall be adopted which prohibit a psychiatrist, psychologist or clinical social worker from employment in a local mental health program in any professional, administrative or technical positions in mental health services." As of August, 1975 the implementing regulations still had not been formalized, though a draft was agreed to by the CSPA in the fall of 1974. There was word that they might be set for public hearing in October, 1975. The CSPA has had no little difficulty gaining timely response from the department of health, since personnel have been shifted in their assignments. AB 1762 (1973) and AB 3475 (1974) of Assemblyman Frank Lanterman were also passed, reinforcing these requirements, among other things. Public hearing of the proposed regulations was finally scheduled for November 14, 1975.

In other instances, failure to achieve desired change may not be due to law or formal regulation, but to administration policy or agency interpretation. The outcome may run the gamut from preferential selection of certain vendors to determination of the qualifications of appointees to senior positions in the absence of required specifications. The formal requirement for the state director of mental health, for instance, may be no more than a well-educated person. But the pressures are usually strong for the appointment of a psychiatrist.

Scope of Legislative Concern

Involvement in the legislative process is not a one-time, simple matter. Regulation adds operational specifics to law, and so can administrative directives. The courts can provide a further clarification by order, injunction, award, or decision. And there is always room for formal or informal negotiation or agreement within the law. The increasing recognition of professional psychologists as independent collegial health practitioners will be achieved in part by negotiation, in part through statutory change, and in part through the judicial process. These three approaches should proceed concurrently at both federal and state levels so that the extent of precedence achieved generates a "common law" recognition of psychology in all prepaid and insured health services. To further illustrate the complexity, the manifold ramifications of health insurance, involving governmental and nongovernmental groups, and at national, state and local levels are charted in Table 1.

Accord Within Psychology

The examples of legislative action in this chapter have had broad accord within organized psychology, a factor critical to success, though by no means guaranteeing it. There are, however, issues on which psychology finds itself divided. The outcome, then, is usually a stalemate. Licensing for practice, perhaps because it defines and regulates psychology per se rather than opens new vistas, has been a subject on which statewide accord has been achieved often only with internal struggle and difficulty. In fact, even though psychologists are now licensed or certified in forty-seven states and the District of Columbia (see Chapter Three), the struggle is not over. Laws departing from the doctoral standard were passed in recent years in Pennsylvania and Iowa. Many states are considering update revisions that always bring issues to the fore anew. Congress itself is defining psychology by the legislation it passes (see Chapter Three).

Then, Ohio's experience in reaching an internal consensus

Table 1. Organization of Health Insurance Activities

	Governmental			Nongovernmental			
	A. Executive	B. Legislative	C. Judicial	D. Insurance Carriers	E. Certification Bodies	F. Consumer Groups	G. Citizens Groups
I. National	Federal employees health contracts Regulations of laws (Medicare Title XVIII, vocational rehabilitation, and so on) Community mental health services Veterans administration outpatient service Consumer protection agency CHAMPUS	National health insurance bills Amendments to Medicare Other health enabling legislation (Rehabilitation Act, HMO Development Act, and so on)	Class action suits	National Association of Blue Shield/Blue Cross Plans, also HSI/MIA Teachers Insurance and Annuity Association Health Insurance Association of America	Professional associations Joint Commission on Accreditation of Hospitals, Psychiatric Facilities, and so on National Register of Health Service Providers in Psychology	Corporations engaged in interstate commerce Unions	National Association of Mental Health White House conferences

Table 1 (*continued*)

	Governmental			Nongovernmental			
	A. Executive	B. Legislative	C. Judicial	D. Insurance Carriers	E. Certification Bodies	F. Consumer Groups	G. Citizens Groups
II. State	Medicaid, Title XIX Crippled children, Title V Vocational rehabilitation Disability insurance Title II State employees' insurance Workers' compensation	Practice laws Freedom-of-Choice laws Mandatory mental health coverage Facility licensing	Writ of mandamus re: insurance commissioner Workers' compensation claims Right to treatment, amicus curiae briefs Class action on restraint of trade Suit for public hearing	State Blue Cross/Blue Shield Insurance company home offices	Professional associations training accreditation	Unions headquartered in state	State health, mental health/mental retardation organizations
III. Local	Professional standards review organization Health service areas	Legislative contact and advocacy (federal, state and local officials)	Small claims courts resolution on reimbursement Malpractice suits	Contact with claims offices Foundations for medical care (FMCs) Health maintenance organizations	Credentials committees Hospital staff privilege	Union contracts Fraternal benefit societies	Local health/mental health organizations and advisory boards

while concurrently addressing external opposition in order to gain passage of their licensing law in 1972, highlights most of the common "splits" within psychology. If Ohio's experience has some claims to uniqueness, it is because the experience came late in the legislative process (the forty-sixth state association to secure legal recognition).

Briefly, the historical situation in Ohio was that medicine had systematically opposed the licensing bills that the Ohio Psychological Association (OPA) had been proposing, and had succeeded in blocking passage of several previous bills. The primary concern in 1969, however, was with the school psychologists, who had blocked passage of an OPA bill in 1967 and 1968. The Ohio School Psychology Association (OSPA), a vigorous and politically alert group representing predominantly master's-level school psychologists, well-trained and well-respected in their own field, favored master's-level licensing and opposed unilateral doctoral licensing such as recommended by the American Psychological Association (Committee on Legislation, 1967). In the midst of an intraorganizational effort at conciliation, OSPA unilaterally had a compromise bill introduced into the state legislature, by a very strong Democratic senator, who was in effect the patron of educators and school personnel in Ohio. The professional psychologists of Cleveland moved vigorously to abort the bill and to lock it irretrievably in committee until after the legislature recessed for the fall. The school psychologists thus discovered what they had been teaching OPA for years, that it is easier to kill a bill than to push one through.

The problem ahead was relatively simple and yet quite complex. A weak bill could not be sold internally. A strong bill that did not take into account the sensibilities of other groups could not be sold externally. A new bill was very carefully drafted initially, yet it subsequently went through probably twenty major revisions and no less than fifty to one hundred minor revisions in its subsequent passage through the legislative process.

School psychologists clearly posed a special problem, as competently trained, professionally ethical, conscientious sub-specialists who for the most part were not abusing their subspecialist role. Of course, master's-level licensing is contrary to APA standards, although the issue of master's-level subspecialty licensing has never really been adequately dealt with by APA governance. But a danger of subspecialty licensing is the possibility of expansion of the subspecialty to be a general license in practice if not in theory, especially when the processes and definitions of psychology are so difficult to specify rigorously. The final wording for a subspecialty school license at the master's level became: "Practice of School Psychology" means rendering or offering to render to individuals, groups, organizations, or the public any of the following services:

> (1) Evaluation, diagnosis or test interpretation limited to assessment of intellectual ability, learning patterns, achievement, motivation, or personality factors directly related to learning problems in an educational setting; (2) Counseling services for children or adults for amelioration or prevention of educationally related learning problems; (3) Educational or vocational consultation or direct educational services. This does not include industrial consultation or counseling services to clients undergoing vocational rehabilitation.

Anyone who has read the definition of psychological practice in almost any of the state statutes must be impressed by the preemption of such sweeping activities as "application of principles, methods, or procedures of understanding, predicting, or influencing behavior, such as the principles pertaining to learning, conditioning, perception, motivation, thinking, emotions, or interpersonal relationships . . . ." Any law pretending to be a licensing law that attempts to throw a licensing blanket over these activities will certainly be disputed in court. Many of the clearly technical dimensions of professional psychology indeed should be available to the general public and should not be the exclusive province of psychology, even though the psychologist should explicitly have legal access to such procedures. Only a relatively few procedures should truly be restricted by the licensing provision.

Resolution was achieved by the exemption: "Nothing in this chapter shall restrict any person in any capacity from offering services of a psychological nature provided they neither hold themselves out to the public by the title of psychologist or school psychologist nor utilize psychological procedures that the State Board of Psychology judges by uniform rule to be a serious hazard to mental health and to require professional expertise in psychology." This language appears to make the Ohio law probably the only truly enforceable licensing law on the books and allows the tightest certification law in the country. No psychology groups except federal employees are exempted from the essential provisions of the law, except for the teaching of psychology and research when these do not otherwise involve professional practice in which patient or client welfare is directly affected. Thus, state employees, employees of nonprofit or charitable organizations, and similar groups that are often exempted come under the regulation of the Ohio statute.

With the opposition of most organized groups neutralized through appropriate language in the bill that did not really change its basic nature, the most threatening opposition then came from within psychology itself, in the form of a few academics who had not taken the trouble to express themselves during, or to be a part of, the long, arduous preparation of the bill. They essentially were arguing an iconoclastic position, for no regulation of the profession, and did not impress the legislators with their arguments.

One further comment about this process should be made. When a legislative committee is drafting legislation, there is not time to review every wording change and every policy position with all of the psychologists of the state, or even with the association executives or even perhaps with the legislative committee itself. Decisions and literally momentous decisions for the future of the profession must often be made by a single individual in a single moment. That individual *must* be *thoroughly* cognizant of the various attitudes and concerns and biases of his or her colleagues, of the legislative group, of the potential adversaries to the legislation, and of the short-term and long-term implications of almost any and all wording changes that might be made. That person must then be willing and able to act for the best interests of the profession and the public rather than for any private interests or private concerns of his or her own, and the integrity of such action must be apparent in the final product. Some few determined people with ability must be available to exercise the necessary integration and leadership. One cannot ignore the practicalities of impact and flexibility that come from skillful individual leadership exercised with integrity.

Even passage of a major bill is certainly not the end of the necessity for vigorous legislative involvement. Upon entering the legislative arena one discovers that any profession must function within the fabric of statute law before it is a really effective profession. How well psychologists as professionals enter this arena will determine how effective the profession is in serving both the public and ourselves. Such activity is and must remain an indispensable part of our professional existence.

13

Impact of Peer Review on Future Health Practice

Russell J. Bent

How we see the possible sets limits upon how we might achieve the actual. Let us focus on a possible direction professional psychological services may take in the next decade. First let us clarify the definition of a profession. A profession renders, to the public, services that are complex and demand specialized training and skills. Traditionally, the services rendered by the professions relate to sensitive or significant areas of human concern. Furthermore, the consumers of professional services cannot make informed judgments about the adequacy of the services rendered. For these reasons the profession sets high standards for the selection, education, and training of their members and sets procedures for accreditation. Most importantly, standards of ethics and practice are established within the profession.

Over the past several decades organized psychology has worked very hard to establish the essentials of a profession and has done so quickly, relative to other professions. Only recently

This chapter is based, in part, on a paper that was delivered as the Invited Address, Division 12, Section 2 of the American Psychological Association at the 82nd Annual Convention, New Orleans, August 30 to September 3, 1974.

has psychology established our professional independence in several federal health and insurance statutes. Licensed psychologists are recognized as a primary health profession in the Rehabilitation Act of 1973. Freedom-of-choice legislation has been enacted in twenty-three states and on the federal level in the newly enacted PL 93-363, perhaps the most significant legislative recognition thus far accorded psychologists. Psychologists have initiated a uniform procedure to define the profession's health providers through the establishment of a *National Register of Health Service Providers in Psychology* and the first organized APA standards for providers of psychological services recently have been approved by the profession (1974). Psychologists have not one, but two legislative advocacy organizations and even their national organization, largely organized to meet yesterday's priorities, is beginning to respond to today's problems, occasionally even to tomorrow's possibilities—the process of building, influencing, and creating. So, as a profession psychology has arrived.

Of course, psychologists are not the masters of their destiny. For example, legislatures have insisted, as has psychology, on statutory regulation with sanctions against grossly poor practice. Regulations, guidelines, job descriptions, and such hover around the profession like moths around a flame. Relationships between professions—and with administrative agencies, multiple regulatory bodies, planning commissions, various levels of the informed and uninformed public, with local, state, and national legislative bodies—produce a dizzying conglomeration of variable forces that further test the profession's identity. Social priorities and pressures and other groups with their identities and territory confront psychology. How do psychologists compromise or adjust standards and interests to the consumer, to the restraints of priorities, of limited resources, of the social good? How do psychologists react to and affect the macrocosm? In the next decade or so, in what direction might psychology move to insure that the qualities of excellence in the profession survive and make a major contribution to society while providing conditions conducive to the profession's enhancement and development.

Psychologists often find themselves in conflict, with a duty to meet professional standards and interests and an equally compelling duty to adjust to realities outside the profession and in the consumers' behalf. The profession must combat those forces that threaten professional practice and integrity as well as combat those forces that would make professions myopic and narrowly territorial. Jean Jacques Rousseau posed the general question centuries ago when he said: "The problem is to find a form of association which will defend and protect the whole common force, the person and good of each associate, and in which each, while uniting himself with all, may still obey himself alone, and remain as free as before" (1947 [1762], pp. 14-15). This problem is fundamental. As Chris Argyris recently has pointed out: "One of the most urgently needed intellectual crash programs is that of developing new designs of technology, administrative controls, and leadership styles that will lead to organizations capable of being productive and self-renewing, of being effective, and of encouraging self-actualization among the participants" (1970, p. 4).

Psychologists in the service field have shown little awareness of and made slim contributions to the crucial organizational aspects of services, the so-called delivery, systems, and operations problems. The focus of organizational psychology has been either on conditions leading to organizational effectiveness or on conditions leading to individual satisfaction and fulfillment in organizations. Little has been done toward studying conditions that integrate individual goals with organizational objectives, although some exciting theoretical work has been done. How can the microscopic professional goals and macroscopic organizational goals and resource constraints merge in optimal service delivery? This major problem faces our society today in national health proposals and in the pressures to be accountable, to evaluate what psychology is doing in relation to specified objectives. Until recently, many professionals, whether in agencies or in practice, have spent money without accounting to the public for effectiveness. In the process they have minimized the problems, procedures, and controls related to cost. Small wonder that the price of health services has been highly inflationary. The shortage of dollars, however, is bringing a long overdue insistence on cost-benefit relationships and accountability and will force all professionals to take harder, more realistic looks at effectiveness.

Now that psychology has established independence as a profession, a major effort should be made toward a new emphasis in development, a goal in the macroscopic environment, toward objectives beyond the professional, in which the strengths of the profession are seen as means to achieve specified, socially related objectives. Now that psychology has developed independence and a manpower resource of national significance (Dörken and Whiting, 1974), a major effort should be made to construct a more productive and appropriate model for clinical psychology or what more broadly might be thought of as the professional (practicing) psychologist (see Chapter Fifteen). An adequate model should help answer questions such as: How should psychologists organize to bring their contributions and services to the public? What is their model for service delivery? How effective are their professionals? How do psychologists maximize effectiveness at the least cost? Let us consider a model that may be productive in answering such questions.

Peer Review

First, let us make an assumption related to the organization of health and human service systems in the decade ahead. There will be a continuing breakdown of the large bureaucracies. The organizational trend is toward what Alvin Toffler (1970) has called *Ad-hocracy*—that is, a movement toward mobile, flexible organizations with an emphasis upon horizontal, not vertical, lines with less sharply defined, porous roles or divisions of labor. Warren Bennis has spoken of such organizations as "temporary systems" with people differentiated not vertically, according to rank and role, but flexibly and functionally, according to skill and professional training (1966). We will see an increasing collapse of the hierarchy, a shift from up-and-down to sideways, groups working as coequals, the decision maker and the task taker often merging. What we know as the large state, federal, and agency service hierarchies will not be "where the action is." But, the considerable number of psychologists who may leave the bureaucratic botch are not advised to enter independent practice. As John Gardner has pointed out, "It is becoming increasingly doubtful that a large number of small unaffiliated operators can survive in a world of gargantuan organizations. Thus it becomes critically important to explore any possible arrangement by which the individual or small organization can enjoy some of the benefits of large-scale organization without any substantial loss of autonomy" (1964, p. 85). If the future of professional psychologists is not in the large bureaucracy or in solo practice, where is it? How should psychologists organize themselves over the decade ahead to affect, as service providers, those who would profit from psychological services?

The most viable answer for the professional psychology of today and tomorrow is the peer review organization model. This emerging concept has the most relevance, innovative potential, and significance for professional psychology. The organization and development of peer review is new, fluid, and open to ideas —virtually made for the implicit and explicit ideals psychology as a profession has tried to develop. It is a service delivery management system that can integrate development (research) and continuing education with practice. For clinical psychology it would be a vast improvement over the weak, vague, generally irrelevant scientist-professional model to which psychologists have subscribed, a model that has never been integrated into an applied service system with any significant impact. Despite over twenty years of the scientist-professional model, for example, a major problem that continues unabated, with some exceptions in behavior modification, is the lack of integration or diffusion of research results into practice. How do psychologists change service patterns or service provider practices after a good evaluation or research effort has indicated the way to develop? Similarly, the relevant questions of practitioners seldom receive meaningful attention from researchers. How can psychology really get it all together? The creative development of organized review by organized psychology is the timely and relevant way to bring discipline and practice together.

As an introduction to the emerging peer review concept it

would seem helpful to present a short history of PL 92-603 (the Bennett Amendment). This law originated with proposals by the American Medical Association (AMA) for the development of peer review organizations (PROs) by state medical societies. As a mechanism of cost control, PROs were incorporated in the AMA's Medicredit plan, which was introduced in the House of Representatives in 1970 as the Health Insurance Assistance Act of 1970. The PRO proposals of the AMA were also forwarded to Senator Wallace Bennett of Utah for introduction in the Senate. He, in turn, forwarded the proposal to the Senate Finance Committee staff for comment and analysis, particularly in terms of the Medicare and Medicaid programs. The Committee believed the AMA plan was unduly limited. After two years of reworking the amendment was passed in the Senate and accepted in the House after several further modifications by a House-Senate conference committee. The final 1972 legislation expanded the limited PRO concept offered by the AMA and extended the peer review concept to what was named the Professional Standards Review Organization or PSRO. This legislation authorizes the secretary of the Department of Health, Education and Welfare (HEW) to designate specific national service areas by January 1974 and to establish conditional contracts for PSROs in each area by January 1976. The PSROs will monitor the appropriateness of utilization and the quality of institutional services provided to beneficiaries of the Social Security Act (Medicare, Medicaid, and Maternal and Child Health programs). A PSRO is not required to determine the reasonableness of fees or costs, but "only provides standards for the dispensation of federal funds" according to a federal court in Chicago in dismissing a constitutionality suit of the Association of American Physicians and Surgeons. With concurrence of the secretary of HEW, PSROs have the option to monitor ambulatory services. Since it is intolerable to develop two standards of care—tax-supported health care and nontax-supported health care—strong pressures are brought to bear on the private health care sector to conform to the same standards as in the public sector and vice versa. For example, pressure is already developing to require the public agency staff to meet the same licensure standards of private practice. As increased public tax dollars move into the health system, pressures mount to develop a comprehensive health system even though not a single national health care program has been passed. It is critically important to realize that PSRO is connected to Medicare and Medicaid and that the operational aspects and experience gained from these programs will most likely serve as the base for any national health program.

By watching the development of this legislation, and particularly by reading the interim guidelines of the provisions of PL 92-603, dated March 1974 and entitled *PSRO Program Manual,* one can see a comprehensive, liberalized, innovative development of peer review that can have a revolutionary effect on our health delivery system. The development of PSRO is a serious federal strategy to distribute equitably the quality and quantity of health care services without price constraints. The new emphases that recently have emerged in the PSRO concept deserve serious recognition. Fundamentally, PSRO is a managerial method that gives the health professions opportunity for self-regulation. It may be the health professions' greatest (and last?) opportunity to regulate the health system in the face of less workable, restrictive, bureaucratic controls.

Some matters of substantive importance also should be recognized in the evolution of the PSRO concept. Peer review is not claims review, which primarily occurs after a service is rendered, generally reviewed by a clerk, to verify the existence of a contractual obligation on the part of the payor. Only occasionally in claims review is the appropriateness of service evaluated. Psychology's involvement in peer review has been summarized recently by McMillan (1974), who has observed that until now, our approach to peer review has been along claims review lines. To date, psychology has been most concerned that the provider is certified and that costs are reasonable, but has seldom been concerned about utilization or quality control. Review has been regarded as a retrospective, "after-the-service" process. Here too, however, quite rapid changes are occurring in organized professional psychology. Not only is a professional standards review committee providing leadership and coordination, but in

1974 professional standards review committees were established in forty states and in the District of Columbia, and a directory of these committee chairpersons has been distributed by the American Psychological Association. And standardized "request for review" forms were already in use a year earlier, in 1973.

The peer review process that has emerged in the PSRO concept is unlike claims review. It is not designed to be retrospective but rather to be prospective and concurrent—that is, to authorize services before they are rendered and to control continuous, current services according to norms of practice and collective professional judgment. The *PSRO Program Manual* (HEW, OPSR, 1974) states: "PSROs however, will assume full responsibility for all decisions having to do with quality, appropriateness and necessity of services. When a PSRO is carrying out its review responsibilities there will be no retroactive review potentially leading to the denial of payment (Sec. 701)." Further, "In each of its review activities the PSRO will use norms, criteria, and standards which are useful in identifying possible instances of misutilization of health care services or of the delivery of care of substandard quality. The PSRO is responsible for the development and on-going modification of the criteria and standards of the norms to be used in its area (Sec. 702.2)."

The APA's Board of Professional Affairs, at the request of its Committee on Health Insurance, established the Health Benefits Task Force. The task force's purpose was to describe an optimal range of mental health benefits within a national health care plan. The management of these benefits was seen by the task force as a critical component of the benefits themselves. The task force subscribed to the peer review process as central to the management and development of the mental health delivery system. Chapter Eight of this book is a full account of the task force's report. In that report, peer review is defined as:

> . . . a process which applies collective professional judgment to determine and monitor the necessity, quality, and effectiveness of mental health services. Peer review's major function is a managerial one de-

signed to develop and insure the effective and efficient distribution of mental health services within resource availability constraints and with the least interference of bureaucratic control. Peer review differs
from the usual retrospective claims review process in
that its emphasis is upon prospective and concurrent
review. Peer review is directed toward the coordination and most effective use of resources and educa-
tional/consultation outputs which modify the mental
health providers' performance. Particularly when
mental health services are provided in non-institu-
tional settings, peer review should be more flexible to
adapt to a different pattern of practice than in most
physical health services. A more functional definition
of peer (the service a mental health provider renders)
might often lead to the mixed discipline composition
of a mental health peer review committee, particularly in group or interdisciplinary practice settings.

The task force definition is quite consistent with the developing
PSRO definition and should foster congruent development of
the review process.

Although at this point psychologists are not afforded full
membership in the PSRO program, psychologists are perceived
as independent nonphysician health care practitioners in the
PSRO. As stated in the *PSRO Program Manual* (1974):

730.31 *PSRO Responsibility.* The PSRO is responsible for assuring, over time, that non-physician
health care practitioners are involved in the establishment and on-going modification of norms, criteria
and standards for their discipline. This is true both
for PSRO direct development and when development
is delegated to hospitals.

709.18 *PSRO Development of Norms, Criteria,
and Standards.* The PSRO will be expected to utilize
non-physician health practitioners for the development of the criteria and standards and the selection
of the norms to be used for the review of the care
provided by such practitioners. For those conditions

in which care is often provided by physician and non-physician practitioners, the norms, criteria and standards should be jointly developed.

520.08 *Non-physician Health Care Practitioner Review Eligibility and Restrictions for Review.* Non-physician health care practitioners must be involved in the PSRO review of care provided by their peers. Continuing recruitment of reviewers of each type shall be performed to ensure a large and representative pool of eligible reviewers. PSROs shall involve these health care practitioners in the development of standards and criteria for their peers and, to the extent it is efficient and effective, have such practitioners perform the review where the care is provided by one type of practitioner (e.g., dentist, optometrist, podiatrist).

In summary, then, peer review is a rapidly developing concept that crosses professional lines. It has broad implications for professional psychology. Some of the activities expected in organized peer review will be enumerated. Review by members of the profession would evaluate the quality and utilization of services rendered by that profession. Organized review would cover the relevance of individualized services to each patient's specific needs; the volume of services provided; the appropriateness of the outcome objective, including dispositional planning; the appropriateness of the services provided to populations as a measure of the comprehensiveness of services; and the collection of data on individuals receiving service and of data describing the performance of a provider (individually and organizationally) in the total services rendered to a population.

Organized peer review would establish implicit criteria by recognized experts and service providers and would establish increased reliance on the development and application of objective criteria, norms, and standards. Here, the methodology of the discipline could be integrated into day-to-day professional activities, mutually enhancing each other. Outputs of peer review would be integrated with provider education, their impact measurable in terms of improved professional practice. Under organized review there would be an overview of the total service system in a designated area and an analysis of provider service to that total service system area. Program-related research relevant to significant process or outcome service variables would be systematically carried out. Program research would be supported with a national interchange of efforts, results and problems.

The demands of the peer review organization model will make it necessary to develop a more standardized, universal language and explicit criteria. Consider what effect an organized peer review model might have on the profession of psychology. Some general effects would be to focus our concern and responsibility on a "community" or a specified population of consumers—that is, the total range of persons who need services, an "at-risk" population. An interesting account of a service organization facing problems posed by an "at-risk" population and a peer review management system is reported by Newman (1974). Further, peer review would redistribute major resources in the discipline. Such a move would involve the diffusion of research into application, which is generally neglected in psychology and other disciplines (HEW, HSMHA, 1971*b*). Psychology's parochial and often irresponsibly narrow definition of research would be expanded to focus upon problems and methodology related to service and service delivery, such as evaluation and including organizational-management problems (Bent, 1974; Raush, 1974). Identification and accountability of service providers would have to be supplied, as well as their characteristics and patterns of activity. Moreover, psychology would be responsible for developing continuing educational efforts to improve and correct provider services. Criteria, norms, and standards of the profession would be connected closely with the practicing profession itself. An increased awareness of costs, resources, and other constraints and of innovation would be inevitable. A closer relationship would be promoted among service organization, methods, educational facilities, and training. The often narrow resources in which most of practitioners are trained would be expanded, opening up a comprehensive base of resources for training and educational purposes. Such relationships would underline the social responsibility and accountability of psychologists to the broader public in our pluralistic society, increasingly emphasizing that psychologists are accountable to more than the universities, students, and journals.

The task force recommended that the management and administration of mental health services within a national health plan be based on the basic assumptions of consumer freedom, a pluralism of service provider systems, program management organizations, peer or program review procedures, and on state and national policy and standard setting councils. The administration of mental health benefits should be interwoven with the delivery of these benefits, to develop organizational effectiveness. The administrative process of bringing the mental health service benefits to the consumer should be managed in such a way that administration is the program and the program is administration. The consumer should be able to "spend" benefits as he or she chooses within an environment of authorized mental health providers and provider management organizations wherein the provider is subject to a review of both the quality and quantity of the services he delivers. Although the review should be carried out by small committees of the providers themselves, the development, the support, and the organization of the review process itself should be coordinated through specialized management organizations designed to support the review process and to involve consumers in the total mental health benefit program.

The specialized management organizations of provider (peer) review would assume that varied mental health providers can be more effective and efficient if combined into voluntary, cooperative systems. Of course, authority and management support must be vested in some organizational structure. The proposed mental health program management organization (MHPMO) is conceived of as an autonomous, corporate body whose board and staff plan, manage, and implement the comprehensive mental health service benefits authorized under the national health care plan. The MHPMO would elect its board of directors and indicate its functions, organizational structure, management staff, provider arrangements, "subscriber" population, and other relevant information within broad state and federal regulations. It would also be responsible for such activities as provider support and education; the development and implementation of the review process, including technical assistance and monitoring of the review process; standardized data sets and automated management information applications; provider and patient monitoring; evaluation and program research studies; coordination activities; community education; operations information; procedures for assuring compliance with basic standards and benefits; and cost-utilization studies and assurances of proper fiscal management. Further, the MHPMO is seen as a dynamic, flexible organization encouraged to develop diverse organizational patterns and to be maximally adaptable and innovative in providing the mental health benefits. Essentially, it is the successful attainment of the benefit objectives and not the organizational structure of the MHPMO that would receive emphasis on evaluation. Consumer satisfaction as reflected in their selection of MHPMOs also would serve as an important evaluative index of effectiveness.

Levels of Review: Outpatient Services

In order to manage the peer review process it is necessary that: (1) relevant standards, norms, criteria, and results of evaluation be developed; (2) levels of review be established, developed, and directed by authorized providers; (3) the decisions of review be timely and not delay service (less concern with usual, short-duration services and more emphasis on extended, more costly, intensive service methods); and (4) peer review for long range impact be fundamentally consultative or educational, constructively involving the provider. Most review systems have been developed primarily for hospital services. Outpatient review in mental health, particularly peer review, is almost virgin territory.

A peer review model does not begin with a rationale to develop some sort of "criteria sets" based on psychiatric diagnostic categories. Such a starting point is rejected as a disastrous dead end, given the gross unreliability of psychiatric diagnostic categories and the selection of service methods for these categories. It is not surprising, for example, to find that no relationship exists between length of outpatient treatment and diagnosis. (Bailey, Warshaw, and Eichler, 1959; Garfield and Affleck, 1959; Rosenthal and Frank, 1958). It seems utter folly, then, to pretend that a reasonable reliability of psychiatric diagnostic categories exists or even that the unreliable categories are accurately reported, and to expect that realistic utilization criteria (let alone quality care criteria) can be the product of such pretense. Instead of starting with diagnosis, one must focus on the objectives of service by authorized providers and the methods used to achieve those objectives in an optimal fashion. Starting from this strategy, empirical norms and other criteria can be developed by peer review operations and from standardized, automated, data-processing procedures.

A time-and-resource application framework for outpatient services could be divided into three practical management levels based on estimates of the general outpatient utilization patterns of at-risk populations. The three apparent cutoff levels would be 1 to 6 units (a unit being equivalent to the service effort of an individual therapy or assessment "hour" by a mental health professional); 7 to 15 units; and some specified number of units beyond 15. These service or benefit levels might be called the short-resource level, the intermediate-resource level, and the high-resource level. Monitoring and peer review need to be appropriate and practical for each level.

In the short-resource level, the benefits would be 1 to 6 units of service. These units might include, but not be limited to, determination of disability, consultation, crisis service, or brief psychotherapy. The provider should be able to render these services without prior peer review authorization and without prior filing of a service plan. Using empirical methods and expert professional judgment, numerous usual methods or procedures used by mental health professionals in the initial phases of client service or in short-duration services would be established and be assigned resource (cost and effort) unit relative values. Service providers, authorized according to national standards (which meet or exceed state and local statutory standards), could use their professional judgment and skills quite independently within the resource constraint of the short level (6 units of service). The provider could determine if he is able to provide a reasonably positive mental health service(s) with his client in order to meet generally or specifically agreed on (between provider and client) objectives. These objectives should be written, clear, attainable within the units of service anticipated, agreed on between provider and client and briefly evaluated on the termination of the short level by the provider and (when possible) by the client. These procedures would be reported, after short-level services are completed, to the MHPMO on a brief (one-page) document, along with basic identifying data. The MHPMO would forward payment or credits payment (depending on the service system structure, whether salaried in an organized setting, or independent fee-for-service) on receipt of the document. Information related to each short-level service pattern would be filed in a computer. Computer programs could output periodic client and provider profiles as audit documents to be compared against empirical, short-resource service patterns. Individual client and provider profiles could be randomly audited for accuracy, including "spot-check" site visits. Provider profiles that deviated from reasonable norms and standards would be referred for review by a peer reviewer. If the reviewer could not make a recommendation, the provider would be reviewed by a peer review committee. Depending on the size and structure of the MHPMO, a specific appeals procedure would also be available, if necessary. The peer reviewers and peer review committee members would be selected on a rotating basis from the authorized mental health providers in the MHPMO. Reviewers would be reimbursed for their review activities at a level consistent with reimbursement for a similar amount of time in client service activities. A peer review committee would consist of from four to six authorized providers. The principle review function at the short level would be assessing appropriateness of resource level use and quality of care. Although indirectly the reviewer would influence cost by recommending educational and other corrective action for deviant provider profiles, at no point would the review process be concerned with unit dollar costs. Rather, it would be concerned with quality and appropriateness of the service and level of resource use intended to meet the objectives specified—as related to empirical norms and criteria, professional standards, and MHPMO guidelines for overall cost impact.

It is estimated that the majority of outpatient services would occur at this short level with minimal use of prospective and concurrent peer review. By "batching" the provider reporting at the short level, both reporting time and data processing time would be minimized. Further, in mental health outpatient services where large, diverse, at-risk populations are involved, underutilization rather than overutilization has been the problem (Reed, Myers, and Scheidemandel, 1972). Most cost and quality care concerns have been at the high level. Many practitioners, especially those in independent practice, have biased their practice toward serving groups prone to high utilization and believe, because of their experience, that at-risk populations will be or should be high utilizers. Until recent years mental health service providers were most influenced by a psychoanalytic orientation favoring high-level resource use for most clients. New orientations and emphases on group and family therapy, behavior intervention methods, crisis and goal limited therapy, to mention but a few examples, have moved the field away from heavy reliance on the high level of resource use.

Now let us return to the assertion that services for most clients would fall into the short level when a representative at-risk population is considered. Garfield (1971) has summarized the findings of investigations studying the number of psychotherapy encounters and has concluded "that in those studies that excluded all those patients who were offered therapy but refused it, and included only actual therapy patients, the median number of interviews was between five and six." The analysis of the annual statistical reports for psychiatric clinics in New York and Maryland show that the majority of patients are seen for less than 5 interviews (Gordon, 1965). These findings are replicated in other large-scale surveys such as those by Rogers (1960) and by the National Center for Health Statistics

(1966). According to this latter survey a total of 979,000 persons consulted a psychiatrist during the year ending June 1964, with an average number of visits per person of 4.7. The Rogers survey of 10,904 referrals in six states found an average number of 12.9 interviews. Utilization data from insurance carriers show similar results. For example, even in liberal plans with minimal deductibles and coinsurance, such as the United Auto Workers in Michigan with an at-risk population of 1.1 million persons, the average session rate was 8.5. A recent analysis of the Civilian Health and Medical Program of the Uniformed Services (CHAMPUS), with benefit population of 7,800,000, the largest single group health insurance plan in the nation, found that the average number of visits for outpatient mental health services in this liberal benefit program ranged from 7.4 to 11.9 visits (Dörken, 1974a). The recent (Hanson, 1974) California five-county evaluation found that 74 percent of all outpatients received less than 5 units of service and only 5.2 percent received over 11 units. The average number of outpatient visits per year in five sample federally-funded community mental health centers showed an average of 69.2 percent of the clients used 5 or less visits with 89.8 percent of the clients using 15 or less visits (National Institute of Mental Health, 1974). In a study by the American Psychiatric Association of private-office psychiatrists (reported in the NIMH study and based on 1973 data of a sample including analytic and ecclectic psychiatrists), the results showed that the mean number of visits for patients first seen less than a year ago in a year period was 22 visits, with a median of 12 visits. When nonanalysts only were considered under the same criteria, the mean number of visits was 15 with a median of 9 visits (National Institute of Mental Health, 1974). The private-office psychiatrist providers, expected to be the provider subgroup most likely biased toward a high utilization pattern, do not show excessive high utilization patterns. In conclusion, it can be expected that in a national health plan with a variety of authorized service providers and a heterogeneous at-risk population of clients using outpatient services the majority of clients will utilize less than 6 units of service.

In the intermediate-resource level, the benefits would be 7

to 15 units of service. At this level the provider would have to file a plan, subject to peer review, detailing service objectives and procedures to meet those objectives. In effect, the provider would follow virtually the same procedures as in the short level, but at any time after the first unit of service and before the seventh unit of service a service-by-objective plan would have to be filed with the MHPMO and would have to receive prior authorization to assure reimbursement. The mere filing of the service plan should force the provider to more carefully plan and consider the intermediate level of resource use. Further, with more knowledge and involvement of the client, intermediate-range planning should be more precise and warrant closer quality control. At this level of review, trained mental health technicians would randomly review a moderate percentage of the filed plans to insure their completeness and their clarity. Deficiencies or questionable plans would be forwarded to the peer reviewer. Computer profile patterns, as in the short level, would be employed with spot checks and deviant patterns handled by the peer reviewer, who could decide an issue or refer it to the full peer review committee. Again, if necessary, an appeal process would be available.

The intermediate level was set at 7 to 15 units for a number of reasons. Empirically, the evidence does not show as clear a "break" in utilization at around 15 units as it does a break at 5 or 6 units. However, there is much evidence that a significant "batch" of utilization occurs between 7 and 15 units so that from 70 to 90 percent of outpatient services will have occurred by unit 15, allowing a reasonable size increment for the development of profiles, norms, and criteria.

Finally, the high-resource level would apply to benefits beyond 15 units of service. Such long-term or unusual service plans requiring more than 15 units of service would be managed by prior review authorization made under close, individualized peer review. In addition to prospective review, concurrent review cycles would also be established for authorized high-level plans that are more extensive or for which significant outcome questions are raised in peer review. Each plan would be reviewed by a peer reviewer together with individual and provider profiles and presented by the reviewer, with recommendation, to a full peer committee for final authorization. The same procedure would be followed for concurrent review cycles. It is expected that providers would be requested to appear before the peer review committee with moderate frequency at this level of review. Excessively high unit values and plans that have high probability of needing review would require providers to appear before the full review committee. Although guided by standards, norms, and criteria, peer review of high-level resource use would depend on the collective professional judgment of the authorized providers serving as reviewers. This level of review would be consultative and educational, fostering a collegial level of interchange as might exist in smaller organized care settings. It would serve a continuing educational function for reviewer and reviewed. An example of what such a level of review can be with independent providers is reported by Newman (1974). It is estimated that 2 to 3 percent of all service plans would be high-level plans that would require provider appearance before the full peer review committee. As with other review levels, an appeals process, if necessary, would be explicitly provided.

The provider appearing for review would be reimbursed for his time in the review process with modest compensation for travel. The high-level peer review system would compensate all providers for their participation in service review, thus reducing excessive "staffing" time in many organized service settings and expanding such collegiality for providers functioning in more isolated, independent settings. Peer review is not punitive but a process integral to proper professional functioning. Upon the authorization of high-level service plans, a monthly progress form would be completed by the provider, indicating the service rendered and an estimate of progress toward the service objective as judged by the provider and the client. Reimbursement would follow upon receipt of this form. Information also would be abstracted for computer processing to aid in continually establishing the empirical aspects of review and service evaluation. Obviously, this peer review system model would rely heavily on the automated information filing and processing.

Thus, the attempt to develop a systematic procedure to

bring mental health services or benefits to the consumer, especially under a national health plan, involves broad management and development issues. The key concept both in the federal development of the professional standards review organization and the task force on mental health benefits is that of organized peer review. In effect, the development of a peer review organization model for psychology would bring us into the creative, leading edge of service delivery. The initial concepts presented here of peer review, the mental health program management organization, and levels of outpatient service review, provide developmental concents on which organized psychology may build.

14

Professional Autonomy and Medical Supervision

Russell J. Bent

Some health insurance carriers require that services rendered by a psychologist be carried out under the supervision of a medical doctor. Similarly, a number of state and local governmental agencies in particular, require M.D. supervision. Very rarely does the M.D. have to qualify as a psychiatrist or have any meaningful psychiatric experience. In effect, such insurance guidelines produce the paradox that M.D.s not trained or experienced in mental health work must supervise psychologists highly trained and experienced in mental health work. These policies, then, require that one profession's practitioners exercise controls over another profession's practitioners. Although organized medicine generally has en-dorsed such a concept of control, a significant number of M.D.s see the obvious unreasonableness of such a position.

Patients of psychologists are indignant about having to pay for and suffer the inconvenience of having to see an already overworked M.D. to satisfy this control requirement. There has been a gradual and continual deletion of these supervisory regulations through administrative and legislative action, but progress has been slow. To many nonpsychologists the M.D. super-

Republished with minor revision and some additions by agreement of the American Psychological Association, from the *Journal of Professional Psychology,* 1972, *3*, 351-356.

visory regulation seems plausible. But this regulation needs more than a cursory examination.

Those who support medical referral and supervision believe that this practice is a way of controlling overutilization and keeping costs under control. But there is no consistent evidence to indicate that psychological services are overutilized. On the contrary, experience with the mental health benefits of Aetna, Prudential, Occidental, and Massachusetts Mutual insurance plans, as provided by psychologists, presented no problem from an economic, actuarial, or managerial standpoint. The representatives of these companies so testified before the Senate Sub-Committee on Compensation and Employment Benefits in November 1971. Moreover, to require a medical referral or impose medical supervision upon a psychologist-client relationship adds unneeded professional visits and featherbeds the cost of services. There is another unsound economic effect of the medical referral requirement. By arbitrarily restricting the availability of psychological services, it affects the supply-and-demand balance that can inflate the rates of physician and psychiatric services.

Such considerations were evident in the Senate subcommittee hearing on S 2619 (McGee). Now law (PL 93-363), it assures free choice and direct access to clinical psychologists for covered services in all federal employee health plans. On reviewing the objections of Blue Cross and Blue Shield to removal of the medical referral and supervision clause in their policy the United States Senate Committee on Post Office and Civil Service reported (1972) that, "the evidence disclosed at our hearing seems to indicate that there is little if any benefit derived from the practice of supervision of such service other than earning of money by doctors of medicine and the avoidance of payment by Blue Cross/Blue Shield." There is some reason to believe that the insistence on medical supervision is an effort to secure or retain monopoly of the health field. This effort is generally justified in terms of "medical responsibility" but the effect is an intrusion into the practice of other health professions. Formal clarification of medical responsibility, which often carries an overreaching territorial interpretation, has been achieved in California. Because it is nowhere defined in the California State Medical Practice Act, the term was recently defined by regulation. Under Title 9, Sub-chapter 3, Community Mental Health Services, under the Short-Doyle Act, medical responsibility (in regulation 522) is defined as "A physician meeting the qualifications of Section 620(a) [a board-eligible psychiatrist] shall assume responsibility for all those acts of diagnosis, treatment, or prescribing or ordering of drugs which may *only* be performed by a licensed physician" [Explanation and emphasis supplied]. The acts thus specified can be summarized as the cutting, severing, and penetrating of tissue; injecting substances; and prescribing medications.

Indeed, in filing suit against the Blue Cross Association in November of 1973, the Council for the Advancement of Psychological Professions and Sciences (CAPPS) alleged economic boycott and restraint of trade, among other charges. Though adoption of PL 93-363 has resolved the issue for federal employees from January 1975, thus placing certain aspects of the original lawsuit in doubt, the move by Blue Cross to dismiss was denied by the court and this class action, antitrust suit is proceeding as of this writing in the U.S. Court of Appeals.

Medicaid (see Chapter Five) is another program in which the imposition of medical referral (or outright denial of psychological services) is all too common. A state's Medicaid plan, is typically drafted by the state government health or welfare agency in accord with federal guidelines. These guidelines are permissive insofar as the inclusion of psychology is concerned. Nonetheless, even despite a state licensing or certification law recognizing psychology as an independent profession or despite a freedom-of-choice law regulating health insurance, some states have continued to impose a condition of medical referral on Medicaid recipients or have as yet failed to recognize the services of psychologists in the state plan.

The medical referral or supervision issue is, then, neither casual nor minor. A host of arguments and facts can and have been submitted to establish the impracticality of the M.D. supervision policy. Two frequently cited effects are: (1) decreased availability of services to the public in a field already fraught with critical shortages and (2) increases in costs in a field already plagued with critically high costs. Elimination of the middleman is still a good efficiency and business principle. These points are adequately argued elsewhere in this book. Therefore, the balance of this discussion will be directed to two further issues raised by the M.D. supervision policy: (1) the legal propriety of the M.D. supervisory relationship over psychology and (2) the ethics of the professions involved in such a supervision policy.

Is it appropriate for an M.D. to assume the role of supervisor over a psychologist? Conversely, is it appropriate for a psychologist to establish this relationship as a supervisee? In legal terminology, the psychologist in such a relationship assumes the role of a "servant" employed to perform services for another (the M.D.), and in the performance of services is subject to the M.D.'s control or right to control. The term *independent contractor*, from a legal point of view, is the antithesis of the term *servant*. In contradistinction to the servant, the independent contractor carries out his work without the supervisory control of a master.

To determine whether a person is a servant or an independent contractor, the law considers the facts and circumstances of the relationship. Definitions and clarifications of the supervisory relationship have a long history and have come to be codified and organized in the law of agency. The *Restatement of the Law, Agency 2d* (American Law Institute, 1958) authoritatively restates the law of agency. Written by experts with the highest legal academic credentials, it is looked upon by the courts as the authority in this specialized area of the law.

If one applies the restatement's definitional points regarding the differentiation between servants and independent contractors to the matters of fact in the M.D. supervision requirement under consideration, it is clear that a psychologist is in the role of an independent contractor and from a legal point of view his work cannot assume a relationship of supervisee to a physician. Let us take up, one by one, the restatement's definitional points in determining whether a servant or an independent contractor condition exists or not. The related matters of fact in the M.D.-psychologist supervisory relationship follow each definitional point. It is important to realize that in legal reasoning the circumstances that contribute to a particular master-servant relationship are thought of as "matters of fact" that form a totality—the fact situation. The triers of fact relate the fact situation to the definitional points in order to make a judgment about the relationship. The "hardness" or objectivity that a psychologist usually associates with the term *fact* is not connoted in the following discussion.

S 220—Definition

(1) A servant is a person employed to perform services for another in his affairs and who, with respect to his physical conduct in the performance of the service, is subject to the other's control or right to control. (2) In determining whether one acting for another is a servant or an independent contractor, the following matters of fact, among others, are considered: (A) The extent of control which, by agreement, the employer may exercise over the details of the work . . .

Matters of Fact. Basically, this language is the point at issue. In fact, psychologists strenuously object to control over their work by another profession and do not agree to the attempt of unilateral imposition of such control by insurance carriers. There is no agreement between the parties on an extent of control.

(B) whether or not the employed is engaged in a distinct occupation or business . . .

Matters of Fact. Psychology is an independent profession, a distinct occupation. A profession has an accumulated body of knowledge, techniques, and skills based on disciplined methods and theory. Almost every large university in the United States has an extensive undergraduate and graduate program in psychology that meets university accreditation standards as well as the high standards of the American Psychological Association's Education and Training Board and the National Commission on Accrediting. The American Psychological Association (APA), founded in 1892, is the national organization for psychology, representing over 40,000 psychologists. In order to exchange scientific and professional information the association publishes fifteen journals and maintains numerous committees and a large central office staff in Washington, D.C. The American Board of Professional Psychology, established in 1947, grants diplomate status, through examinations, to those psychologists who have qualified themselves as advanced specialists in clinical, counseling, industrial and organizational, or school psychology.

A profession is concerned with the proper application of its knowledge, theory, and techniques. Standards of application within ethical principles of practice must be set by the profession, particularly when professional activities involve the public. Psychologists require of themselves that their practice conform to the highest ethical standards, subscribing to APA's code, "Ethical Standards of Psychologists" (American Psychological Association, [1953] 1963). State and local psychological associations and societies and the national society maintain ethics committees. The APA's Board of Professional Affairs is responsible for the establishment and maintenance of professional standards, including a Committee on Health Insurance. The latter committee has helped establish and coordinate psychological regional insurance review committees covering the entire nation. The APA has considered seriously many insurance issues and has made its position clear on these issues (American Psychological Association, 1971). The association has adopted as policy on September 1974, a detailed set of standards for providers of psychological services (see Chapter Two) in which the profession is clearly held to be independent and autonomous.

Governmental control of a profession is generally demanded by the public in the form of licensure or certification. Psychology is regulated in forty-seven states and the District of Columbia through statutory regulation, with the remaining states subject to nonstatutory regulation. The American Association of State Psychology Boards represents the various state boards of examiners in psychology. A nationally standardized examination has been developed. This brief summary should be sufficient to establish that psychology is a distinct professional occupation.

(C) the kind of occupation, with reference to whether, in locality, the work is usually done under the direction of the employer or by a specialist without supervision . . .

Matters of Fact. Virtually all the consumers of psychological services using third-party reimbursement see psychologists in private practice. Psychologists in private practice are not supervised by another profession. A minority of psychologists in private practice do associate themselves with other professions in their office arrangements—usually with psychiatrists or social workers. Such arrangements facilitate interdisciplinary collaboration, the professionals sharing space and office support services while maintaining independence of practice. Some practicing psychologists do supervise technicians and persons with psychological training less than a doctorate degree in the course of their practice. It should be noted that psychologists carry their own professional liability insurance in keeping with the independent status of their practice and its responsibilities.

(D) the skills required in the particular occupation . . .

Matters of Fact. The skills required to practice psychology require many years to develop. Considerable skill is required, for example, in carrying out consultation activities employing psychological tests or therapeutic activities such as client-centered therapy or behavior modification. Psychology has developed a wide range of skills, many of which do not overlap with any of the other helping professions. Psychologists begin to develop such skills during the four-year period in which they are enrolled in their graduate degree studies. A training or internship period under the close supervision of senior psychologists in programs with rigorous professional standards follows graduate academic studies. To further develop their skills most psychologists work for years in settings with more senior psychologists before moving into independent practice. Most psychologists in full, independent practice are boarded or board-eligible for the diplomate status of the American Board of Professional Psychology (ABPP). ABPP requires the Ph.D. in psychology and five years (four postdoctoral) of acceptable experience to be considered for board eligibility.

> (E) whether the employer or workman supplies the instrumentalities, tools, and the place of work for the person doing the work . . .

Matters of Fact. Psychologists providing service for third-party reimbursement provide their own office, which they privately rent or own and furnish as the place where their services are carried out. Similarly the supplies and instrumentalities connected to their work are provided by them. Many mental tests offered commercially are available only to persons with the training and professional qualifications of psychologists.

> (F) the length of time for which the person is employed . . .

Matters of Fact. Most independent psychological services are offered on an hourly basis or fraction thereof. Some evaluation and consultation services are offered by the "job" or on a per diem basis. In either instance the time required for services rendered by psychologists is set by the individual psychologist providing that service. The psychologist controls how much time his work will take.

> (G) the method of payment, whether by the time or by the job . . .

Matters of Fact. Almost all psychological services offered to the public for a fee use a fee-for-service system based on an hourly rate. In some evaluative or consultative services payment is "by the job," but this system constitutes a very small proportion of rendered psychological services. Again, in either instance the fee for services rendered by a psychologist is set by the psychologist providing the service. Whether a third-party carrier establishes a similar fee for service is incidental to the psychologist's fee setting.

> (H) whether or not the work is a part of the regular business of the employer . . .

Matters of Fact. The services a psychologist renders are imbedded in a professional relationship that is always more than any particular aspect of work provided. In this sense, therefore, any particular service rendered by a psychologist within the scope of this competency is unique to his profession.

Some psychological work is unique to psychology. Other work done by psychologists overlaps the work of other professions. For example, much counseling or psychotherapeutic work done by psychologists is also done by psychiatrists and psychiatric social workers. Most outpatient treatment of mental disturbance is treated by psychotherapy. Psychotherapy is not within the province of any one profession. When M.D.s have tried to restrict psychotherapy as medical practice only, the opinions of state legal officers (for example, Michigan, New York, and California) have held that the practice of psychotherapy is not restricted to M.D.s. Medical doctors, outside of psychiatrists trained in psychotherapy, have minimal skill and training in psychotherapy.

Given these matters of fact, is the psychological work rendered by psychologists in the point at issue part of the business of the physician (acting as supervising agent for the insurance carrier)? The answer is, for the most part, No. The great majority of physicians are not trained in psychological work or psychotherapy and do not practice in such areas. A smaller number of physicians specializing and trained in psychiatry are competent psychotherapists, and it is here, when we consider psychotherapy apart from other psychological service, that some work overlaps exist. In reality, psychotherapy consists of many psychotherapies. Some of these psychotherapeutic methods are more practiced by one profession or another—for example, the behavior therapies and use of biofeedback in the case of psychologists. In any case, no adequate justification (derived from education, training, experience, development, effectiveness, statutory definition, agency policy, and so on) supports psychotherapy as solely a medical (psychiatric) treatment method whose only competent practitioners have medical backgrounds. Even in the more conservative times of fifty years ago, Freud did not limit psychotherapy, even psychoanalysis, to medical practitioners.

> (I) whether or not the parties believe they are creating the relationship of master and servant . . .

Matters of Fact. Psychologists, as members of an independent profession, cannot carry out their professional responsibilities nor represent themselves as psychologists when supervised by another profession. They do not believe they are creating a master and servant relationship with M.D. supervisors when they provide service to patients eligible for third-party payment. The supervisory relationship has not been created by psychologists nor with their consent, but has been imposed upon psychologists by some insurance carriers and some agency regulations.

> (J) and whether the principal is or is not in business.

Matters of Fact. The principal is in business—that is, the practice of medicine. The principal is not in the practice of psychology nor is he licensed or certified to practice psychology.

The matters of fact related to the ten definitional points just described present a more than sufficient total fact situation necessary to conclude that practicing psychologists are independent contractors and not servants. The psychologist's particular professional training, experience, statutory status, and judgment, imbedded within the ethics and social milieu of his profession, dictate his actions in providing psychological services to his patients. From a legal viewpoint the practicing psychologist cannot be subject to the supervisory control of an M.D. Insurance carriers or agencies requiring that M.D.s must supervise psychologists when psychologists render services for mental and emotional disorders are acting in an inappropriate and improper manner.

Moreover, one must be free to form and carry out decisions and to control the details of one's work in order to be held ethically responsible. Therefore, if a psychologist is under supervision, he is not considering his ethical responsibilities. In order to function as a professional psychologist and be subject to the profession's ethical standards, the psychologist must not allow another, untrained and unlicensed in the profession of psychology, to judge or dictate the psychologist's manner of performance. "As a member of an autonomous profession, a psychologist rejects limitations upon his freedom of thought and action other than those imposed by his moral, legal, and social responsibilities" (American Psychological Association, 1968b, p. 9).

As for the M.D. supervisor, Section 7 of the *Principles of Medical Ethics* states that "In the practice of medicine a physician should limit the source of his professional income to medical services actually rendered by him, or under his supervision, to his patients" (American Medical Association, 1958, p. 39). Therefore, if the M.D. receives a fee for "supervising" a psychologist, he is violating his medical ethics by participating in such an inappropriate relationship. That is, he should not receive payment for a service that he is not qualified to supervise or does not directly render himself. It would be in keeping with the fact situation and intent of both professions to recognize that the M.D. refers a patient to a psychologist for treatment or consultation largely because he cannot provide such a service himself and is seeking an appropriate service in the interest of the patient, while recognizing the limitations of his own competency in the area of the psychologist's expertise. Rather than supervisory, the relationship between the two professions should properly be one of collaboration.

15

Issues Facing
Professional Psychology

Herbert Dörken and David A. Rodgers

In retrospect, it seems evident that the developments of the past several years serve to establish psychology as a health profession today. Professional standards have been formulated and substantial statutory recognition at both federal and state levels has been gained. The numbers of psychologists involved in health practice have multiplied and this increase is reflected in their utilization in a wide range of health insurance and related programs. The legislation passed by the 93rd Congress (1973 to 1974), for example, did not simply advance the recognition of psychology but established psychology as a health profession. Moreover, the progress and change recounted in the preceding chapters did not occur by chance, but by intent and action. Still, there remain significant unresolved issues and a potential for considerable further change. Many implications for the future of psychology can be drawn from the foregoing discussions. It seems clear that the United States is moving toward universal entitlement to health services. Equalization of fiscal access must lead to a redistribution and more equal utilization of health resources. Freed from the bonds of indigency, health services will probably shift away from the current forced reliance on public services and toward private care. If survival is in any way tied to utilization revenue, then, many state hospitals and community mental health centers are likely to be foreclosed by a shift to care in general hospitals and by community practitioners. The magnitude of the shift, however, is also likely to underscore the impracticality of relying on independent solo practitioners for systematic health delivery. The expected thrust will be to private sector care, but such care will have to be offered as an organized service. Health maintenance organizations have, of course, been a pioneering model, but the advent of foundations for medical care (individual practice associations) promises a viable fee-for-service alternative.

Both the public and the private sector are now typically charging for direct clinical services and to that extent are clearly in competition. The system is clearly archaic, since many public services are not required to meet standards of licensure at least equivalent to the private sector. The continued existence of a dual (inferior) standard serves only to discredit the public sector. Since this inferiority is coupled with costs that may be higher, costs for staff and programs that have less flexibility in addressing changing needs, government may be prompted to divest itself, to the extent practical, of mental health services. According to the recent study by Levine and Levine (1974), the direct costs of mental health services in 1971 were $10,100,000,000 or 14 percent of national expenditures for all health services. Not to be overlooked is the fact that 46 percent of the funding came from the private sector, which undercuts the general assumption that state funding predominates in mental health services.

Furthermore, psychologists and other practitioners generically licensed or certified will soon have to face up to a definitional problem. Just as not all physicians are trained and truly competent in the evaluation and treatment of mental disorder, it is equally obvious that all psychologists are not prepared by training or experience for health care. For all major professions, then, the day of specialty certification based on credential review, if not on examination, seems close at hand. In the case of psychology, negotiations to date with the insurance industry, medicine and government underscore the fact that only doctoral-level training, coupled with clinical experience in an organized health setting, will be recognized as the standard for future practice. Indeed, we can expect continuing education to become a requirement for relicensure. It already is mandated in Colorado, Minnesota, Nevada, Oregon, and Utah. The *National Register of Health Service Providers in Psychology* (1975) attempts to address this problem, including "grandfathering" certain nondoctoral licensed psychologists. On October 3, 1975, the Blue Cross and Blue Shield administration for the Federal Employee Program (Washington, D.C.) advised all its offices that "psychologists in the Register do qualify as clinical psychologists. . . ."

The definitional problem has another dimension. In terms of mental disorder, neither the *International Classification of Diseases* (ICD) nor the *Diagnostic and Statistical Manual of American Psychiatry* (DSM II—American Psychiatric Association, 1968) have sufficient reliability (consistency) for either effective clinical or research use. A functional classification of mental disability is needed, but not yet developed. Moreover, the extent to which those mental disorders, which might be termed *functional problems in living,* will be recognized as health problems is doubtful. In any event, the inconsistent use of present diagnostic and classification systems is such that from the insurer's perspective, the carrier is not really insuring services (in coverage for mental disorder) but providers. Thus, at this intermediate stage it becomes necessary to control (limit) practitioners as a way of controlling utilization. The recoverable benefits will then be less than the public need for service.

Present utilization data does show that even the extended mental health coverage of the CHAMPUS or federal employee programs, on a per capita basis, are quite feasible in terms of cost. And although, the available utilization data are sparse and perhaps not exactly comparable, levels of utilization seem sufficiently consistent to enable implementation of rational peer review and utilization control. It also seems obvious that mental health services are effective both in terms of reducing or offsetting other health utilization and in increasing income and improving employability, not to mention personal factors bearing on the quality of life.

As yet, we have not delineated a clear, single, best way to deliver mental health or health services. Consumers also hold strong views on personally preferred models. These are reasons enough for insisting that multimodel systems open to consumer choice be developed. We must also introduce true competition among health systems by such mechanisms as prepaid, at-risk contracting, proscriptive rate and fee negotiations, and capitation and health incentive funding. Nationalization or federalization might seem like the obvious solution, offering some early advantages in greater uniformity and economy that would, however, soon be outweighed by the diseconomies and inaccessability of bureaucracy. Moreover, in this country, widespread continuing practitioner cooperation seems unlikely toward government service.

The two oldest health professions—medicine and nursing—are heavily involved in direct health care delivery. Short of a massive increase in their training programs, they can do little on short notice to significantly increase their man-hours available for health care. Psychology is unique in having perhaps more than one-third of its members now engaged in part-time fee-for-service practice. With new incentive, such as inclusion in national health insurance, psychologists could rapidly increase their participation in health service. There has also been a dramatic increase in enrollment in graduate training programs for psychologists and an increase in the proportion of clinical students. Thus, while the number of doctoral graduates in psychology will likely double by 1978, the clinical component will probably soon triple that of 1974.

Psychology, then, has come a long way. But all of the gains the profession has made must be actively guarded and extended. In a November 1974 speech the recent assistant secretary for health (HEW) Charles Edwards, lent encouragement when he said, to the Conference of State and Territorial Alcohol, Drug Abuse, and Mental Health authorities, "The tradition that all services must be provided by a physician or under his guidance is now giving way to practical reality. As an example of this trend, as of January 1, 1975, all government employees' insurance plans will permit payments to psychologists, without requiring a physician's supervision." And he went on to say, "This more practical attitude should be encouraged by all of us."

Major attitudinal and territoriality obstacles are still advanced by medicine in general and by some segments of psychiatry in particular to "this more practical attitude." The issues are well reviewed, addressed, and dispelled by Mariner (1967), who notes that "a knowledge of human behavior, thought, and emotion would be the logical and necessary foundation on which a professional practice dealing with disturbance of behavior, thought, and emotion would to have to rest. Thus psychology —or, "behavioral science"—would seem, unquestionably, to be the basic academic discipline of choice" (p. 278). The term *medical responsibility* is often used but seldom defined. Since it was nowhere to be found in the California Medical Practices Act, care was taken to define it in regulation No. 522 (California Administrative Code, Title 9, Subchapter 3): "A physician meeting the qualifications [of a Board eligible psychiatrist] shall assume responsibility for all those acts of diagnosis, treatment, or prescribing or ordering of drugs which may *only* be performed by a licensed physician" (emphasis supplied). The "only" in essence is to cut, sever, penetrate tissue, inject substances, and prescribe medications—hardly a sufficient factual or preparatory basis on which to exercise claims for the direction and supervision of mental health care services and control over its nonmedical practitioners.

Whether psychologists are included in a national health insurance program will depend not simply on professional competence or accomplishments in the mental health field, but upon psychology's efforts to be included. The profession has, however, begun to establish itself in "common law" as health providers. Since legislators often use preexisting laws and regulations as models, and as psychology begins to become part of law, the likelihood of acceptance into new legislation as a matter of precedent increases.

The issues are complex and the problems are many in building a national health care system. Money is problem enough, but in the main, we are already spending it. The more fundamental questions relate to organization of delivery systems, accessible distribution of practitioners, and benefit entitlements encouraging early intervention and community-based ambulatory care. The largest component in health costs is hospital care. The limited ambulatory services of most health insurance plans provide incentives for the wrong direction—toward inpatient care. Deductibles prior to coverage and followed by coinsurance probably also exert greater restraint on ambulatory care utilization than on hospitalization. Undercutting hospital usage and costs should be the first consideration in cost control efforts.

Public Service and Health Insurance

As prepaid health service organizations increase their coverage for mental disorder, and as wider benefits become available in major medical and general group disability (health) policies, the community mental health center (CMHC) movement may find itself faced with a dilemma. Will CMHCs subcontract? If mental health services are covered universally in the private sector, will the need for these public services continue? Will it not become more appropriate for CMHCs to concentrate on the indirect services (Dörken, 1971) such as inservice training, resource development and coordination, and consultation with primary caretakers, or to focus on social action intended to improve the quality of life rather than attempt to compete in the direct patient service arena? The broadening availability of insurance could entail a marked increase in private sector health care delivery, but this increase is likely to involve corporate and organized practice systems. National health insurance could also entail a redistribution of services from upper-income to lower-income groups, as occurred in Great Britain, Montreal, and Saskatchewan when full-coverage ambulatory plans became available (Newhouse and others, 1974). And it could mean, to the extent services are funded from general revenue, some inherent redistribution of income. To date, some of the public programs such as Medicare have been "a better mechanism for insuring the providers than [for insuring] the patients" (Hodgson, 1973).

In health services based on client fees, the model of direct remuneration to the practitioner—the private practice model—predominates. Care for the indigent has been a separate public or governmental service. The progressive inclusion of benefits for emotional and mental disorder under health insurance has already made many employed persons independent from public mental health services—both hospitals and clinics. The advent of national health insurance seems very likely to catalyze the development of organized health, mental health, and rehabilitation services by the private sector to provide communitywide coverage. In a way, the private and public (state or local) mental health services have actually been in a strange competition. Some public mental health clinics will not accept those able to afford private care—even though such citizens have probably contributed more heavily to their tax support. Most public services, however, up to actual cost, will ordinarily charge for their services according to ability to pay whether from earnings, insurance or assets. National health insurance would provide the economic basis for universal coverage. If it also provides for multimodal delivery systems and consumer choice, the marketplace, which is influenced by past performance and consumer attitude, is likely to see a sharp erosion in general use of many public mental health facilities. There is also reason to believe that many public services will not be able to compete effectively with the private sector from either a cost or benefit perspective. On the other hand, universal coverage will bring not only prepayment for the insureds but prospective rate negotiation to providers and facilities, the need for integration of resources to assure twenty-four-hour access to care, the credentialing of providers by peers, and incentives for redistribution. While not prohibitive, these forces are essentially contrary to *independent* fee-for-service practice. After all, the health industry is the third largest employer in the economy and, with a record of inflationary price increases, it would be unrealistic to expect that external controls will not be introduced.

What are some of the factors, then, that place the public model at a disadvantage? Requirements for licensure have often been lowered for physicians (Torrey and Taylor, 1972) and typically waived entirely for some of the other health professions—hardly a way to secure the best qualified staff. Then, while salary ranges in government services are typically competitive at the lower end of the scale, their arbitrary ceilings often compact physician and administrative salaries. There is little financial incentive for the physician to assume programmatic responsibility, while for nonmedical personnel the salary adjustment in such positions may be significant but seldom at parity. Moreover, advancement rewards are generally reserved for supervisory and administrative roles with only limited incentives for clinical competence or workload, whatever the discipline. The "merits" of such a system sound more to the second half of Webster's definition of *merit,* "just reward and due punishment." These organized public settings have become a place where the young professional can acquire a broad experience often unmatched elsewhere. For those with programmatic interests there is typically some opportunity for competitive advancement—but the system is weighted heavily on the side of seniority and competition for middle management is too often restricted to those in the system, preventing open competition on the basis of available talent within a profession. Top positions are too often appointive or subject to political pressures rather than to needs for quality health care administration and equitable service delivery.

What does such a system do to its professional personnel? It creates a rapid turnover of young professionals at entrance level positions—a costly and wasteful personnel practice; it drives out the ambitious and the competitive; to reward seniority, it establishes eligibility lists and a structure to support the organization; and at some expense to client service, it retains archaic methods and senior personnel, thus tolerating obsolescence and discouraging innovation. The presumed economies of scale become diseconomies under the weight of administrative overload and bureaucracy. A double standard of service is continued—one that has no need to compete with or match the private sector, one whose costs are higher at least on an outpatient unit service basis. And generally, there is no evidence that the public services have a better treatment outcome record. Rather, they have been created and sustained to meet a public need where public funds were required. That economic reason for being could change abruptly.

The various national health insurance proposals introduced before Congress in 1974 and 1975 do not differ widely in total cost; their variance appears to be within a 10 percent range (Committee for Economic Development, 1973; *Consumer Reports,* 1975). Their sources of revenue and focus of administrative control, although distinctly different in some respects, are hardly likely to change the health infrastructure. The benefit structures differ somewhat but are open to compromise. In any event, as Ginzberg (1975) points out, "Reform of the health system runs headlong into the entrenched interests of a great many powerful constituencies, including physicians, health insurance agencies, hospitals . . . which can no more be ignored than they can be easily neutralized or co-opted." And, "Most state and local governments have demonstrated little capacity for effective planning . . . the effective power resides in the nongovernmental sphere . . . ."

Utilization and Staffing Models

Various reports, as summarized in Chapter Eleven, provide encouraging data on the utilization of mental health services by consumers, on the frequency or duration of utilization, on the service delivery capacity of certain professions, on their manpower base (Chapter One), and on the cost of services. These data all point to the need for mental health services, the feasibility of their inclusion under health insurance, and their potential cost-benefit advantages. Seldom, however, is the data sufficiently complete or drawn in a manner that allows a reliable comparison between studies. Most reported data are idiosyncratic to a specialized service, type of population, or area. They are seldom broad enough, based over sufficient time, to enable generalized conclusions. Moreover, most coverage and services are either limited in benefit or appeal, so that the utilization reported is very likely not complete. Finally, longitudinal or cohort studies are rare. All these limitations notwithstanding, there seems to be a gradual accumulation of promising indices for utilization of mental health services.

Both the North California Kaiser Health Plans and the

CHAMPUS ten-state data are sufficiently consistent or comprehensive to make comparative projections interesting. Kaiser follows a private practice model of mental health service delivery using a closed panel of highly trained practitioners from several professions (three-fifths are clinical psychologists). While the experience is restricted to a relatively small working population and their dependents (about 350,000 persons), the long-term consistency of their experience and the integration of mental health as part of total health care in this prototype HMO model holds special significance. The Kaiser program does not, it must be noted, provide for long-term inpatient or chronic care. CHAMPUS, on the other hand, involves a very wide range of largely independent fee-for-service practitioners (psychologists provided services for 16.3 percent of all mental health visits, 2.5 and 23.1 percent of inpatient and outpatient services respectively) in serving a population derived from a military employment base. In 1974, the mental health coverage was essentially unlimited for most conditions. In both plans the reported utilization should be reasonably complete. For illustrative purposes, both models were projected to the national population.

It is evident in Table 1 that while the comparative utilization in terms of persons receiving mental health services in the Kaiser model is about half those in CHAMPUS, the number of outpatient visits required was but 30 percent that of CHAMPUS, and inpatient services less than 10 percent that of CHAMPUS, the coinsurance provisions of the latter notwithstanding. HMO proponents will claim that this substantial differential is due to the superior ability of such organized settings to deliver more effective services in a coordinated manner and to deliver services of shorter duration (since costs are prepaid and lack the possible incentive of fees to continued service). Proponents of professional practice will note the broader diversity of CHAMPUS therapists, many without concentrated training in mental health care (the sharp curtailment in therapists recognized by CHAMPUS in February and March 1975 may be reflected in future utilization changes) and might argue that the level and specificity of training contributes to the Kaiser efficiency, noting in particular that visit frequency is less, even for

Table 1. Mental Disorder Utilization: Projected Comparison of
an HMO and Fee-for-Service Model to a National Base

Category	Kaiser	CHAMPUS
1973 census population	209,581,000	209,581,000
Outpatient visits	12,465,149[a]	41,403,983[b]
Inpatient visits	1,657,823[c]	20,391,866[d]
Total visits	14,122,972	61,795,849
Annual practitioner visit capacity	1,200[e]	1,500[f]
Practitioners required	11,769	41,197
Proportion psychologist services	60%[g]	16.3%[h]
Psychologists required	7,061	6,715
Utilization of mental health services, unduplicated user	.95%	1.87%
Hospital days for mental disorder	828,911[i]	42,262,717[j]
Practitioners required at 5% utilization level	61,942	110,152

[a]Equals 9 insureds per 1,000 utilization, average 6.6 visits each per year.

[b]Based on 643,638 visits per 3,262,200 insured.

[c]Equals .5 hospitalizations per 1000 insureds per year, average stay 7.9 days, two
visits daily (A.M. group therapy, P.M. individual therapy).

[d]Equals 316,998 visits per 3,262,200 insured.

[e]Equals 25 visits per week, each full-time equivalent mental health specialist, 48
weeks, not including case consultation, inservice training, other indirect services.

[f]Psychiatrists in private office practice reported to carry 30 to 33 visits weekly and
1,500 per year.

[g]Ph.D.-licensed clinical psychologists.

[h]Licensed or certified psychologists. From March 7, 1975 requires Ph.D.-licensed
clinical psychologists with two years' experience in organized health setting.

[i]Half of [c]

[j]Equals 46,592 admissions (though only 14,296 user beneficiaries) at average 14.1
days of stay.

users served. Kaiser services are essentially active treatment rather than continued care services. In contrast, there is a low frequency but extended utilization of residential care among young dependents in the CHAMPUS program.

The staffing requirements also differ sharply. In terms of just direct treatment services it might appear that Kaiser needs only 39 percent of the staff needed in the CHAMPUS model, whose support services are not evident and form part of practice overhead. When the Kaiser specialist staffing ratio of 1:7,200 insureds is applied, staffing requirements are 71 percent of the CHAMPUS model.

Both models, it should be noted, recognize licensed clinical psychologists as primary practitioners though the Northern California Kaiser program makes substantially greater use of their services. In terms of manpower, today there is clearly sufficient trained mental health manpower (see Chapter One) to meet the staffing needs of either model, if the utilization held firm for national application of such delivery systems. The distribution of this manpower may be quite another matter, however. Though more equitable distribution is badly needed, the notion that there are sufficient well-qualified staff appears to hold, when nationwide needs are projected from other indices. Both the Aetna governmentwide indemnity program and the Blue Cross and Blue Shield program for federal employees report recent utilization as 1.2 and 1.1 percent of those insured—both drawing from a select employee base. Whereas days of hospital care in the Blue Shield and Blue Cross high-option plan were about one-third that in the CHAMPUS program, they were, at 14,695 days (1969 data projected to a national base), almost eighteen times greater than the Kaiser experience. (Given that hospitalization costs are very substantially greater than outpatient care, there should be strong incentives to shift health insurance benefits towards ambulatory care.)

Kramer (1973) reported a national utilization in 1971 among organized settings of 2 percent of the population. The private sector and some other services were unreported (see Chapter One). In addition to the over 4,000,000 episodes reported by Kramer, an additional 5,000,000 episodes in the private sector can be inferred from the numbers of professionals in private practice. Components of other reports indicate that utilization among adult dependents of employees is on the order of 4 to 4.5 percent. All things considered, then, given universal coverage under a national health insurance program, it is probable that total population utilization of mental health services could be around the 5 percent level. On such basis the Kaiser and CHAMPUS models project to a manpower need of 61,942 and 110,152!

The total of employed, qualified, mental health professionals involved on a full-time equivalent basis in direct patient services is on the order of 63,000 (psychiatry—19,000; psychol-

ogy—15,000; clinical social work—20,000; and psychiatric nursing—9,000). Barely enough to staff the Kaiser model; 57,000
short of staffing the CHAMPUS model. No wonder the United
States Public Health Service was able in 1974 to report 9,000
budgeted, unfilled positions. Rational planning would include
augmented training support for these specialties, and equitable
distribution of the new trainees. The manner in which care is
delivered by type of setting warrants not simply cost but outcome review to maximize cost-benefit effectiveness. Duration of
stay in state hospitals and private psychiatric hospitals has been
substantially greater than in psychiatric services of general hospitals, but the differential has narrowed considerably in recent
years. In contrast, the average number of visits to community
mental health clinics is typically reported as four or five, less
than the visit duration when private resources are used.

Rather than foreclose further development by emphasizing
only one model of mental health service delivery, it would seem
wiser to encourage competition and treatment effectiveness and
especially to pay closer attention to planning for service delivery. Also, strong incentives should be provided at the earliest
possible date to those now in training to locate in underserved
areas when they are professionally qualified. Similar incentives
should be provided to assure that training programs prepare
health professionals to meet the broad public need, not simply
to congregate in prestigious urban institutions. Without a reasonable distribution of personnel, sound health services cannot
be delivered across the country.

Organization Strategies

The National Health Planning and Resources Development
Act of 1974 (PL 93-641) is likely to have a profound impact.
Adopted on January 4, 1975, this law calls for the sectorizing
of each state into health service areas of 3,000,000 to 500,000
people (less, in unusual circumstances); for the governance of
the health systems agencies to include a majority of consumer
representatives (but not more than 60 percent); for capitation
health planning grants (basically $.50 per capita); and for the

channeling of certain former federal categorical funding, such as now exists under the Community Mental Health Center Act, through a state agency (no project may be assisted that is not in the state plan).

Clearly, sweeping change is intended in the organization of health care delivery and in the means for designating service and manpower needs. From the perspective of psychology, some amendments are needed, such as specific listing of psychologists among the designated "providers of health care" in Section 1531 and provision for the direction of outpatient and rehabilitation facilities by psychologists in Section 1633. These amendments must be actively sought.

However, such sectorized health planning will facilitate the training of future health professionals within community settings rather than in isolated university hospitals and clinics. The law may also hold the promise, by decentralizing training, of preventing the development of enormous health organizations as might occur if national health insurance became a single federalized governmental system (HEW, 1971).

In more economically favorable times or with a larger allocation of funds to health, it may even be possible to shift treatment and care from large mental hospitals to services in general hospitals—when inpatient services are necessary (Bennett, 1973). Moreover, if all services are community-based, there will be no escape from the treatment responsibility to patients and their families. Without the development of effective, active-treatment, local mental health resources (whether public, private, or a combination thereof) we may well soon see a shift to greater usage of state mental hospitals among the unemployed, who are also likely to be without health insurance. Brenner (1973) has shown a clearly inverse relation between the level of economy and admissions to state mental hospitals. Thus, given the United States economy of 1973 to 1975, the demand for admissions to state mental hospitals could rise sharply as the tolerance level of people breaks down under economic stress. (Correctional systems also experience a correlation between the unemployment level and prison populations.)

Supportive living and residential treatment settings other

than the mental or general hospital warrant consideration. The absence of insurance coverage for institutionalization of the emotionally disturbed in nonmedical facilities has virtually precluded the development of residential psychological facilities for the care and treatment of such patients, facilities that would provide a useful alternative to traditional psychiatric hospitals. Psychologists could establish such institutions in terms of professional competence, but such "psychological settings" have not been economically feasible under traditional funding arrangements and governmental regulations, which tend to support the maintenance of a medical monopoly in institutional practice in the health care field. Such a monopoly is unfortunate in those areas of health care that are not uniquely medical, such as emotional distress, because it discourages cost-effectiveness, competition, creative innovation, and optimal expansion of the professional mental health manpower pool. Should residential psychological facilities become economically feasible, they would constitute an important additional setting for psychological practice. Certainly, they would not entail the high cost and heavy capital investment of a hospitallike structure nor the overhead of such a facility, which requires heavy construction and costly support services.

Changes in the involuntary commitment process can have complex outcomes. Thus, although one intent of California's Lanterman-Petris-Short Act, a bill of rights for mental patients passed in 1969, was to protect patients from being locked up in hospitals without their consent, the bill seems to have had an unintended outcome. Only a small proportion of patients meet the required definition of "gravely disabled." As a consequence it now appears that many mental patients, exercising their civil right to refuse treatment, later run afoul of the law and wind up in county jails and state prisons. The state hospital population may have declined dramatically, but California authorities now claim that several thousand inmates of correctional facilities are mentally disordered (Williams, 1975). Of course, such facilities are not staffed to deal with this situation. Moreover, reduction in the state hospital population might seem to hold out the prospect of reduced public cost. But many of the long-term care patients, when discharged, become foster home residents receiving aid to the totally disabled. As welfare recipients, their health services are also provided for, but under Medicaid. At the least, the cost-benefit aspects of the situation as well as those involving the quality of life warrant careful review.

Staff Privilege

The nature of staff privilege defines and delineates the scope of one's practice within a hospital. One may be licensed to practice in a state, and the definition may encompass a broad range of services—in private practice. But in a hospital or other organized facility, further controls may be placed on the clinician in addition to credential review by peers and other measures to assure clinical competence. Extended control is especially prevalent in the private sector. The standards of the Joint Commission on Accreditation of Hospitals (JCAH) and its separate councils on accreditation of psychiatric, long-term care, and other types of facilities, sharply delineate the services of the nonmedical professions. In actuality, the commission standards could be looked on as an extralegal restrictive covenant on the practice of psychology and other nonmedical professions— except for the fact that they are becoming referenced into law or agency regulation as in Medicare or CHAMPUS (see chapters Five and Nine).

In a Veterans Administration hospital, any licensed professional on the admission unit can admit a patient. He or she may be a psychologist, but rarely is. Once admitted, psychologists and other professional staff may carry treatment responsibility within the scope of their license. Hospital discharge, however, is only on a physician's order.

Another all-salaried, closed-panel staff model is that of the Kaiser Foundation Health Plan in Northern California (see also Chapter Ten). Any one of the staff psychologists at a Bay Area Kaiser facility can arrange for hospitalization at Kaiser's inpatient mental health unit in Richmond. At the inpatient unit any other psychologist can carry full treatment responsibility and also make the discharge determination for his or her clients. A staff psychologist may also admit and discharge in the emergency unit.

In open-panel private sector settings staff privileges for psychologists typically are sharply reduced. The 1973 manual of the JCAH Council on Accreditation of Psychiatric Facilities can allow some latitude if requested by local administration. Thus, in the department of psychiatry at the Peninsula Hospital and Medical Center in Burlingame, California, qualified psychologists and clinical social workers—all in private practice—are members of the affiliate staff and may arrange for admission of their patients, treat them while in hospital within the scope of their license to practice, and arrange for their discharge when appropriate. These nonmedical affiliate staff participate in peer review and other standard settings within the department (Vaughan and others, 1973). Indeed, a psychologist has chaired the peer review committee.

The 1973 JCAH accreditation manual, however, essentially encourages a narrower and strictly medical model. Thus, eligibility criteria require that "the medical responsibility for patients rests with a psychiatrist or other physician." This requirement can be all-encompassing if anything a physician does or might do is subsumed under the concept of medical responsibility. However, it is at the same time surprisingly narrow if medical responsibility is limited to those acts of diagnosis, prescription, or treatment that may *only* be performed by a physician. Similarly, in the interpretation of Standard IV (p. 21), "the diagnosis and treatment of psychiatric disorders are (held to be) the ultimate responsibility of psychiatrists." But when the standard diagnostic nomenclature is reviewed it clearly subsumes a wide variety of behavioral and adjustment problems that no less appropriately may be claimed to be within the province of another profession, such as psychology. The interpretation of standards for outpatient services is perhaps even more brazen. In a multidisciplinary setting, few would quarrel with the requirement (profession unspecified) that "The director of the outpatient services shall be a qualified mental health professional who has at least two years of administrative experience." But requiring that the "Responsibility for the diagnosis and treatment of patients shall remain with a qualified psychiatrist" is clearly a blunt attempt to infringe on the practice of other licensed health professions. Perhaps we are overdue in formally questioning whose interests such councils serve, in reviewing the composition of their membership, and in ascertaining whether the standards truly serve to assure improved treatment and care or rather are guild trappings. What is the rate of accreditation denial? On what grounds? Can the Joint Commission Accreditation Council on Psychiatric Facilities stand the light of such a day?

In the fall of 1974 the American Psychological Association (APA) applied for membership on this council. The application has been set aside while the council reviews the criteria for membership! Meanwhile, this APA stands ready to buy two seats on council ($2,500 apiece) if admitted and has submitted its *Standards for Providers of Psychological Services* (1974*b*; see Chapter Two). Several of these standards, notably 2.4 and 4.2, bear on the issue of staff privilege and, if followed, would clearly call for some change in the JCAH standards: "The psychologist will bring his professional background and skills to bear on facility goals by participating in the development and the delivery of services" (2.4). This standard addresses the issue of representation on facility committees concerned with service delivery and membership in its governing body. "Psychologists are members of an independent, autonomous profession" (4.2). The intent is to eliminate arbitrary referral and supervision requirements that discriminate against the profession. It also supports the principle that "each participating profession shall have equal rights to vote, hold office, administer service programs in their respective areas of competence, and share the privileges and responsibilities of full membership in the human service facility." The issue may also be approached by statutory mandate. Thus, a bill (AB 1570, Paul Carpenter) was introduced in the California legislature in the spring of 1975, seeking to amend the health and safety code, Section 32128, to read: "The rules of the hospital, established by the board of directors pursuant to this article, shall include: 1. Provision for the organization of physicians and surgeons, *psychologists,* podiatrists, and dentists licensed to practice in this state who are permitted to practice in the hospital into a formal professional staff . . . ." Podiatrists had been added to this section in 1974. Clinical psychologists, although they have gained a broad recognition in both service delivery and direction of public mental health services, will find that they face a new round of resistance as they enter the organized health facilities of the private sector.

In passing, it should be noted that a hospital cannot offer the services of a radiologist (or other medical specialist) because to do so would mean the illegal practice of medicine. Only an individual is licensed to practice (or in some states, unidisciplinary professional corporations). Hence it might be argued that hospitals, if they offer the services of psychologists for a fee or charge, are practicing psychology illegally.

Perspectives on Psychological Training

Simply increasing the supply of health manpower, however, does not solve problems of health care delivery. Increasing personnel per se gives no assurance, for example, that the needs of children and the elderly will be better met. There have already been increases in the numbers of health personnel trained. In medicine it has been accompanied by an aggravated geographic and specialty maldistribution that in turn has led to an increased use of hospital and emergency outpatient services and progressive reduction in the availability of primary health care. Perhaps rather than think in terms of medical specialties, one should reflect on the frequency of types of disability. By all accounts, mental disorder is the largest, most frequent disability category. It is generally agreed that 50 to 60 percent of persons seeking health care do so because of emotional or mental disorder either as the primary or a concurrent problem. Similarly, national data show that a good half of the clients served by rehabilitation programs are categorized as mentally disordered or retarded. And the two specialties with the most comprehensive and pertinent training are psychiatry and clinical psychology. A reconceptualization of these two specialties as primary health providers would warrant not only a different perception of their roles, but in national priorities regarding their training. Despite the growth already apparent in 1972, clinical psychology was turning away close to 80 percent of its candidate population. According to Nyman (1973) the medical school candidate acceptance ratio was 2.7, but it was 4.6 in clinical psychology. A partial response to this pressure has been the creation of professional schools.

Psychology is a relatively young and growing profession and its graduate training capacity is growing rapidly. Fifteen new doctoral programs were accredited in 1973. The total of APA-accredited United States doctoral programs in clinical psychology reached ninety-eight in 1974 (American Psychologist). Whereas enrollment in many graduate programs has declined in recent years, that in psychology has shown a most dramatic increase, with over 39,000 graduate psychology students in 1973, an increase of only 1,200 over the prior year but 12,200 above that of 1970 (Cuca, 1974). Graduate enrollment in psychology is beginning to approach the size of student enrollment in this country's medical schools. Because of the increased graduate student body some 5,000 Ph.D.s can be anticipated in 1978 of whom close to 40 percent will be clinical/ professional. One interesting contrast is that perhaps 9 percent of medical graduates become psychiatrists. There will be some 12,000 United States medical graduates by 1978. This estimate suggests that while the current United States production is comparable between the two specialties, it could well shift to 2:1 in favor of psychology in several years. Thus, if the future brings an increased demand for clinical psychologists they will be there —and in even greater numbers when the impact of the newly developing professional schools becomes evident. This sharp increase in doctoral graduates over the next several years, coupled with the potential reallocation of man-hours from the substantial proportion of psychologists now engaged in part-time health service delivery (practice) suggests that psychology may be unique in having "at the ready" a sizeable health manpower resource, trained in the United States, that could be attracted to health service delivery on quite short notice. Professional psychology's potential for further "penetration" of the health market is thus very substantial. New training support, such as inclusion of clinical psychology in the existing Health Manpower Training Act, would usher in a new stage in the growth of psychology as a health profession.

The progressively increased numbers of psychologist practitioners engaged in health services will likely face the growing public demand for prior assurance of competence. Not only continuing education requirements but also specialty certification criteria will be regularly expected. The *National Register of Health Service Providers in Psychology* (1975) seeks to answer the need for specialty credentialling in the face of generic practice licenses. Quite narrow definitions have already appeared in the 1975 CHAMPUS directives and are similarly explicit in the health insurance industry's proposed bill on national health care (HR 5990, Burleson-S 1438, McIntyre). Nor are the pressures exclusive to psychology. For physicians, such specialty review may become a condition of acquiring or retaining hospital staff privileges. For nurses, the specialty certification process could well lead to greater practice responsibility in selected areas.

Optometry and podiatry are two doctoral level nonmedical professions that share with psychology many of the same legislative concerns and health care delivery problems. It is of interest to note their size as a health manpower resource. By the end of 1970 there were 18,400 optometrists, with 12 schools of optometry in 1971-1972 and 817 expected graduates in 1973-1974. In the case of podiatry the same figures respectively were 7,100, 5, and 309. If psychology is experiencing special difficulty in gaining recognition as a collegial health profession, then, it is not due to insignificant size!

The Professional Schools of Psychology

California saw the establishment of the first graduate School of Psychology in a university when the Fuller Theological Seminary, in Pasadena, admitted its first class in the fall of 1965. All regular faculty were practicing clinical psychologists except for one, a practicing psychiatric social worker. The only psychology program ever offered there has been professional training leading to a Ph.D. in clinical psychology. (Fuller also has graduate schools of theology and world mission.) Their first doctorates were awarded in 1969; some twelve to sixteen psychologists now graduate annually. In February 1974, Fuller became the first professional school of psychology to be accredited as such by the American Psychological Association (APA). Training facilities on campus include a child development center and the Pasadena Community Counselling Center.

Despite this pioneering development there was a mounting concern in the professional community in the last half of the 1960s that not nearly enough clinical or related specialists were being trained to meet the manpower needs of the major state agencies and the rapidly growing community mental health programs, to say nothing of the needs and potential opportunities in the correctional field or the private sector. It was time for action. Sponsored by the California State Psychological Association (CSPA), the California School of Professional Psychology (CSPP) became incorporated as a private nonprofit institution in March of 1969—psychology's first autonomous free-standing professional school, which has since grown to four campuses. By the end of 1974, its two senior campuses had graduated 150 Ph.D.s. The school is now part of a trend that is gathering momentum. In 1973, Adelphi University, long noted for its strong and professionally oriented clinical program, which graduates about twenty-five clinical Ph.D.s annually, established the second professional school of psychology within a university setting. Beginning with the 1974-1975 academic year, the New Jersey Graduate School of Applied and Professional Psychology opened at Rutgers University, unique in being the first graduate school of psychology, independent but coordinated with a university, and offering, after the master's, the Psy.D. degree (Schaar, 1974). By the fall of 1975, ninety graduate students were enrolled from among about 1,500 applications. These four professional schools, whose programs are headed by a dean or other person of higher academic rank, represent a distinct new development in the training of professional psychologists.

Stricker (1975) predicts that professional psychology will extend well beyond clinical psychology and into more settings in which appropriate training can be obtained. Students are likely to be older and have attained more maturity and life experience before entry into graduate school. Practicum experience and field work will probably be emphasized and acceptable dissertation projects broadened to cogent life topics. Indeed, student selection will probably emphasize life experience and selective use of interviews rather than the more current standardized but nondiscriminating tests. Stricker's "forecast" is actually a good description of the current situation and procedures at CSPP. The professional school of psychology may well be the next major force behind the growth and development of psychology.

Some 134 universities in the country are reported to have a doctoral program in clinical psychology, 98 being accredited by the American Psychological Association (APA). Several offer a professional degree. The first university, however, to offer a Psy.D. degree was the University of Illinois. This program began operation in 1968, but as of 1974 had graduated but four doctorates (Peterson and Baron, 1975). This professionally focused program, now APA-accredited, is parallel to the more traditional, experimentally oriented graduate program leading to the Ph.D. Illinois was followed by Baylor University and the Hahneman Medical School of Philadelphia in offering the Psy.D.

In the fall of 1974, the University of California at Davis, separate from the department of psychology, inaugurated a clinical program in the department of psychiatry at the medical school, drawing on faculty resources in this department and in sociology and child development, among others. At the same time, in collaboration with Mount Zion Hospital in San Francisco, the University of California at Berkeley planned a new professional school. This multidisciplinary program drawing on bases in behavioral science, social science, and pharmacology would award a doctorate in mental health. With faculty changes, it now seems probable that this new program will be transferred to the San Francisco campus as part of the department of psychiatry in the school of medicine.

Though not state-approved until September of 1975, the graduate school of the Wright Institute (Freedman, 1975) was established in 1969 at Berkeley and has graduated thirteen Ph.D.s. These applied psychologists are trained to work with human and social problems. And the movement does not end here. Professionally oriented programs are under consideration by the Ohio Psychological Association's Professional School Committee and a steering committee for the Massachusetts School of Professional Psychology is active. At the University of Minnesota, long regarded for its quality Ph.D. program in clinical psychology, the new Division of Health Care Psychology has recently formally proposed establishment of a professional doctoral program in health care psychology. Though not to be a separate professional school, the division is hopeful that its proposed interdisciplinary program in the graduate school will receive university approval to open in the fall of 1975. Its focus would be to train professional psychologists for work in non-psychiatric general medical settings—in effect to integrate psychological practice in the broad mainstream of health care, unlike its more commonly segregated functioning in mental health or psychiatric services.

With the assistance of a grant from the National Institute of Mental Health, the APA convened the National Conference on Patterns and Levels of Training in Psychology at Vail, Colorado, in July 1972. This conference asserted that the science of psychology had progressed sufficiently to justify creation of an explicit professional training. The Vail conference differentiated the professional model from previous models such as the scientist-professional model of the Boulder Conference some twenty-five years ago. The ingredients and parameters of professional training in clinical psychology are well summarized by Campbell and Hodges (1975) from a student's perspective.

Beyond Mental Health

While psychologists have been active for some time in the field of child development and have worked closely with pediatricians in some settings, there are recent indications that the profession is broadening its clinical interests beyond the problems of mental disorder per se to psychological intervention and support in conditions such as dying and chronic pain, to give but two illustrations. Studies of those dying and their families, such as children with leukemia (Miller, 1975b), have helped to chart the stages of mourning following the death of a loved one. This research has focused the need for more effective intervention in the psychological reactions experienced by family members, consultation with hospital staff treating the dying, and anxiety reduction among patients themselves. Psychologists are also investigating chronic pain, which is often disproportionate to the pathologic stimulus or persists after the stimulus disappears. Fordyce (1973) has shown that operant conditioning can be an effective method for managing chronic pain, since pain occurring over long periods of time affords an opportunity for learned behavior. One common example is the heavy laborer with chronic back pain. Well behavior (working) may be disliked. And disability compensation provides a secondary gain. Thus, if the organic element is missing or questionable, pain may be leading to time out from an aversive (disliked) activity or situation. (The area of restorative services was reviewed in Chapter Four.)

The proposed professional degree program leading to a doctorate in Health Care Psychology at the University of Minnesota addresses the need for training professional psychologists in health care administration, preventive care research, illness management, and health care delivery. The program may well be a major advance toward the involvement of psychology in the mainstream of health care delivery. And one should look beyond treatment. No major human health disability has ever been adequately controlled by attempts to treat the affected individual. The clinical approach is simply best suited to dealing with phenomena of very low prevalence. There are ethical reasons for support of direct treatment, and certainly many persons seeking and "needing" care, but if the objective is control of the condition in the population, the fundamental approach is through definition of the nature and extent of the problem and recognition of positive factors in prevention. A program based on treatment of major mental disorder in an individual may be good clinical practice, but it is poor public health. In the search for causes, then, we must look to the ultimate causes of disorder: the living and working conditions of people, their homes, their economic insecurity, their social alienation, and their ignorance. We must gain control of the general environmental factors that precipitate or can control disability. Stallones (1972) stated the issue well: "The assumption that effective treatment of illness vastly improves community health is incorrect . . . community health is more directly a function of disease prevention . . . advances in . . . knowledge and the decline of disease are simultaneous results of a general improvement in the quality of life." Society needs to focus on health maintenance and to maximize the effectiveness and viability of the large majority.

Redefining Professional Psychology

Psychology has struggled to become a health profession that is defined by a body of knowledge, using only validated techniques and scientifically researched premises following the scientist-practitioner model of professional training formulated at the 1950 Boulder Conference. This body of knowledge concerns the nature of human behavior and especially its cognitive and emotional dimensions. Among other defining parameters, such as a body of knowledge, a code of ethics and standards for identifying membership, perhaps the most critical identifier of any profession is a field of need to be served. For example, the teaching profession serves those needing to learn, the profession of law serves people who have legal problems. Often, the available body of knowledge is not adequate to serve fully the area of need to which a profession relates. Teachers still have not agreed on the best way to teach reading. Attorneys cannot solve all legal problems. Indeed, it can be argued that where a body of knowledge is adequately validated and adequately comprehensive to serve a field of need, then experts in that knowledge are basically technicians rather than professionals. It is the responsibility for making decisions about problems of uncertain solution, from an inadequate even if extensive knowledge base, that truly defines a profession. In this sense, psychology's commitment to validated procedures and scientifically researched approaches tends to be a commitment to a technology rather than a profession, and indeed psychologists have been hired as technicians in many other professional "houses" such as medicine and education.

If psychology is to be a profession, then the consuming public and the profession must both be able to identify the unique field of need that psychology serves and to have the expectation that psychology will *attempt* to deal with that entire field of need as expertly as possible, even when effective solutions to the problems presented are uncertain. The field of need is improving the effectiveness of any less-than-optimal behavioral pattern. Such behavior might be that of a regressed schizophrenic who must cope with life in spite of or in terms of his or her distorted mentation, whether or not such distortion represents a medical illness; that of a "tired housewife" whose mode of behaving aggravates mental discord while not adequately providing for her need for a sense of achievement or self-respect or enjoyment; that of a child whose patterns or modes of acquiring information do not fit comfortably the mode of teaching in the normal classroom and who must face at least ten or twelve years of functioning in a school system; that of an acutely depressed patient whose depression effectively blocks effortful behavior toward change to eliminate the cause of the depression; that of an alcoholic who consumes alcohol as a short-term solution to problems and thereby creates even worse problems on a long-term basis, or that of an adolescent whose drug use or rebellious behavior is disruptive to his or her immediate situation and destructive to his or her long-range best interests. From this perspective, these are behavioral not medical syndromes.

In the clinical area, this focus on improving the effectiveness of behavior would provide a culturally important alternative to the medical model. Anxiety, depression, phobias, and emotional upset are all conditions that have been more or less assigned to the domain of medicine, because they all represent states that are not willfully summoned by the individual involved; that lie outside of his mind-guided capacity to manipulate or control, and therefore must be examples of illness or pathology. Medicine's response to these conditions has been that if they are pathologies then they are wrong and should be eliminated, like any other illness. Drugs can and do eliminate or at least suppress anxiety. Hospitalizations can and do take people out of anxiety-provoking situations and thereby reduce the anxiety. Electroshock treatment can substitute for pharmacology when the tension is manifested as depression. Even the primary form of psychotherapy with which medical practice is identified, psychoanalysis, offers the promise of eliminating all emotional upset, by clearing out all repressed material and producing a tranquility of personal knowledge that is free of the pathology of neurotic unconscious influences and therefore free of the "pathology" of emotional upset. The psychological perspective suggested here would focus on a goal to be achieved rather than a condition to be eliminated.

Psychology clearly does not have validated methodology for dealing with this broad scope of problems, but people with these problems are increasingly turning to psychology because it is the most appropriate profession to deal with this field of need. Psychology seems best prepared to identify the areas of ignorance regarding human problems and to plan strategies whereby effective response can replace less-than-optimal human behavior.

The approach to these areas of need, planned from a psychological perspective, would often be dramatically different from the approaches of other professions. It would focus on improving the quality of life and increasing the effectiveness of the individual's behavior for accomplishing life goals. For example, a focus on helping a schizophrenic function more effectively should provide a highly useful competitive orientation to the present medical focus on drug therapies, electroshock, or custodial care. A focus on improving the effectiveness of adolescent behavior (and what is effective for the adolescent must ultimately of course take into account, and be effective for, the culture as well) should provide a useful competitive orientation to the penal approach of punishing wrong-doing or the medical approach of "curing" the "pathology" of stressful growing up.

In these and other examples, accepting as the primary defining parameter of psychology a field of need rather than a validated body of knowledge, would greatly increase the burden on the profession of psychology to struggle with major cultural and social health problems for which we do not now have solutions but concerning which our profession seems best qualified to seek solutions and to devise at least partially effective temporary approaches until adequate knowledge is developed. Such an approach would move psychology from a technology to a true profession, would force it to "build a house of its own," and would ultimately provide an inestimable gain for both the culture and the profession. This gain could probably be purchased only at the expense of considerable anxiety on the part of professional psychologists about the knowledge vacuum that hampers effective professional decision making in these areas of need. The anxiety might stimulate both the professional and the academic community to an unprecedented forward thrust in both applied and basic research and technology, to fill the vacuum that must ultimately be filled. Neither the profession nor the culture can much longer afford the luxury of professional psychology remaining aloof from the truly professional dilemma of struggling with real problems to which we do not know the solutions while we remain scientist-practitioners of a high-level technology that, as such, is an inhibiting defense against the realities of professional practice. The range of problems with which professional psychology currently deals is of course much broader than a strict interpretation of the scientist-practitioner model would allow, and conversely this scientific knowledge base is less adequately established. Indeed, psychology has already moved a long way toward becoming a true profession, dedicated to dealing with any problem of less-than-optimal behavior. There is no area of human need that is ultimately of greater importance. It bears ultimately on the quality of life, both personal and societal, with potential for enhanced effectiveness, adaptability, and health.

Annotated Bibliography

Alander, R., and Campbell, T. "An Evaluative Study of an Alcohol and Drug Recovery Program: A Case Study of the Oldsmobile Experience." *Human Resource Management,* 1975, *14*, 14-18.

Refers to studies by W. Winslow, United States government, and J. Vitek that show the increased costs associated with problem drinker employees. At Oldsmobile's Lansing plant, changes were compared in on-the-job behavior for voluntary participants in the recovery program and in a control group of abusers. Community resources were used for treatment and rehabilitation services. The control group (N = 24) had one full year each of pre- and post-program involvement. Post-program behavior is reported for three experimental groups (total N = 117) having a follow-up period of one year, six months to a year, and less than six months, respectively. In all categories, all study groups showed a substantial decline in lost man-hours, sickness and accident benefits paid, leaves of absence, grievances, disciplinary action, accidents, and wages lost. Collectively, wages lost decreased 52 percent from an employee average of $3,851 to $1,862. Collectively, the difference was in excess of $250,000. By contrast, the control group showed a substantial increase in sickness and accident benefits, leaves of absence, and disciplinary actions. The average wages lost increased almost 10 percent to an average of $3,450 per person. Clearly, the program paid off for both the company and participating employees.

Albee, G. "The Uncertain Future of American Psychology."
    Unpublished document presented to APA Policy and Plan-
    ning Board, 1972.

    Reviews the remarkable growth in first-year graduate stu-
dents in doctoral programs between 1970 and 1971, from 7,588
to 11,800, this level being more than sustained in 1972. These
data enable a prediction of 5,000 to 7,000 doctorates annually
in four or five years (1977). The author comments that psychology is a young profession, losing but 1 percent of faculty annually, in contrast to the 5 to 6 percent loss of other disciplines.
"Well over half of all living Ph.D.s in psychology have been
awarded . . . in the past decade!" Albee speculates on various
projections and opportunities and notes that graduate programs
must adapt to the changing job demands of tomorrow and to
the interests of students today.

Alexander, R. J., and Sheely, M. D. "Cost per Hour for Delivery
    of Service in a Community Mental Health Center." Dis-
    eases of the Nervous System, 1971, 32, 769-776.

    Cost comparisons between fee-for-service provision and
services offered by one community mental health center were
made for various mental health specialists. The standard charges
in the community were: psychiatry—$30 per hour; psychology
—$25 per hour; and social work—$20 per hour. Authors concluded that this clinic could not provide services for less than
the private sector; in fact, physician costs were higher at the
clinic.

Alter, J. Narrowing Our Medical Care Gap. Jericho, New York:
    Exposition Press, 1972.

    Notes that psychosocial factors, as expressed in smoking,
drinking, overeating, alcohol and drug intake, and interpersonal
and intergroup frictions, contribute to morbidity and mortality.
This brief, easy-to-read account is designed to show the inadequacy of current health insurance measures and to show that
government funding of hospital construction, Medicare, and
Medicaid have helped raise hospital utilization without improv-

ing health care. Also notes that excessive specialization has fragmented health service and suggests training health providers in community settings rather than in hospitals.

American Law Institute. *Restatement of the Law, Agency 2d.* Vol. 1. Philadelphia: American Law Institute, 1958.

The authoritative compilation of and commentary on administrative law on agency and related topics.

American Medical Association. "Principles of Medical Ethics. Opinions and Reports of the Judicial Council." *JAMA,* 1958, *167,* 6.

The official code of ethics of organized medicine, with extensive commentary by the Judicial Council of the American Medical Association.

American Psychiatric Association. *Diagnostic and Statistical Manual of Mental Disorders.* (2d ed., DSM-II). Washington, D.C.: American Psychiatric Association, 1968.

Prepared by the American Psychiatric Association's Committee on Nomenclature and Statistics, this booklet provides instructions for use, definitions of (diagnostic) terms, a listing of mental disorders and their code numbers (for example, *307.3: transient situational disturbances [307], adjustment reaction of adult life [.3],* tables comparing information with the previous DSM-I (1951) and with the International Classification of Diseases (ICD), and related information. The DSM-II is a move to greater uniformity with the World Health Organization's eighth revision of its ICD-8, which became effective in 1968 .

American Psychiatric Association. *Equal Coverage for the Mentally Ill, A Position Statement.* Washington, D.C.: American Psychiatric Association, 1972.

A position statement summarizing the L. Reed study of federal contracts. Points out that first-dollar coverage of members by the United Auto Workers (UAW) provides for outpatient mental health care at from $2.00 to $2.50 a covered person per year.

American Psychiatric Association. "Recent Data Documenting the Feasibility of Nondiscriminatory Coverage of Mental Illness." Unpublished document prepared for the American Psychiatric Association, Washington, D.C., March 1975.

Data from the federal employee Blue Cross plan shows a plateau of use in 1972 and 1973. Equal coverage for mental disorder is provided for hospital and outpatient services in 68 percent and 41 percent of the plans, respectively, among 148 large employers surveyed by the Bureau of Labor Statistics. Canada's federal-provincial health insurance programs provide all needed care for mental conditions on the same basis as other conditions. The proportion of total payout for mental disorder is 5 percent or less depending on the province.

American Psychological Association. "Report of the Committee on a Directory of Psychological Service Centers." *American Psychologist,* 1953, *8,* 682-685.

Contains the criteria tentatively recommended for voluntary listing in a directory of psychologists and agencies certified as competent to deliver health services. The content of directory entries and the structure and functions of the reviewing board are specified.

American Psychological Association. *Ethical Standards of Psychologists.* Rev. ed. Washington, D.C.: American Psychological Association, 1963.

This eight-page policy statement presents the APA's current position on the psychologist's obligations to serve the best interests of his or her colleagues and of society. The nineteen specific principles address: responsibility, competence, moral and legal standards, misrepresentation, confidentiality, client welfare, client relationship, impersonal services, announcement of services, interprofessional relations, remuneration, test security, interpretation and publication, research precautions, publication credit, responsibility to organizations, and promotional activities. First issued in 1953; updated in 1959, 1963.

American Psychological Association, Committee on Legislation. "A Model for State Legislation Affecting the Practice of Psychology 1967." *American Psychologist,* 1967, *22,* 1095-1103.

Traces the history of state legislation affecting psychology and recommends that future laws and law revisions seek to secure licensing in which psychotherapy is included within the definition of practice. Preference was expressed for a one-level law requiring the doctorate and two years of supervised experience. Provisions for reciprocity, privileged communication, a code of ethics, and an injunction authority were also recommended. The committee reported that antagonism from other professions, notably medicine and psychiatry, appears to have decreased.

American Psychological Association. *The Psychologist and Voluntary Health Insurance.* (Rev. ed.) Washington, D.C.: American Psychological Association, 1968*a*.

Summarizes the growing recognition of psychologists under health insurance. Notes the emergence of the psychologist as an autonomous practitioner, citing state legal opinions in Michigan, New York, and California that the practice of psychotherapy is not restricted to physicians. Lists fourteen insurance companies that have recognized the services of psychologists in some of their plans, with testimonial notes of favorable experience from Continental Assurance and Occidental Life. The appendix includes *Ethical Standards of Psychologists* (APA, 1963), state laws regulating practice, and state association insurance chairpersons.

American Psychological Association. *Psychology as a Profession.* Washington, D.C.: American Psychological Association, 1968*b*.

A broad policy statement by the American Psychological Association on the professional aspects of psychology.

American Psychological Association. "Psychology and National Health Care." *American Psychologist,* 1971, *26,* 1025-1026.

A position statement of the APA recommending certain guidelines for a comprehensive national health care program: equal access by all, protection of individual rights, comprehensive services, freedom of choice, consumer participation, evaluation of quality, peer review, inclusion of mental health care, participation of all health professionals, and so forth.

American Psychological Association. *The Consolidated Roster for Psychology.* Washington, D.C.: American Psychological Association, 1973.

Based on a 1972 survey of psychologists in the United States and Canada, this locator reference lists 35,206 APA members and 10,480 nonmembers, a total of 45,686. Includes address and phone numbers, data on current employer, highest degree, diplomate and licensure status, and a geographical (state) cross-reference.

American Psychological Association. "APA-Approved Doctoral Programs in Clinical, Counseling and School Psychology: 1974." *American Psychologist,* 1974a, *29,* 844-845.

Lists the ninety-four United States APA-accredited doctoral programs in clinical psychology, as well as three in Canada and four provisionally approved programs. Twenty-two counseling and six school psychology programs are also listed.

American Psychological Association. *Standards for Providers of Psychological Services.* Washington, D.C.: American Psychological Association, 1974b.

A policy statement in two major parts: the "preamble" outlines history, rationale, guiding principles, and implications of the *Standards.* The balance of the document contains a glossary of terms and sets forth standards for providers, programs, and service environments. A special section notes four major areas of accountability for practitioners.

American Psychological Association, Health Benefits Task Force, Committee on Health Insurance. "The Integration of Mental Health Services in a Comprehensive National Health Plan." Unpublished document, ed. R. Bent and A. E. Shapiro. Washington, D.C.: 1974.

The report of APA's Health Benefits Task Force, describing an optimal mental health benefits "package" and how to organize the delivery these benefits within a national health plan.

Argyris, C. *Intervention Theory and Method.* Reading, Mass.: Addison-Wesley, 1970.

A theoretical approach to intervention in organizational structures (primarily business, industrial, and corporate) in order to bring about increased human and output effectiveness.

Auster, S. L. "Insurance Coverage for 'Mental and Nervous Conditions': Developments and Problems." *American Journal of Psychiatry,* 1969, *126,* 698-705.

Reviews the evidence for the probable acceleration of insurance coverage for mental illness treatment. Points out the flaws in some of the arguments advanced by insurers against increased coverage and stresses the need for peer review as a control measure.

Avnet, H. H. *Psychiatric Insurance: Financing Short-Term Ambulatory Treatment.* New York: Group Health Insurance, 1962.

This landmark study indicates that less than 1.5 percent of those covered during the thirty months of the project filed claims for mental health benefits. A high percentage of individuals advised to seek professional treatment never did so. Patients with mental conditions used substantially more (176 percent) medical or surgical services than patients not diagnosed as having a mental condition. Only slightly over one-third of the patients were referred by family physicians. Approximately an equal number were self-referred, while the remaining one-third were referred by other sources. Neuroses accounted for 42 percent of the cases; psychoses, 20 percent; personality disorders, 14 percent; and transient situational disorders, 11 percent.

Avnet, H. H. "Psychiatric Insurance—Ten Years Later." *American Journal of Psychiatry*, 1969, *126*, 113-120.

Cites the Health Insurance Plan of Greater New York premium rate of $10.80 per capita or $32.40 per family, along with an estimated cost of $50 per clinic service. Unit cost of clinic services in the Retail Clerks Union in Los Angeles in 1968 were $30.86 per visit and $39.76 per clinician treatment hour, while fee-for-service rates in New York and Los Angeles in 1968 were from $25 to $30 per hour. Data suggests that prepaid plans do not deliver services at less cost.

Bailey, M. A., Warshaw, L., and Eichler, R. M. "A Study of Factors Related to Length of Stay in Psychotherapy." *Journal of Clinical Psychology*, 1959, *15*, 442-444.

A study of demographic variables related to terminators and remainers in psychotherapy. Diagnosis was not related to length of therapy; in fact, only educational levels suggested a significant correlation.

Balint, M. *The Doctor, His Patient and the Illness*. New York: International Universities Press, 1957.

Years of experience with national health care in the United Kingdom led Dr. Balint and his associates to the discovery that patients with personal problems learn quickly that their doctors will only listen to complaints of physical distress. Consequently, patients unconsciously somaticize their emotional problems and thereby are accorded their doctor's attention and sympathy. This process is encouraged by the fact that doctors provide health care under insurance (government or otherwise) and are poorly motivated to get involved in the patient's problems.

Baynes, T., Jr. "Continuing Conjectural Concepts Concerning Civil Commitment Criteria." *American Psychologist*, 1971, *26*, 489-495.

Reviews state involuntary commitment codes and underscores their deficiencies. None of the statutes explicitly defines the criteria for deviant behavior on which commitment will be based. Moreover, until recently these laws have failed pragmatically to guarantee the patients' civil rights. The majority lack a statutory definition of mental illness, but rather are addressed to the person who is a personal or public nuisance. Behavioral aspects—that is, nonmedical criteria—are the dominant modes of definition. The construction of most codes is circular. The authors conclude that these codes are "conflicting labels that are the social excuse for incarcerating the gauche."

Beach, F. A. "The Snark was a Boojum." *American Psychologist*, 1950, *5*, 115-124.

A delightful and informative discussion of some of the characteristics and foibles of the comparative psychology movement in the United States.

Bennett, A., Hargrove, E., and Engle, B. "Voluntary Health Insurance and Nervous and Mental Disease." *JAMA*, January 17, 1953, *151*, 202-207.

Gives an excellent, though dated historical perspective on health insurance for mental disorders.

Bennett, D. "Community Mental Health Services in Britain." *American Journal of Psychiatry*, 1973, *130*, 1065-1070.

Describes how Britain evolved the plan of "sectorizing" services to population groups of 60,000. Both mental hospitals and general hospitals are managed by the same regional wards. The major aims are prevention of chronic patienthood and the closing of mental hospitals. The inclusive localism prevents professionals from getting rid of undesirable patients by referring the patients elsewhere.

Bennis, W. G. "Organizational Developments and the Fate of Bureaucracy." *Industrial Management Review*, 1966, *7*, 41-55.

A historical and trend analysis that predicts the future of the bureaucratic form in western society.

Bent, R. J. "One Approach to Evaluating Mental Health Delivery Systems." In F. T. Crawford (Ed.), *Exploring Mental Health Parameters*. Atlanta: Paje, 1974.

Offers a systematic approach designed to help psychologists carry out relevant evaluation in actual health service organizations.

Binner, P., Halpern, J., and Potter, A. "Patients, Programs and Results in a Comprehensive Mental Health Center." *Journal of Consulting and Clinical Psychology*, 1973, *41*, 148-156.

Using a value output index, the authors found that "the best return for the program dollar invested can be realized by giving treatment of very low intensity to all patients regardless of their level of impairment." They argue for maximum possible use of outpatient and partial hospitalization resources and minimum use of inpatient care. In no case, however, did the analysis find less than a dollar's worth of value returned for each program dollar invested. This article provides a means of measuring therapeutic outcome according to the intensity of the treatment process, while also taking into account the degree of severity of the mental condition.

The BLK Group. "Survey of Clinical Psychologists Receiving Payments Under Title XIX of the Social Security Act: Draft Final Report to National Institute of Mental Health." Unpublished report, Contract No. ADM-42-74-74 (MH). The BLK Group, Inc., 1730 M Street NW, Washington, D.C., August 25, 1975.

Notes inaccuracies and problems in identifying states that grant independent vendor status to psychologists. Of nine states identified by the National Institute of Mental Health (California, Colorado, Georgia, Kentucky, Nevada, New Mexico, New Hampshire, Maine, and Wisconsin) BLK found that only four (Nevada, New Mexico, Maine, and Wisconsin) covered both testing and treatment on an independent basis. [At date of report, independent status was in effect also for New Jersey, Ohio, and Michigan, as BLK later found out, but not Nevada.—Ed.] It proved impossible to obtain comparative utilization data among all states, and frequency and cost data for psychologists was often not identified. Maine has differential therapy rates of $35, $25, and $23.75 for psychiatrists, psychologists and social workers. New Jersey differentiates psychology generalists from specialists, $26 and $37 per hour, respectively. New Mexico requires prior authorization after three visits (found too expensive for initial visit); Connecticut and Nevada recognize only Ph.D.-level psychologists. Payments to psychologists as a percent of total vendor payments in four states (Maine, New Jersey, Nevada, and Montana) in 1974 averaged only .17 percent of the Medicaid budgets in those states.

Blue Cross Association. "Blue Cross Plan Psychiatric Benefit Surveys." Unpublished report. Blue Cross Association, Chicago, May 20, 1969, and December 29, 1969.

This study analyzed the conditions for inpatient and outpatient services under seventy-four Blue Cross plans and found a wide variation among the plans for these services. One hundred and twenty days of inpatient care per calendar year and an aggregate of $400 for outpatient services per calendar year were modal benefits. There was even a wider variation for psychiatric day care and psychiatric night care, with as little as $6 per day for 30 days under one plan for psychiatric day care and night care, which could either be charged as half day of benefits or as a whole day of benefits, depending on the plan.

Bodenheimer, T. "The Hoax of National Health Insurance." *American Journal of Public Health,* 1972, *62,* 1324-1327.

This critical study of National Health Insurance suggests that it is designed to meet a health care crisis caused by financial instability, influential providers and payers of health care. Author sees the common element of all such plans as the transfer of money from working Americans to powerful payers and

providers. Forecasts the evolution of a tax-subsidized, monopo-
listic, health industry empires.

Boneau, A. "Job Market Holding Firm." *APA Monitor,* 1974, *5,*
18.

Using data from 198 doctorate-granting departments, reports that from 1971 to 1974 the proportion of new doctorates
in academic settings has steadily declined, while the number in
nonacademic settings has risen (almost equal in 1974). While
18.5 percent of these graduates were not placed as of June, previous experience has demonstrated that virtually all doctorate
recipients find employment by September after graduating.

Boring, E. G. *A History of Experimental Psychology.* New
York: Appleton-Century-Crofts, 1929.

An excellent, informative history of the development of
psychology as a profession until 1929. Should be familiar to all
psychologists.

Boroson, W. "Diagnosing Your Health Insurance." *Money,*
1974, *3,* 39-51.

Describes coverage by "layers": (1) minor expenses such as
occasional doctor visits and maternity benefits; (2) hospital
charges and basic protection; (3) major medical expenses in
thousand-dollar brackets; and (4) catastrophic expenses in tens
of thousands. Notes that typical group insurance plans return
more than 95 percent of all premiums in benefits, whereas the
comparable "loss ratio" for commercial individual insurance is
only somewhat over 55 percent. Cites the basic insurance principle that insurance is best when it protects against a large loss
that is unlikely to happen and least effective when it protects
against a small loss that is likely to happen.

Brenner, H. *Mental Illness and the Economy.* Cambridge, Mass.:
Harvard University Press, 1973.

Studying a period of 127 years, Brenner documents the
strong inverse and stable correlations that occurred between
changes in the economy and the use of mental hospitals. This

relation is so consistent for certain segments of society that virtually no major factor other than economic instability influenced variation in mental hospitalization rates. Moreover, this relationship has not been affected by any of the major changes in psychiatric practice or society as a whole. The problems of mental disorder are placed clearly within social policy.

Burnell, G. M. "Financing Mental Health Care—An Appraisal of Various Models." *Archives of General Psychiatry,* 1971, *25,* 49-55.

Indicates that the financing of psychiatric care is an important variable in determining the type of treatment, the duration of hospitalization, and the length of outpatient psychotherapy. Despite many clinical innovations, new legislation, and increased federal funding in the last decade, there are only scant research data on new methods of financing mental health care. Current economic models include: (1) fee-for-service plans, (2) commercial and governmental insurance plans, (3) prepayment plans, and (4) public subsidy plans. The advantages and disadvantages of each economic model are analyzed. Author concludes that there is a close relationship between economic models and the types of delivery of mental health services and that there is an urgent need for systematic studies of cost, utilization, and clinical effectiveness within the framework of each economic system.

California Medical Association. California Relative Value Studies: 1969. California Medical Association, San Francisco: 1969.

Of special interest to psychology is the 90800 series for psychiatric services, consultations (90600 series), the medicine modifiers, and special services and billing procedures. Procedures within these series are assigned a relative unit value (or weight) based primarily on time involved and also complexity. A conversion factor applied to the unit value may be used to derive fees within a section. The factor will vary between communities. This relative value study is widely used to provide fee guidelines.

Campbell, L., III, and Hodges, W. "Professional Training in Clinical Psychology: A Student's Perspective." *The Clinical Psychologist,* 1975, *28,* 7-8.

Suggests that a training model for providing the clinician with the wide repertoire of therapeutic, diagnostic, and consultative skills necessary for effective clinical functioning is sorely lacking. The university clinic or teaching hospital rarely provide a valid representation of the clinical environment in which most graduates find employment. Use of the attending psychologist recruited from the professional community is the only method by which a truly professional training program can be implemented and operated, with training in relevant, real-world situations. The resistance to change in universities from the traditional scientist-practitioner, referred to as the Boulder model, is commented on.

Cant, G. "An X-Ray Analysis of Doctors' Bills." *Money,* 1973, *2,* 23-27.

Notes that public support and insurance after World War II have in the main eliminated charity medicine for the physician. Describes the inflation in medical costs. Notes that fee ceilings tend to become the floor, insurance adds bookkeeping costs and the concept of usual and customary, or reasonable (UCR) does not serve to lower fees. Rise in hospital costs have been sharpest. Reports fees for ten common procedures (including psychiatric office visit) by four broad regions of the country.

Carey, K., and Kogan, W. "Exploration of Factors Influencing Physician Decisions to Refer Patients for Mental Health Services." *Medical Care,* 1971, *9,* 55-66.

Reports that emotional problems were identified in 822 of 10,667 patients who had health checkups. Half (411) of these cases were made known to the examining physician at the time of the check; half were not. This information "*did not* result in an alteration of the pattern of referral already in existence." (This data suggests that information alone is insufficient to have the primary physician change his or her attitude toward referral of patients for mental care, and raises serious questions as to whether the "primary physician" referral concept is viable for dealing with mental problems.—Ed.) In the Group Health Cooperative of Puget Sound, the general practice group saw treatment of emotional problems as part of their role more than did medical specialty groups. The general practice group was the greatest prescriber of psychotropic drugs; the surgical specialty group was the most frequent prescriber of placebo drugs.

Cates, J. "Psychology's Manpower: Report on the 1968 National Register of Scientific and Technical Personnel." *American Psychologist,* 1970, *25,* 254-263.

Intended as a complete census of psychologists, this report is based on 23,077 registrants from a mailing list of 35,529. In terms of relation to principal employment, 29 percent were clinical psychologists. Provides data on degree level by specialty, income ranges (interquartile range and median for clinical subfield, Ph.D.'s, clinical practice were: 12,100 to 20,200 and 15,600; 13,900 to 21,100 and 17,000; 12,000 to 21,000 and 16,000, respectively), and ratio by population among states (1.7 per 10,000 nationally).

Civilian Health and Medical Program of the Uniformed Services: Performance Data Fiscal Year 1970 and 1971. Personal communication from Vernon McKenzie, Principal Deputy Assistant Secretary for Health and Environment, Department of Defense, to Jack Wiggins, Chair, APA Committee on Health Insurance, December 6, 1971.

Data are for the year immediately prior to removal of the medical referral requirement and for the year immediately after. Statistics are not completely clean because of partial fiscal years involved but are suggestive. All outpatient health services increased 19 percent and mental outpatient services increased 22 percent. Expenditures for psychologist outpatient and inpatient visits increased 46 percent and 25 percent to 1.9 and .15 million dollars, respectively. Expenditures for psychiatrist outpatient and inpatient visits increased 24 percent and 73 percent to 5.7 and 5.7 million dollars, respectively. Of total expenditures for

visits to both professions, the proportion to psychologists was
at 15 percent in both years, though by type of care the trend
was to an increased use of psychologists for ambulatory care,
when referral requirements were eliminated. In contrast, psychiatric inpatient visits showed a sharp rise in 1971.

While the cost of psychological services increased in fiscal
year 1971 following removal of the requirement for medical
referral in June 1970, the increased cost of psychiatric services
was even greater, reflecting overall increased utilization. Psychological outpatient and inpatient visit costs increased from 1970
to 1971, from $1,300,000 to $1,900,000 and from $121,000 to
$151,000, respectively; for psychiatry the comparable figures
were $4,600,000   and $5,700,000   and $3,300,000   and
$5,700,000. Of the two professional service components com-
bined, with elimination of the referral requirement, psychological outpatient services increased from 22 to 25 percent of the
combined cost, but its inpatient proportion decreased from 3.5
to 2.6 percent approximately. The overall increase was due to
general cost increases and to an increase in the persons served.
The implication clearly is that the referral requirement was not
an effective means of cost control. In fiscal year 1972, the average cost per beneficiary user of outpatient services was $478,
the majority of users served within 15 visits. The average yearly
cost of inpatient users of mental health services was $2,258.

Clampitt, R. "1975 MPA Fee Survey." *Minnesota Psychological
Association Newsletter,* September 4 to 6, 1975.

Reports data on 469 usable returns; 57.4 percent of those
surveyed in June 1975. Of MPA members, 47 percent have
some private practice activity, in contrast to 30 percent of nonmembers. Since there was a clear tendency for those devoting
less than 20 hours weekly to practice to charge lower fees, average fees were calculated on a weighted basis of hours devoted to
practice. The fees at the tenth, fiftieth, and ninetieth percentiles
of doctoral-level clinicians providing hourly consultation were
$19, $28, and $48; for evaluation, $19, $30, $41; for group
therapy, $9, $14, $19; and for psychotherapy, $23, $33, $41.
The weighted means of doctoral practitioners for psychother-

apy and group therapy were $38.05 and $17.91 as compared to $32.78 and $13.95 for master's-level practitioners.

Clark, C. "Courts of First Resort." *Money,* 1973, *2,* 32-35.

Includes a tabulation by state of the claim limit and court name. Typically, trials are held for a modest fee, within a few weeks after complaints have been filed. Formal rules of evidence are usually relaxed, no stenographic accounts are made, no jury is involved, attorneys are not necessary, and settlement is prompt.

Clark, K. E. *America's Psychologists: A Survey of a Growing Profession.* Washington, D.C.: American Psychological Association, 1957.

Founded in 1892, with 31 members, the American Psychological Association had almost 15,000 members in 1956, the membership doubling every seven to eight years. Boring therefore extrapolated that by 2100 A.D. there would be more psychologists than people. By detailed surveys of psychologists and retrospective comparisons, Clark draws a number of conclusions that appear to hold valid today: significant contributions emerge early in their careers; team and cooperative research appears to heighten productivity; the activities of colleagues and availability of time are more conducive to research than financial support for research; diversity within the association will increase; the experimental-physiological-general psychologists (once the exclusive membership) are now a minority; applied psychologists are more involved in state associations and experimental psychologists in regional associations; and successful applied psychologists easily match or exceed the salary of significant contributors. A 1954 survey of 100 Los Angeles psychologists in private practice found the modal hourly therapy session fee to be $10, with 77 percent of these practitioners charging $7.50 to $15.00. Overall, the average fee was $10.33.

Clarke, G. *Health Programs in the States: A Survey.* New Brunswick, N.J.: Center for State Legislative Research and Service, Eagleton Institute of Politics, Rutgers University, 1975.

Highlights disparities among states in their Medicaid programs; cites problems of rate and cost regulation; summarizes
the development of health maintenance organizations; and provides statistical data by state on mental health programs. Also
includes sections on other health data, by state.

Cohen, J., and Hunter, H. "Mental Health Insurance: A Comparison of a Fee-for-Service Indemnity Plan and a Comprehensive Mental Health Center." *American Journal of
Orthopsychiatry*, 1972, *42*, 146-153.

Report on why a local union with a prepaid insurance supporting a comprehensive mental health center switched to a fee-
for-service indemnity plan. Compares the experience of two
Retail Clerks locals. The cost per eligible member serviced was
$245.73 in the comprehensive plan and $452.70 in the indemnity plan. The difference was largely due to the high hospital
utilization in the indemnity plan (31.3 days per 1,000 eligibles,
compared to 20.8 days in the comprehensive plan). The comprehensive plan, however, had a generous array of services, resulting in five times greater utilization (5.6 percent as compared
to 1.0 percent) than for the indemnity plan, with the intention
of providing saturation-level services. This approach resulted in
a higher cost per eligible for the comprehensive plan: $13.80 as
compared to $3.88 for the indemnity plan.

Commission on Accreditation of Rehabilitation Facilities. *Standards Manual for Rehabilitation Facilities.* Chicago, Ill.:
Commission on Accreditation of Rehabilitation Facilities,
1973.

This 127-page document is the revision of the original
1965 manual. It is comprised of five major parts: (1) an intro-
ductory section, including a glossary and criteria of eligibility
for accreditation; (2) the standards, organized under nine basic
areas; (3) an interpretation section for each major standard; (4)
a checklist for preliminary self-survey; and (5) the commission's
policies and procedures for conducting surveys. The definition
of *psychologist* appears on Page 15.

Committee for Economic Development [CED], Research and
Policy Committee. *Building a National Health Care System.* New York: Committee for Economic Development,
1973.

Finds that nearly half the increase in expenditure for personal health care since 1950 is due to price rather than to
greater utilization or new techniques. Notes a functional as well
as geographic maldistribution of manpower and resources and
national inadequacy in primary care. Advocates prospective rate
setting and national policy in the support of health manpower
training. Provides data and analysis on manpower, costs, hospital use, mental health, and so on. Objective is an integrated,
prepaid comprehensive health care system developed on a
phase-in approach. A carefully developed study report and pertinent reference.

Conley, R. *The Economics of Mental Retardation.* Baltimore,
M.D.: Johns Hopkins Press, 1973.

Based on a 1971 study, commissioned by the President's
Committee on Mental Retardation, which estimates that the
social well-being of the United States was reduced by an annual
rate of $7 billion due to mental retardation. Of this amount,
$4.8 billion was caused by the loss of productivity by underemployment, and $2.2 billion by "excess costs" of programs.

Conley, R. W., Conwell, M., and Arrill, M. B. "An Approach to
Measuring the Cost of Mental Illness." *American Journal
of Psychiatry,* 1967, *124,* 755-762.

In 1966, the estimated costs of mental illness were $20 billion, including the estimated costs of direct treatment services,
loss of earnings, and other losses of productivity.

Consumer Reports. "National Health Insurance: Which Way to
Go?" *Consumer Reports,* 1975, *40,* 118-124.

Notes that health expenditures now claim 7.8 percent of
the GNP. Claims that the marriage of public funding and private
administration, wide variance in health under welfare, and lack

of incentive to preventive care are major problems. Analyzes the major national and health insurance proposals, noting that the United States is the only major industrial nation without a comprehensive national plan. Points out that "the significant difference among the plans is not the total cost, but who pays it—and how." Analyzes the five main national health insurance proposals of the 93rd Congress in terms of how they meet consumer goals; describes these goals; compares costs; and offers certain recommendations. A concise, salient, and readily understood review of the issues.

Council for the Advancement of Psychological Professions and Sciences [CAPPS]. "Principles for National Health Insurance." Unpublished document. Council for the Advancement of Psychological Professions and Sciences, 1200 17th Street NW, Washington, D.C. 20036, December 13, 1973.

The twelve national health insurance principles described are: universality of coverage, freedom-of-choice of practitioner, dual choice among plans, utilization controls on providers, different systems for active treatment and continuing care, prepayment, minimal government intrusion, mental health service an integral component, continuity of care, prevention orientation, ambulatory alternatives to hospitalization, market demand, and consumer use determination.

Crawford, J. L., Morgan, D. W., and Gianturco, D. (Eds.) *Progress in Mental Health Information Systems: Computer Applications*. Cambridge, Mass.: Ballinger Publishing Company, 1974.

A detailed overview and commentary on existing automated mental health information systems.

Cuca, J. "Graduate Enrollments Leveling Off." *APA Monitor*, 1974, *5*, 16-19.

An association survey of graduate study enrollment; shows that 33 percent of the doctoral enrollment is in clinical and professional programs, with 833 such doctorates awarded in 1973 from a total of 2,612. Total graduate student enrollment was 37,188.

Cuca, J. "Clinicians Compose 36 Percent of APA." *APA Monitor,* 1975, *6,* 4.

Based on 1972 data: 80 percent of clinicians have a doctorate, 74 percent were licensed or certified, and 55 percent engage in fee service therapy some of the time. Only 3 percent were unemployed but only 31 percent of these were seeking employment (less than 1 percent). Moreover, 40 percent of the employed had a full-time position and one or more part-time positions as well.

Cummings, N. A., and Follette, W. "Psychiatric Services and Medical Utilization in a Prepaid Health Plan Setting (Part II)." *Medical Care,* 1968, *6,* 31-41.

Reports that attempts to increase the number of referrals to psychotherapy by the use of computerized early detection and referral resulted in zero increase in the number of patients seeking psychotherapy. The authors concluded that in a prepaid comprehensive health plan setting already maximally employing educative techniques to both patients and physicians, and already providing a range of prepaid psychological services, the number of insured persons seeking psychotherapy will reach an optimal level and remain constant year after year.

Davidson, H. "Health Insurance and Psychiatric Coverage." *The American Journal of Psychiatry,* 1957, *114,* 498-504.

This time-dated article provides a useful historical perspective.

Davis, K. *National Health Insurance: Benefits, Costs and Consequences.* Studies in Social Economics. Washington, D.C.: The Brookings Institution, 1975.

Underscores that the present diverse public health programs lack a unifying policy. The growth of the private health insurance industry to $32,000,000,000 in 1975 has been closely linked to the work place, with resultant major gaps in coverage. Health services are now a $100,000,000,000 industry. It follows then that to be accepted and functional a national health insurance (NHI) plan must be equitably financed, easy to understand and administer, and acceptable to the providers. Revamping the payment system might enable reorganization of health delivery but these are not primary NHI goals.

An analysis of the implications of the major NHI proposals placed before Congress suggests that those neither poor enough to qualify for governmental assistance nor with sufficient assets to afford the full costs may be most adversely affected. Major cost implications are specified, such as the inflationary potential of covering the entire costs of short hospital stays, the UCR fee practice, and excessive use of advanced technology under catastrophic coverage. Then, because of their current substantial role, any NHI plan that does not involve the private companies is likely to result in substantial displacement effects. There is a substantial degree of uniformity in goals of the bills before Congress, and they appear to differ little in real costs. Rather, they differ markedly in methods of financing, administration, and reimbursement of providers.

Decker, B., and Bonner, P. *PSRO: Organization for Regional Peer Review.* Cambridge, Mass.: Ballinger Publishing Company, 1973.

A comprehensive study on PSRO (Professional Standards Review Organization) and factors related to peer review. A streamlined version of the Arthur D. Little, Inc., report for the U.S. Department of Health, Education, and Welfare on developing a working model of peer review under Medicare and Medicaid. Extensive coverage of quality care assessment, cost control methods, data processing systems for medical care appraisal, and suggested PSRO guidelines.

Dominick, P. H. "High-Quality Medical Care." *Congressional Record,* March 22, 1973, S. 5488-5493.

Peter Dominick, retired senator from Colorado, details an eloquent account of the history of the foundation for medical care movement and declares his confidence in the delivery of quality health services by these Individual Practice Associations (IPAs). Underscores their use of peer review to effect control of utilization and quality of services. A subsequent vote on the senator's amendment led to a revision of the Health Maintenance Organization Development Act to include foundations for medical care (PL 93-222).

Dörken, H. "Problems in Administration and the Establishment of Community Mental Health Services." *Mental Hygiene,* 1962, *46,* 498-509.

Describes the development of Minnesota's Community Mental Health Program and draws certain generalities regarding: mental health boards, qualities of good administration, features of decentralized administration, paradoxes in community mental health programs, center-hospital relationships, and levels of public health concern. Concludes that small units of well-trained personnel are more effective and less costly than large units.

Dörken, H. "Insured Peace of Mind: Review of *Psychiatric Insurance: Financing Short Term Ambulatory Treatment,* ed. H. Avnet (New York: Group Health Insurance, Inc., 1962). *Contemporary Psychology,* 1963, *8,* 405-406.

Despite no-cost addition of mental benefits and their advertising, Group Health Insurance, Inc. (GHI) could not drive up utilization any higher than 1.5 percent of the eligibles in the thirty project months, five per 1,000 annually. For four out of five clients, individual office psychotherapy was the sole procedure. The cost per subscriber enabled an estimate of $.36 per person per month coverage. Problems of interprofessional coordination are noted. In July 1963, GHI offered psychiatric coverage at $.35 per month for single persons and $.60 per month for families.

Dörken, H. "Utilization of Psychologists in Positions of Responsibility in Public Mental Health Programs." *American Psychologist,* 1970, *25,* 953-958.

Reports, by state, on the appointment or opportunity for psychologists to head departments, divisions, mental hospitals, or community mental health centers (CMHCs) or to participate as a signatory in the commitment process. In 75 percent of the states psychologists were or by law could be directors of CMHCs.

Dörken, H. "A Dimensional Strategy for Community Focused Mental Health Services." In G. Rosenblum (Ed.), *Issues in Community Psychology and Preventive Mental Health.* New York: Behavioral Publications, 1971, pp. 75-87.

Advocates a public health model with emphasis on the "indirect" services rather than the usual almost exclusive focus on direct treatment services in order to meet community mental health needs, reorganize health care delivery, and achieve program control.

Dörken, H. "Reorganization of California State Hospitals: Impact on the Allied Health Professions." *Administration in Mental Health,* 1973, Fall, 42-51.

Describes the change in reorganization of state mental hospital services from discipline-oriented departments to programs each having a specific type of patient population. Selection of program directors was based on competence. The new system still failed to provide advancement for excellence of clinical performance, but did so provide for administration and supervision. Certain aspects of civil service structure such as inflexibility, seniority, classification of the job rather than the person, and lack of market gradation by profession (except for medicine) have hampered reorganization and curtailed potential results. A substantial shift away from totally medical program direction occurred. Among the nonmedical professions, psychologists became well-represented among program directors and assistants.

Dörken, H. "CHAMPUS Ten State Experience for Mental Disorder: FY 1973." Paper presented at the Symposium on Psychology as a Primary Health Provider. Annual Meeting of the American Psychological Association, New Orleans, Louisiana, 1974*a*.

An analysis of utilization of mental health direct service benefits under the Civilian Health and Medical Program of the Uniformed Services CHAMPUS program in the ten survey states. Although utilization of psychologists to psychiatrists for outpatient visits was on an average ratio of 1:2, or 19 percent and 40 percent of all such visits, there was substantial variation among the states. The average fees of psychologists for outpatient psychotherapy at $31.65 were within $1.92 of parity with psychiatry.

Dörken, H. "Psychologist, Is There a Foundation in Your Future?" *Journal of Community Psychology*, 1974*b*, *2*, 99-103.

Summary review of the foundation for medical care (FMC) movement and its evolution as an "Individual Practice Association." Reports on the opening of membership to psychologists in the pioneering San Joaquin FMC and on the membership standards.

Dörken, H., and Whiting, J. F. "Psychologists as Health-Service Providers." *Professional Psychology*, 1974, *5*, 309-319.

Based on returns from the 1972 survey of members. A pilot study of fee service practice was conducted. Illustrates the iceberg phenomenon of practice: those psychologists in part-time practice are about five times the number in full-time practice. Provides some data on third-party reimbursement fees charged and practitioner income and outlines manpower projections.

Dorsey, J. L. "The Health Maintenance Organization Act of 1973, (PL 93-222) and Prepaid Group Practice Plans." *Medical Care*, 1975, *13*, 1-9.

Concludes that unless requirements similar to those imposed on Health Maintenance Organizations (HMOs) for certification are imposed on other private insurance carriers, then competitive marketplace forces cannot work on a publicly regulated but privately operated system. The act is seen as an alternative organizational structure for health services delivery and a potential forerunner to the benefit packages for national health insurance. Analyzes the law section by section.

Eisdorfer, C., and Lawton, M. P. (Eds.) *The Psychology of Adult Development and Aging.* Washington, D.C.: American Psychological Association, 1973.

This important resource book presents data, by various age groups, on utilization of mental facilities, including outpatient clinics, day-care facilities and hospitals, and nursing homes. Current 2 percent utilization for the elderly is considered unrealistically low; utilization could approach 5 percent. Manpower projections to meet current and future needs of the elderly are presented, indicating that less than half of the personnel needed are available or will be available in 1980 according to present training rates.

Eisenberg, H. "There's a Medical Foundation in Your Future." *Medical Economics,* 1971, *48,* 88-98.

Describes the medical foundation from its origins to its expansion as a health care delivery system across the United States. Contends that the foundation movement will be the largest and most acceptable model for United States health care providers.

Evenson, R. C. "Program Evaluation Using an Automated Data Base." *Hospital and Community Psychiatry,* 1974, *25,* 80-83.

Describes basic requirements and overview of the Missouri Automated Mental Health System and how the system outputs are used for program evaluation.

Feldman, S., and Windle, C. "The NIMH Approach to Evaluating the Community Mental Health Centers Program." *Health Services Reports,* 1973, *88,* 174-180.

Outlines methods for analyzing the effectiveness of the

community mental health center program and lists thirty-two references.

Fink, R. "Financing Outpatient Mental Health Care Through Psychiatric Insurance." *Mental Hygiene,* 1971, *55,* 143-150.

Describes research findings from studies on comprehensive psychiatric insurance. Focuses on the experience of the Health Insurance Plan (HIP) of Greater New York in a demonstration program that provided outpatient and inpatient psychiatric treatment with no upper limit on the number of visits and with no cost to the patient. The average annual utilization rate was between 1.5 to 2 percent per year, with about 15 visits per year for each patient treated. Results of the program, which gave a total of 16,264 services in a period of almost three years (with 60,000 eligible subscribers), led to an adoption of the plan for all subscribers to HIP. Premium rates for outpatient services were $.90 per month for a single person and $2.70 per month for a family of three or more.

Fink, R., Goldensohn, S., and Shapiro, S. "Family Physician Referrals for Psychiatric Consultation and Patient Initiative in Seeking Care." *Social Sciences and Medicine,* 1970, *4,* 273-291.

Examines the role of doctor and patient initiative in the family physician's referral decision in a prepaid medical group practice. Patients referred to the psychiatrist are classified according to whether the referral was patient-initiated or doctor-initiated; those who were not referred were classified according to whether or not they had ever wished a referral. Data are presented showing that physician referrals accounted for *only half* of enrollees needing mental health care. Therefore, physician referral requirements for psychotherapy artificially restricts services and creates a large unmet demand for care.

Fink, R., and Shapiro, S. "Patterns of Medical Care Related to Mental Illness." *Journal of Health and Human Behavior,* 1966, *7,* 98-105.

Indicates that the family doctor provides the only care received by 75 percent of the patients diagnosed as having mental conditions. Thus the family physician is not successful in obtaining the specialized care required for individuals with nervous and mental disorders.

Fink, R., and others. "Treatment of Patients Designated by Family Doctors as Having Emotional Problems." *American Journal of Public Health,* 1967, *57,* 1550-1564.

States that psychiatric referrals tend to go to those with conditions regarded by the family doctor as being of importance and with conditions that interfere with life activities. Unfortunately, 65 percent of the group in the sample of patients with psychiatric diagnoses had never discussed psychiatric referral by their family doctors. In another 9 percent of psychiatric diagnoses sampled, discussion had taken place but no referral made. In only 26 percent of the psychiatric sample had a medical referral been made. (These data suggest that the primary physician referral concept is an inadequate method for dealing with mental conditions in a health delivery system.—Ed.)

Fink, R., and others. "The 'Filter-Down' Process to Psychotherapy in a Group Practice Medical Care Program." *American Journal of Public Health,* 1969, *59,* 245-257.

Documents the fact that how patients see their problems affects their acceptance of treatment. Those regarded as having mental conditions were high utilizers of medical services. Important differences were found among patient groups in how fully they utilized psychotherapeutic services.

Follette, W., and Cummings, N. "Psychiatric Services and Medical Utilization in a Prepaid Health Plan Setting." *Medical Care,* 1967, *5,* 25-35.

Classic study showing that psychotherapy groups were high utilizers of medical facilities. For the "one-interview" and "brief psychotherapy" groups there was subsequent significant decline in overall utilization. For the long-term psychotherapy group, inpatient utilization declined significantly, to a level comparable to the general health plan population.

Follman, J. R., Jr. *Insurance Coverage for Mental Illness.* New York: American Management Association, 1970.

Provides a quick overview of the problems of mental illness, its treatment, and financing of care. Describes insurance coverages and other types of protection and cites some actuarial experience. Some of the findings include the facts that 50 percent of patients treated by general practitioners have emotional components; 43 percent of Army disability discharges during World War II were for neuropsychiatric reasons; there are 5,000,000 mentally retarded persons in the United States; emotional illness causes more absenteeism from work than any other illness except the common cold, costing American business $10,000,000,000 yearly; about 80 to 90 percent of industrial accidents originate in some type of mental or personality problem (these accidents kill 15,000 and disable 2 million each year at an estimated cost of $3,000,000,000); a total of 1.7 million alcoholics are employed in American industry, these employees losing, on the average, 22 days of work a year because of alcoholism or its physical effects.

Fordyce, W. E. "An Operant Conditioning Method for Managing Chronic Pain," *Postgraduate Medicine,* 1973, *53,* 123-128.

Holds that it is not necessary to have personality problems to have a pain habit. In chronic pain there is an opportunity for learned behavior. Describes an operant conditioning method for managing chronic pain where there is no organic base for the pain.

Foreyt, J., and others. "Cost-Benefit Analysis of a Token Economy Program." *Professional Psychology,* 1975, *6,* 26-33.

Reports that cost savings were $108 for each dollar spent on a program of tokens for acceptable behavior from seventy-four "untreatable" regressed mental patients in a custodial institution. Within one and a half years, 91 percent were living in the community. During this period, only 9 (11 percent) returned to a state mental hospital, compared to a 49 percent rate for the hospital as a whole. The cost of the program was $29,205 and cost savings were estimated at $3,137,935. If these regressed individuals had spent the rest of their lives as custodial patients (likely had there been no therapeutic intervention), the cost savings could be estimated to be $8,860,796 or a savings of $302 for each dollar spent. The method of analysis of data is useful and instructive.

FP. "Insurance Committee Report." *FP—Newsletter Journal of Florida Psychological Association,* 1974, *25,* 26.

Survey of fees charged for individual psychotherapy by psychologists found the median to be $40, though in the Orlando and Broward areas it was $30 and $35, respectively. Results sent to Blue Shield of Florida, and since accepted as the fee basis for CHAMPUS claims (previously would allow only 75 percent of fees paid psychiatrists with a maximum of $30).

Freedman, M. "The Graduate School of Wright Institute: Certain New Ways of Conducting Graduate Education in Psychology." *State Psychological Association Affairs,* 1975, *6,* 1-2.

Established in 1969 by Nevitt Sanford and the author with thirteen students, enrollment has increased to seventy-five. Most of their thirteen graduates are employed in academic settings even though the goal of the school is preparation for careers of research and action on human problems. Describes the faculty and student organizational model.

Fry, J. "Twenty-One Years of General Practice—Changing Patterns." *Journal of the Royal College of General Practitioners,* 1972, *22,* 521-528.

Presents detailed records of Fry's practice under the National Health Service. Makes the significant observation that, "It is of interest that the rates of attendance for psychiatric conditions have remained constant in spite of the advent of the newer psychotropic drugs."

Gamlin, J. "Claims Are Up, But Payments Are Down for Insurer's Health Maintenance Plan." *Business Insurance,* April 21, 1975, p. 56.

Reports Pacific Mutual Life Insurance Company's five-year experience with a health maintenance plan that placed a $100 deductible on hospitalization. First-dollar coverage for outpatient treatment for sickness or accident yielded a 30 percent increase in claims, but a reduction in costs. Enrolled firms report employee satisfaction. The Orange County Medical Foundation administers and pays all claims.

Gardner, J. *Self-Renewal: The Individual and the Innovative Society.* New York: Harper & Row, 1964.

Analyzes contemporary society and argues for a more optimistic, constructive approach to changing basic institutions and organizations, by redirecting the individual's assets and skills toward more open development.

Garfield, S. L. "Research on Client Variables in Psychotherapy." In A. E. Bergin and S. L. Garfield (Eds.), *Handbook of Psychotherapy and Behavior Change.* New York: John Wiley & Sons, 1971, p. 271-298.

An authoritative, comprehensive review and summary of empirical research on client variables in psychotherapy.

Garfield, S. L., and Affleck, D. D. "An Appraisal of Duration of Stay in Outpatient Psychotherapy." *Journal of Nervous and Mental Disease,* 1959, *129,* 494-498.

Relates the length of one's stay in psychotherapy to a number of critical variables. Diagnosis shows no significant relationship to length of stay in psychotherapy treatment in a general population of psychiatric patients.

Garfield, S. L., and Kurtz, R. "A Survey of Clinical Psychologists: Characteristics, Activities, and Orientations." *The Clinical Psychologist,* 1974, *28,* 7-10.

Survey taken in late 1973, sampled every third member of the division of clinical psychology of the APA. Ninety-seven percent were Ph.D.s, 2 percent foreign graduates; for 23 percent private practice was their main occupational setting while 47 percent engaged in such practice part-time, collectively 70 percent of the sample. Slightly less than half held but one position.

Gibson, R. "Can Mental Health Be Included in the Health Maintenance Organization?" *The American Journal of Psychiatry,* 1972, *128,* 33-39.

Claims it is difficult for enrollees to get psychiatric benefits in most HMO plans. Cites a cost of $10 per year per enrollee to cover mental health costs of hospital benefits, outpatient services, and some educational and consultative services.

Ginzberg, E. "What Next in Health Policy?" *Science,* 1975, *188,* 1184-1186.

Economist holds that national health insurance would not involve basic change in the health infrastructure but more likely would provide financial coverage for catastrophic illness and some broader entitlement for ambulatory care. The realities of the current economy and entrenched interests contraindicate major change. Improvements in the quality of life are prerequisites for improving national health.

Glasser, M. A., and Duggan, T. "Prepaid Psychiatric Care Experience with UAW Members." *American Journal of Psychiatry,* 1969, *126,* 675-681.

Reports that during the first year of the outpatient benefit, there was a utilization rate by Michigan UAW members of 6.4 per 1,000 eligible persons. The average number of visits was 8.5 and paid claims averaged $136. Total outpatient claims amounted to $940,000, indicating the cost of outpatient care received amounts to only about one-third the cost of inpatient care. Inpatient care costs rose from $1.8 million in 1965 to $2.8 million in 1967. The 53 percent increase, to $603 per hospital claim, was caused primarily by escalation of hospital costs as well as increase in the size of the population-at-risk and the median number of days hospitalized (12.6). The changes in the hospital benefit coverage, from 30 to 45 days, had no meaningful cost impact.

Goldberg, I., Krantz, G., and Locke, B. "Effect of a Short-Term Out-Patient Psychiatric Therapy Benefit on the Utilization of Medical Services in a Prepaid Group Practice Medical Program." *Medical Care,* 1970, *8,* 419-428.

Duplicates studies by Cummings and Follette and indicates that medical utilization declines as much as 30 percent following mental health consultation. The year after referral, study patients showed a marked reduction in utilization, primarily in the diagnostic, X-ray, and laboratory studies. Results (at the Group Health Association—District of Columbia) support the thesis that inclusion of mental health services leads to more appropriate and efficient overall utilization.

Goldensohn, S. "A Prepaid Group-Practice Mental Health Service as Part of a Health Maintenance Organization." *American Journal of Orthopsychiatry,* 1972, *42,* 154-158.

Notes that a premium of $32.40 for a family of three or more averaged $7.50 per person per year and provides inhospital and outpatient care and psychotropic drugs. Points out it is financially feasible and economic for prepaid group practice insurance to provide, without deductible or coinsurance charges, an open-ended "return-to-function" treatment of the mentally and emotionally disturbed. Author notes the opportunity to do research in such a setting. Limitations exist for chronic hospitalized patients and for psychoanalytic and intensive, long-term therapy, life-time supportive care, treatment for hard drug addicts, day hospital care, half-way house facilities, and special education and vocational services.

Goldensohn, S., and others. "Referral and Utilization Patterns in the First Year of a Mental Health Center in a Prepaid Group Practice Medical Program." *Medical Care,* 1967, *5,* 36-43.

Reports that about 1 percent of the eligible group

(43,000) of 15 years of age and older were referred for psychiatric consultation in this first year. Seventy-six percent of those referred were accepted for treatment and 70 percent actually were treated. Treatment was typically psychotherapy, with 40 percent of the cases receiving adjunctive psychotropic medication. Medication control was the primary treatment in 24 percent of the cases. Seventy percent of the diagnosed cases reported were classified as having a neurosis, with 28 percent listed as *depressed,* 24 percent as *anxiety reactions,* 17 percent as *adolescent behavior disorders,* and 13 percent as *family conflict.* Thirty percent of the diagnosed cases were reported to be psychotic, either with depression or schizophrenia. Average length of treatment was fifteen sessions.

Goldensohn, S., Fink, R., and Shapiro, S. "Referral, Utilization and Staffing Patterns of a Mental Health Service in a Prepaid Group Practice Program in New York." *American Journal of Psychiatry,* 1969, *126,* 135-143.

Notes that among adults fifteen years of age and older, the average annual consultation rate was 11 per 1,000 enrollees and the treatment rates were 11.5 per 1,000. Treatment visits in one year averaged 14.2 services, with psychiatrists having fewer visits (12.5) than social workers (15.9). Family doctors in the medical group altered their referral practices slightly after two years of contact with the mental health service.

Goldensohn, S., Fink, R., and Shapiro, S. "The Delivery of Mental Health Services to Children in a Prepaid Medical Care Program." *American Journal of Psychiatry,* 1971, *127,* 93-98.

Studies a New York prepaid group practice plan that offered mental health services to children under age fifteen during a twenty-four-month demonstration period. On an annual basis, the psychiatric consultation rate was 12.6 per 1,000 enrollees and the treatment start rate was 8.6 per 1,000. The average number of services per patient during the first twelve months was 14.5. Among the children receiving treatment, 39 percent had another family member who was also in treatment.

Goodwin, I., and Rosenblum, A. E. "A Method of Measuring and Comparing Costs in Mental Health Clinics." *Hospital and Community Psychiatry*, 1972, *23*, 47-49.

Compares cost per service unit for different types of patient contact. Intensive psychotherapy was three to four times more costly than group psychotherapy or supportive psychotherapy. The same services provided by psychologists and social workers were significantly less costly than those provided by psychiatrists.

Gordon, S. "Are We Seeing the Right Patients? Child Guidance Intake: The Sacred Cow." *American Journal of Orthopsychiatry*, 1965, *35*, 131-137.

An empirical, descriptive study of patient flow from intake demonstrating the high drop-out rate and low utilization rate of child patients and related adults in an outpatient children's clinic. Discusses the inappropriate delivery model of the child guidance clinic in not properly serving "short stay" patients.

Goshen, C. "The High Cost of Non-Psychiatric Care." *GP*, 1963, *27*, 227-235.

Presents laboratory studies of 36 patients with psychiatric conditions. Finds that $9,616 was spent on unnecessary laboratory studies only to negatively confirm diagnoses already made. These costs would have offset the charges of a full-time psychiatrist for six months. These costs were an unnecessary expense superimposed upon the costs of psychiatric services. The author estimates a 25 percent reduction in total costs of medical care if adequate diagnoses of mental conditions are made.

Goshen, C. E. "Functional Versus Organic Diagnostic Problems." *New York State Journal of Medicine*, 1969, *69*, 2332-2338.

Presents data showing that a cost savings of up to 25 percent is possible if psychological conditions are routinely diagnosed along with physical conditions. Following the publication of findings to the hospital staff, there was a 53 percent reduction in costs of diagnostic procedures for psychiatric patients, representing an average cost saving of $212 per patient. Medical diagnosis alone merely forced the patient with functional disturbances to develop new complaints and hence more laboratory studies. Author emphasizes the necessity of simultaneous mental and physical diagnosis.

Goshen, C. E. "Diagnostic Overkill and Management of Psychiatric Problems." *Mental Hygiene,* 1970, *54,* 306-309.

Analyzes patients admitted for psychiatric problems, medical and psychiatric problems, and medical or surgical problems only. Indicates that the search for nonexistent pathology in neurotic patients adds substantially to the cost of diagnosis. Concludes that physicians use unnecessary laboratory tests merely to convince patients that nothing is wrong rather than dealing with the neurotic elements and thus causing patients to feel that something is the matter with them. By catering to the patient's neurotic tendencies, the doctor remains popular with the patient, but at high cost.

Green, E. "Psychiatric Services in a California Group Health Plan." *American Journal of Psychiatry,* 1969, *126,* 681-688.

Reports that federal patients utilized mental health services at a rate of 23.6 per 1,000 and that UAW members had a rate of 21.8 per 1,000. The high utilization rates (higher than those reported by Avnet) are attributed to a higher acceptance of mental health services in this locality. Only one major group, the UAW, was permitted self-referral. In actual practice, many outpatients ask that their internist or family physician refer them, and he or she readily obliges. "The administrators of our health plans have less fear that we are going to bankrupt the plan: The fact is that it has been proven over an 8 year period that our department [mental health] can function without taking resources from the health plan at large."

Green, E. "Experience of the Southern California Permanente Medical Group." Paper presented at the annual meeting of the American Psychiatric Association, Honolulu, Hawaii, May 1973.

Estimates that low-income groups will have a 2 percent utilization rate of outpatient services, resulting in five consultations for the user. Inpatient service utilization for low-income groups is estimated at .2 percent with an average of eighteen days per patient. Among the common fallacies noted were the following: there is no need for mental health services in a health maintenance organization (HMO); patients flood clinics with unnecessary requests for treatment; treatment to low-income groups does not help and is free in an HMO clinic; and every patient who is evaluated for a mental condition undergoes therapy and patients get treatment on demand. Author emphasizes that psychologists and social workers are competent therapists and much of a psychiatrist's training is of the wrong kind; that our clinical model is the private practice model; that the team approach is too costly.

Green, M., Haar, E., and Hyams, L. "Psychosocial Aspects of Medical Practice." Unpublished study supported by the United States Public Health Service Research Grant IR01 MH16624-01. National Institute of Health, Rockville, Maryland, 1972.

States that "A common pitfall of medical authority is characterized by a repetition of the same prescription—usually a mild sedative or psychotropic drug—over a period of many years. The primary physician trained in illness-centered medicine could not achieve much, but he kept on trying anyway— attested to by the high frequency of multiple diagnoses in this group." Furthermore, "the first treatment choice for a typical physician when confronted with emotionally disturbed patients is to provide physical examination and reassurance. The second choice is to give opportunity for ventilation and the third choice is advice. Drugs are listed fourth. The physician is very cautious in his use of drugs, naming more correct drugs for anxiety than for depression and even fewer for schizophrenia." (More than a third refused to deal with schizophrenia.) The typical physician would prefer to refer patients with emotional problems than to treat these patients. Yet 31 percent of the doctors did not refer more than two patients in a six-month period. (This fact suggests the primary physician concept is not effective in dealing with mental conditions.—Ed.)

Greenberg, I. G., and Rodberg, M. L. "The Role of Prepaid Group Practice in Relieving the Medical Care Crisis." *Harvard Law Review*, 1971, *84*, 889.

An extensive review of the current "nonsystem" of health care in the United States, carefully documented. Argues for the "Kennedy Bill" approach to health care, emphasizing the development of a new national health care system similar to the HMO model.

Group Health Association. "Evaluation of the Costs of Medical Care Provided to D.C. Medicaid Enrollees in a Prepaid Group Practice." Contract No. SRS-71-14. Washington, D.C.: United States Department of Health, Education, and Welfare, Social and Rehabilitation Service, January 27, 1975.

Compares the annual medical costs of Medicaid enrollees in the Group Health Association plan to the medical costs for the Medicaid fee-for-service universe and shows a 30 percent savings in costs for the prepaid group practice plan. The hospitalization utilization rates for the Medicaid enrollees were 50 percent higher than for the high-option Group Health Association members. Costs for mental health services were nominal in comparison to the costs for other conditions.

Gurin, G., and others. *Americans View Their Mental Health: A Nationwide Interview Survey*. New York: Basic Books, 1960.

An epidemiologically focused study of a representative sample of the American population. Highlights the critical referral role of the clergyman and medical doctor for those seeking mental health care. Notes influence of culture on utilization.

Though they did not seek help, 9 percent of population felt they had a problem for which help could have been used.

Hall, C. "Deductibles in Health Insurance: An Evaluation." *The Journal of Risk and Insurance,* 1966, *34,* 253-263.

An evaluation of existing evidence in general health care regarding the effectiveness of deductible features in reducing costs. Analysis leaves doubts for any firm conclusion at this time.

Halliday, W. R. "Rehabilitation of Injured Workmen with Psycho-Social Handicaps." In Leedy, J. J. (Ed.), *Compensation in Psychiatric Disability and Rehabilitation.* Springfield, Ill.: Charles C Thomas, 1971, pp. 338-348.

Presents data on medical care under Workmen's Compensation in Washington State. Although one in four workers is treated annually for industrial injury, only 1 percent, or 1,500, are disabled annually for as much as sixty days. Six thousand have severe, long-term disabilities. Another 3,000 to 4,000 have apparently minor injuries but prolonged complaints. These so-called problem cases are potential victims of "the disability process." A program of "medico-vocational" rehabilitation is described. Rehabilitation of eleven cases to gainful employment obviated the necessity of pensions that would have required pension reserves of $583,306.

Halliday, W. R. "Compensation Medicine Today." Paper presented at the 13th International Conference on Legal Medicine, San Francisco, May 5, 1973.

Reports that conjoint multispecialty medical examinations were ineffective in rehabilitating "industrial back" cases. The average attending physician was not in a position to recognize psychosocial problems or to do much about them when diagnosed. Advocates direct observation of the patient in a rehabilitation center and use of medicovocational teams.

Halpern, J., and Binner, P. R. "A Model for an Output Value Analysis of Mental Health Programs." *Administration in Mental Health,* Winter 1972, 40-51.

Establishes an effectiveness index for mental health treatment by comparing estimated economic productivity and estimated potential response to treatment to the actual outcome of treatment. This approach allowed comparison of the effectiveness of one treatment center to another treatment center. Comparisons were also made for various diagnostic categories. Psychoneuroses (excluding depression) and paranoid reactions yielded the highest output value, while acute and chronic brain syndromes and mental deficiency had the lowest output values. This study is important for methodological considerations.

Hannaford, M. *Characteristics of Patients of Selected Types of Medical Specialists and Practitioners: United States, July 1963-June 1964.* Produced by National Center for Health Statistics. Public Health Service Publication No. 1000, Series 10, No. 28. Rockville, Md.: United States Public Health Service, 1966.

A large, descriptive, compilation of health statistics including psychiatric (mental health) services.

Hannings, R., Ash, P., and Simick, D. *Forensic Psychology in Disability Adjudication: A Decade of Experience.* HEW Publication No. 72-10284. Washington, D.C.: U.S. Department of Health, Education, and Welfare, Social Security Administration, 1972.

Outlines the history of disability determination under Social Security and the involvement of psychologists as vocational experts. Under Social Security, *disability* means "inability to engage in any substantial gainful activity by reason of any medically determinable physical or mental impairment . . . ." Following judicial establishment of the Kerner criteria in 1960, not only must the claimant be able to work, but work must be available. In effect, an employability rather than a disability test is required. Rehabilitation potential is not the issue, but rather the transferability of skills—the transliteration of medically determined impairment into functional terminology and residual capacities, and an appreciation of concomitant psychosocial overlays such as a motivation to remain disabled. Hearings are concerned with availability of work the claimant is able to do. Effective performance as a vocational expert requires an intimate knowledge of the job market and skills required by job. From a legal standpoint, vocational expert testimony is considered the best type of vocational evidence obtainable. Experts are appearing in a higher percentage of hearings on disability claims: 2.9 percent in 1963 and 24.5 percent by 1971.

Hanson, M. R., and others. "Five County Cost-Effectiveness Study." Unpublished document prepared for the California Department of Health, Health Planning and Intergovernmental Relations, Sacramento, California, October 11, 1974.

This November 1974 final report of the Butte, Fresno, San Diego, Santa Barbara, and Siskiyou county programs was mandated by California law. The budget proportion allocated to inpatient care ranged from 31 to 68 percent, partial care 4 to 16 percent, outpatient care 26 to 55 percent. Of the 8,748 patients, over 30 percent were treatment dropouts. According to ratings, little change in impairment occurred until eleven or more units of service were acquired. However, 75 percent of outpatients received five or less units and only 5 percent over eleven units. A major finding was that while clinicians had a high level of agreement on the manifest problem, they were unable to discern between life crisis and mentally disordered target groups. Of the 11,652 treatment episodes, 49 percent occurred in inpatient services. Follow-up data revealed that 5.2 percent of males and 2.2 percent of females were reported to have often hurt another person.

Hardwick, C. P., Myers, J., and Shuman, L. J. "The Effect of a Copay Agreement on Hospital Utilization." Research Series No. 9, Blue Cross of Western Pennsylvania, Pittsburgh, Pennsylvania, 1971.

A comparison of utilization between two Pennsylvania Blue Cross plans, showing no utilization differences. One plan had full coverage while the other plan had a copayment feature.

Harper, R., and Balch, P. "Some Economic Arguments in Favor of Primary Prevention." *Professional Psychology*, 1975, *6*, 17-25.

Describes a means for assessing the dollar costs of prevention and mental health in comparison with the costs of direct services for already existing mental conditions.

Harsham, P. "What, Me Incorporate?" *Money*, 1973, *2*, 55-58.

Notes that most professionals are eligible to incorporate in every state and in the District of Columbia, and have increasingly done so since 1969 when the Internal Revenue Service was obliged to liberalize its rules on corporate status. Advantages include much larger tax-sheltered contributions to retirement plans and the inclusion of tax-deductible fringe benefits for members and employees.

Health Insurance Institute. *Group Health Insurance Policies Issued in 1962.* New York: Health Insurance Institute, n.d.*a*.

Identifies the forty-four companies surveyed that underwrote 75 percent of the total group health insurance premiums in 1961. Nearly one million persons were insured in these new plans, and of those with comprehensive or supplementary major medical plans 96.6 percent were covered for nervous and mental disorder, a slight increase over 1960. Report summarizes trend data and provides tabular information on persons covered, type of coverage, and so forth.

Health Insurance Institute. *Source Book of Health Insurance Data 1974-75.* New York: Health Insurance Institute, n.d.*b*.

Represents 327 member companies that issue about 85 percent of the health insurance written by insurance companies in the United States. Traces history of health insurance and growing involvement in HMOs. Reports data from 1940 to 73 on hospital expense—182,000,000 insured; surgical expense—169,000,000 insured; regular medical expense—152,000,000 insured; and major medical expense—82,000,000 insured. Ratio of primary insured persons to dependents ranged from 1.51 to 1.73. Total United States health insurance payments in 1972 were $10,600,000,000 and $10,400,000,000 by insurance companies and Blue Cross-Blue Shield respectively. Americans spent 3.19 percent of disposable personal income on health insurance premiums. Sourcebook contains a glossary of common insurance terms.

Health Insurance Plan of Greater New York. "Demonstration and Research in Psychiatric Care: The Psychiatric Demonstration Program." In R. Fink and others, eds., *HIP Statistical Report*. New York: Health Insurance Plan of Greater New York, n.d.

Reports that a mental diagnosis rate of 16.9 per 1,000 was established for the medical group of enrollees aged 20 and older in the HIP plan. Women were more likely to receive a mental diagnosis from the family doctor than were men and were more likely to reach consultation in a health center than were men. Younger age groups appeared to accept psychotherapy more readily than older age groups. Study covers the period of October 1965-February 1967. For those having at least a full year of exposure to treatment, the average annual utilization was 15.8 visits—15.1 to psychiatrists and 16.7 to social workers.

Hess, A. E. "Medicare and Mental Illness." *American Journal of Psychiatry*, 1966, *123*, 174-176.

Discusses the provisions for the diagnosis and treatment of mental conditions under Medicare. Because of the lack of actuarial data regarding the incidence and utilization services for mental conditions, especially on an outpatient basis, mental health benefits were set arbitrarily low to reduce the exposure of risk to the plan and at the same time to acquire actuarial data. (See also Chapter Five of this book—Ed.)

Hett, W. S. *Aristotle on the Soul, Parva Naturalia, on Breath*. Cambridge, Mass.: Harvard University Press, 1957.

Comments on some of Aristotle's thinking, including material that is of special relevance to psychology.

HEW. *See* United States Department on Health, Education and
    Welfare. *See also* HEW subagencies:
    HSA (Health Services Administration)
    HSMHA (Health Services and Mental Health Administration)
    OCD (Office of Child Development)
    OHD (Office of Human Development)
    OPSR (Office of Professional Standards Review)
    RSA (Rehabilitation Services Administration)
    SRS (Social and Rehabilitation Services)
    SSA (Social Security Administration)

Hodgson, G. "The Politics of American Health Care." *Atlantic,*
    1973, *232,* 45-61.

This penetrating analysis notes two recent and major shifts
in political attitude: that government should guarantee the
availability of health care to all citizens and that government
should actively encourage replacement of at least some fee-for-
service practice by prepaid group health service. Medicaid and
Medicare, while having done incalculable good, made no attempt to increase the number of providers or hold down costs
by imposing controls—with a predictable inflationary result.
Too many people are being hospitalized because of the way insurance policies are written. The medical-industrial complex or
health empire networks, rather than patients, effectively hold
decision-making power over demands for treatment. The availability of health insurance obscures the noneconomic deficiencies of the medical system. Gradual change provides no leverage
for reform.

Iglehart, J. K. "Heralded HMO Programs Beset by Unexpected
    Problems." *National Journal Reports,* 1974, *6,* 1825-1830.

Notes that in the four years since the administration declared its commitment to HMOs, some twenty-nine new facilities have opened with federal aid, serving some 400,000 people
at expenditures thus far of $21,700,000. Barriers to implemen-
tation are the mandated expensive benefit package and community rating, federal administrative discontinuity, and union

concern that individual assignment undercuts the collective bargaining process among others.

Jacobs, D. F. "The Agony and Ecstasy of Professional Role Change." A. I. Rabin (ed.). In *Clinical Psychology: Issues of the Seventies.* Lansing, Mich.: Michigan State University Press, 1974, pp. 75-85.

Summarizes the history of clinical psychology in human service settings. Discusses the challenges that practicing psychologists will face in attempting to meet rapidly expanding service demands. Claims that a permanent place inevitably will be developed for paraprofessions within psychology.

Jacobson, A. "The Failure of the Psychiatric Community Clinic." *Psychiatric Quarterly*, 1965, *39*, 621-631.

While replete with put-downs of "ancillary" personnel, this is a perceptive analysis of the differential effectiveness of private practice as contrasted to clinic service. Jacobson notes that the team approach is lengthy and that complete work-up is an extravagant waste of time. "If a patient is willing to persevere through a long intake and work-up process . . . he rarely is acutely ill . . . ." Of eighty-three consecutive applicants to a New Jersey clinic, only twenty-five were ever seen in treatment. Concludes that "the actual cost of seeing a patient in a clinic setting . . . must be enormously higher than the cost of seeing a patient in treatment privately." Notes also that many clinic personnel see their roles as simply preparatory to private practice. Asks whether it would not be less costly to the community to underwrite private therapy for those unable to afford the care than to refer such patients to psychiatric clinics. Is of the belief that this "would provide for far better quality of care at an over-all reduction in the expenditure of public funds."

Joint Commission on Accreditation of Hospitals. *Accreditation Manual for Psychiatric Facilities 1972.* Chicago: Joint Commission on Accreditation of Hospitals, 1972.

Holds that "policies and procedures should be consistent with professionally recognized standards of psychology, and shall be in accordance with the legal requirements governing the practice of psychology in the state." Nonetheless, claims that in diagnosis, treatment and rehabilitation of the psychiatrically ill, medical responsibility should rest with a psychiatrist or other physician. Holds that "psychiatrists have the ultimate responsibility for patient care." Requires the establishment of a medical staff with consequent staff privileges. In these ways the criteria appear to exert a restraint in trade upon the practice of psychology.

Joint Commission on Accreditation of Hospitals, Accreditation Council for Facilities for the Mentally Retarded. *Standards for Residential Facilities for the Mentally Retarded.* Revised ed. Chicago: Joint Commission on Accreditation of Hospitals, 1973.

Delineates the council's administrative policies, standards for resident living and professional and special programs, among other subjects. By noting that identical or similar services or functions may be competently rendered by individuals of different professions and calling for competent performance without regard to profession (Section 3, 3.1.2.2, page 42), these standards are in sharp contrast to those of the psychiatric facilities council and other councils calling for strict medical program direction and ultimate medical responsibility for all services. The American Psychological Association is among the organizations represented on the Standards Review Committee. Requires that all psychologists providing services meet the APA membership standards. Holds that professional services rendered to the retarded in a residential facility must be at least comparable to those provided the nonretarded in the community.

Joint Commission on Mental Illness and Health. *Action for Mental Health.* Final Report. New York: Basic Books, 1972.

This ten-volume commission report laid the basis for a new direction in mental health care towards community-based services, with emphasis on ambulatory care. Six volumes written by a psychologist, a seventh coauthored by a psychologist.

Karon, B., and Vandenbos, G. "The Consequences of Psychotherapy for Schizophrenic Patients." *Psychotherapy: Theory, Research and Practice,* 1972, *9,* 111-119.

Studies thirty-six patients randomly assigned to a treatment program of (1) psychotherapy; (2) psychotherapy and medication; and (3) medication only. The twenty-one patients receiving psychotherapy had an average of 78 days of hospitalization. The twelve medication-only patients averaged 113 days in the hospital. A follow-up two years later revealed that medication-only patients spent nearly twice as many days in the hospital subsequent to the experiment than the patients receiving psychotherapy. (These data suggest that medication alone is not enough—Ed.)

Karon, B., and Vandenbos, G. "Treatment Costs of Psychotherapy versus Medication for Schizophrenics." *Professional Psychology,* 1975, *6,* 293-298.

Reports three main findings: (1) 75 percent of the patients treated by medication alone received welfare benefits in the first twenty months of treatment as compared to 33 percent of their randomly assigned counterparts who received psychotherapy; (2) there were no differences in effectiveness between the professions according to the outcome data in dealing with this hospitalized population; (3) total treatment costs of using experienced therapists at private practice rates were less than costs of using inexperienced therapists, without including their training costs; and (4) experienced therapists using psychotherapy produced cost savings of up to 36 percent over using medication alone.

Kennecott Copper Corporation. "Performance Outcome Data." Unpublished report, Utah Copper Division, Salt Lake City, Utah, 1972.

Compares 150 employees undertaking counseling and 150 employees considered to need treatment but who did not participate. The groups were matched in terms of work situation though the participants were select in that they sought help.

Data is for the period six months prior to treatment, the one year under study, and the period six months following treatment. Essentially, community facilities and practitioners were used. On a per man per month basis, absenteeism of the participants decreased in the before-during-after phases from 3.18 to 1.49 to 1.54 days, respectively. Similarly, indemnity costs declined from $26.08 to $12.44 to $6.63; also health, medical, and surgical costs declined from $93.22 to $49.91 to $41.62. This change represents a 52 percent attendance improvement and a 75 percent and 55 percent decrease, respectively, in weekly indemnity costs and in health, medical, and surgical costs. Values for the nonparticipants were substantially lower in the before phase and showed a slight increase in the after phase except for indemnity costs of $6.01 to $3.70, reflecting a plant-wide effort to reduce them. In the before phase for the nonparticipants, absenteeism was .74 days and health, medical, and surgical costs were $36.25.

Kogan, W., and others. "Impact of Integration of Mental Health Service and Comprehensive Medical Care." *Medical Care,* in press.

Reports that individuals seen in mental health service tend to be higher utilizers. Noted a tendency two years prior to being seen on mental health service for a rise in utilization that two years later, dropped to its former level. Life crises can be precipitants. Finds that prepayment (absence of a fee) does not prolong treatment. In 1972, 4.2 percent of the insureds used the mental health service for an average of three and a half visits (median, three visits) some discontinuity of cumulative frequency at fourteen, thus set low, middle, and high utilizers at none to three, four to thirteen and fourteen or more visits per year.

Kohn, N. "Organization and Operation of the American Board for Psychological Services." *American Psychologist,* 1954, *9,* 771-772.

Spells out the four major purposes of the independently

incorporated board, the standard for listing certified persons and agencies, and how to apply for evaluation.

Kramer, M. "Historical Tables on Changes in Patterns of Use of Psychiatric Facilities: 1946-1971." Unpublished report prepared for Biometry Branch, National Institute of Mental Health, Rockville, Maryland, October 1973.

Table 1 shows sharp decline in state hospital use and corresponding increase in use of outpatient mental health facilities. Overall utilization from approximately 1 to 2 percent. Care of aged shifted to nursing homes but a 250 percent increase in psychiatric care of the twenty-five- to forty-four-year age group. Ratio to population and proportionate use is given by diagnosis and type of facility. Estimates percent of unmet need (Table 13), manpower requirements (Table 14), and population age segments shifts (Table 15).

Laska, E. "An Overview of the Multi-State Information System." Unpublished report prepared for the Information Sciences Division, Rockland State Hospital, New York, 1973.

An authoritative summary description of the Multi-State Information System by its developer and director.

Levine, D., and Levine, D. "The Cost of Mental Illness." Prepared for National Institute of Mental Health, Rockville, Maryland, under Contract No. ADM-42-74-82 (OP), 1974.

Concluded that direct costs in 1971 for mental health services amounted to $10.1 billion or 14 percent of national expenditures for all health services and supplies; 46 percent or 4.6 billion came from the private sector (1.1 billion from health insurance). These conclusions contradict the traditional pattern of predominance of state funding for mental health services.

Ley, P. "What the Patient Doesn't Remember." *Medical Opinion and Review*, 1966, *1*, 69-73.

Concludes that the patients remember best what they are

told first and that patients also recall best what they consider to be the most important.

Ley, P. "Comprehension, Memory and the Success of Communications with the Patient." *Journal of Institution Health Education,* 1972a, *10,* 23-29.

Review of sixty-eight studies shows that a median rate of 44 percent of the patients did not follow medical advice. Nine of these studies show a similar median rate among patients for whom psychiatric drugs were prescribed did not take the medication as prescribed. Evidence is presented that failure to follow advice is largely a matter of poor communication between doctor and patient. Describes a method for significantly increasing recall of medical advice.

Ley, P. "Primacy, Rated Importance and the Recall of Medical Statements." *Journal of Health and Social Behavior,* 1972b, *13,* 311-317.

Three investigations show that laymen, presented with medical information, recall best (1) what they are told first, and (2) what they consider most important. The findings from volunteer subjects recalling fictitious information are confirmed with patients recalling real information. In the real-life situation, it was possible to manipulate recall of certain kinds of information by using the primacy and importance effects. While 86 percent could recall their diagnosis, only 62 percent could recall other information they were told, with just 44 percent remembering the instructions for treatment they were given.

Ley, P., and Spelman, M. S. "Communications in an Outpatient Setting." *British Journal Social and Clinical Psychology,* 1965, *4,* 114-116.

Demonstrates that doctors, when they try to communicate specific information to patients, tend to tell the patient the things the doctor wants the patient to know, rather than to answer the questions the patient has. As a result, the patient does not listen or heed the doctor's advice and tends to remain dissatisfied.

Ley, P., and Spelman, M. S. *Communicating with the Patient.* London: Staples Press, 1967.

Notes that patients frequently fail to understand what is said to them. The reasons for poor success of common-sense measures is that the patient frequently forgets what he or she is told and that it is very easy to forget unfamiliar material couched in technical language. Only 35 percent of the general patients and 38 percent of psychiatric patients felt their complaints were adequately handled.

Ley, P., and others. "A Method for Increasing Patients' Recall of Information Presented by Doctors." *Psychological Medicine,* 1973, *2,* 217-220.

Reports that within minutes of leaving the consulting room, patients are frequently unable to recall what their doctor has told them. Describes a simple, practical method of increasing recall from 25 to 50 percent by the organization of medical information in "labelled" categories. The success of this technique was demonstrated first in a laboratory experiment with volunteer subjects, and then in a naturalistic setting with general practice patients.

Lipsitt, D. "Curing the Patient Who Clings to Ill Health." *Medical Opinion,* April 1971, *7,* 46-49.

Studies 800 chronic complainers, problem patients, and others needing psychological assessment who were referred to the Integration Clinic over a period of four years. In 86 percent the isolated somatic symptoms represented components of a single syndrome of masked depression. "As soon as patients realized that acceptance by the physician did not depend on the intensity of symptoms, complaining diminished . . ."

Lipsitt, D. R. "Fragmented Medical Care: A Retrospective Study of Chronic Outpatients, Parts I and II." Bureau of Health Services, U.S. Department of Health, Education and Welfare, Contract No. PH-108-67-70. Washington, D.C.: U.S. Department of Health, Education and Welfare, 1900.

Some of the points presented are that outpatient clinics tend to be the "hospital's step-child"; that we are unaware of ethnic and cultural differences in the concept of illness and the role of the physician; and that "While physicians generally acknowledge that anywhere from 25-85 percent of their practice consists of emotional problems, their preference is to deal with the 75-15 percent of the 'physical' problems and to look with disdain on the 'neurotics' of medical practice." Moreover, "it would appear that in many cases the physicians do not know what the patients are really looking for, but they (the physiccians) are none the less racing pell-mell to provide them with better (more) service of what the *doctors* or administrators think they need." It is also noted that "problem patients constituted only 8 percent of annual referrals to the Integration Clinic. Heavy clinic service users tended to be women over 60 years of age. Marital problems are a significant determinant of clinic utilization rates. Number of visits to clinics is a poor index of 'chronic complainers.' A more accurate index is the number of different clinics, often 10 or more, that the patients use (thick charts)."

Little, K. "Editorial." *APA Monitor,* 1975, *6,* 2.

Describes the incremental change process of the democratic APA structure in accommodation to internal stress and social pressures. Provides summary data on the rapid recent membership increase.

Locke, B. Z., and Gardner, E. A. "Psychiatric Disorders Among the Patients of General Practitioners and Internists." *Public Health Report,* 1969, *84,* 167-173.

Discusses how internists and general practitioners view the mental conditions of their patients and raises questions regarding the ability of the physician providers to detect mental symptoms.

Locke, B. Z., Krantz, G., and Kramer, M. "Psychiatric Need and Demand in a Prepaid Group Practice Program." *American Journal of Public Health,* 1966, *56,* 895-904.

Attempts to assess the frequency of mental problems among subscribers to a prepaid group health practice. Results for the first eight months of operation for the outpatient mental health services are presented.

McCaffree, K. M. "The Cost of Mental Health Care Under Changing Treatment Methods." *International Journal of Psychiatry*, 1967, *4*, 142-157.

Compares the costs of custodial and intensive mental health care. The costs considered are: (1) subsistance and depreciation; (2) treatment costs of professional services and supplies; (3) loss of income; and (4) transfer of payments (economic costs that may result from taking income from one unit in society and giving it to another). Presents data on Washington State mental hospitals, showing that psychotherapy and intensive care cost 30 percent less than custodial care. Argues for the development of mental health insurance coverage of private practice and nongovernmental inpatient services as being cheaper and more efficient than state hospital systems.

McKeachie, W. "Admission to Graduate Work in Psychology." *American Psychologist*, 1972, *27*, 1078-79.

Argues that if there is student demand for doctoral training in psychology, despite job market uncertainties, universities have a responsibility for preparing them with transferrable skills. Notes there is no shortage of human problems and that graduates may fan out beyond academia to find new functions in society.

McMillan, J. "Peer Review and Professional Standards for Psychologists Rendering Personal Health Services." *Professional Psychology*, 1974, *5*, 51-58.

A historical review of the development of peer review by organized psychology through 1973.

Malan, D. H. "A Study of Brief Psychotherapy." *Mind and Medicine Monographs*. Springfield, Ill.: Charles C Thomas, 1963.

This classic study of brief psychotherapy honestly examines the prejudices of a group of psychiatrists toward brief psychotherapy: the kinds of benefit possible, the kinds of clients who utilize it, and the permanency of the results. Concludes that traditional attitudes about brief therapy are mostly in the nature of unjustified prejudices. It would appear that therapeutic effects of brief therapy that can be labeled "transference cure," "flight into health," "intellectualization," and other derogatory terms can often be long-lasting and result in a major change in the person's symptoms, relationships, and even lifestyle.

Malan, D. H. "The Outcome Problem in Psychotherapy Research, An Historical Review." *Archives of General Psychiatry,* 1973, *29,* 719-729.

Presents a critique of over eighty outcome studies in psychotherapy and finds that most of them lack meaningful outcome criteria. Concludes that most of the negative findings regarding the outcome of psychotherapy are largely caused by unresolved methodological problems. In contrast, controlled studies in adult patients with internal psychosomatic disorders indicate positive results for peptic ulcer, ulcerative colitis, and asthma.

Manson, H. "Manpower Needs by Specialty." *Journal American Medical Assn.* 1972, *219,* 1621-1626.

Claims that manpower problems are more related to maldistribution than to shortage. Practicing physician-to-population ration is 1:766 nationally. Cites some major HMOs that have physician-to-member ratios averaging 1:1061. Psychiatrist-to-population ratio is 1:10,384 (though only 48 percent are board-certified), while the ratio in the District of Columbia, New York, and California is 1:2636, 1:4,399, and 1:7,306, respectively.

Mariner, A. "A Critical Look at Professional Education in the Mental Health Field." *American Psychologist,* 1967, *22,* 271-281.

A detailed and insightful review and discussion of the relevance of medical education to the practice of psychiatry and to the other mental health professions. Underscores much of the ironical and illogical posturing of psychiatry to exert territoriality. A thorough evaluation of the factual situation of practice, written by a psychiatrist, in plain language, it is relevant not only to the mental health professions but also to legislators and consumers concerned with the planning and development of mental health services.

Maxwell, M. A. "A Study of Absenteeism, Accidents and Sickness Payments in Problem Drinkers in One Industry." *Quarterly Journal of Studies on Alcohol*, 1959, *20*, 301-312.

Compares matched groups of problem drinkers and problem-free employees for a major corporation. Reveals that problem drinkers had two and a half times as many cases of illness or injury-caused absence lasting eight days or more than did the control group. The cost of sickness payment to the problem drinkers was three times greater than for the control group. The accident rate for the problem drinkers was 3.6 times that of the matched controls.

Medicine and Health. Washington, D.C.: McGraw-Hill.

A short summary weekly newsletter, often referred to as *Washington Report on Medicine and Health*, that announces current developments, with emphasis on Congressional action and committee hearings.

Milgram, S. "The Small World Problem." *Psychology Today*, 1967, *1*, 61-67.

Demonstrates that people in society are linked by mutual acquaintances. There is better than a 50:50 chance that any two Americans can be linked up with two intermediate acquaintances. Only five intermediaries will on the average, suffice to link any two randomly chosen individuals no matter where they live in the United States.

Millett, J. "The Public Interest in Graduate Education." *Educational Record*, 1974, *55*, 79-86.

Forsees that with over 50 percent of university research expenditures coming from the U.S. Department of Health, Education, and Welfare, there will be a growing need to demonstrate instrumental accomplishment. Public interest leans towards educating experts who will contribute to the solution of practical problems. Notes the distinction between research-oriented and practice-oriented programs.

Miller, J. "Insanity Defense: Mad or Bad? Congress Considers Reforms." *APA Monitor*, 1975*a*, *6*, 6, 14.

Reviews the changes in insanity proceedings from the M'Naghten through the Durham and Brawner decisions of the mid-nineteenth century, 1954 and 1972 respectively. Discusses the disputed intent of S.1 before the 94th Congress to curtail an alleged abuse of the insanity defense by criminals.

Miller, J. "Study of Death Draws Interest of Psychologists." *APA Monitor*, 1975*b*, *6*, 1, 5.

A study of the mental distress accompanying death. Focuses on children dying of leukemia and on their families. Suggests an area of research for psychologists seeking to strengthen the profession's involvement in direct therapeutic care.

"*Moore* v. *Metropolitan.*" *New York State Psychologist*, 1974, *26*, 4. Also published as "Insurance Law Upheld," *New York State Psychologist*, 1973, *25*, 1, 11.

Reports that the Metropolitan Life Insurance Company, having denied reimbursement on the grounds that it only covered psychiatric care, lost the claim in small claims court and appealed to the New York State Supreme Court, which decided for the client in August 1972. The company then appealed to the appellate division, which (February 1973) decided unanimously for Moore, and appealed later to the New York State Court of Appeals, which found likewise. Before April 1974, Metropolitan had filed but later decided not to appeal to the

United States Supreme Court. The company then began processing all claims dating back to the first renewal of contracts following September 1, 1969. Meanwhile, as a result of the appellate court decision, the New York State insurance department ordered Travelers to comply with the 1969 amendment (a freedom-of-choice law).

Morris Associates, Inc. "Erroneous Data Used to Cut MH Benefits by Blue Cross/Blue Shield." *MH-MR Report.* Washington, D.C.: Morris Assoc. Inc., 1974.

Finds that the Blues' claim that mental health benefits would constitute 8.6 percent and 10 percent of total plan costs in 1973-1974, respectively, is "apparently both incorrect and misleading."

Muller, C. "Health Insurance for Drug Addiction: A Survey." *American Journal of Psychiatry,* 1972, *12,* 66-73.

Notes that coverage for drug addiction is fairly common in both commercial and other health insurance policies, but benefits are often limited. There are frequent restrictions pertaining to treatment in specialized facilities or after incarceration and to care by less traditional types of health personnel. Improved coverage will require ambulatory benefits and other adaptations of present insurance practices to newer settings and modalities of care.

Myers, E. "Insurance Coverage for Mental Illness: Present Status and Future Prospects." *American Journal of Public Health,* 1970, *60,* 1921-1930.

Reports that voluntary health insurance met only 36 percent of medical care expenses in 1967. It met 74 percent of hospital expenses and 38 percent of physicians services, but only 4 percent of expenditures for other types of care. In contrast, patients with psychiatric admission to general hospitals were insured in 35 percent of the cases and had 70 percent of their bill paid. Sixty-nine percent of patients with admissions to psychiatric hospitals were insured and had but 58 percent of their bill paid. Coverage for outpatient care was less. Of 12,917 patients seeing psychiatrists, 26 percent had insurance coverage. In 44 percent of insured cases, 50 percent of the charges were paid, 36 percent had 80 percent paid, and 20 percent had less than 50 percent paid. Various group insurance plans for mental health care are reviewed.

National Association of Blue Shield Plans. "Blue Shield Benefits, Enrollment for Mental and Nervous Disorders as of 12/31/66." Unpublished report prepared for Blue Shield Association, Chicago.

Reports the following enrollment by millions of persons involved for certain benefits: inpatient visits for mental disorders, 45.3; inpatient electroshock, 26.0; outpatient electroshock, 17.7; inpatient psychotherapy (above general medical care), 12.8; outpatient psychotherapy, 8.3; psychological testing, 7.0; outpatient and prescription drugs, 9.7; and psychiatric social workers, 4.3.

National Commission on State Workmen's Compensation Laws. "The Medical Care and Rehabilitation Objective," in *National Commission Report on State Workmen's Compensation Laws.* Washington, D.C.: United States Government Printing Office, 1972, pp. 77-85.

Notes that it is "important to prepare patients psychologically for recovery of their capabilities and morale." Among eighty-four recommendations for improvement of workers' compensation (nineteen considered essential), the commission recommended that the worker be permitted the initial selection of his physician; that there be no statutory limits of time or dollar amount for medical care of physical rehabilitation services for any work-related impairment; and that there be no arbitrary limits by regulation or statute on the types of medical service or licensed health care facilities that can be authorized.

National Health Insurance Reports. Washington, D.C.: Plus Publications.

These brief bi-weekly newsletters report on studies pertinent to National Health Insurance.

National Institute of Mental Health. *Financing Mental Health Care in the United States.* The Advisory Panel on Financing Mental Health Care of the American Hospital Association. HEW Publication No. (HSM) 73-9117. GPO No. 1973-505-756. Rockville, Md.: National Institute of Mental Health, 1973.

Provides a summary of mental health needs and resources in terms of the extent of mental disorders, current methods of organization and delivery of mental health care, the supply and distribution of mental health manpower, and mental health research. It also describes existing arrangements for financing mental health care by the federal government, by state and local governments, through private health insurance plans, and through philanthropic endeavors. Briefly discusses financing mental health care through a national health insurance program and makes a series of recommendations for this program. While much valuable statistical information is supplied, the recommendations are traditional.

National Institute of Mental Health. "Insurance for Mental Health: Trends in the Delivery and Financing of Mental Illness Services in the United States: Draft Report of the Work Group on Health Insurance." Unpublished report prepared for National Institute of Mental Health, Rockville, Maryland, November 1974.

Report contains extensive data, most of it not yet available in the literature. Chaired by Henry Foley, the group has assembled data on trends in care and its cost by type of service. In 1971, the direct care costs for mental illness totaled $10,400,000,000, equivalent to 14 percent of all health care expenses nationally. Shows that much insurance is dysfunctional to practice. Traces the flow of Medicare and Medicaid dollars. Provides actuarial data by year on the Federal Employee Blue Cross-Blue Shield plan. Includes CHAMPUS cost data for 1972 and 1974; also, the socioeconomic analysis of Monroe County (New York) utilization.

Reports the number of nonanalysts' patient visits in the

past twelve months, of persons first seen less than a year before, at an average of 15, a median of 9 visits. Notes that the comparable figures for analysts only are 82 and 70. The median number of visits in the past year for analytic patients seen a year or more before, compared to nonanalyst patients, was 160 versus 30.

National Register of Health Service Providers in Psychology. Washington, D.C.: Council for the National Register of Health Service Providers in Psychology, 1975.

Published in the early summer, this first register lists some 7,000 psychologists meeting the credential standards and review for listing as a health service provider. A second volume will be released in the summer of 1976 with interim addendum listing. Eventually it is expected that some 13,000 to 17,000 will be listed. To be listed, the psychologist must be licensed or certified for independent practice by the state board of psychologist examiners and, in addition, must have a doctorate from a regionally accredited university and two years of supervised experience in health services, at least one of these postdoctoral. There is a "grandfather clause" until January 1978, during which time master's-level psychologists with six years experience and licensed prior to January 1975 are eligible for listing.

Newhouse, J., and others. "Policy Options and the Impact of National Health Insurance." *New England Journal of Medicine,* 1974, *290,* 1345-1359.

Estimates the effect of various prototype health insurance plans on the demand for service. Projects a greatly increased demand for ambulatory services, which would stress the system and the redistribution of such services from the affluent to the poor. Suggests that in a full coverage national health insurance plan the government as the principal "buyer" would subject rates of reimbursement to negotiation. Elaborates on a time-price concept, the dependent being "time-rich" as contrasted to the "time-poor" worker. Elimination of financial barriers under national health insurance could favor increased utilization by those having more available time, such as dependents and indigents. Notes that usual deductibles and coinsurance have little effect on hospital utilization, but fails to appreciate the fact that early intervention and ambulatory services can reduce hospitalization and health care expenditures.

New Jersey Department of Institutions and Agencies, Division of Medical Assistance and Health Services. "New Jersey Medical Assistance and Health Services Act, Psychologist's Services Manual." Trenton, New Jersey: Department of Institutions and Agencies, Division of Medical Assistance and Health Services, 1968; rev. 1973.

This manual, proposed in September of 1973, became operational January 1974. It assures the client free choice of qualified facilities and practitioners. Mechanisms for prior authorization by peers and billing procedures are outlined and the range of procedures (services) defined. The range of services recognized was broadened in July 1974. Prior authorization is required for services in excess of $300 in a year. Medicaid benefits are coordinated with other benefits such as workers' compensation. Maximum fees established in 1974 were at $26 per hour for "psychological generalists" and $37 per hour for "psychological specialists." The specialist differential is based on board certification (ABPP). The Prudential Insurance Company through its Millville, New Jersey, office, serves as the program's fiscal intermediary.

Newman, D. E. "Peer Review: A California Model." *Psychiatric Annals*, 1974, *4*, 75-85.

The organized review procedure at the Penninsula Hospital in Burlingame, California, is described, discussed, and analyzed. This system is one of the few operational review systems in mental health for a stipulated at-risk population (including medical).

Nyman, L. "Some Odds on Getting into Ph.D. Programs in Clinical and Counselling Psychology." *American Psychologist*, 1973, *28*, 934-935.

Notes that in 1972 the number of acceptances in clinical

psychology graduate programs ranged from 6 to 33, with the average program accepting 13.3 students (1,209 for the 42 responding programs). Eighty percent of the candidate population were turned away. The candidate acceptance ratio was 4.6, more severe than for medical school.

Ohio Department of Welfare, Division of General Support Services. "Ohio Medicaid, Provider Handbook." Columbus, Ohio: Ohio Department of Public Welfare, Division of General Support Services, 1974.

This handbook is subject to cumulative update. Chapter Two pertains to psychologists and lists procedures that are covered services, ones not covered, visit limitations (ten per month), prior authorization for testing in excess of five hours a year and reimbursement of the department's payment schedule set at the 75 percentile of provider charges for similar services. A provider form is included, as well as general instructions. As of January 1975, illustrative maximum fees were: psychological psychotherapy in office, clinic, home or hospital per session, $25; psychological testing, one hour, $25; psychological group psychotherapy, per person, $9.

Owens, A. "Which Fees Should Raise This Year?" *Medical Economics,* 1974, *51,* 162-169.

Shows impact of Cost of Living Council on fees of general practitioners and several medical specialties, including psychiatry. Based on Spring 1973 data of fee-for-service practitioners. Psychiatric fees for individual psychotherapy ranged from $30 to $45 for 85 percent of those reporting. Forty percent charged $35, which was the median fee.

Ozarin, L., Taube, C., and Spaner, F. "Operations Indices for Community Mental Health Centers." *American Journal of Psychiatry,* 1972, *128,* 1511-1523.

States that data obtained from a survey of federally funded mental health centers in operation for more than two months in 1969 revealed that the 205 centers provided care for an estimated 372,000 persons, 23 percent on inpatient and 73 percent on outpatient status. One-third of the patients sought help directly, without professional or agency intermediaries. Staff time by percent: social workers—15 percent; psychiatrists —10 percent; psychologists—8 percent. Staff salaries accounted for 71 percent of expenditures, psychiatrists, comprising 9.2 percent of all staff, received 20 percent of the total salary expenditures. Per case costs ranged from $87 to $260 according to the sketchy information presented. (Figures cited in Statistical Note 65 show that $238,000,000 was spent serving this population of 372,000, which would make the average per case cost $640.—Ed.)

Pacht, A., and others. "The Current Status of the Psychologist as an Expert Witness." *Professional Psychology*, 1973, *4*, 409-413.

Reviews court decisions that have helped to establish the psychologist as an expert witness in criminal and civil trials. Guidelines for witnesses included admonitions to stay close to data within area of expertise; to confine testimony to area of competence; to avoid unexpected questions by pretrial preparation; to respond briefly and without jargon; to testify about, not for or against, the client; and to attend to detail and intellectual honesty.

Peck, C. "Fee Practices of Psychologists." *Professional Psychology*, 1969, *1*, 14-19, 154.

This survey (in January 1968) was sent to every third licensed or certified psychologist listed in a state roster at APA in the fall of 1967. A total pool would have been just under 8,000, derived largely from 1966 rosters. (Note that in the eight years, 1966 to 74, the pool had increased two and a half times.—Ed.). Whereas the fees reported are time-dated, certain other parameters appear to hold true today: fees are based primarily on time required rather than a procedure; the fees of those in full-time practice tend to be higher; solo practice is more typical of those with small part-time practices than full-time; over one-third of the respondents reported no fee-for-service activity; and only one-tenth were full-time. (Thus the majority of licensed psychologists were in part-time fee-for-service work.—Ed.)

Penner, N. "The CHAMPUS Issue." *Journal of the National Association of Private Psychiatric Hospitals,* 1975, *6,* 17-24.

The Dependents Medical Care Program was established by law in 1956 and authorized use of civilian providers. The Military Medical Benefits Amendments of September 1966 (PL 89-614) expanded coverage to the retired member and dependents, permitted the treatment of mental disorder, and expanded coverage to include outpatient care. These amendments also established certain nonmedical services for the mentally retarded and physically handicapped. The program has been perceived as beneficial and liberal. Funding is from the Annual Defense Appropriation. Of the 7,800,000 beneficiaries in 1972 only some 900,000 (11.5 percent) used the program.

Peterson, D., and Baron, A. "Status of the University of Illinois Doctor of Psychology Program, 1974." *Professional Psychology,* 1975, *6,* 88-95.

Outlines the history of the professionally oriented Psy.D. program in clinical psychology. Since initiation in 1968, forty-two Psy.D. candidates have been admitted, nine having left the program, and four graduating. Academically, these candidates compared favorably to the Ph.D. clinical students.

Peterson, O. "How Effective Will National Health Insurance Be?" *Annals of Internal Medicine,* 1973, *78,* 739-749.

Notes that national health insurance is really medical care insurance. Illustrates implications of major national health insurance bills, including reference to the British experience and to Medicare. The lesson of Medicare and Medicaid is that health insurance is a very poor instrument for solving the problems of medical care organization. A large part of care can be given effectively in physicians' offices. Organized practices allocate a substantial proportion of their doctors to primary care. There is some indication that hospital use in fee-for-service is greater than in prepaid medical care; also, that a significant proportion of hospitalizations are unnecessary.

"Prepaid Plans' Cost Exceed Fee-for-Service, GAO Reports." *American Medical News,* Oct. 14, 1974.

States that the U.S. General Accounting Office reported per capita payments for Medicaid patients enrolled in two prepaid health plans in California were higher in one of the plans than they would have been on a fee-for-service basis. The study raises the question of whether or not prepaid group health insurance is actually less costly than fee-for-service payment.

Raimy, V. C. (Ed.) *Training in Clinical Psychology.* New York: Prentice-Hall, 1950.

The official report of the Boulder Conference on the training of psychologists. The conference established that the scientist-practitioner model overwhelmingly dominated professional training of psychologists in the United States.

Raush, H. L. "Research, Practice, and Accountability." *American Psychologist,* 1974, *29,* 678-681.

A critical discussion of research as related to practice in psychology. Argues for more relevance and for application and integration of research and practice.

Reed, L. S. "Utilization of Care for Mental Disorders Under the Blue Cross and Blue Shield Plan for Federal Employees, 1972." *American Journal of Psychiatry,* 1974, *131,* 964-975.

Reports that in a plan covering over 5,000,000 people, utilization for mental disorder accounted for 7.3 percent of all benefits paid in 1972—$11.92 per covered person. Care of hospitalized inpatients accounted for 65 percent of benefits for mental conditions. Under the high-option plan there were 6.4 admissions per 1,000 population for mental disorder (less than 1 percent).

Reed, L. S., Myers, E., and Scheidemandel, P. *Health Insurance and Psychiatric Care: Utilization and Cost.* Washington, D.C.: The American Psychiatric Association, 1972, p. 411.

This excellent reference book provides analysis of costs and coverages of over forty federally sponsored health insurance plans. Charges for outpatient services amounted to $2.99 per covered person per year, with benefit payments estimated at $2.16 per covered person per year. Charges for hospital care of mental conditions amounted to approximately $4.13 per covered person, equal to 6.3 percent of total charges for all conditions. Group practice plans have about one-third lower rates of hospital admission and days of care for all conditions than do plans that operate on a fee-for-service basis. (These findings support the conclusion that there is overutilization of inhospital mental health services and a corresponding underutilization of outpatient services. If insurance contracts provided benefits for outpatient service visits comparable to inpatient service, cost savings might be achieved, since outpatient services are much less costly.—Ed.)

Reid, J. R. "The Myth of Dr. Szasz." *Journal of Nervous and Mental Disease,* 1962, *135,* 381-386.

Comments on Szasz's rather iconoclastic views about mental illness.

Reiss, B. "Changes in Patient Income Concomitant with Psychotherapy." *Journal of Consulting Psychology,* 1967, *31,* 130.

Indicates that the income of patients undergoing psychotherapy tends to increase, thereby producing new tax monies. These new tax monies on increased earnings amortize the cost of psychotherapy in as little as one and a half years.

Rice, D. P., Knee, R. I., and Connell, M. "Financing the Care of the Mentally Ill under Medicare and Medicaid." *American Journal of Public Health and the Nation's Health,* 1970, *60,* 6-12.

Describes provisions of mental health benefits under Medicare and Medicaid. Points out that administrative controls may circumscribe the availability of the 190-day inpatient lifetime benefit and the $250 a year outpatient benefit. Hospitalization of the elderly increased in the eighteen months after Medicare was established, as compared to the prior eighteen-month period. (This increase is possibly due to the low outpatient benefit compared to the inpatient benefit.—Ed.) In the first six months of Medicare, 1.4 percent of those 65 and older had a primary psychiatric diagnosis; these cases amounted to 1.6 percent of the total days of care. On an annual basis, there were three psychiatric discharges from hospitals representing fifty-one days of care for each 1,000 Medicare enrollees. The aged mentally ill may need medical or surgical treatment in conjunction with mental treatment. "Medicare contains built in limitations that restrict patterns of care and the availability of service for the mentally ill. Such limitations are not imposed on persons with other illnesses."

Rodgers, D. A. "A Psychological Interpretation of Alcoholism." *Annals of the New York Academy of Sciences,* 1972, *197,* 222-225.

Interprets alcoholism as a behavioral and psychological rather than medical problem.

Roemer, M. I., and others. "Copayments for Ambulatory Care: Penny-Wise and Pound-Foolish." *Medical Care,* 1975, *13,* 457-466.

By cohort, studied the absolute and relative utilization of MediCal (Medicaid) health services to the AFDC (Aid to Families with Dependent Children) universe in three California counties six months prior to the imposition of copayment for ambulatory care and prescription drugs and for one year after copayment was imposed only on those Medicaid beneficiaries who had some financial resources beyond their statutory cash benefit (they tended to be older). After three months, prior authorization for more than two visits a month was required by the state, effecting a sharp decline in utilization rates. Additionally, the copay cohort, relative to the base rate, showed a substantially lower rate of doctors' office visits, also, lower rates for common laboratory tests, a preventive screening test, and use of prescription drugs. By contrast, there were differentially higher indices of hospital use for the copay cohort in three of four quarters. Prior to copay, doctors' visits by this population were equivalent to 2,400 per 1,000 persons (much lower than the general population—cost per visit $8.79). The hospitalization base rate was 83.6 patients per 1,000 per year at a cost of $623 per patient. The "controls" yielded a net excess of $935 per 1,000 in hospital costs offset by only a net saving of $88 per 1,000 in ambulatory care under copay. Converted to the state's AFDC population, the projected consequence of copay was an excess of $1,228,150. "Short term savings for lower ambulatory care use were followed by definite increases in costly hospital use" (p. 466).

Rogers, L. S. "Drop-out Rates and Results of Psychotherapy in Government Aided Mental Hygiene Clinics." *Journal of Clinical Psychology,* 1960, *16,* 89-62.

Statistical analysis of five states' drop-out rates, showing that the majority of patients leave treatment before the eighth unit of service.

Rosenblum, M. (Ed.) "Medical Care Benefits." In *Compendium on Workmen's Compensation.* Washington, D.C.: National Commission on State Workmen's Compensation Laws, 1973, pp. 145-160.

Finds that about 5 percent of all injured workers show some residual effect of their injuries. Under full coverage, any disease is compensable that can be shown to have a causal connection with the work of the claimant. A review of state commission use of fourteen types of practitioner found that seven states (Alabama, Louisiana, New York, Oklahoma, South Dakota, Utah, and Ohio) generally would not pay for the services of psychologists in January 1972. Six states excluded optometrists and Louisiana alone excluded psychiatrists. Holds that insurer control is diminished in states that permit the employee choice of doctor. Twenty-four states now recognize employee choice and the legislative trend (six states over the past ten years) is in this direction. There are no significant differences in medical costs in different states on the basis of their methods of physician choice. However, a greater number and variety of specialists are available to injured workers in employee-choice states.

Rosenthal, D., and Frank, J. D. "The Fate of Psychiatric Client Outpatients Assigned to Psychotherapy." *Journal of Nervous and Mental Disease,* 1958, *127,* 330-343.

Reports analysis and follow-up of clients in psychotherapy at the Phipps Clinic.

Ross, W. D. "Some Economic Estimates in Relation to Psychotherapy by General Physicians and Other Mental Health Professionals." *Canadian Psychiatric Association Journal,* 1968, *13,* 17-21.

Shows that aggregate corporate costs of employees with personal or suspected drinking problems are twice as much as those for "problem-free" employees when measured by costs of health compensation claims, grievances, days absent, medical clinic visits, and efficiency on the job. Problem-free employees' daily wages averaged 16 percent more than the employees with identifiable problems. Mean days absent were seven times higher for the miscellaneous problem sample and sixteen times greater for the suspected problem drinking sample than for the problem-free sample.

Rothfield, M. B. "Sensible Surgery for Swelling Medical Costs." *Fortune Magazine,* 1973, *86,* 110-130.

Suggests that Health Maintenance Organizations, by charging a fixed fee whether clients are sick or well, give doctors a powerful incentive to provide quality care more effectively.

Rousseau, J. J. *The Social Contract.* New York: Hafner, 1947 [1762].

A reprinting of Rousseau's classical work on the individual in society.

Sachs, B. "An Experience in Providing Mental Health Care in a

Comprehensive Prepaid Group Practice Plan." *JAMWA,* 1972, *27,* 186-196.

Reports that 60 percent of staff time at the Group Health Cooperative of Puget Sound was spent in direct patient contact and 40 percent in consultation, education, and administration. A staff of four psychiatrists, two psychologists, seven psychiatric social workers, two nurses, and five support personnel saw 4,561 patients for a total of 18,177 visits. The average number of visits was 3.98, compared to 4.01 medical visits per enrollee. Half of the individuals were seen for 2.57 visits or less and half of the utilization was by individuals making 6.7 visits or more. Inpatient utilization data is not presented.

Schaar, K. "Jersey opens Professional School." *APA Monitor,* 1974, *5,* 1.

Reports on the opening of new graduate program for the New Jersey Graduate School of Applied and Professional Psychology. With a pilot class of forty in the fall of 1974 (twenty-five in the clinical psychology program and fifteen in the school psychology program) this professional school, independent but coordinate with Rutgers, began a post-masters Psy.D. program, for psychologists employed in New Jersey.

Scheidemandel, P. "Utilization of Psychiatric Services." *Psychiatric Annals,* 1974, *4,* 58-74.

Summarizes some of the information gathered by Reed and others (1972). Concludes that insurance coverage for mental disorder is feasible and cites supportive utilization data. In a survey of psychiatric practitioners, found that 45 percent had insurance or third-party coverage. Those plans with data on the number of visits per patient to psychiatrists in office practice reported an average of four to fifteen per patient.

Scheidemandel, P., Kanno, C., and Glasscote, R. *Health Insurance for Mental Illness.* Washington, D.C.: The Joint Information Service of the American Psychiatric Association *and* the National Association for Mental Health, 1968.

Provides an analysis of how much of the patient's costs of mental health care is paid by insurance and notes the trends towards increased coverage. The survey reveals the following points. (1) Blue Cross and Blue Shield plans generally provide lower benefits for care in private or state psychiatric hospitals than for care in general hospitals. These restrictions have the potential of limiting hospital care to a relatively small number of facilities in many geographic areas, thus seriously compromising the value of the policies. (2) Services of therapeutic and diagnostic personnel other than physicians are frequently excluded. (3) The limitations in existing group and individual policies are still unduly restrictive both in terms of the number of days covered and the deductible percentage usually applied. (4) Few commercial insurance carriers will write out-of-hospital coverage for mental illness in individual health insurance policies. (5) In certain areas of the country only token or no benefits are provided by Blue Cross and Blue Shield for mental illness. (6) Seventy-four percent of patients seeing psychiatrists in their offices had no benefits and of those who did, many were provided less coverage than for other illnesses. (7) Considerable evidence is uncovered that the plans of some carriers require that copies of physician's reports must be sent to patient's employers and that this procedure inhibits utilization of available coverage.

Schofield, W. "The Role of Psychology in the Delivery of Health Services." *American Psychologist,* 1969, *24,* 565-584.

Defines psychology as a health profession and as distinct from mental health.

Schofield, W. "The Psychologist as a Health Care Professional." *Intellect Magazine,* January 1975, 255-258.

Describes some aspects of psychology's role in the development of the country's health resources. Points to the current opportunity for new models of health care delivery. Holds that when there is adequate recognition for the emotional needs of the patient the total demand on medical resources and the cost of treatment can be reduced. Various developments confirm the competence of clinical psychologists as special health professionals.

Schorr, D. *Don't Get Sick in America.* Nashville, Tenn.: Aurora Publications, 1970.

Offers a consumer view of the health insurance industry. Explodes the myth that Americans are getting the best medical care in the world. Some terms illustrate tone of book: "corner grocery hospital"; "pushcart peddler doctor"; and "health insurance—the shrinking security blanket."

Simmons, S., and others. "California Court Ruling on Dangerousness Stirs Controversy." *APA Monitor,* 1975, *6,* 12-18.

Analyzes a significant court case in California. A patient receiving outpatient psychotherapy at a campus clinic, informed his psychologist therapist that he intended to kill his former girlfriend. At the therapist's request the campus police briefly detained the patient. He was released and the psychiatrist in charge directed that no further action be taken to detain the patient. The victim was not warned. The court found that attempting to confine the patient imposed a duty to warn. Article discusses the predictability of violence and other aspects of what may be a landmark case.

"Soaring Costs of Health Care: Pictogram." *U.S. News and World Report,* January 23, 1974, pp. 28-29.

Portrays the rapid rise in health expenditures to $83,400,000,000 in 1972 (since risen to $104,200,000,000 in 1974—7.7 percent of the GNP), the relatively more rapid increase in medical care (particularly hospital services) compared to other goods and services, and the particularly high impact of the increases on those sixty-five years of age and older.

Society of Actuaries. "Report of the Committee on Disability and Double Indemnity: Experience Under Certain Ordinary Disability Benefits Between the 1930 and 1950 Anniversaries." *Transactions,* 1953, no. 2, 70-88, 130-145.

Data subdivided by length of waiting period prior to disability entitlement. Provides evidence of early involvement of the industry in coverage for mental disorder under disability benefits supplemental to ordinary life insurance policies.

Spingarn, N. "Social Work a Profession Confounded by Contradictions." *Chronicle of Higher Education*, 1974, *8*, 8.

Cites data on undergraduate and graduate study enrollment. Notes changing standards and pressures for diverse involvement. The 81 graduate schools of social work have 16,000 first-year places; 30,000 students are enrolled in the 213 approved undergraduate programs. Although the National Association of Social Workers decided that as of July 1974 the BSW would be fully recognized as professional, the National Federation of Societies for Clinical Social Work would limit membership to MSWs with several years' clinical experience.

Spiro, H. "On Beyond Mental Health Centers." *Archives of General Psychiatry*, 1969, *21*, 646-656.

Presents a conceptual model involving three levels of mental care permitting neighborhood comprehensive health centers, community mental health centers, and specialized mental health programs designed to relate to one another according to size of population served.

Spiro, H., and others. "Fee-for-Service Insurance versus Cost Financing: Impact on Mental Health Care Systems." *American Journal of Public Health*, 1975, *65*, 139-143.

Considers the implications of fee-for-service practice, indemnification financing, cost-financed group practice, and capitation-based financing. Study contrasts utilization of fee-for-service and cost-financed group practice in a union program. Over the four-year period from 1967 to 1970 only 2.73 percent of the population at risk used the mental health benefits. "Utilization never exceeded 1.3 percent per year. Cost remained well under 50 cents per month. The removal of restrictive deductibles and early coinsurance produced none of the predicted dire effects." Hospitalization was substantially higher in the fee-for-service clients but they did not differ demographically from those using cost-financed group practice.

Stallones, R. A. "Editorial: Community Health." *Science,* February 25, 1972, *175.*

Denies the assumption that effective treatment of illness vastly improves community health. Takes the position that enormous improvements would be possible if we were able to understand and control the general environmental factors. Advocates an ecological systems approach.

Stricker, G. "Training the Professional Psychologist of the Future." *Clinical Psychologist,* 1975, *28,* 3.

Summary of a presentation at the American Psychological Association, New Orleans meeting, 1974. Argues for retention of the Ph.D.; for faculty appointments based on professional experience and skill in its communication, and, if the foreign language requirements are not dropped, for functional (spoken) skill in a foreign language.

Tarter, R., and others. "Reliability of Psychiatric Diagnosis." *Diseases of the Nervous System,* 1975, *36,* 30-31.

Studies 256 consecutive admissions interviewed by any two of five psychiatrists. Neurotic and personality disorders were agreed on less than 50 percent of the time, psychotic disorders only slightly better than 50 percent. Raises the possibility that the poor reliability in diagnoses may be attributed to the inadequacy of the *Diagnostic and Statistical Manual—II* as a classification system.

Taylor, R., and Torrey, E. F. "Mental Health Coverage Under A National Health Insurance Plan." Unpublished report prepared for the National Institute of Mental Health, Rockville, Maryland, 1972.

Represents the private observations of two physician specialists employed at the National Institute of Mental Health (forty-eight references cited). Notes that "Psychiatric hospitalization is less effective as a means of dealing with mental problems than are a number of less expensive alternative. Per case costs cited: Outpatient Crisis Intervention—$162, Acute Hospitalization (average 8.6 days)—$943, and Extended Hospitalization (average 58 days)—$1922." Also, "With its emphasis on psychiatric hospitalization and the use of psychiatrists as primary providers of outpatient service, traditional psychiatric care will not be able to meet the demand generated by a national coverage plan." Claims that the requirement—supported by the APA and implemented by most health insurance carriers—that psychotherapy be provided only by physicians or by those non-physician mental health professionals working under supervision of a physician raises costs of services without ensuring greater effectiveness or increased quality control.

Thiessen, D. D., and Rodgers, D. A. "Behavior Genetics as the Study of Mechanism-Specific Behavior." In J. N. Spuhler (Ed.), *Genetic Diversity and Human Behavior*. Chicago: Aldine, 1967, pp. 61-71.

Considers the nature and direction of the developing specialty of behavior genetics.

Toffler, A. *Future Shock*. New York: Random House, 1970.

Suggests ways to apply "thinking ahead" to an analysis of future trends in contemporary society.

Torrey, E. F., and Taylor, R. "Cheap Labor from Poor Nations." *The American Journal of Psychiatry*, 1973, *130*, 428-433.

Reports that since 1967 as many foreign medical graduates (FMGs) have entered the country annually as are graduated from United States medical schools. In 1970 34 percent of all psychiatric residents were FMGs. The FMGs exceeded 75 percent of all psychiatric residents in the state hospital systems of New York, Rhode Island, New Jersey, Massachusetts, Connecticut, and Ohio; possibly others. The imported medical personnel are largely from underdeveloped countries and fare poorly in licensure exams.

Tureen, L. L. "The Role of the Psychiatrist in a Prepaid Group

Medical Program." *American Journal of Public Health,*
1959, *49,* 1373-1378.

Relates the early experience of the St. Louis Labor Health
Institute (LHI). Provides perspective for the later prepaid group
experience in terms of utilization, manpower, and services required. The new patients per year were 1 percent of those eligible, with an average rate of ten consultations per case. Identified mental health problems for the group were at the rates of
6.6 percent and another 4 percent were estimated to be in need
of services. Psychotherapy was the treatment of choice with 40
percent of the cases. Those making one or two visits had a 20
percent improvement rate, in contrast to a 75 percent improvement rate for those making three or more visits. Psychoneurotic conditions dominated the psychiatric case load, with
less than 12 percent of referrals being classified as psychotic.
Stresses the need for psychological testing, especially for the
diagnosis and treatment of children and the need for industrial
intervention.

United States General Accounting Office. "Report to the Spe-
    cial Subcommittee on Alcoholism and Narcotics." Wash-
    ington, D.C., Committee on Labor and Public Welfare,
    B-164031(2) United States Senate, September 28, 1970.

Indicates that substantial cost savings could be obtained
from the establishment of a program for alcoholism for federal
employees. Between 4 percent and 8 percent of federal employees studied had work problems related to alcohol. It was
estimated that these problems with alcohol increased the cost of
the annual salary of these employees by 25 percent due to absenteeism, sickness benefits, and inefficiencies. The estimated
cost for establishing the program was $15,000,000 annually,
which could result in a savings of $135,000,000.

United States Department of Health, Education and Welfare.
    "Towards a Comprehensive Health Policy for the 1970's:
    A White Paper." HEW Publication No. 0-427-047.
    Washington, D.C.: U.S. Government Printing Office, May,
    1971.

Defines problems, outlines solutions, and reports that the administration's strategy is to modify the entire system of health, viewing the major problems as systemic. Presents considerable factual material. Health occupations accounted for 3.6 percent of the workforce by 1966. Cites decline in the ratio of primary care physicians and disparity in geographic location of resources. Health insurance is a financing market that often excludes or limits outpatient care and preventive services wherein ". . . one party sets prices for services, a second receives them and a third pays for them, so that no one is concerned about rising costs." The strategy is to preserve and strengthen pluralistic private sector resources to avoid a single governmental system, which is seen as a diseconomy and bureaucratic encumbrance.

United States Department of Health, Education and Welfare. "Records, Computers, and the Rights of Citizens: Report of the Secretary's Advisory Committee on Automated Personal Data Systems." Washington, D.C.: U.S. Government Printing Office, 1973.

A "definitive" and thorough study of confidentiality, especially of automated data systems, by a select committee. Detailed, thoughtful recommendations and policy guidelines are suggested.

United States Department of Health, Education and Welfare, Health Services Administration. *Inclusion of Mental Health Services in Health Maintenance and Related Organizations: A Review of Supplemental Benefits.* Publication No. (HSA) 75-13019. Rockville, Md.: Health Services Administration, 1974.

Reviews the benefits, services, staffing patterns, and utilization of mental health services available in prototype health maintenance organizations. One important finding reported was that travel time has different return effects on different groups. For medical care, the distance to travel was shown to be related to case severity. Nonemergency mental health services are more easily postponed than other medical services and are compared to nonemergency dentistry. Implies that it is necessary to have mental health specialists readily accessible in order to assure appropriate treatment for mental conditions. Includes an annotated bibliography.

United States Department of Health, Education and Welfare, Health Resources Administration. *The Supply of Health Manpower: 1970 Profiles and Projections to 1990.* HRS 75-38. Washington, D.C.: Health Resources Administration, December 1974.

Prepared in 1972-73, this 222 page health manpower reference provides "detailed occupational profiles" not only on physicians and medical specialists but also on optometrists, podiatrists, etc. Of 323,210 physicians active December 1970, 21,150 and 2,100 were in psychiatry and child psychiatry, collectively 7.2 percent of the physician total. By the end of December 1972, their numbers were reported at 22,570 and 2,268, a total approaching 24,850. Optometrists numbered 18,400, podiatrists, 7,100. (In such context, professional psychology is a substantial health manpower resource.) Projected as a ratio of all psychiatrists to 10,000 of population, there were 1.14:10,000 in 1970. The study was undertaken to provide baseline data for the development of optional strategies and policies in health manpower production. The four year medical school attrition rate is reported at 5.3 percent; 90 percent of physicians are involved in the direct care of patients. An attempt was made to estimate also the supply of active allied health manpower. Clinical psychologists are listed under "other personnel" also medical social workers. The estimated active personnel count in 1970 for these two professions was 13,000 and 25,200. States said to be requiring a license for these professions in 1971-72, numbered 46 and 9.

United States Department of Health, Education and Welfare, Health Services and Mental Health Administration. *Health Maintenance Organizations: The Concept and Structure.* Superintendent of Documents, HEW No. 1720-0030. Washington, D.C.: U.S. Government Printing Office, 1971a.

A concise description of the salient features of an HMO.

United States Department of Health, Education and Welfare, Health Services and Mental Health Administration. *Planning for Creative Change in Mental Health Services: A Distillation of Principles of Research Utilization.* Vol. 1. Washington, D.C.: U.S. Government Printing Office, 1971*b*.

An exhaustive annotated review. Some analysis of literature related to change, organizational reorganization, and the diffusion of research results into applied settings.

United States Department of Health, Education and Welfare, Office of Child Development. *Head Start Program Performance Standards.* (OCD Notice N-30-364-4). Washington, 1975 (July).

This policy manual for the Head Start Program cites the standards verbatim from the *Federal Register* (June 30, 1975, Vol. 40, No. 126, Pt. II) in the left-hand column and interpretive guidelines for their implementation alongside on the right. Psychologists are explicitly stated in the guidelines for Section 1304.3-4 (a)(1) obtaining or arranging for treatment of all health problems detected, and in 1304.3-8. Mental health services.

United States Department of Health, Education and Welfare, Office of Professional Standards Review. *PSRO Program Manual.* Washington, D.C.: U.S. Department of Health, Education and Welfare, 1974.

Sets forth statutory requirements and interim guidelines for organizations and professional groups desiring to participate in the implementation of the provisions of PL 92-603 relating to professional standards review. Chapter 7, Section 730 deals with "Involvement of non-physician health care practitioners in PSRO review."

United States Department of Health, Education and Welfare, Social and Rehabilitation Services. *State Data Book, Federal-State Vocational Rehabilitation Program, Fiscal Year 1972.* HEW Publication No. (SRS) 75-25403. Washington, D.C.: United States Department of Health, Education and Welfare, Social and Rehabilitation Services, n.d.

Provides tabular data on the 326,138 persons rehabilitated in 1972, by state, by type of disability, by state earnings at referral and closure, and by other criteria. The average cost for mental conditions was $581 and for mental retardation was $678, indicating that mental disorders and mental retardation are not excessive in comparison with the average cost of all major disabling conditions of $666.

United States Department of Health, Education and Welfare, Social and Rehabilitation Services. "The Profile of Mentally Ill Persons Rehabilitated in the Fiscal Year 1969: Statistical Note No. 23." Washington, D.C.: U.S. Department of Health, Education and Welfare, Social and Rehabilitation Services, March 1971a.

Indicates that the weekly incomes of rehabilitated mentally ill persons increased as much as $58 per week. Even when the person who was treated for a mental disturbance was employed before rehabilitation, there was still an average gain in weekly income of over 10 percent. The gain in annual income would produce tax monies that would amortize the average cost of $581 spent on the rehabilitation of the mentally ill in under two years.

United States Department of Health, Education and Welfare, Social and Rehabilitation Services. "Major Disabling Conditions of Clients of State Vocational Rehabilitation Agencies Rehabilitated and Not Rehabilitated During the Fiscal Year of 1969: Statistical Note No. 27." Washington, D.C.: U.S. Department of Health, Education and Welfare, Social and Rehabilitation Services, June 1971b.

Indicates that mental illness was the most common disabling condition among both rehabilitated and nonrehabilitated clients. Mental illness accounted for 23 percent of those rehabilitated and 39 percent of those not rehabilitated. Many of the conditions listed in this study as requiring physical rehabilitation, such as digestive problems and mental retardation, may also be classified as mental conditions.

United States Department of Health, Education and Welfare,

Social and Rehabilitation Services. "A Profile of Mentally Retarded Clients Rehabilitated During the Fiscal Year of 1969: Statistical Note No. 29." Washington, D.C.: U.S. Department of Health, Education and Welfare, Social and Rehabilitation Services, September 1971c.

Shows that clients diagnosed as being mentally retarded had weekly income gains, as much as $47.50, following rehabilitation. Even when the person diagnosed as mentally retarded was working prior to rehabilitation, the weekly income gain was as much as $15 or a 35 percent gain in weekly income. The diagnosis and treatment of mentally retarded clients is therefore financially feasible, since the average cost of rehabilitation of mentally retarded clients was $678.

United States Department of Health, Education and Welfare, Social and Rehabilitation Services. "Expenditures in Federally Funded Community Mental Health Centers, 1970: Statistical Note No. 64." Washington, D.C.: U.S. Department of Health, Education and Welfare, Social and Rehabilitation Services, July 1972a.

The 255 operating community mental health centers spent an estimated total of $224 million in 1970, an average of $877,000 per center. About 66 percent of these expenditures were for staff salaries, 26 percent for other operating expenditures, and the remaining 8 percent for capital and other expenditures. Salaries for psychiatrists were (in millions of dollars) $26.8; for psychologists, $14.8; for social workers, $20.9; registered nurses, $18; practical nurses, $3.6; and for clerical, fiscal and maintenance personnel, $21; and other salaries, $43. (The number of patient care episodes reported for community mental health centers in 1971 were 797,000—130,000 of these being inpatient. Holding the cost constant would yield an average episode cost of $281.—Ed.)

United States Department of Health, Education and Welfare, Social and Rehabilitation Services. "Source of Funds, Federally Funded Community Mental Health Centers, 1970: Statistical Note No. 65." Washington, D.C.: United States

Department of Health, Education and Welfare, Social and
Rehabilitation Services, July 1972*b*.

Lists total government funds, $175,000,000 (including
$71,000,000 federal, $76,000,000 state and $25,000,000 lo-
cal). Total receipts from services, $54,600,000 including
$18,700,000 from patient fees, $15,600,000 from insurance,
$4,000,000 Medicare, and $8,900,000 Medicaid); other receipts
(including fundraising), $8,300,000. Number of centers was
255. Total funds were $238,000,000.

United States Department of Health, Education and Welfare,
    Social and Rehabilitation Services. "Selected Characteris-
    tics of Clients Closed from Active Caseload Statuses, by
    Major Disabling Condition, Fiscal Year 1972: Statistical
    Note No. 43." RSA-IM-76-11. Washington, D.C.: U.S. De-
    partment of Health, Education and Welfare, Rehabilitation
    Services Administration, 1975.

The average case cost of rehabilitated clients was $771 as
opposed to $501 for those not rehabilitated. Mentally ill clients
were more likely than other disability groups to receive services
without cost to the state agency. For every dollar rehabilitated
clients were earning at referral, they were earning $4.73 at
closure. Case costs for mental disorder and retardation were 37
percent of the total for 40 percent of the clients rehabilitated.
For mentally ill clients reporting earnings, they averaged $11.43
weekly at referral and $79.44 at closure, an increase of $68.01.
Comparable figures for the mentally retarded were $3.02,
$53.40, and $50.38. Mean costs of rehabilitation were substantially higher for cases of blindness, asthma and hay fever, and
heart disease, all over $1,000 and all common conditions.

United States Department of Health, Education and Welfare,
    Social and Rehabilitation Service, Rehabilitation Services
    Administration. *Characteristics of Clients Rehabilitation in
    Fiscal Years 1968-1972: Federal-State Vocational Rehabil-
    itation Program.* HEW Publication No (SRS) 74-25079.
    Washington, D.C.: Social and Rehabilitation Service,
    n.d.

Provides tabular data on persons rehabilitated over the five-year period from 1968 to 1972, together with some explanatory text and graphic illustration. The "mentally ill" are considered the "major disabling condition." Gives breakdowns on services provided, occupations at closure, and other demographic data.

United States Department of Health, Education and Welfare, Social and Rehabilitation Services, Rehabilitation Services Administration. *Standards for Rehabilitation Facilities and Sheltered Workshops.* HEW Publication No. (SRS) 72-25010. Rev. ed. Washington, D.C.: U.S. Department of Health, Education and Welfare, 1971.

Presents an update of the standards first issued in 1967 to encourage facilities and workshops to upgrade their program. The standards were recommended for adoption by the National Policy and Performance Council, a citizens group appointed by the secretary of the Department of Health, Education and Welfare. This twenty-one page booklet contains a brief preliminary section with definition of services, and standards for organizations, services, staff, clients, community relations and safety. The definition of *psychologist* is on page 14.

United States Department of Health, Education and Welfare, Social Security Administration. "Ambulatory Current Medicare Survey Report, Impact of Cost-Sharing on Use of Ambulatory Services under Medicare, Preliminary Findings, 1969." HEW Publication No. (SSA) 74-11702. Baltimore, Md.: U.S. Department of Health, Education and Welfare, Social Security Administration, October 10, 1973.

Tests the hypothesis that for the comparatively affluent or those for whom the deductible and coinsurance of the supplementary medical insurance program (Part B) involves little or no out-of-pocket expense will tend to use more service. The impact was greatest on those with low to moderate family incomes. For enrollees who meet the deductible, coinsurance apparently does not affect the number of services used. Public medical assistance enrollees (for whom part or all of the cost-sharing was paid and who were older and in poorer health as a group) had the highest utilization, at an average of twenty-two physician visits in 1969.

United States Department of Health, Education and Welfare, Social Security Administration. "Independent Health Insurance Plans in 1973: Research and Statistics Note No. 15." HEW (SSA) 75-11701. Washington, D.C.: U.S. Department of Health, Education and Welfare, Social Security Administration, 1975a.

Health insurance plans other than Blue Cross and Blue Shield and insurance company plans hold a small and slowly growing share of the private health insurance market. In 1973, this share amounted to nine million persons covered for hospital care, eleven to twelve million for physicians' services. While such plans held only 4 percent of the gross enrollment of all insurance plans for hospital care, they held 10 percent of the coverage for physician's office and home visits indicative of the emphasis placed on ambulatory care. Group practice plans paid a higher rate of return (91 percent) than individual practice plans (87 percent), with the IPA's (Individual Practice Association) putting 51 percent of their expenditures into hospital care. Tabular comparisons of group and individual practice plans are made.

United States Department of Health, Education and Welfare, Social Security Administration. "Utilization of Short Stay Hospitals under Medicare: 1968-71." HEW Publication No. (SSA) 75-11702. Washington, D.C.: U.S. Department of Health, Education and Welfare, Social Security Administration, 1975b.

Reports a trend to proportionately more brief stays (seven days or less) and fewer long stays (thirty days or more), from 40 to 42 percent and 9 to 7 percent respectively. Half the short-stay discharges, however, are due to death. A basic weekly pattern in the use of hospitals was evident. The requirement of earlier physician certification of hospital need (at twelve and eighteen days instead of at fourteen and twenty-one days) yielded no evidence that the physician certification regulations influenced the distribution of short-stay discharges.

United States Department of Health, Education and Welfare, Social Security Administration, Office of Research and Statistics. *Financing Mental Health Care Under Medicare and Medicaid.* Research Report No. 37 (Stock No. 1770-0167). Washington, D.C.: United States Department of Health, Education and Welfare, 1971.

Delineates inconsistencies in these programs and provides some utilization and cost data relevant to the population over sixty-five years old. The Medicare lifetime maximum of 190 days of inpatient care in a psychiatric hospital does *not* apply to inpatient psychiatric care in a general hospital where benefits are the same for patients with mental disorder and those with other disabilities. Under Medicaid, states are not permitted to differentiate or exclude services on the basis of diagnosis. As a result of the Long Amendments (1965) elderly patients became eligible for direct assistance payments under the Social Security Act (Titles I or XVI) while hospitalized in a mental institution and federal aid was made available to states in meeting the costs of caring for elderly patients in mental hospitals after Medicare benefits were exhausted. In contrast, patients under sixty-five are specifically excluded by statute from such coverage. As for outpatient services there is a statutory provision limiting out-of-hospital treatment of mental illness to $312.50 or 62.5 percent of actual expense in a calendar year. Since only 80 percent of incurred expenses can be paid by the Social Security Administration the maximum in effect becomes $250 or 50 percent of actual.

Only 2.1 percent of outpatient psychiatric clinic services were to the elderly in 1968. Of the total Medicare and Medicaid reimbursements, those for all psychiatric services were 4.5 percent in 1967, and 3.7 percent in 1969 (1.4 percent of Medicare and 7.6 percent of Medicaid). In 1969, 70 percent of inpatient Medicare psychiatric expenditures went to general hospitals. All hospital reimbursements totalled $4,000,000,000 but only 0.6 percent of this went to psychiatric hospitals. Under supplementary medical insurance only two persons per 1,000 received one or more psychiatric services in 1967. But 0.2 percent of all supplementary medical insurance enrollees used one or more outpatient psychiatric services.

United States Department of Health, Education and Welfare, Social Security Administration, Office of Research and Statistics. "Age Differences in Health Care Spending: Fiscal Year 1974." HEW Publication No. (SSA) 75-11701. Washington, D.C.: U.S. Department of Health, Education and Welfare, Social Security Administration, May 13, 1975.

Reports that the average health care bill for those aged sixty-five and over was $1,218, almost seven times the average health care expense of persons under nineteen and almost three times that of those in the intermediate group. Hospital expenditures were almost ten times that of the young person. Health care expenditures for the aged rose 11.7 percent in fiscal 1974. Medicare alone accounted for 62 percent of hospital expenditures for the aged and 52 percent of doctor bills. For persons under 65, by contrast, third-party payments accounted for 64 percent of health care expenditures.

United States House Armed Services Committee. *CHAMPUS and Military Health Care*. HASC No. 93-78. Washington, D.C.: Government Printing Office, December 20, 1974.

Outlines historical development of Civilian Health and Medical Program of the Uniformed Services (CHAMPUS) and notes rapid increase in the size of retired insured in the ten years from 1964. Escalating costs necessitated setting visit limits and elimination of some procedures. Subcommittee has sought changes to equalize cost sharing between inpatient and outpatient services.

United States Senate Committee on Post Office and Civil Service. *Access to Psychologists and Optometrists Under Federal Health Benefits Program*. Reports 92-861 and 93-961. Washington, D.C.: U.S. Government Printing Office, June 25, 1974.

Outlines the rationale by which the committee unanimously approved direct access to licensed clinical psychologists and optometrists in the Federal Employees' Health Benefits program. The previous restrictions were found to not stand the test of service to the employee. Those psychologists licensed or certified under grandfather clauses are recognized provided the basic standard is the doctoral degree. Any provider shall also meet "applicable national and state professional and ethical standards relevant to independent practice as clinical psychologists providing mental health services."

University of Minnesota, Division of Health Care Psychology. "Proposal for a Professional Degree Program Leading to the Doctor of Psychology in Health Care Psychology." Unpublished document, produced by the Division of Health Care Psychology, Health Sciences Center, University of Minnesota, Minneapolis, June 1974.

Suggests that a basic goal should be the foresighted and thoughtfully developed application of psychological research and practice to the entire spectrum of health-related behaviors. Notes that, of 1,300 psychologists employed in medical schools in 1972, 800 were in psychiatry and that six medical schools offer doctoral programs in psychology. Would train professional psychologists for health administration, preventive health care, and illness management with skills in the design of delivery systems, their evaluation, applied health research, training of caretakers and the public, consultation to physicians and other health professionals, and application of psychological procedures in treatment. There would be a significant proportion of field experience at all training levels. Details the curriculum drawing on courses in psychiatry, public health, medicine (including family practice), sociology, and psychology as well as in health care psychology, interdisciplinary programs, and electives. (Implementation could open new vistas to professional psychology in the mainstream of health care.—Ed.)

Van Buskirk, D. "Training and Treatment Costs in a Community Mental Health Center." *Administration in Mental Health,* 1974 (Summer), 28-36.

Derives a cost-per-hour-of-service rate by dividing total dollar input by total hours of service delivered per year, omitting the unmeasured by-products. Nonetheless, the all-staff average cost per hour of direct service in 1972 was $43 and $35 per hour for short-term versus long-term therapy respectively. Gives comparative training cost figures on psychology trainees, social work students, and third-year medical students.

Vaughan, W., Jr., and others. "The Private Practice of Community Psychiatry." *American Journal of Psychiatry*, 1973, *130*, 24-27.

Describes the multidisciplinary organization of practitioners at Peninsula Hospital in Burlingame, California. Patient care is paid for at cost in this federally funded, accredited, comprehensive, community mental health center. Services are provided under prepaid contract to the county. In June 1969, the professional staff voted by-law changes establishing a department of psychiatry and affiliate membership for licensed psychologists and clinical social workers. By July 1971, there were forty-five attending psychiatrists and forty-five affiliated nonphysician, licensed, mental health practitioners. Every patient has a private attending mental health practitioner. A peer review committee for prior authorization and utilization review was established in February 1971. Potential new staff are carefully proctored before membership is voted. (An important model for the collaboration of practitioners of several disciplines in private practice.—Ed.)

Vetter, B. "Survey Paints Fiction of Psychology Manpower." *APA Monitor*, 1973, *4*, 3, 7.

Notes that the 1972 survey of members gained response from 77 percent or almost 27,400. Almost 80 percent had a doctorate or professional degree; just over half were currently licensed or certified; 53 percent worked for government (all levels); about one-half and three-fourths have held no more than two or four previous jobs; 74 percent report more than a 40 hour average work week; and the voluntary unemployment rate was 1 percent.

Walsh, J. "Medical Education: Carnegie Panel Urges Expansion Acceleration." *Science,* 1970, *170,* 713-4.

Urging expansion in medical education, this Carnegie report notes that the Flexner model of training largely ignores health care delivery outside the medical school and its hospital and sets science in the medical school apart from science on the general campus. Recommendations include telescoping both medical education and residency training from four to three years each; incorporation of the internship into the residency; reconceptualizing health care training in university health science centers; and developing functional relations with community agencies in improving health care.

Walsh, J. "TIAA-CREF: for Richer, for Poorer, Married to the Market," *Science,* 1974, *186,* 513-515.

Describes the origin and scope of these plans and their relationship to market values. More than 2,200 educational institutions have TIAA/CREF (Teachers Insurance and Annuity Association *and* College Retirement Equities Fund) retirement plans. These plans also underwrite group life and major medical health insurance.

Wamocher, Z. "Emotionally Disturbed Found to Visit M.D. Twice as Often." *Medical Tribune,* 1973, *14,* 2.

Surveys 769 patients of two villages and one kibbutz who had been treated by one doctor over a period of ten years. It was determined that 35 percent of the population suffered emotional disorders. Rates were 25 percent for the men and 45 percent for the women. The doctor contact rate was 5.6 times a year. Emotionally disturbed persons averaged 8.7 visits per year and the undisturbed averaged 3.7.

Warren, J. "Learned Societies in Transition: the APA." *Educational Researcher,* 1975, *4,* 14-16.

Describes the continued growth of the American Psychological Association while other associations are faced with declining membership. APA membership exceeded 39,500 in 1975

and, with 12,000 first-year graduate students in doctoral programs, there are in training almost as many psychologists as
M.D.'s. The signs that the APA is becoming more and more of a
professional association are undeniable.

Watson, J. B. "Psychology As a Behaviorist Sees It." *Psychological Review,* 1913, *20,* 158-177.

Watson's original behaviorist manifesto, a major turning
point in the evolution of psychology as an academic discipline.

Watson, R. I. *The Great Psychologists from Aristotle to Freud.*
Philadelphia: J. B. Lippincott, 1963.

A good history of psychology that focuses on persons, a
good companion to Boring's *A History of Experimental Psychology.*

Webb, J. "Distribution of Psychologists and Psychiatrists by ZIP
Code Areas in Ohio." *Ohio Psychologist,* 1974*a, 20,* 5-12.

Compares the membership of the Ohio Psychiatric Association with the roster of licensed psychologists by county of resi-
dence and finds that of the 88 counties, 56 percent have no
psychiatrists (18 percent of the population) and 28 percent
have no psychologists (6 percent of the population). Maldistribution is indicated by location of 79 percent of psychiatrists in
the five metropolitan areas of the state as compared to 43 percent of the population and 59 percent of the psychologists.
Author refers to his 1970 study of over 12,000 patients of
psychiatrists and psychologists compared on two point codes of
the MMPI (Minnesota Multiphasic Personality Inventory) and
finds that there were no essential differences in patients treated
by psychologists as compared to patients treated by psychiatrists.

Webb, J. "Supply and Demand of Psychologists in Ohio: It
Affects All Psychologists." *Ohio Psychologist,* 1974*b, 21,*
1, 40-43.

Drawn from the *National Register of Scientific and Tech-*

nical Personnel, 1970 salary data for academic and applied doctoral scientists in 15 fields showed a +.899 correlation. In all fields but linguistics (which had the lowest ranked pay), the median salaries of noneducational employers were higher. Webb suggested that "as the value of a discipline increases in society as a whole, salaries for that discipline in academic settings increase."

Weisbrod, B., and Fisler, R. "Hospital Insurance and Hospital Utilization." *American Economic Review,* 1961, *41,* 126-132.

Presents data and other evidence to support the view that minimal cost sharing by the consumer is as effective as a large copayment in controlling utilization.

Wetherille, R., and others. "Part II. Growth Across the Nation." *Prism,* 1975, *3,* 15-17, 54.

The authors are staff of Interstudy, a Minneapolis center specializing in the study of health policy. As of March 1, 1975, there were 179 operational HMOs in the country (42 percent of them in California) and another 314 in formational or planning stages. Almost seven million people were enrolled in HMOs at the start of 1975, a 12 percent increase in one year. Half the HMOs responding to survey had less than 5,000 members, while only 6.6 percent had over 100,000. The greater number of HMOs in large population areas suggests that they locate where they can compete with other health care providers.

Wheelwright, P. (Trans.) *Wheelwright's Aristotle, Natural Science; the Metaphysics; Zoology; Psychology; the Nicomachean Ethics; on Statecraft; the Art of Poetry.* New York: Odyssey Press, 1957.

Translation of some of Aristotle's more significant writings.

White Paper on Workers' Compensation: A Report on the Need for Reform of State Workers' Compensation. Interdepartmental Study on Workers' Compensation, May 13, 1974.

GPO-875-745. Washington, D.C.: United States Government Printing Office, 1974.

Notes that each year two million employees miss one or more days of work due to work-related injury or illness and that the cost of state workers' compensation programs was $6,000,000,000 in 1973. Occupational disease concepts are being broadened from those that are almost solely occupationally related, to include those concepts that are more prevalent in certain occupations and those that occur frequently in the general population, but that can be aggravated by work conditions. Only the largest firms, which tend to have low accident rates, can afford self-insurance, and only one-quarter of all firms subject to workers' compensation are experience-rated. Available evidence indicates that vocational rehabilitation (VR) is more cost-effective for workers' compensation claimants than for the general population of federal-state VR programs. On the average, the net economic benefit of rehabilitation services to workers injured in 1965 to 1966 was $15,200 (in 1966 dollars). Compensation laws have largely removed fault as an element of controversy.

Whiting, F. *Psychiatric Services, Systems Analysis, and Manpower Utilization.* Washington, D.C.: American Psychiatric Association, 1969.

Reports that as of March 1968 there were about 22,400 United States psychiatrists—7.5 percent of medical manpower. Recent growth rate was 4.6 percent (since August 1965). Direct patient service accounted for 67 percent of psychiatry manhours. Private practice accounts for 42 percent of overall psychiatric time.

Whiting, F., and Boneau, A. "Psychology's Human Resources: A Social Psychological Analysis." Unpublished report prepared for the American Psychological Association, Washington, D.C., 1973.

Contrasts the work effort of psychologists and psychiatrists in five key roles. Because of the broad involvement of psychologists in education and research beyond intraprofessional concerns, psychology is "contributing to a much broader range of societal goals." Estimates that the dollar value investment by the United States economy in psychology as a discipline exceeds $1,000,000,000 annually.

Whiting, F., and others. "Psychology's Human Resources for Service Provision: The Empirical Base for Standards Development." Unpublished report prepared for American Psychological Association, Washington, D.C., 1972.

Identifies 55,496 United States psychologists. Finds that two-thirds participate in service provision. Full-time equivalent (FTE) service providers number 19,800. Thirty percent of providers practice in hospital-clinic settings. Reported that psychologist providers were distributed by region closely parallel to the general population.

Williams, G. "Mental Patients Wind up in Prisons." *Sacramento Bee,* April 20, 1975, p. 1.

Reviews the impact of changes in mental health laws on the prison population, presenting the opinion of various authorities in California.

Williams, R. "A Comparison of Hospital Utilization and Costs by Types of Coverage." *Inquiry,* 1966, *3,* 23-42.

A comparison of Blue Cross plans with different cost-sharing features. Results showed lower utilization with cost sharing.

Wyatt v. *Stickney.* 344 F. Supp. 373, 344 F. Supp. 387 (M.D. Ala. 1972), 325 F. Supp. 781 (M.D. Ala. 1971) Appeal pending 5th Cir.

A court case that is likely to have profound impact on mental health care generally and specifically on care and treatment of patients who are committed to treatment institutions under state mental illness commitment laws. Establishes the right to treatment, defines essential minimal institutional conditions, mandates minimum staffing ratios, and defines a fully "qualified health professional." The psychologist with a doctorate is so recognized.

Index